The FABRIC *of*
CIVIL WAR
SOCIETY

CONFLICTING WORLDS

NEW DIMENSIONS OF THE AMERICAN CIVIL WAR

T. Michael Parrish, Series Editor

UNIFORMS
BADGES
AND
FLAGS
1859–1939

The FABRIC *of* CIVIL WAR SOCIETY

SHAE SMITH COX

LOUISIANA STATE UNIVERSITY PRESS

BATON ROUGE

Published by Louisiana State University Press
lsupress.org

DESIGNER: Michelle A. Neustrom
TYPEFACE: MillerText

Cover photographs courtesy of the author.

Portions of chapters 6–8 have appeared, in somewhat different form, in "Outfitting the Lost Cause: The Re-creation of Southern Identity through Confederate Veterans' Uniforms, 1865 to the 1920s," in *Buying and Selling Civil War Memory in Gilded Age America*, ed. James Marten and Caroline E. Janney, copyright © 2021 by the University of Georgia Press.

Visit the companion site for this volume at thefabricofcivilwarsociety.com.

LIBRARY OF CONGRESS CATALOGING-IN-PUBLICATION DATA
Names: Cox, Shae Smith, author.
Title: The fabric of Civil War society : uniforms, badges, and flags, 1859–
    1939 / Shae Smith Cox.
Other titles: Uniforms, badges, and flags, 1859–1939
Description: Baton Rouge : Louisiana State University Press, [2024] |
    Series: Conflicting worlds : new dimensions of the American Civil War |
    Includes bibliographical references and index.
Identifiers: LCCN 2023045181 (print) | LCCN 2023045182 (ebook) |
    ISBN 978-0-8071-8117-1 (cloth) | ISBN 978-0-8071-8164-5 (pdf) |
    ISBN 978-0-8071-8163-8 (epub)
Subjects: LCSH: United States—History—Civil War, 1861–1865—
    Antiquities. | Material culture—United States—History—19th century.
    | United States—Armed Forces—Uniforms—History—19th century. |
    Confederate States of America—Armed Forces—Uniforms. | United
    States—History—Civil War, 1861–1865—Flags. | United States—
    History—Civil War, 1861–1865—Medals. | United States—History—Civil
    War, 1861–1865—Societies, etc. | Collective memory—United States.
Classification: LCC E646.5 .C68 2024 (print) | LCC E646.5 (ebook) |
    DDC 306.4/6097309034—dc23/eng/20231012
LC record available at https://lccn.loc.gov/2023045181
LC ebook record available at https://lccn.loc.gov/2023045182

For my boys, Henry and Sebastian

CONTENTS

ILLUSTRATIONS

ACKNOWLEDGMENTS

I t is with immense joy and relief that I acknowledge my community and all of the people who made this book possible. I am thankful for the time and impressive archival skills from the American Civil War Museum in Richmond; the Manuscripts and Folklife Archives Department of Library Special Collections at Western Kentucky University; the North Carolina History Museum; the Oklahoma Historical Society Research Center; Larry Campbell at the Lynn, Massachusetts, Grand Army of the Republic Post Museum; and the South Carolina Confederate Relic Room and Military Museum. Your assistance, patience, and willingness to help made a world of difference. A special thank you to Mark Andrews for photographing my objects and editing the images and to Clifton Theriot for scanning my paper items. This project would not be complete without them. I am thankful for the financial assistance from the National Society of the Colonial Dames of America and, at UNLV, the College of Liberal Arts, Graduate School, and Department of History; their contributions provided me the opportunity to venture into the archives and immerse myself in objects. I treasure the continued support of my undergraduate advisors and mentors Bradley Clampitt and Christopher Bean. Our conversations, questions, and encouragement mean more than you could possibly know. Michael S. Green, Deb Young, and Elizabeth White Nelson cared for me as one of their own. I am so fortunate to have the three of you to teach, guide, and support me. Thank you for being my people.

I would also like to thank my reviewer for LSU Press, Anne Sarah Rubin. I appreciate your honest feedback. You saw potential in this project and asked me to do something exceptionally challenging. Your suggestions and concepts made this a better book; I am indebted to you. I would also like to thank the team at LSU Press for making this book a reality.

Thank you to my Nicholls State University Museum Studies students for your hard work and to my dear students Ashlyn, Rae, Gabby, Madeline, Mia, John, and CLIO History Club for your cheers, check-ins, and care throughout this process. My dear colleague Kevin McQueeney deserves special acknowledgment. Thank you for asking critical questions and challenging me to add just one more example. You humored me, read every word multiple times, and consistently encouraged me to center my voice. I am forever grateful to and for you.

We often benefit from the assistance and kindness of others. That said, I greatly appreciate Laura Edwards. Her earnest and unexpected request to read my manuscript and help me throughout this process brought clarity and improved this book. I am blessed to have wonderful friends. Thank you to Evan Rothera, first for his friendship and encouragement, then for reading and offering suggestions to improve this work. My gratitude extends to Adam Domby, who dropped everything to take a phone call, offer advice, and check in on me. And thank you to Jenni Tifft-Ochoa, Heather Nepa, Carolyn Fisher, Nancy Labauve, Rebecca Picou, and Lauren Rizzuto for the texts, calls, pop-in visits, crawfish, king cake, and support. I needed you all, and like magic, you appeared.

Finally, thank you to my family. My mom, Robin; my sister, Taylor; Clint; my two precious boys, Henry and Sebastian; and my faithful pup, Chase. You listened or provided me with breaks from work, and for that, I am grateful and in your debt. To anyone who I may have forgotten, I truly appreciate you and your assistance. You all share in this accomplishment.

The FABRIC *of*
CIVIL WAR
SOCIETY

INTRODUCTION

On Sunday, April 9, 1865, "the two greatest men produced respectively by the North and South during this war met face to face, . . . [o]ne to yield up his sword, and the other to receive it. They met as victor and vanquished."[1] Across the country, newspapers brought the story of Appomattox into people's homes, using descriptive language that set the scene and gave special attention to the attire of both men. "Gen. [Robert E.] Lee was sitting by the table, dressed in a suit of gray—coat, pants and vest all of gray," wearing "an elegant sword," while Ulysses S. Grant had "left his sword behind," appearing "in the same suit he had worn in the field through the eventful days—a plain blue frock, with double row of buttons, and shoulder straps bearing the three silver stars—the insignia of his rank as Lieut. General."[2] The vivid description of these men at this momentous event confirmed the popular opinion of them: Lee was a southern gentleman, and Grant was a no-nonsense soldier.

It should come as no surprise to a modern reader that the uniforms these formidable adversaries wore were important details in the recounting of the surrender of Lee's army. Although no photographer documented the exact moment of this historic event, engravings and portraits of the scene in Wilmer McLean's parlor remain popular to the present, as has the appearance of these two generals. The contrast between the uniforms worn by Lee and Grant has become shorthand for each man's character, a thumbnail sketch of two sides of the conflict. We know the story of what they wore that day better than we know the story of what they said.

Contemporary images and tokens of the Civil War hold a fascination for Americans who study this era.[3] The uniforms worn not just by the great generals who led the armies but also by ordinary soldiers were preserved in great numbers, in attic trunks filled with mothballs or in the back of a closet, ready to be worn at a commemorative event. Photographs and regimental histories preserved the visual details of these uniforms, and antiquarians cataloged these details for future generations. In the twentieth century, film and television animated these uniforms once again, offering the general public knowledge of "the blue and the gray" as two sides of a tragic conflict, reducing the war to opposing opinions and colors. If the war is to be understood as a tragic conflict between brothers, the uniforms these men wore have become shorthand for the ideological battles over its meaning.

That said, the argument presented in *The Fabric of Civil War Society*—material items, especially uniforms, badges, and flags, had a more important role during the Civil War than is currently acknowledged in the scholarship—is threefold. First, the complications and struggle of logistics—specifically, deciding who would pay for uniforms and where they would come from—placed an unexpected financial burden on the soldiers and their families, plaguing both factions of Civil War society. Second, uniforms physically and metaphorically transformed their wearers and influenced those who saw or interacted with them, inducing both positive and negative emotions and reactions. The rules and power dynamics of uniforms, badges, and flags were felt both individually and in society, allowing the objects fluidity in meaning and interpretation. Third, by using these material objects as a lens, we can trace their change in meaning to individuals and communities over time from practical tools of warfare to symbols of sentimentality. By paying close attention to how they were used in narrative construction for Union and Confederate memorial societies and veterans postwar, we can see how these objects performed the heavy lifting in promoting nostalgia through the 1930s.

Overlooking the significance of material culture, especially uniforms, badges, and flags, to Civil War society is a blind spot in the literature. These artifacts are a form of discourse and a means of understanding a larger historical narrative. Although uniforms might seem inconsequential in relation to wartime economics, politics, or military strategy, they not only were important in their own right, much like firearms or ammunition, but also innately influenced those considerations for the United States and the

Confederacy. First, the process of obtaining material objects, including uniforms, was one of the most significant financial drivers of wartime expenditures. In the readymade society of the twenty-first century, people take for granted their ability to access clothing. Yet this was not the case in the nineteenth century. At the beginning of the war, the U.S. Army only had 16,000 soldiers. Lincoln's call for 75,000 troops sparked the production of uniforms in a way that had no precedent. This affected both the northern and southern economies by creating an internal need for the textile industry on a new scale while also influencing international policy for raw materials and finished products. In addition, the opposing forces needed to decide how their soldiers would look and how they would differ from each other. Because of their necessity, uniforms shaped the Confederacy's international relationships and contributed to their financial ruin because of the national leadership's willingness to go into debt. Combining the total U.S. and Confederate forces over the course of the war, a conservative approximation of 3,500,000 troops demonstrates the magnitude of the demand for uniforms.[4]

As the field of Civil War and Reconstruction scholarship continues to grow, the incorporation of material culture into these studies has taken hold, serving as the historiographical foundation of this book. Two edited volumes, *Objects of War: The Material Culture of Conflict & Displacement* and *War Matters: Material Culture in the Civil War Era,* are substantial works that provide both background and a community for the current book, each examining the use of objects as a method of understanding war on societal and individual levels.[5] In addition, scores of other works address the big picture of secession, the war's military history, and its political history, occasionally mentioning uniforms, badges, and flags but not in a way that makes them central or even marginally important to the larger narrative. Historian Mark Wilson has studied the mobilization and preparation of Union efforts for the Civil War. While uniforms have a place in his book, again, they are not the central focus. One of the ways in which the current volume differs from his is its contention that material preparations for the war began immediately after John Brown's raid on Harpers Ferry, Virginia, much sooner than Wilson suggests.[6]

The economics of Civil War uniforms bled into cultural significance because these garments claimed the bodies that wore them for a particular side, signifying that individual's politics. These material objects possessed economic, social, and cultural powers by denoting more than individual identity. Uniforms, badges, and flags provided their possessors with legitimate personhood. Even as individuals defined themselves and their larger communities by their material trappings, the objects themselves spoke loudly as well, demonstrating various points of conflict, disagreement, and discontinuity that one might not otherwise notice.

Because of rules, laws, and customs, those in uniform became an extension of the state and the war aims for which they fought. Uniformed individuals were subject to the rules of war and to the command of their superiors, meaning that they were not allowed to bend to the whims of civilians. African Americans in the uniform of the United States acquired a military status and the legal protection of the federal government, but this also provided U.S. authorities the opportunity to impart rules and laws on them. Native soldiers in uniform understood their clothing as an extension of sovereignty and equality to white men, yet the respective national governments viewed this clothing as a claim on Native service and personhood. Even women in uniform ardently adhered to the social constructs of masculinity because clothing themselves in the authority of the uniform gave them power and freedom that petticoats could not. Many women participating in the home war joined volunteer organizations, a trend that increased during Reconstruction and through the turn of the century.[7]

Uniforms provide this study with insight into the public self and the private self because clothing speaks to, reflects, and affects human identity. Material-culture studies demonstrate the many ways in which physical evidence is central to understanding human experiences.[8] They assist us in grasping how and where particular things are valued in society and the meanings constructed from these objects. This also lends itself to the cultural understanding that even those who are illiterate or unfamiliar with a particular language can read physical items, which allows those objects to become imbued with more meaning because they represent those individuals'—and our own—tangible understanding of their world. An explanation of clothing and its meanings in the nineteenth century is necessary because of the different way modern society grapples with them. According to historian Laura Edwards, throughout the nineteenth century, retailers and manufacturers of cloth and clothing built their businesses around the concept that everyone in society, even those without property or property rights, possessed clothing and had the same cultural understanding of its value. She asserts that between the American Revolution and the Civil War, cloth and clothing held substantial value and served an economic purpose beyond simply their utility or desirability. Because of this, textiles gained legal qualities, which imbued them with various social understandings, such as status. This cultural understanding then reinforced the notion that clothing was a central concept in defining individual identity. Edwards states that simply by wearing clothes, there was a "verifiable relationship between a person and the garments in question." This then allows us to analyze not only individuals but also the larger social, cultural, and economic issues from the Civil War and Reconstruction era. Women specifically reinforced this idea, which was a central reason for their deep involvement in manufacturing wartime and veteran's uniforms for commemorations: they not only understood but also highly valued the cultural currency and symbolism of clothing.[9]

Historian Sarah Jones Weicksel has discussed the "visceral nature" of the American Civil War. She specifically focuses on how Black and white individuals used garments and dress customs to "rework and resist the shifting boundaries between slavery and freedom, the gendered dimensions of daily life and citizenship, and the government's role in civil society." While this book shares similar views in terms of conceptualizing identity and the role the uniforms play in soldier's lives, it differs from Weicksel's work by including Indigenous Peoples, through examining these objects with a longer conceptualization of the era, and postwar memorialization.[10]

Uniforms, badges, and flags allow us to track the evolution of these objects from necessary tools of physical warfare to instruments of memory and identity manipulation. They highlight narrative shifts for both individuals and society toward acceptance of the Lost Cause mythology. After the war, the social significance of veterans' uniforms increased as people and communities attached individual and communal memories to them as well as to badges and flags, which assisted Americans in transforming soldiers into veterans and the creation of a postwar society in complicated ways. Psychological studies have shown that clothing is important to the narrative of human life: "apart from their aesthetic value, clothes have the ability to evoke issues of identity, of the relation to self to body and self to the world." Meaning is woven throughout our clothing and stitched to our identities. Because clothes have the ability to conjure memories, "garments become autobiographical narratives 'rooted in sensory and emotional associations,'" which means that people "save these threads of the past in order to keep our memories alive."[11]

Union and Confederate memory machines reimagined garments for veterans, crafting uniforms for memorialistic rituals such as commemorations, parades, and reunions. The United Confederate Veterans (UCV) designed a veterans' uniform to create a singular perfect image for the Lost Cause to rally around. By creating a set of tangible symbols for their culture of honor, the women who made, paid for, or repaired these uniforms drove most of the country to rally around their new narrative. While receiving far less credit for this than the white southern men featured in the story, women provided the visual underpinnings for the Lost Cause. Material culture in the form of uniforms, badges, and flags proved crucial to this ideology. After the Civil War, former rebels maintained their "Confederateness" and celebrated their new form of southern nationalism through such objects. This book extends the existing discussion of memory and women's associations to include material culture because those women created the tangible symbols that furthered what they and their fellow southerners considered their "true history." Their form of cultural politics still influences our current memory of the Civil War in important and perhaps irreparable ways.

Uniforms, badges, and flags did the heavy lifting of conveying the desired narratives of the Union and Confederate memory machines through the 1930s. As ambassadors for their respective causes, these material constructs, so significant during the war, provided visual legitimacy to the Lost Cause narrative and assisted the Grand Army of the Republic (GAR) and Woman's Relief Corps (WRC) in combating the stories told by the UCV and the United Daughters of the Confederacy (UDC). There are ample books within the field that discuss the reformation of life during and after Reconstruction in connection with the Lost Cause and Civil War memory. These studies provide the intellectual framework for the second half of this work and the prioritizing of uniforms, flags, and postwar badges.[12] The theory of the Lost Cause, the movement that describes the Confederate quest as a heroic struggle against insurmountable odds, has significantly influenced the memory of the Civil War. While the federal government sought to re-unify the country after the war, cultural concepts of the Lost Cause ideology invaded the dialogue and found a great deal of acceptance throughout the country during the period of reunification.[13]

The concepts of commemoration are paramount in understanding societal roles in the postwar period. Cornerstone works focusing on the centrality of women to the memorialization of the Civil War and the Lost Cause narrative inform this project. Caroline E. Janney has argued that the Ladies' Memorial Association (LMA), founded in the immediate post–Civil War period, were the original leaders of the memory movement, not the male veterans' organizations or the UDC, as many have believed. The LMA deserves attention and study as the first group to honor the Con-federate dead, to redefine the Confederacy's military defeat as a "political, social, and cultural victory for the white South," and to differentiate clearly between reunion and reconciliation; these women sought to distinguish the southern past from the northern past. Karen L. Cox concretely shows the importance of southern narrative preservation to the LMA, UDC, and other women's groups. In another study, Janney asserts that reconciliation reflected a "veneer of civility," with grievances from the war still simmering beneath the surface of postwar interactions as each side actively promoted its narrative. *The Fabric of the Civil War* builds on these ideas by focus-ing on the tools the various commemorative groups used to promote their narrative, specifically what people wore and held dear, such as uniforms, badges, and flags.[14]

Objects and the concept of the souvenir are extremely important to this study by helping balance the public and the private spheres in terms of memory, objects, and narrative. According to Susan Stewart, in "the de-velopment of culture under an exchange economy," there is a "search for authentic experience and, correlatively, the search for the authentic object" that becomes "critical." With the passage of time, experience becomes less tangible, and "the memory of the body" or event "is replaced by the mem-ory of the object," which represents "a memory standing outside the self and thus presenting both a surplus and [a] lack of significance"; thus, it is only as valuable or meaningful as the person who possesses it by evolving into its possessor's narrative. Objects or souvenirs allow the "external expe-rience" to be internalized and "authenticates the experience of the viewer."

Souvenirs do not represent "the lived experience" but display the romance of its representation.

Thus, authentic items from the Civil War and those created after the war for the consumption and display of narrative form a divide in this book. Both types of objects assist in their owner's narrative control of the Civil War. Those from the war become sentimental souvenirs kept in the privacy of homes, while newly produced veterans' items are intended for public consumption. Yet postwar badges and uniforms are also invested with sentimentality. The creation and movement of these later objects allowed women the flexibility to move between home and public service in a natural progression. The use of uniforms, badges, and flags as identity markers was completely normal for all fraternal organizations throughout the nineteenth and twentieth centuries.[15]

The first four chapters of this book are constructed thematically around discussions of the logistics and sentiments of uniforms, flags, and regimental badges, while the rest of the volume continues the analysis in chronological order. Chapter one discusses a brief history of uniform policy, the rush to dress troops during the secession crisis, and the logistics from the beginnings of war. Chapter two concludes the discussion of governmental and individual struggles to uniform troops during the war. Emotions and power dynamics are the central themes of chapter three, as people became attached to or rejected the understandings of those who wore the blue or gray. Chapter four provides a short history of badges and flags, returning the focus to the beginning of the war and documenting the process of crafting wartime badges and flags and the emotions behind their use.

We already know Civil War–era chronology well, so this thematic approach to wartime history lays the groundwork for the eras of Reconstruction and the memory machines to better explain the continued use of wartime material culture and the creation of veteran uniforms as both symbols and dividers through the 1930s. Chapter five concludes the war years by discussing the clothing of demobilization. Chapters six, seven, and eight dive deeply into the creation and focus of memorial organizations, intimately describing how the development of veteran uniforms and badges provided representation for GAR, WRC, UCV, and UDC members, including the return of captured Confederate battle flags. The postwar meanings of uniforms, badges, and flags are woven throughout the final chapters to detail how the work of the memorial societies successfully conveyed their desired narrative and forever altered perceptions of the war. The book concludes with a discussion of the continued commodification of Civil War and memory-machine objects.

The timeframe and scope of this book are wide, but they do not encompass everything. For purposes of recognition, uniform coats, hats, and badges (wartime and postwar) are most important to this study because they easily distinguish with which side a soldier or veteran identified. The specific politics and material reasonings of deserters are not mentioned at length. The material trappings of the navy are not discussed in depth, though this does not mean that they were unimportant during the war or to the postwar memory machines. Uniforms, badges, and even some flags were displayed on the physical person, so how they were worn and any personal touches are political identity markers. Ultimately, this book continues the work of many historians by discussing everything from the logistics of manufacturing and supply during the war to soldiers' identity while also assessing the motivations of the GAR, the WRC, the UCV, and the UDC. Hopefully, it also illuminates at least some of the neglected aspects of Indigenous Peoples, Black people, and women's participation from 1859 to 1939.

Most of the attention we pay to these items, however, is in the service of our present understanding of the war or our obsession with reenacting the battles. The currency of these objects in contemporary culture has obscured the history of their meaning to the men—and women—who wore them in combat. For those people, uniforms were not uniform. This book traces the history of how Americans in both the North and the South procured, wore, felt about, and remembered uniforms, badges, and flags, from the secession crisis through the 1930s. This is a story of the centrality of these objects to how soldiers on both sides of the war negotiated their identity. For all Americans, these items embodied patriotism or treason, status or degradation. Far from the tidy concepts of a Hollywood costume department, the realities of how soldiers wore their uniforms on the battlefield were myriad. Americans used the symbolism of uniforms to negotiate the complex terrain of identity formation in a country torn apart by internecine warfare and redefining its national and regional concepts. By recovering the processes through which soldiers received, kept, lost, and replaced their uniforms, badges, and flags, this book offers a way to see how soldiers and civilians crafted their own understanding of these items' significance.

ASSUMING
THE CLOTH
OF WAR

U nder the expanded headline "The War Begun—Engagement at Fort Morris—Attempted Reinforcement of Ft. Sumter—Star of the West Fired into and Driven Back—A Reliable Narration of Facts," editor Joseph Clisby of Georgia's *Macon Daily Telegraph* published an account, reprinted in newspapers across the United States, provided by an eyewitness to Fort Morris firing upon the Union ship *Star of the West* in Charleston harbor, South Carolina. Under the protection of the Palmetto Guards and the Irish Volunteers, the men at Morris Island buzzed with excitement at the sight of the supply steamer. Their mission was to keep "strict surveillance over the harbor, and to make such signals as had been agreed upon in the event of the approach of reinforcements to the fortress in possession of the United States troops" and to "report the approach of any vessel that may appear." Southern troops in a small boat signaled the entire camp on the island. Soldiers already at their stations in anticipation of a fight remained ready for a volley from the artillery at Sumter. The *Star of the West* positioned itself directly opposite the Morris Island fortifications. When the steamer came within range, the men received the command to open fire. "As soon as the Stars and Stripes were run up the masthead the act of defiance was met with a succession of heavy shot from the fortification." The unarmed vessel attempted to get closer to Sumter, but the southerners drove it back when struck. To avoid additional fire and damage, the *Star of the West* lowered its colors to half-mast and sped out of the harbor. News of this confrontation traveled quickly to the city, resulting in "several companies of troops never before in actual service" called out and sent to different locations as a precaution. "In the streets, military uniforms were numerous. Old and young assumed the 'cloth of war,' and took their places in the ranks" because "war, actual war, seemed inevitable."[1]

This story serves as an example of an immediate decision by citizens to "assume the cloth of war" as a sign of their willingness to fight, their commitment to their cause, and their vision of what the resulting war would be like. The immediate reaction of these men highlights the value of their uniforms to the Civil War narrative. Their feelings permeated every aspect of society, from language to preparation, but they are best highlighted in tangible forms such as uniforms, physical manifestations of political alignments and individual beliefs. Uniforms also represented the practical problems created by gearing up for war: soldiers not only needed to identify rank, military organization, and whom to fire upon but also could not fight naked. The Civil War created a need to clothe thousands of soldiers in short order, revolutionizing the textile industry and creating a new market for mass-produced clothing.

PREWAR MILITIAS & THE MEXICAN AMERICAN WAR

The history of volunteer militias in the United States is inseparable from the story of raising and clothing troops during the Civil War. The units' purpose could vary, but by the 1850s, white US-born men and immigrants attached themselves to independent volunteer militias in an attempt to express communal identity and assist with local protection. They maintained public order by enforcing quarantines or quelling riots, and in the South volunteer militias patrolled enslaved people and prevented escapes. These groups offered status for their participants, sustaining "traditional white masculine power and control."[2] According to historian Lesley Gordon, "Membership cost money, and so did equipment and uniforms," so that volunteer companies drew its ranks from middle-class men. For many at this time, the French Zouave became the ideal model to these American citizen-soldiers. Their tactics and dress were attractive to many, embodying masculinity and the military movements of the era. Gordon describes the life and journey as part of this movement of young Illinoisan Elmer Ellsworth, who asserted that "the citizen soldiery would and could serve at a moment's notice, should a national crisis erupt."[3] When the crisis indeed erupted, uniforms were an important but often overlooked issue: what would they look like, what would they cost, and who would pay for them? Such questions long predate the Civil War.

Throughout U.S. history, uniform regulations have undergone revision multiple times, often reflecting civilian fashion or the climate in which the soldiers fought. According to Captain Oscar F. Long, who researched and wrote a booklet published in 1895 by the U.S. Army Quartermaster's Department, "little uniformity [existed] in the clothing, and none whatever in the colors of facings," of the Continentals and militias of the Revolutionary War. He states that those who fought at Lexington and Concord did not have a uniform and even Continental troops engaged at Bunker Hill were without them, fighting in the "plain and ordinary dress of citizens." In 1775 the men of one Virginia regiment were "uniformed at their own expense in hunting shirts and leggings." The lack of uniforms became confusing to the soldiers because there was no way to distinguish who was in charge. By November 1775, Congress "resolved that the clothing for the Army should be paid for by stoppages from the men's pay [three dollars per month]," amounting to ninety cents withheld for clothing; the U.S. Army placed a similar financial burden on its soldiers during the Civil War. While the popular decision among soldiers was a blue coat, each regiment looked a little different in blue, light brown, dark brown, or gray. The "great scarcity" of "proper cloth from which to make uniforms" also affected their appearance. At the urging of General George Washington, those who did not have uniforms used hunting shirts in black, white, yellow, green, or blue; long breeches; and gaiters. Soldiers became so desperate that charitable citizens donated "old and cast-off garments for the Army." Indeed, by 1776, it was "impossible to import material for clothing from the mother country, and little but any, except the homespun, had been made in the Colonies," making the "cast-off clothing" a necessity. The Continental Congress desperately tried to "obtain for the troops proper uniform suits" whatever the color, creating an army that "varied tints of the rainbow." During the Valley Forge winter of 1777–78, Inspector General Baron von Steuben reported seeing one guard in a dressing gown crafted from an old blanket and some men who were "literally naked." The inspector from the Rhode Island Infantry discussed "the naked situation of the troops" and their need for breeches to make them decent. Congress did not pass a *uniform* uniform resolution until early 1779, requesting woolen overalls for winter and linen for the summer, blue coats, waistcoats, and breeches, depending upon supplies and at a maximum cost of approximately four guineas.[4]

The War of 1812 was the next large military conflict, and army regiments were outfitted differently, with the exception of militia uniforms. The ideal uniform was a regulation dark blue coatee, but there was a dye shortage, which meant that some coats were gray, brown, or green. Waistcoats, neck stocks, and white, blue, or gray trousers with gaiters completed the uniform.[5] Officers and their staff members wore cocked hats without feathers, single-breasted coats complete with tails, high military boots, and white or buff breeches. The common soldiers wore completely gray uniforms. It remained expensive for soldiers to pay for their clothing. Enlisted men made $8.00 a month, but the bare minimum uniform cost them $16.87.[6] There were slight changes in the outfit until the Mexican American War, when the military created detailed descriptions of uniforms down to the letter on the buttons.

The army uniform underwent changes in 1847. Infantrymen wore dark blue coats, epaulets, and light blue-gray pants, much like what regulars wore during the Mexican American War. This reflected stylish menswear during the period. Often, noncommissioned officers, musicians, and privates simply wore "coat and trousers" of "dark grey cloth," with other aspects of their uniform the same as infantry styles. This attire was considered comfortable and adaptable.[7] The army updated regulations again in 1851, then once more in August 1861 because of the increased scale of requirements. Prior to the Civil War, both government authorities and private actors purchased war supplies. It was common for states to fund some of the expenses of outfitting and transporting troops, although they could be reimbursed. The national government took responsibility for "arming volunteers" during the Mexican American War, but individual soldiers had to purchase their uniforms, with a clothing allowance that supplemented their pay. So when the Civil War erupted, it was unclear to many within the North who was financially responsible for the uniforms.[8]

JOHN BROWN TO SECESSION

After the long history of the volunteer militia movement, what happened on the night of October 16, 1859, accelerated preparations and advanced the military readiness of white men across the country. John Brown led fourteen white men and four Black men in a quest to overrun the armory at Harpers Ferry and dispatch messengers to local plantations to begin an insurrection of the enslaved. The ill-fated venture left much of the Brown party dead and sparked panic and apoplectic rage throughout the South. It was a catalyst for groups in both the North and South to begin preparing for war. New home guards, governors' cavalry, and other militia companies organized throughout the country.

With a few exceptions regarding troops from northern states, anyone who volunteered for a unit was expected to "pay out his own pocket nearly all the various expenses which attend the existence of the company."[9] This literally meant putting their money in line with their political beliefs. Newspaper reports throughout the United States chronicled a similar story about organizing these new protectors, the expensive nature of outfitting them with new uniforms, and how excited the men were to show them off to the public. Putting men in uniform became a nonverbal cue of lines being drawn and identities aligning with separate sides. The *Macon Daily Telegraph* reported, "this company, whose organization is of recent date, drilled in full uniform at the Fair Ground on yesterday forenoon." The men "presented their usual fine appearance" in the regular U.S. artillery uniform.[10] While this case does not demonstrate a distinct identity, it shows military readiness, which also had economic implications: outfitting a new company with uniforms was expensive.

Yet other newspapers suggest that this was not the case throughout the South. For example, both houses of the Virginia legislature "voted to present the Jefferson Guards with new uniforms for their services at Harper's Ferry."[11] Rewarding these men for their performance was a metaphorical pat on the head from plantation culture for putting down villainous abolitionists. For volunteer companies such as the Perote Guards, it was a point of pride and a mark of "true patriotism" to "furnish themselves with uniforms made of Southern manufactured goods," especially if the material was from their home state. Not only did this promote regional pride but also signaled that northern goods were not necessary for southern defense.[12] The concept of southern manufacturing and utilizing their own goods over northern products was prominent throughout the war and a motivational point of pride for southerners.

During the 1860 presidential campaign, Republicans benefited from the support of young men who formed paramilitary campaign groups. The Wide Awakes were "the first major campaign organization to adopt a military motif. Upon enlistment members became soldiers in the Wide Awake army—complete with ranks, uniforms, and duties," as historian Jon Grinspan observes. "The movement's dangerous use of militarism for political purposes unintentionally bled into powerful cultural agitation that terrified southerners. Young northerners equipped with uniforms and torches sent an ominous message to those already apprehensive about the Republican party's antisouthern attitudes." Grinspan points out that this group increased sectional tension—the uniforms they wore were crucial to their view of themselves and how others viewed them.[13]

Lincoln's 1860 presidential victory sent shockwaves throughout the South. On December 20, 1860, South Carolina seceded from the Union, blazing the way for six more states to quickly follow its example over the next two months.[14] This act of defiance galvanized states in both the North and the South to redouble their efforts in preparing for war—specifically, in obtaining uniforms.

Southerners demonstrated commitment to their cause in a variety of ways, and one of the key methods being their concern about clothing their soldiers. Crucially, pleas from individuals for uniforms appeared on the day that South Carolina seceded: to clothe soldiers was to claim those men, solidifying their separation from the United States, and further committing them to the cause of saving slavery—more than four months before Fort Sumter. Wealthy white southern men implored their neighbors through newspapers as part of their commitment to their cause. In "An Appeal to the Public," which appeared in many different southern papers, petitioners urged their fellow citizens to "give your last dollar to aid in the noble cause" of clothing soldiers for war. One South Carolina newspaper, the *Anderson Intelligencer*, published a staunch statement along with the article, declaring that all uniforms for the volunteer corps of infantrymen "will be made of Southern cloth, with Southern-made hats." It estimated that each uniform would cost "between $12 and $16," seeking to "raise by subscription $300" to "uniform 24 men." If someone did not wish to give money, it asked for the benefactor to "select some worthy young man and present him with a uniform." The Palmetto Riflemen appointed James A. Hoyt, who was also editor of the *Intelligencer,* as well as W. W. Humphreys, J. C. C. Featherston, and James H. Whitner to pen an earnest request to South Carolinians to assist in paying for the unit's uniforms. Even if a person could only purchase a subscription of ten dollars, the authors believed "the whole amount [could be] raised with little effort."[15]

Still others raised companies by digging into their own pockets. Officers like Frederick Townsend of Albany purchased uniforms for the new regiments when he "organized a Zouave corps." A San Francisco newspaper picked up the story that "General Townsend has ordered eighty uniforms at his own expense, from Paris, and they will arrive in time for his company to participate in the inauguration ceremonies at Washington."[16] The *National Republican* reported on a meeting of the capital city's Fourth Ward leaders and their discussion to propose a design and appoint a committee to "solicit subscriptions to buy uniforms for those unable to furnish themselves."[17]

In addition to soliciting such subscriptions for purchasing uniforms, wealthy white men called on women for assistance in physically creating them. Regiments placed newspaper advertisements for women to volunteer their time and sew uniforms; some even offered payment for the work. In January 1861, newspapers throughout the country began advertising for women to assist in preparing for war. The Emmet Guard, under the command of a Lieutenant Brennan, called "upon the ladies to complete their fatigue uniforms without delay."[18] An advertisement by J. W. Aderhold, captain of the Independent Volunteers of Georgia, sought "ladies who are willing to make the uniforms for the Independent Volunteers," stating that they "will receive three dollars for each suit made." It also noted where to pick up the precut pieces to fashion together.[19] Such advertisements only increased in quantity once the war began and continued to appear throughout the war.

Manufacturing companies led larger-scale efforts, advertising in newspapers to offer to produce uniforms or to tout their efforts in outfitting regiments from several states. Georgia's Eagle Manufacturing Company claimed to have supplied military companies from Louisiana, Mississippi,

Alabama, and Florida with "8,000 yards of cassimere for uniforms since the secession movement began." The article described the material as "'a substantial fabric, of the cadet mixed or green color.'"[20] Reports of new uniforms manufactured in Maryland for various regiments differed from that in other parts of the country, as those in Baltimore bragged about making them for the Chesapeake Rifles of Kent County "of a blue cloth coat and pants, trimmed with gold." Marylanders also produced uniforms for the Clifton Guards, "a new dragoon corps in Factory District, St. Mary's [C]ounty," whose "uniform is of gray cassimer [*sic*], trimmed with black braid."[21]

On March 4, 1861, Lincoln took the oath of office as the sixteenth president of the United States. As a response to this, two days later the newly organized southern government called for 100,000 volunteers to serve in a provisional army "to repel invasion, maintain the rightful possession of the Confederate States of America in every portion of territory belonging to each State, and to secure the public tranquility and independence against threatened assault." These troops would "serve for twelve months after they shall be mustered into service, unless sooner discharged." The "volunteers shall furnish their own clothes," then if they were mustered into service, the unit's home state or the Confederate government would ensure they were properly armed. Authorities planned to clothe their troops "when called into actual service, and while remaining therein, be subject to the rules and articles of war, and instead of clothing, every non-commissioned officer and private in any company shall be entitled, when called into actual service, in money to a sum equal to the cost of clothing of a non-commissioned officer or private in the regular army of the Confederate States of America."[22] From the start, Confederate officials knew the importance of military uniforms to their soldiers, and they were willing to furnish them or pay for the existing uniform of those mustered into service.

While prewar preparations assisted in getting supply chains underway, once war broke out, both the North and the South confronted their own specific challenges to expansion. Supply lines and manufacturing relationships from prewar contracts often were unavailable, and fighting the war required men to leave their traditional occupations and women and children to pick up the slack. In the beginning, Union and Confederate troops often looked the same on the battlefield because colors had not yet been decided, leading to deadly confusion in early battles. Each belligerent faced the tribulations of finding funds, procuring supplies, and gathering a labor force to craft their uniforms. While enduring some of the same problems, both the average citizens as well as the highest leadership of the Union and the Confederacy crafted creative solutions.[23]

SUMTER TO 1862

During Lincoln's inaugural address, he vowed to maintain control of the federal property in the seceded states. To make good on that assertion, a resupply ship set out from New York for Fort Sumter, South Carolina, on April 9, 1861. When Brigadier General P. G. T. Beauregard learned of this, he ordered Major Robert Anderson, commanding the fort and its garrison, to evacuate, but Anderson refused unless he received orders from Washington. In the early morning of April 12, the battery at Fort Johnson fired a round high above Sumter, and by morning light, the fort was under heavy fire. The bombardment continued for thirty-four hours until the afternoon of the thirteenth, when Anderson surrendered. The Civil War was underway, with Lincoln answering the loss of Fort Sumter with a call on April 15 for 75,000 military volunteers.[24] This would mean that by the end of the month, the two armies needed approximately 200,000 uniforms combined.

The rest of April and May brought a significant amount of activity and posturing between the Union and the Confederacy. Virginia seceded from the Union on April 17. Two days later, at Major General Winfield Scott's recommendation, Lincoln enacted the Anaconda Plan, which among other things called for the blockade of southern ports and would prove critical to upsetting the Confederate supply process. On May 3 Lincoln called for an additional 42,000 volunteers to make a three-year commitment to serve the United States, after which, on May 6, Arkansas and Tennessee seceded, requesting to join the Confederacy, as did North Carolina two weeks later. On May 16 the Confederate Congress authorized recruiting 400,000 volunteers.[25] The calls for troops and their immediate mustering meant a flurry of hurried activity to prepare men for war without a clear understanding of how a regiment should look, since the uniform design for either side was not yet standard or decided.

Wartime uniform production boomed with Lincoln's call to arms: the practical need for military clothing, the adaptability of existing production facilities, and the initial omission of uniform design directly benefiting the New York textile and clothing industry. The outpouring of cash from the federal government to make government contracts to buy uniforms for its soldiers flooded the garment industry with funds. This led smaller mills to combine forces to obtain these contracts. One such collaboration, Mack, Stadler, & Glaser, understood this concept and gained enough contracts to be considered the Union's second-largest supplier in 1861. The combination of the three firms and the Mack Company's reputation with Ohio governor William Dennison as an "honest contractor" assisted their prosperity.[26] Indiana procured uniforms from several Ohio companies, including Stadler Brothers and Glaser Brothers.[27] Between August and December 1861, Mack, Stadler, & Glaser manufactured 191,548 pieces of clothing for the Union military. By the close of the Civil War, the Union had purchased vast quantities of clothing, including "six million pairs of trousers, eleven million shirts, and twenty million pairs of stockings," from this firm and others.[28]

Larger firms also reaped the benefits of government contracts. Most contractors sold directly to their own state unless it was permitted to sell outside of the state or if they did not have the facilities necessary to fulfill the contract. The popular readymade New York City clothing manufacturer and wholesaler Brooks Brothers acquired one of its state's larger contracts, numbering twelve thousand uniforms. This upset other clothiers in the area not only because they did not have a bidding opportunity but also because Brooks Brothers misled officials about its ability to produce all of the garments from heavy wool broadcloth. Upon the next need for a large uniform purchase, state officials took bids and split the $270,000 order between six firms, specifying the price of the uniforms at $18 each.[29] Clothing establishments, such as those in Detroit owned by clothier Samuel Sykes, also contracted to manufacture uniforms. Sykes quickly became the largest Union military contractor in Michigan, a pursuit so profitable that he retired in 1862 and moved his family to Europe, leaving his business to his brother-in-law Samuel Heavenrich.[30] Between Samuel Sykes & Company and E. S. Heineman & Company, the federal government placed $180,000 worth of orders for uniforms and blankets.[31] In addition to obtaining uniforms manufactured in the North, Washington officials sent purchasing agents to England and secured agreements with a few Yorkshire woolen mills to supply the Union with goods. Many of the mill owners sympathized with the Confederacy, however, and delayed their Union production to benefit the South. This proved counterproductive by necessitating the growth of the North's textile industry and establishing its importance to the Union cause.[32]

In the interest of efficiency, the states shouldered the burden when furnishing uniforms for new Union regiments. They did this through quartermasters who were required to procure, store, and issue war goods, including uniforms. According to historian Mark Wilson, the quartermaster system used during the Civil War originated because Secretary of War John C. Calhoun developed the new staffing and bureau system in 1818.[33]

In 1861 national regulations were not yet in place for uniform color, just style, which meant that northern armies looked less consistent than they are imagined today. Because of regulations created in the late 1850s, the standard style for U.S. soldiers typically included a frock coat with branch piping, uniform jackets with branch coordinating lace, sky-blue trousers, a blue wool four-button sack coat, and a forage cap, also known as a kepi. The army issued shirts that were cotton or cotton-wool blend in a pullover style and bootees that were black leather, ankle height, and with soles.[34] The lack of regulations allowed some U.S. quartermasters to furnish "gray uniforms." Occasionally, "generously patriotic" citizens donated funds to the state on behalf of the soldiers "towards defraying the expenses of fitting out her sons for battle."[35] Gray cloth was popular, cheap, and readily available in the majority of all states, making it an attractive option for clothing troops on both sides.

A sampling of newspaper articles describing newly formed regiments reveals the variety of uniforms. The *Watertown Republican* in Wisconsin proudly told of its men going to war "uniformed in heavy gray cloth" and being "well provided" with almost everything they needed. Observers reportedly praised the regiment's appearance and said it "presented a striking contrast to those sent from Illinois," who wore dark blue.[36] Due to the lack of uniformity in dress, those men recruited from throughout the state to form the Eighth Maine Regiment were "attired in gray uniforms, with the army regulation hat."[37] Indiana regiments bound for Virginia "were handsomely dressed in gray uniforms, with hats, instead of caps."[38] In one instance Union troops from Wisconsin were called for service, and the commander's answer was that since "no regulation has yet been made . . . I think we shall adopt a cheap uniform for field service; probably a blue blouse, woolen pants, of dark grey cloth, and the army hat."[39]

The lack of direction and the variety with which the Union faced supplying its troops with adequate uniforms was compounded by the lack of material, the use of poor materials, and the question of who would pay the bill. At the start of hostilities, textile manufacturers and clothiers had difficulty completing contracts for hundreds of thousands of uniforms for two reasons: first, secession created a cotton shortage that hurt their ability to make quality garments; second, a robust ready-to-wear industry did not yet exist, so fulfilling an order that large in a limited time span was a strenuous task. The majority of Civil War–era uniforms utilized mixed fibers. Woolen coats, cotton or linen shirts, and woolen or denim pants were common.[40] This forced suppliers to come up with creative options to fulfill government contracts. The solution the textile industry designed was to combine the "fibers of recycled woolen goods into a material called 'shoddy.'" This term became synonymous with a terrible product because the garments ripped or fell apart after a few weeks of wear due to "shoddy" construction. In Ohio the *Highland News* reported that Hillsborough's volunteer troops were "now naked, the poor material of which their uniforms were manufactured not being strong enough to hold the stitches together." The newspaper explained that the soldiers had "worn out their own clothes in the service, and yet are unable to procure any from the Government."[41] On visiting a soldiers' camp in York, Pennsylvania, another reporter commented on observing men wearing their overcoats on a warm day: "I was surprised to see many of the men wearing their overcoats. Upon inquiring the reason, I found to my amazement that it was a matter of absolute necessity" because the "pantaloons which had been furnished them were so rotten that many of them would burst at the first stoop made by the wearer." He added that there was no point in mending the pantaloons because "the cloth, or shoddy . . . , was too rotten to hold the stitches, and as a necessary consequence, the poor fellows were obliged to wear their overcoats to hide the rents."[42] Once word spread about the poor quality of such uniforms, it became a source of pride to report on good ones. A Vermont newspaper boasted, "the overcoats and uniforms are of an excellent material, of Vermont manufacture, with no indication of 'shoddy' (or rag wool), of strong texture, closely woven."[43]

All of these complications were just for temporary soldiers, most of whom had only signed up for a three-month term. Underscoring the importance of material and matériel, these issues prompted one newspaper to suggest that the "delay in the three-year's enlistment is undoubtedly the neglect of the part of the proper authorities to furnish the uniforms and arms."[44] If the basic needs of soldiers to be clothed and armed for three months could not be met, then outfitting troops for the duration of the war appeared an impossible task. On July 22, 1861, the day after the Union defeat at the Battle of Bull Run, Congress authorized a volunteer army of half a million men serving three-year terms. This call to arms prompted states to gear up production and spend time and money clothing new regiments.

By that fall, Union uniform production grew smoother, but the lack of regulation from the War Department meant that soldiers still were not all dressed the same. Many troops from Maine, Vermont, Indiana, and Wisconsin continued to be outfitted in gray or a mixture of blue and gray, which led to fatal mix-ups on the battlefield.[45] Lieutenant Colonel Wilder Dwight perfectly expressed the problem with this inconsistency when describing the Battle of Bull Run. In this letter he painted a horrifying scene. A regiment appeared in front of Captain Charles Griffin's battery, its cannon loaded and preparing to fire, when an officer began begging Griffin to hold because the men were his own troops. The artillerymen had no way of visually distinguishing them as friend or foe by their uniforms, and they "carried no flag." Griffin's men then turned their guns and fired in a different direction, at which time the unidentified regiment opened fire on them, shooting down many cannoneers and taking the battery. Dwight claimed that the destruction of that regiment would have "changed the result in that part of the field" and demonstrated "the importance of a *uniform* uniform."[46]

The solution, ordered by Major General George B. McClellan, began trickling through northern newspapers in August and September 1861, but it did not make headlines. Below the section title "No More Gray," it proclaimed, "McClellan forbids the use of gray uniforms—the rebels' color." The War Department issued this order "to prevent confusion on the field" and to inform everyone "that the national uniform is to be blue."[47]

This decision corresponded with the revised regulations for the U.S. Army published in August 1861. In the quartermaster's section several line items detail the allowance of uniform clothing, when a soldier would receive new items, and how many he could have over the course of five years, stating that everyone should go through the quartermaster for their clothing. The manual makes clear that soldiers would shoulder the greater burden of their clothing because what they were allotted twice a year would not keep them physically covered, given the amount of wear and tear expected normally. If a soldier was transferred or discharged, "the amount due to or by him for clothing" was "stated on his descriptive lists" or certificates to the "settlement of his accounts." If a soldier deserted, his clothing would be "turned into store" because the military uniform was the "property of the [War] Department."[48]

As more than 300,000 Ohioans would leave their homes to fight in the Civil War, they paid not only a physical and mental price but a financial one as well. In 1861 Governor Dennison approved contracts "made for 8,000 uniforms with the 'scales' at $16 each."[49] The *Daily Ohio Statesman* published General Orders No. 20, concerning the cost of uniforms for Union soldiers and how they should look. Adjunct General H. B. Carrington noted, "this uniform can be procured at a price ranging from seven to ten dollars, according to quality of material."[50] What the officers failed to acknowledge was that those producing the clothing raised their prices to make money during the war.

The high costs of uniforms burdened Union soldiers financially, which did nothing to improve morale when their state asked them to pay for regimental regalia upon enlistment. Alfred Castleman, a soldier in the Army of the Potomac, wrote in his diary that the men used "all our little private means to buy uniforms and outfits for the war."[51] According to an item in the *Indiana State Sentinel,* those in the artillery and infantry—that is, men serving on foot—at the rank of private received eleven dollars a month. The advertisement stated that "in addition to the pay," men would receive "one ration per day and an abundant supply of good clothing is allowed to every soldier." The caveat was that the government provided "quarters, fuel and medical attendance," all "without deduction from the soldier's pay"; the absence of a reference to clothing suggests that they would be required to pay for it.[52] The *Cleveland Morning Leader* also provided information about the monetary burden to soldiers, stating, "commissioned officers are obliged to clothe, equip and arm themselves . . . at their own expense." Noncommissioned officers and privates were "allowed the uniform clothing stated" in the table provided them upon enlistment, including but not limited to "2 coats; 3 pairs of trowsers; 3 flannel shirts; 3 do. drawers; [and] 4 pairs bootees." This clothing discussion ended with the warning, "only such articles of clothing as are indispensable for immediate use will be issued to recruits at the rendezvous," but not stating who was to pay for the items.[53] If privates (the majority of the army's men) were paid only eleven dollars a month in the beginning of their enlistment, which later increased to thirteen dollars a month, the initial cost of uniforms at sixteen to twenty-five dollars each could leave them indebted to the government and affect their families.

The army's needs heavily influenced the textile industry's ledgers, but they also had a significant effect on its workforce. As men enlisted to fight, women proved to be a significant labor source for the Union. Some of them remained in the industry in which they already worked and began making uniform garments, while others entered the workforce, which expanded to meet wartime needs, for perhaps the first time. Marcus Kohner's clothing business in Madison, Wisconsin, sold its state's government approximately $100,000 worth of uniforms, some of them produced by seamstresses in Milwaukee and Madison.[54] While the men were at war, the Merrimack Manufacturing Company in Lowell, Massachusetts, brokered a government contract "to supply the soldiers with cotton-flannel drawers." Women at the factory accepted the work, although many of the mills were closed "for lack of cotton."[55] Philadelphia's Schuylkill Arsenal employed about 3,000 women to make uniforms and assist the war effort in 1861.

Many of these women were contract workers who earned only $1.50 a week, barely enough to keep them out of the poorhouse. They sought to work directly for the U.S. government because war contractors paid so little in comparison. President Lincoln intervened in the dispute between the factory women and government contractors and raised their pay, but the army's expensive contracts with manufacturing conglomerates continued to provide low compensation for the workers fulfilling them.[56] Women who made shirts in Philadelphia in 1863 earned an estimated $2.40 weekly, while those in New York who were a part of the Working Women's Protective Union who did "military work" that same year made $6.00-7.00 per week.[57] In 1860 the going rate for "good quality cotton and wool suits" created by a tailor was $8.00, while "medium all wool suits" were $12.00. The general process for creating these garments began with the cloth being cut in the factory, then "made up by the piece under contract by tailors who run their own shops, furnish tools, and employ their own workmen." In New York in 1860 male tailors made $1.50 per week, while female tailors made sixty-six cents per week. On average they worked ten-hour days. This amount held steady until 1862; the weekly wage increased to $1.83 for men and eighty-three cents for women by 1863 and remained there through the end of the Civil War.[58] With no standard pricing, it is nearly impossible to determine how much money was spent and made on uniforms throughout the Civil War. But overall figures leave no doubt that uniforms were an extremely costly venture, with much of the expense driven by the expanding clothing industry. Due to the high demand, producers repeatedly raised prices, leading to great wealth for clothing manufacturers and emptying the pockets of the men serving in the uniform that poorly paid workers, predominantly women, created.

Despite these opportunities for great wealth, production only slowly increased in 1861. Even Union officers had a challenging time obtaining uniforms for their troops and thus were even prouder of their efforts when the materials finally arrived. The situation grew so dire at one point that Major General Benjamin Butler was forced to quell a mutiny in one of his regiments in August 1861. One of the major complaints from soldiers was the "want for proper clothing." The men waited more than two months for their clothing, but it never arrived, and they did not have extra trousers.[59]

As a result of this constrained supply, the federal government relied on other sources for uniforms. Women also organized various charitable efforts to clothe their community's soldiers. Many not only received contracts form the Union army but were also personally hired by individual soldiers to attend to their clothing needs.[60] Because of the limited availability of readymade items generally, many women were proficient in cutting, sewing, and mending clothes. Some ladies' groups and societies held fundraisers to procure money for purchasing cloth and materials in order to make uniforms.[61] "The Work of the Patriotic Women," as one newspaper headline put it, was a point of pride for the people of Philadelphia: "the Guard House was literally besieged with women" who were "anxious to make up 'some of that army clothing upon any terms.'" The paper reported that "five hundred of the ladies of Germantown are sewing for the volunteers of the Twenty-second Ward" and those of "the West Spruce Street Church, who are desirous of offering their services to the public authorities in making up garments for the soldiers," were in the lecture room of the church ready to help where they could.[62]

Union soldiers resorted to other methods of obtaining uniforms or the materials to make them. Several southern newspapers reported the theft of clothing and uniforms by northern troops. A North Carolina newspaper published an account by H. C. Ferrell of his experience as a prisoner of war. For a short time before his capture by enemy soldiers, because of his similar uniform, Ferrell was mistaken "for a member of their own regiment." While he was confined, his Union captors at first allowed his friends to visit and bring provisions. This eventually stopped, and "several boxes of clothing and other articles, sent afterwards, were taken from the prisoners and appropriated to the use of their own troops."[63] Another common cause of stolen uniforms were bounty jumpers—men who would enlist, then skip out on service. The *Nashville Daily Union* reported that "three men dressed in Federal uniform were arrested" because they had lost their leave-of-absence papers. It went on to speculate that the men were "bounty jumpers who have stolen their uniforms and were endeavoring to escape."[64] The irony of that statement is while Union soldiers purchased their uniforms, they were still considered the property of the government.

The Confederacy also worked from the start on raising funds and trying to equip white volunteers and soldiers with uniforms, but just like the Union, it had no official regulation that determined the color of the uniform, just the design. On August 30, 1861, the Confederate Congress amended a previous resolution that "authorized and required" the secretary of war "to provide, as far as possible, clothing for the entire forces of the Confederate States, and to furnish the same to every regiment or company upon the requisition of the commander." Lawmakers even added, "in case any state shall furnish to its troops and volunteers in the Confederate service such clothing, then the Secretary of War is required to pay over to the Governor of such State the money value of the clothing so furnished." Each unit commander had "the privilege of receiving commutation for clothing at the rate of twenty-five dollars per man for every six months, when they furnished their own clothing."[65]

Outfitting troops with adequate clothing was a priority for the Confederate government, so much so that the South continued their solicitation

of women's time and labor to assist the official war effort.[66] White southern townswomen freely provided traditional domestic labor for the cause
to craft military uniforms. Early in the war, newspapers published advertisements, one of which proclaimed "Females Wanted to Make Coats &
Pants."[67] Ladies of the Methodist Episcopal Church offered their assistance
crafting uniforms for the volunteers, requesting only that the materials be
provided and "cut to fit the parties."[68] In order for women to participate
and wage their own war, prominent white men requested their assistance
for the military. "Ladies! Attention!!" was splashed across a corner of South
Carolina's *Abbeville Press*, with James C. Calhoun issuing a call for action
to women whose relatives and friends served in Captain Samuel J. Hester's
company. He promised to furnish everything, asking only "for the ladies
to do the sewing."[69] Confederate soldier David Johnston wrote in his diary
about the women of his town, stating that they worked in "earnest and with
energy to make our outfits" for the cause.[70]

According to Virginian Thomas Almond Ashby, in April 1861 volunteers throughout his county volunteered in large numbers, organizing two
companies fully officered and equipped with uniforms and arms. Many of
these men could not furnish their own horses and uniforms, so the county
authorities provided an appropriation from the local treasury with enough
money for feeding and clothing the volunteers. The "gray cloth suitable for
uniforms" was unavailable in his county, so his father was selected as chairman of a material-purchasing committee. This group's efforts included a
visit to a large woolen mill near Winchester to purchase the necessary gray
cloth. Ashby's town then employed tailors "to cut out the gray cloth for the
uniforms," which were "all made by the [local] women and girls," who were
"aided by some negro women who were trained to do needlework." Within
a few days, the companies had their uniforms and were sent to join the
army at Manassas.[71]

In a patriotic effort to assist the Confederate cause, white men traveled
the countryside pleading for donations. One individual in communication
with the editor of the *Abbeville Press* proudly announced that he had "received about Nine Hundred Dollars in cash and due notes. One hundred
of this sum has been contributed to pay a balance due on the cost of the
Uniform of the Southern Guards."[72] An advertisement placed in a Virginia
newspaper by order of an E. McConnell requested that new soldiers report

for drill but boldly stated, "Uniforms and equipments [sic] furnished free." Another advertisement in the same issue asked that new volunteers report for duty, also adding, "uniforms and accoutrements [sic] cost nothing."[73] Southerners took pride in their uniforms and the support the home front provided. North Carolina soldier Zenas T. Haines reported in a letter home that a "large number of the regiment will wear uniforms made to measure, and of better stock than that furnished by Uncle Sam."[74] Soldiers who heard of the Union's "shoddy" debacle made such comments as Haines did, which only fueled their sense of superiority.

In September 1861 Confederate officials aligned their organization with their military vision by producing the *Uniform and Dress* manual, detailing specific instructions of uniform cuts and colors for each branch of the military, including ornate drawings denoting rank and the correlating uniform. Enlisted men dressed in a "double breasted tunic of gray cloth" or "cadet gray, with the skirt extending halfway between the hip and the knee; two rows of buttons on the breast, seven in each row." The description continued for several more detailed sentences, suggesting how much Confederate leaders were concerned about the appearance of their military personnel. By December, the war began taking its toll on southern forces, and the Confederate Congress needed to reassess recruiting efforts due to "companies reduced by death and discharges." Lawmakers thus authorized the secretary of war to take over recruiting measures "and enlisting men for companies in service for the war, or three years."[75]

Comparing the Confederate manual with the sketches of Union uniforms suggests that the South was dressing its men for glory and parades, not for practicality or military readiness. Adding to this self-inflated notion, an editorial published in the *Memphis Daily Appeal* stated that "true southern independence requires that our uniforms shall consist exclusively of southern material."[76] While an admirable notion, this concept was nothing but a pipe dream. No longer able to rely on northern textile mills to produce uniforms, Confederate officials both established a relationship with European and Central American textile mills and pursued policies to expand their own industry to craft uniforms. To these ends, state and Confederate governments seized or impressed steamers into service as blockade-runners.[77]

Southern textile manufacturers took a great risk by crossing the ocean, obtaining uniform materials, and assisting the cause by exchanging raw goods for finished products and purchasing mill equipment. Leading manufacturer William Gregg advised other textile owners to run the Union naval blockade to reach England to update their machinery for the war effort as well as to sell and trade goods. North Carolinians were persistent in blockade-running and buying goods they could not find in the Confederacy.[78] In April 1861 Gregg requested that members of the Whitten and Sons textile manufactory "complete the first shipment of our machinery" and "forward it to New York to come out here by steamer" because the textile owners "employed a special agent to enter at the custom house in Charleston."[79] These actions entailed risks, including the seizure of goods. A South Carolina paper reprinted a story from the *New York Times* about the vessels *Vixen* and *Bibb* being watched and detained because of suspicious behavior, reporting that "a lot of uniforms for the Southern army have been seized."[80]

Purchasing orders, invoices, and blockade-runners began crossing the Atlantic in August 1861 for large quantities of shirts, cloth, forage caps, and trousers. Caleb Huse, the Confederacy's most influential purchasing agent, began a partnership with British textile manufacturer Samuel Isaac of S. Isaac, Campbell, & Company. Richmond authorities placed large requests, including detailed measurements, with the company in December 1861, not only for bolts of blue and gray cloth but also for artillery and infantry great cloaks, shell jackets, blue serge trousers, boots, woolen socks, mitts, and blankets, making Great Britain the South's largest European supply source.[81] This happened at a financial loss to the Confederacy because the company charged the government far above market value due to the risks.[82] Because of the Union blockade, British suppliers exported goods to the Confederacy through Bermuda and the Bahamas. Running through those ports was easy because they favored the South and had strained relations with the United States.[83] But there were problems that could be difficult to overcome, especially since the Union blockade often made it difficult to get products shipped from Nassau.

The Confederate government spent over $1 million on clothing and uniforms for troops in 1861. This does not account for the $21 (later $25) stipend granted every six months to each volunteer who used his own clothes or had them furnished by their communities, a figure that is not calculable with surviving records. The government paying its soldiers for their provided uniforms could have been a practical, strategic plan due to the South's lower manufacturing capabilities and the effects of the blockade. This stipend and its provisions would assist in making many regiments look more alike, although consistency in Confederate uniforms did not last. This raises the question of how this beginner nation could afford to pay so much money to outfit its soldiers. The answer was that it could not. Many Confederate decision makers came from the planter class.[84] Planters were accustomed to being in debt personally and did not give careful consideration to accruing more obligations nationally for outfitting troops for war.[85] The Confederacy was willing to go into debt at the beginning of the war for uniforms because those grand garments allowed its people not just the perception of justice and glory but also a tangible representation of wartime nationalism.[86]

Making matters worse, Confederate purchasing agents struck deals with southern textile manufactories to promote their domestic industry, but the mills only produced enough material to partially fulfill the Confederacy's needs. Alfred Davis, the quartermaster in Greenville, South Carolina, wrote several letters at the request of General Beauregard to area cotton and woolen mills. He inquired about the district and its ability to assist in meeting the necessities of the war. Davis also requested that mill owners or operators "advise me in writing of the charges of your establishment and its capacity for making cloth or yarn."[87]

Losing skilled textile workers to the military was a blow to the southern war effort in that it threatened the domestic production rate of uniforms. Although the Confederate Conscription Act of April 1862 was enforced, it "exempted from military service all persons employed in cotton and woolen manufacturing upon their application to Quartermaster General [Abraham] Myers."[88] The textile mills needed all of the assistance they could get: over the course of the war, women and children worked eighty-hour weeks, which took a toll on their health and morale and highlighted the need for laborers.[89] Ramping up southern cloth and uniform manufacturing took longer than anticipated, resulting in the continued need to supplement home goods with imported items run past the blockade.[90]

At the beginning of the war, General Scott's Anaconda Plan took a while to put into place. His approach would supposedly squeeze the Confederacy, as a constrictor snake squeezes its prey to cut off its air supply, and cut off access to international resources and aid, damaging the southern war effort. By late 1861 and into early 1862, the Union snake had tightened its coils, causing shortages of goods and higher prices for any materials that made it through the naval blockade. Cloth and clothing became a significant portion of the goods that Confederate blockade-runners transported.[91] Uniforms became an essential facet of Richmond's foreign policy, requiring precious time and resources to risk the blockade. Steamers running the cordon ramped up operations in 1862, enhancing the relationship between the Confederacy and S. Isaac, Campbell, & Company. But more steamer voyages meant more chances of getting caught and cargoes being confiscated. The Confederate quartermaster's importation efforts started taking hits in January and March, when patrolling Union warships picked off rebel supply boats between the coast of Florida and Nassau. The first intercepted vessel carried a full cargo of cloth, accoutrements, and armaments, while the second contained "1,546 yards of gray army cloth, 11,543 yards of steel mixed gray cloth for uniforms," CSA buttons, shoes, blankets, and small arms.[92] Isaac, Campbell, & Company aligned further with the Confederacy in November 1862 when it petitioned Richmond authorities "to furnish [the Confederate army with] clothing and equipments for 100,000 men, deliverable at Bermuda or Nassau." Company leaders had heard about the Confederate government creating a payment system of cotton certificates, which appealed to them as they had already advanced the South about 400,000 pounds of materials.[93] By the end of 1862, Agent Huse had purchased nearly $5 million in supplies, and the Confederacy owed the company approximately $2 million for uniforms and arms.[94]

England was not the only country the Confederate government contracted with to obtain uniforms and material for its troops. Mexico played in important role as an overland outlet for transporting and supplying goods transportation to the South. It was not until 1862 that the Confederacy dispatched an emissary who was well received by Mexican officials. This relationship opened the seaport of Matamoros to southern vessels and allowed significant amounts of European goods passage through consignment in Havana, then shipped through the blockade relatively undetected to the Trans-Mississippi War Department. Trade between Texas and the Mexican states of Nuevo León and Coahuila expanded quickly, bringing in valuable supplies such as cloth for uniforms and blankets by wagon.[95] With the loss of New Orleans and its ocean access in the spring of 1862, the Mexican ports became even more important to Confederate textile supplies.

As an alternative to blockade-running, southern women continued to gather in 1862 to assist their "noble" cause and contribute their skills and resources to their communities. Eliza E. Harper issued a plea to southern women to do all they could for the war effort, declaring that they "must . . . ply the busy shuttle and the shining needle to shield him [the Confederate soldier] from the wintry blast."[96] Often women took on other tasks than sewing uniforms, including blockade-running for materials needed to make uniforms. The wife of a Confederate officer ran the Union gauntlet under the guise of escorting her sister and visiting her mother, but her real mission was to "buy a Confederate uniform in Yankeeland" from a tailor. Although under suspicion from Union authorities, this tailor assisted the woman in conceiving a plan to smuggle home cut cloth for a uniform and shirts as well as gold buttons. "You ran the blockade to get here," said a Union officer, Major Brooks, when the woman was later interrogated. "That's so," she replied. "I managed to cross at Berlin because you had such a nice provost marshal there. He knew two little women couldn't do any harm."[97] Because the blockade began to work, the Confederacy enacted a new law directed at the troops in October 1862, stating that the clothing required to be furnished to them "may be of such kind as to color and quality as it may be practicable to obtain, any law to the contrary not withstanding."[98]

The difficulty of obtaining uniforms led to numerous cases of Confederate troops stealing those of Union soldiers throughout the war. One lady who had recently returned from Richmond recounted her trip to search for her missing husband. She had to walk through the battlefield at Bull Run past the bodies of Union soldiers who "were stripped entirely naked" and "swollen by the . . . rains." She described the southerners who escorted her as "ragged and dirty" because they "were clothed in the bloodstained uniforms they had stolen from the reeking bodies."[99] The *New York Herald* reported difficulties distinguishing between Yankee and rebel troops at the Potomac River crossing between Conrad's Ferry and Point of Rocks because of "the stolen blue uniform[s]" that Major General J. E. B. Stuart's cavalrymen wore.[100] Sanitation Commission inspector Lewis Henry Steiner kept a diary during the Confederate occupation of Fredrick, Maryland, in

1862, on September 10 giving a detailed account of the rebel force as it vacated the town: "over 3,000 negroes . . . were clad in all kinds of uniforms," including "cast-off or captured United States uniforms."[101] By then, many divisions in the Confederacy were short of clothes, and despite the prohibition against stealing Union uniforms, an entire division arrived at the Antietam battlefield dressed in Union blue.[102]

Obtaining proper uniforms was difficult for everyone at this point, so adding more soldiers only increased the problem. While white Union and Confederate forces obtained their materials, the South also sought Indigenous alliances in Indian Territory during the spring of 1861. The United States had pulled all troops and resources from the region, physically and financially abandoning resettled Native People there to prepare for war. This absence left the Indigenous Peoples vulnerable and created an opening for the Confederate government to attempt negotiations, seeing these groups as a possible resource for supplies and troops. Because of the tumultuous relationship the Five Tribes previously had with the U.S. government, the new threat the Lincoln administration brought by opening their lands to white settlers, and the Republican commitment to abolishing slavery, the Indian Territory groups faced an uncertain future in the Union. These fears were not helped by the fact that some of the wealthy tribe members shared the southern commonality of enslavers. Confederate representative Albert Pike began courting the Five Tribes by visiting their capitals and meeting with their leaders, soon concluding treaties with the tribes. The Chickasaw and Choctaw tribes quickly aligned with the Confederacy, but the decision to terminate the relationship with the Union split the Cherokee, Creek, and Seminole tribes. The Confederacy pledged to protect the Natives, defend Indian Territory, and take on the annuity obligations previously promised by the U.S. government. In return, the Native Peoples pledged to support the southern cause and raise units to fight the Union.[103] From July through October 1861, the Confederate Congress ratified treaties with a plethora of Indigenous groups and began preparing them for service in the military.[104]

In December Pike submitted the treaties of the Five Tribes and a report on his actions to the Confederate Congress. He "most urgently and anxiously" advised lawmakers "that the treaties now made may be speedily ratified . . . and that all the Indians who desire to enter into our service may be received and armed, in order that they feel that their interests and ours are identical." Pike further pushed authorities that the Natives should "stand upon equal footing with ourselves, defending the same rights and receiving the same treatment as their fellow soldiers of our own race."[105] In response, the Confederate Congress prepared provisions to pay the Indigenous troops for their service and to allot them an "allowance in lieu of clothing" payable to officers and men mustered into service, discounting deserters or those who "disbanded without permission, or have taken sides with the insurrectionists among the Creeks." This meant that the Confederacy did not give Native People uniforms when they enlisted because the government needed first to outfit its white troops in the eastern theater.[106] To them, clothing Indigenous troops was a different endeavor than for white soldiers. Historically, when the British colonies or the United States allied with Indigenous People for war, they neither gave them uniforms nor otherwise physically claimed them for their side.[107] This changed during the American Civil War. When the Native troops began fighting for the Confederacy, only a few of Pike's orders for their uniforms had actually arrived in Indian Territory by the spring of 1862. This meant that many wore their own clothes and were insufficiently armed. Conditions worsened enough that Indigenous soldiers began stripping prisoners of clothing to upgrade their selection. Consistently, the primary piece of clothing used by Indigenous troops and allotted to them by the government was the standard-issue wool hat, which became cone shaped when wet. This was a proud piece of clothing to the men, signifying their service to the Confederacy; Indigenous troops were often allowed to add personal tokens or decorations to them.[108] But this was meager compared to what they had been promised, such as the $500,000 sum to arm and equip Choctaw Confederates. According to historian Fay Yarbrough, more than one thousand members of the First Choctaw and Chickasaw Mounted Rifles "received a $25 clothing commutation," mirroring larger trends for white soldiers within the Confederate military at that time and assisting with filling the ranks.[109] That said, the contrast between the average Indigenous soldier and their commanders of significant rank was often striking, these senior officers fully outfitted with adequate clothing.

In contrast, other places within the Confederacy outfitted Native troops more completely. One example is William Thomas, who worked feverishly to enlist eastern Cherokees. On October 8, 1861, he procured clothing for his Indigenous soldiers, a feat not easily accomplished in Indian Territory. Thomas's Legion became infamous during the war, even though the men saw little combat.[110]

The Union was leery about using Indigenous troops, but that did not stop Native Peoples from states throughout the North from enlisting. Company K, First Michigan Sharpshooters began organizing in the winter of 1862–63, becoming an all-Indigenous unit numbering approximately 140 men from various tribes and including, but not limited to, Ojibwa, Odaawaa, and the Bodawatomi (Potawatomi). Many of these men were not subject to the draft but wanted to enlist. Just like white soldiers, this company's troops received complete uniforms and accouterments, which they quickly personalized.[111] Creeks in the Union Indian Home Guard regiments also had problems obtaining uniforms because of a lack of resources and ill-fitting clothing, stemming from the quartermaster's indifference to outfitting the Native American soldiers properly. Many of the items they received were oversized or too short, which gave these troops a "comical" appearance.[112]

By 1862, the Union began arming loyal tribes for fighting in Indian Territory to protect the border. The Battle of Pea Ridge occurred in March 1862 in Arkansas, where Confederate Cherokee regiments wore a range of garments, from regular suits to buckskin leggings. Getting these troops together for the battle proved a struggle, and the rebels suffered heavy losses in the two days of fighting, which ended in a Union victory. This precluded Confederate commanders from using Indigenous soldiers as primary forces of defense for the rest of the war.[113]

Positions for Indigenous soldiers in the armies of both the Union and the Confederacy were tenuous. Those troops who did serve in the Civil War did so as a means of gaining favor from the respective governments. They fought in numerous battles in various capacities spanning from 1862 to the end of the war in either all-Indigenous units or mixed in with white soldiers. While the Native Peoples fought for their respective sides, both governments created policies dictating tribal annuities and land. Inhabitants of Indian Territory endured forces from each side warring with and raiding them, enacting violence and hardships throughout 1862. The ravaged region by the end of the year floated as an autonomous state, and its people were left to work themselves out by 1863.[114]

RECRUITING AFRICAN AMERICAN SOLDIERS

On July 1, 1862, President Lincoln called for another 300,000 volunteers to serve a three-year term. This request was sent to the governors of seventeen states and the president of the Military Board of Kentucky.[115] Obtaining troops was much harder than expected by mid-1862, so because of this waning number of white volunteers, the Union government began considering letting Black men to serve in the military. In July 1862 Congress approved the Militia Act, which allowed employment of "persons of African descent" in the army and navy. Their duties were restricted to the grunt work of cooking, cleaning, and digging ditches. Lincoln suggested to congressmen that he did "not want to arm negroes unless some new and more pressing emergency" arose.

That viewpoint changed when the Confederates achieved significant victories during August. Later that month, the War Department gave permission to recruit Black soldiers throughout the South Carolina Sea Islands. This momentous occasion presented a new problem: what were these Black Union soldiers going to wear? Clothing these troops in the established uniform became a point of contention for white soldiers. Many believed this would require a symbolic and ideological transformation of these African Americans from enslaved, to a man, and then to a soldier, which meant that the white men's own tangible understanding of citizenship and sacrifice would now be shared to empower Black Americans.[116]

By the end of 1862, the war was well underway, and the process of providing uniforms and equipment to Union troops gradually became smoother because of practiced manufacturing. But this system experienced new challenges and questions with the Emancipation Proclamation and the mustering in, arming, and uniforming of Black soldiers. But those in the Confederacy had not experienced relief in their struggles to clothe troops. With domestic production unable to meet the demands of war, Confederate officials, civilians, and foreign companies sought to import the necessary supplies by running the Union blockade deeply but struggled once the Anaconda Plan found its grip. This forced southerners into a reliance on alternative methods for outfitting troops, creating a variety of shades for Confederate uniforms.

THE COST
OF WAR

A n 1863 article from the *Philadelphia Inquirer* raised the quandary that "no one seems to know how many men are engaged in the Rebel armies" or how they could afford to pay to uniform all of them. It noted that "the cost of their army is enormous" and "the simple article of clothing is a heavy item of expense." The author estimated that an "army of three hundred thousand men will require an outlay of eighteen millions of dollars for each new cloth uniform, exclusive of overcoats." After adding coats, underclothes, and shoes, the total estimate aggregated "thirty-three million seven hundred and fifty thousand dollars" for one uniform per soldier. This struck the writer as unbelievable, adding that "not even the economy of a member of the Southern chivalry—so famous for the practice of that virtue—could make one suit last for more than six months." With that in mind, requiring "two suits of clothing for each of these soldiers annually makes, therefore, a demand on the Rebel Treasury for the sum of sixty-seven and a half millions." While that was a "small portion of the expense of an army," it would be "gnawing rapidly into the already vastly diminished resources of the Rebels."[1]

While the Philadelphia journalist could only speculate on the costs, he raised an important question: how could the Confederacy afford to clothe such a large army? Cost was a valid question for both the Union and the Confederate governments as well as for African American troops and for the Indigenous soldiers of either side. How did the continued logistics of simply putting men in uniform influence the war? Who was most important to clothe? How did the actual process work, and what happened when it did not? Both sides had anticipated a quick war, which meant that outfitting troops posed a continuing struggle. Some production issues for the North smoothed out, but long-term planning was still difficult since these volunteer forces were not a permanent standing army. Thus, the need for uniforms continued and grew, while the circumstances of obtaining them through theft became increasingly dire. The U.S. War Department's outlook on the standard Union uniform revolved around the notion that it belonged to the government, even if the soldier paid for it, as did the person wearing it until their death. While the process of producing uniforms proved arduous for both sides, once the war began, the Confederate policy of paying for soldiers' uniforms, and having to run the Union blockade to obtain machinery and materials for them, created a major expense for the South that proved unsustainable.

THE USCT & INDIGENOUS SOLDIERS

On January 1, 1863, President Lincoln issued the Emancipation Proclamation, which declared "all persons held as slaves within any State or designated part of a State, the people whereof shall then be in rebellion against the United States, shall be then, thenceforward, and forever free." This shifted the goal of the war from reuniting the Union with or without slavery to reuniting the country without the burden of slavery. The proclamation also announced that "such persons, of suitable condition, will be received into the armed service of the United States to garrison forts, positions, stations, and other places, and to man vessels of all sorts in said service."[2] Black men in service became another resource for the government and removed "contraband" resources, in the form of men, from the southern war effort. This authorization energized the efforts of Black community members to recruit men for the Union army as an outlet for them to exercise their newfound freedom and assist the northern war effort.

Five "African Descent" or "Colored" regiments were formed in 1861 and 1862. With the authorization of the Emancipation Proclamation and the prompting of the Black community, twenty-six more regiments followed within the first six months of 1863, the bulk of those in May and June.[3] The mustering of Black men into the Union army changed after May 22, when

General Orders No. 143 established "a bureau in the Adjutant General's office for the organization of colored regiments, whereby the system of employing them as a part of the forces of the United States has become a fixed and permanent policy of the Government."[4] This meant that those units already raised by states prior converted their state regiments from "African Descent" or "Colored" to U.S. Colored Troops (USCT). This also meant that the federal government put a small amount of effort into recruiting African American men for service.

The call for Black regiments forming and mustering into service began appearing in Black and white newspapers across the country. One report described the "Zouaves d'Afrique" of Kansas and the excitement that they "have finally been mustered into the service of the United States." The First Regiment of Kansas Colored Troops pleaded with military authorities to "muster and pay them" because of their actions defending their home state. Their adjutant, Richard J. Hinton, argued, "We have worn the Federal uniform, carried its flag and have used its arms in defense of that flag," and so the men deserved to be treated as Union soldiers instead of a state organization; weapons mattered, but so did fabric.[5] A Philadelphia newspaper told of a celebration to "commemorate the departure of the 54th Massachusetts (colored) Regiment for South Carolina." Journalists were pleased that the ranks were full and that "the men were dressed in regular United States uniform," which gave the soldiers "a magnificent appearance."[6]

The Bureau of Colored Troops was responsible for handling all matters related to Black soldiers and regulating their process. General Orders No. 143 proclaimed that "recruiting stations and depots will be established by the Adjutant General as circumstances shall require."[7] But it said nothing about uniforms, which means they probably considered neither the financial and material struggles of outfitting more men nor what those uniforms would mean to their new Black soldiers or the communities that encountered them.

A major question arose when considering Black military service: who funded the uniforms for these soldiers? The federal government still considered Black troops as lesser than white soldiers and was not inclined to assist them in the same way in terms of pay and clothing. Often African Americans were not allotted clothing and equipment that satisfied their needs. During the early period of their service, the appearance of Black soldiers was more like that of laborers because they were outfitted with uniforms that wore out quickly.[8] According to Susie King Taylor, a formerly enslaved woman who obtained freedom early in the war and worked in the Thirty-Third USCT's camp, "the first suits worn by the boys [she attended] were red coats and pants, which they disliked very much, for, they said, 'the rebels see us, miles away.'" This was a common situation for Black troops. King here refers to the extremely bright Zouave uniforms worn by regiments on both sides during the war. Most white regiments had discarded them by 1862 for the standard Union blues, but the regiment for which Taylor cared was forced to use castoff clothing because they were not a high priority for Washington authorities.[9] When African American soldiers eventually received proper uniforms, they were the standard issue, consisting of a dark blue dress coat, light blue trousers, blue shirts, and a blue forage cap with black visor.[10]

Until the federal government sufficiently supplied the Black regiments, their men obtained the necessary regulation blues from community members. Newspaper reports on the raising of Black regiments often simply said that they "have been provided with uniforms." Sometimes journalists suggested that prominent members of the local African American community in the area had begun "raising regiments of colored soldiers . . . with considerable vigor," but that was often the extent of the information given unless someone directly volunteered to fund an African American regiment.[11] One article reported that abolitionist Gerrit Smith gave "five hundred dollars toward raising the 1st colored regiment in Massachusetts." Smith offered to provide two hundred dollars more for raising an entire company for the same regiment.[12]

To counter the government's injustice, African American women took up the needle like their white female counterparts to raise money for the war effort and to provide clothing relief to the soldiers and the community by sewing. Often, they did this in association with a congregation. Ministers and their communities administered the call, for example: "Dear ladies, are you busy with your needles, for these poor, hungry, half-clad souls?" They encouraged women to "be energetic at the 'Sewing Circle' for there are the Refugees, the Freedmen, the Orphans, and last, but by no means least, our sick soldier boys, all to be cared for."[13] Not only did Black women provide basic clothing for soldiers but also many of the items they made in sewing circles were sold to raise funds for the troops.

Throughout the entire course of their military service, Black troops struggled. The difficulty of timely payment is commonly known, but the arduous process of being properly clothed dragged on and hurt morale.[14] August 1864 brought little change or hope for African American soldiers. Out of their ten-dollar payment each month, the government only deducted Black troops roughly three dollars for clothing, depending on their date of escape and registration for the army. This means their take-home pay was seven dollars a month.[15]

Historians often have noted the discrepancy in pay between soldiers based on race, but overlooking the role and expense of uniforms means misunderstanding that Black soldiers had it even worse than previously thought. The $3.00 monthly withholding caused frustration and resentment among Black troops and their communities because white soldiers received not only $13.00 pay a month but also a $3.50 clothing allowance on top of that. This discrepancy solidified uniforms as a financial burden for USCT soldiers, especially the recently emancipated who had few resources. The army's official pricing for 1863 states, "the allowance of Clothing to all enlisted men of VOLUNTEERS is $3.50 per month, or $42 per year." Once the Bureau for Colored Troops was created, USCT soldiers obtained their uniforms through the U.S. government. The amount each man spent for obtaining his first uniform was $31.63, rising to $35.23 if a blanket was included. The soldier owed that money, and the army expected him to pay it off.

Making matters still harder for Black troops were extras or other parts of the uniform at an additional charge. After a private in the infantry took one of each item that was offered for clothing, all other equipment for camp, garrison, horses, and arms cost the soldier extra. The monetary value of clothing could add up to as much as $57.67 during the first year, but only $42.00 per year was covered for white troops (through clothing allowances) and $36.00 for Black soldiers (through pay deductions).[16] Black troops might need a whole new uniform for their second year in service, so their debt could compound over time. USCT troops had a take-home pay of $84 per year after the clothing deduction. If formerly enslaved refugees joined the military with no money or acceptable articles of clothing, they started off their enlistment in debt and could never catch up. A Black soldier could die in debt to the government for their uniform fighting to free people who were just like them.

One newspaper detailed the unfairness of this. The reporter explained that at the time they enlisted, members of the Fifty-Fourth Massachusetts "were promised $13 a month, and the usual allowance for clothing," but every man who perished in that regiment "died in debt to the government" because the army "had charged more for their uniforms than it had allowed for their pay." At the end of 1863, "there remained due to the soldiers . . . seven months service, [or] $17 each, fifty-three [dollars] having been charged for clothing." The First North Carolina Regiment enlisted with the understanding that they "were to be placed on equality with whites with regard to pay." This was not the case: after seven months of service, each man was charged $51 for his clothing, $15 over what the allowance covered, suggesting that the soldier needed more than the bare minimum to be properly clothed.[17]

Much like with African American troops, clothing issues persisted for Union and Confederate Native soldiers. Specifically, in Indian Territory they negotiated material items to their advantage, but the northern and southern governments did not care for them or aid them as they did white troops as the treaties promised. Unlike Black troops, however, Native troops could and did realign their allegiances for a better agreement with the respective governments.

Providing Indigenous regiments and the soldiers' families with essential goods such as food and clothing to maintain fidelity drove the war effort in Indian Territory. By 1863, both sides had abandoned the region, making it difficult for soldiers to replenish supplies. For example, Union brigadier general Fredrick Steele's division of Indigenous troops accepted a baggage train of used garments from Major General James Blunt's old division because they were expected to hold their position until the spring of 1863, which meant that they could not travel for fresh supplies.[18] In a letter to Blunt that March, Colonel William A. Phillips pleaded for supplies so he could take command and journey through Indian Territory to prevent the Confederate organization of "Indians south of the river." He "could organize a Creek and Choctaw regiment" if he had the means, but he said, "if we do not, we must fight these men this summer." The colonel appealed earnestly to his commander for assistance because the success of this venture "to a great extent depends on our clothing them neatly, feeding them, and to some extent their starving families. After all, a little goes a great way. It is cheap recruiting." Phillips also reported that the Confederates were "alarmed" and "trying the same game."[19] Once he figured out that the rebels were "giving the Choctaws and Creeks corn and clothing to keep them from turning," Phillips pressed for more supplies. Otherwise, Union authorities ran the risk of having to fight pro-Confederate regiments from those tribes.[20]

In November 1863 Confederate brigadier general William Steele received an "estimate for clothing" from Brigadier General Douglas H. Cooper's brigade "for over 6,000 men" after receiving no reports from that command with the exception of occasional communication. Cooper asked for "suits of gray clothing" as a means "to be used to coax the Indians together," implying that by providing the Native American troops with material for uniforms, they would be more willing to work with the Confederates. Excerpts from letters Cooper sent Steele explain that some of his Creek and Chickasaw regiments had scattered but now reported to Colonel Stand Watie—this Cherokee leader would become the only Native American promoted to brigadier general during the Civil War. Cooper wanted clothing, shoes, and accouterments issued to their camps to entice their return to his ranks.[21]

The idea of controlling Indigenous soldiers with clothing suggests the importance of uniforms as a tool of warfare. Clothing Indigenous troops in gray suits not only contained them but claimed them for the Confederacy. Some of their leaders believed that the Confederacy occasionally used uniforms as a test for determining the fidelity of respective Indigenous groups. Writing to Commissioner of Indian Affairs S. S. Scott on behalf of Cherokee soldiers, Waite stated that "the Indian troops who have been true to the South from the very first have been treated in many instances as though it were immaterial whether or not they were paid as promptly and equipped as thoroughly as other soldiers." He lamented that clothing was "procured at great trouble and expense, to cover the nakedness of Indian troops" and that on several occasions it was "distributed among less necessitous soldiers." Watie believed that "this treatment has been such as to test to the utmost their fidelity" to the Confederacy but affirmed that Cherokee soldiers "remained true as steel."[22]

In December 1863 Confederate secretary of war James A. Seddon received a communication, intended for President Jefferson Davis, from leaders of the Creek Nation expressing their concerns about uniform and food status in Indian Territory. They described a terrible state of affairs and asserted that Creek troops were "'bare-headed, bare-footed, without bread, and body in rags.'" Commissioner Scott proclaimed that this description was "simply a piece of the greatest exaggeration." Still, he acknowledged that at times throughout the war, "the Indian troops were in want of clothing" and "may not be as well clad now as is desired," but he assessed them as "tolerably comfortable" for a time of war.[23] The fact that Creek Nation leaders wrote a letter intended for President Davis to describe their uniform situation speaks volumes because they were attempting to exert the same power concerning clothing that the Confederate government held over them. If they lacked proper food or clothing, the Indigenous troops would be unable or unlikely to complete the tasks assigned to them.

Much like the Confederacy, this struggle for power is reflected in the Union's quartermaster practice. Federal authorities used clothing to supervise their Indigenous soldiers through lending and returning the items that made up a uniform, much as they did for white soldiers. This allowed the government to keep Indigenous troops tied closely to their white officers and supply chains. It also created a loose alliance with the Native Peoples, instilling them with the illusion of identity and authority.

The federal record book for Captain Huckleberry Downing's Company F, Indian Regiment, posted at Fort Gibson in the Cherokee Nation, sheds light on this concept. The book contains typical regimental accounts of enlistment and clothing records from May 30, 1863, to May 31, 1865. Of particular interest is the section "Monthly Return of Clothing Camp and Garrison Equipages Received and Issued in the Field." It denotes the dates issued and received of the different types of clothing and equipment that could be checked out and returned by Indigenous troops. These articles include great coats, pairs of drawers and pants, hats, flannel shirts, and pairs of bootees and boots, although not all of these were constantly available due to supply issues. The total number of items issued when checked against the company's roster provided Captain Downing with an idea of who had what and how many articles drifted in and out of stock each month.

A difference in the treatment of white and Native—that is, officers and soldiers—is evident in this record. The commissioned officers of Indigenous units were also required to check out uniform items, but their names were noted in the log, and they signed next to the articles they received. As the process continued throughout 1863, noncommissioned officers and privates began signing their names or had them copied in the ledger next to their loaned materials. Yet the return page of what the Indigenous soldiers brought back includes no names, just a numerical assessment of the articles returned. Occasionally it lists the roll number, one through three, and how much was issued to the men on each roll, which could then be checked against how many articles were to be returned the following month.

The individual clothing accounts are telling. In an October 1863 entry, a soldier named Rabbit received one lined blouse, one flannel shirt, and two stockings, and in December 1863 he checked out one great coat, one blouse, one wool blanket, something illegible, and a white shirt. In October 1863 Arch Bigfoot received a lined blouse, a flannel shirt, and stockings, and that December he checked out a wool blanket and two white shirts.[24] One difficulty of keeping track of the soldiers and their items is that they do not always appear in the same roll number they were originally counted in or may not reappear on the issued-clothing list again for months; this is the case with Arch Bigfoot, who disappears from the record until April 1864.

Both Union and Confederate officials understood that clothing Indigenous troops allowed their respective government dominion and authority over them. Providing uniforms to the Native Peoples meant extending white identity and fostering Indigenous allegiance to the cause or nation with a visual device that claimed them for a specific side, even if they were not fighting. What cannot be stated strongly enough is that those white officials did not see this as extending their own national loyalty to the Indigenous troops, but merely as an opportunity to use or extort the Native Peoples as tools of warfare.

THE UNION STRUGGLE

White troops also wound up marked and indebted to the federal government for their clothing, but with the significant differences that they entered the military without having to prove themselves worthy of other rights and officials tended to their issues much faster. Thanks to the efficient management of Secretary of War Edwin M. Stanton, the War Department began hitting its stride by 1863, and the process of outfitting Union soldiers with uniforms became smoother. But soldiers sometimes remained unable to obtain proper uniforms for duty, and in these situations the states often intervened while women were still needed to sew, either for individuals or for factories. And unfortunately, problems continued with uniform theft and desertion for the rest of the war.[25]

By 1863, as soldier enlistment waned, states with more resources provided uniforms as an incentive. Throughout 1863 and 1864, the New York Quartermaster's Department again sought service bids. S. V. Talcott placed newspaper advertisements for "the manufacture and delivery" of uniform clothing items. He wanted "three hundred and forty light blue Kersey Overcoats," "three hundred and forty blue cloth Chasseur jackets," and "three hundred and forty light blue Kersey Chasseur Trowsers." The garments would be manufactured in the designated style, with all "proposals for uniform clothing" sent to the Albany office in the state arsenal. Different articles of the uniform were supposed to be manufactured in separate locations throughout New York, such as a call for "fatigue caps" in an adjacent advertisement for items to be made in Brooklyn.[26]

This corresponds with the readymade uniforms advertised throughout northern newspapers. Benham & Boardman were merchant tailors who offered "Army and Navy Uniforms, made to order at short notice."[27] Kelsey & Carpenter provided "Gentlemen's Garments, also Officers' Uniforms in the best material and in the best style."[28] In June 1863 the New York state government called the militia to Harrisburg. Some were "unable to obtain uniforms and clothing or arms . . . from the United States authorities," so they instead drew from the state's resources.[29] By mid-1863, many units began advertising for recruits in the newspapers, promising that they would be "fully uniformed and equipped, and receive $10 city bounty."[30] The Zouaves unit of the 165th Regiment of New York State Volunteers not only advertised bounties but also assured that "the splendid uniforms of this regiment are furnished at these headquarters for new members: it makes a saving of $23 a year on their clothing account."[31]

In the field, regimental quartermasters struggled to keep track of garments lent and returned. According to the revised regulations of the U.S. Army, the unit quartermaster reported on monthly returns, trimonthly reports, recruiting accounts, and current accounts of clothing issued, among other things. They directed the estimates of clothing, necessary equipment, clothing-receipt rolls, and quarterly returns of clothing. These staffers had to account for the "quarterly return of clothing and camp and garrison equipage" and all property in their possession. While the quartermaster kept track of everything, the company commander procured and issued clothing to his men at least twice a year or "when necessary in special cases." When a soldier surpassed his clothing allowance for the year, additional items were extra and charged to him on the next muster roll. Each man had a clothing account kept by his commander, who tracked the monetary value of the clothing received. If a soldier was transferred or detached, "the amount due to or by him on account of clothing" appeared on his list. Deserters' clothing was "turned in to store" or set aside for use by someone else. Quartermasters kept track of damaged clothing to determine if they were "fit for issue, at a reduced price."[32]

Captain Channing Clapp of Massachusetts kept thorough records noting the number of specific articles taken in by that state's quartermaster and their current condition. While occasionally new, many of the items he received were "partially worn" or "serviceable."[33] The revised army regulations included more detailed information on uniform wear and use. Rule 115, "For the Army, Soldiers' Mess," states that "soldiers will wear the prescribed uniform in camp or garrison, and will not be permitted to keep in their possession any other clothing." This essentially marked the men as soldiers, as a sort of property, thus making desertion difficult.

These specific rules allow a closer look at the process and the money spent by the U.S. government and white soldiers to properly clothe themselves for war. According to historian Mark Wilson, in the four years of war, "the Quartermaster's Department spent roughly $350 million on clothing and equipage (including items such as tents and knapsacks)."[34] Several items came under the umbrella of "clothing and equipage," but this does assist in illustrating the expense and importance of uniforms to the war effort.

The chaotic nature of the war made the issue worse for both the quartermasters and the individual soldiers. Forced retreats and long marches combined with the weight of their packs often led to men discarding their heavier clothing items. Lightening their load in this way hurt soldiers' pocketbooks because, through credit or out of their own pocket, they had to pay when they needed more uniform pieces. While stationed at Camp Bridgeport, Alabama, Union soldier Robert Walker wrote to his mother in late 1863 that he was "still well and hearty." The excitement for the day stemmed from the "pay-master" coming, but he did not expect to get much, "for our clothing bill has to be settled this time and it is pretty high." He lost "about twenty dollars worth [of items] at Lexington, Ky, and about eleven dollars worth at Stone river, and some at the Battle of Chickamauga," covering around a one-year period. Walker mentioned that the men were only allowed "forty dollars per year for clothing," but their current "bills range from sixty-five to ninety-five dollars"; his own came to about seventy-two dollars. He added that while settling these debts would not "leave us much this pay day," he "did not come to the army to make money." After a few more lines, he closed his letter "subscribing" himself "your disobedient son."[35]

Much like the struggles of Private Walker, Union soldier David Lane recorded the length and difficulty of marching throughout Kentucky in April 1863. His April 13 entry noted that they "marched to this place [Lebanon], twenty-eight miles, in two days." For the thirtieth he wrote, "at five we were on the move, bound for Columbia, forty miles away." On this "forced march" the soldiers had no teams to carry their luggage, which meant that the men "could not carry all our winter clothing, therefore hundreds of good blankets and overcoats were thrown away." He reported that after proceeding three or four miles, "many of the men found they still had too much load, and then the work of lightening up began in earnest. For miles the road was strewn with blankets, dress coats, blouses, pants, drawers and shirts."[36] This served as a physical reminder of the weight of the material and the toll it took on their bodies. Wearing summer clothing while carrying winter coats and personal effects, as well as the strain from marching long distances with heavy packs, created a tremendous physical burden. The U.S. government allotted two blankets, eight uniform coats, and only one great coat to use per man for five years of service, so when they jettisoned those items, the troops were literally throwing away money.[37]

Rule 123 allowed tradesmen in the ranks to be relieved of typical military duties to "make, to alter, or to mend soldiers' clothing," providing that their fellow soldiers would pay them the following day. By 1863, enlistments had declined significantly, and the army needed as many men as possible. Amid the increased use of the draft and the controversy it created—the New York City draft riots were hardly the only example—government officials clearly viewed the production of uniforms as important, aware of how manufacturers still had not adequately addressed that need.

The revised regulations even made provisions for four women who were "allowed to each company as washerwomen" to receive one ration per day and to be paid for their service "by the month, or by the piece" at a price set by the Council of Administration.[38] In addition to working in camps, women labored tirelessly for the Union and were recognized for their work. "When the history of the war shall be written, the name of woman will shine conspicuous on its pages," proclaimed the *Marshall County Republican*. The Indiana journalist applauded how "many true, patriotic women have toiled and laid down their lives" for the Union.[39] Women continued as the main producers of war materials throughout 1863 and 1864, regularly aiding the war effort by knitting, sewing, and repairing uniforms in camps, in sewing circles, and in factories. Newspapers pushed their female subscribers to make these contributions and readily acknowledged them for doing so. An article in a Pennsylvania publication claimed that their textile and clothing work was "the woman's part in the patriotic struggle we are in." It quoted the president of the U.S. Sanitary Commission as saying, "as long as the men fight the women must knit and sew" because creating uniforms was a physical manifestation of their patriotic duty to their soldiers and their country.[40] Women across the Union also joined "relief societies," sending boxes of goods to hospitals and making "drawers large enough for poor, wounded, swollen limbs" to wear comfortably.[41] Their "labor and generous contributions" to the various aid societies benefited the troops as "they humbly toil, stitch and contribute at home, for the common store."[42]

The enormity of time, labor, and organization that it took to uniform troops through official channels and women's assistance is undeniable, but the difficulty of supplying regiments in the field required still more resources. Men selling military goods and equipment to the army traveled the countryside, carrying letters of character references from their friends, such as, "Mr. H is a Loyal union man & worthy of full confidence," or, "Henry is formally known to our dear old General, and in fact stands highly in the estimation of all who have met him as an honorable and liberal gentleman." Men like Henry A. Huntington often developed profitable relationships with and through their military connections. To fulfill the uniform need, in July 1863 Huntington requested permission to ship his supply of "Officers Military Goods," valued at approximately fifteen thousand dollars, from Nashville and Murfreesboro to the army in the field. Receipts from the transactions of these merchants indicate that thousands of dollars, often five thousand at a time, were spent on "Officers Uniforms and Military accouterments." Once a supplier proved to be a trusted source, his services were recommended to other generals. In a January 1864 letter to Brigadier General Grenville Dodge, George H. Storie introduced Huntington, explaining that his business was "the sale of military goods, etc.," and vouching for him after "several years personal acquaintance." Storie was "able to recommend him" to assist with the purchasing of goods. Like many receiving wartime government contracts, Huntington lacked a sutler's license and supplied uniforms to the Union army in the South based on his reputation and his network of powerful friends.[43]

Official channels and salesmen could only provide a certain amount of supplies, which meant that soldiers would step outside of typical supply chains to clothe themselves if necessary. In the event that Union troops captured and kept Confederate uniforms, the War Department created, from the beginning of the war, rules to provide guidance on using them and prevent issues. These provisions were established in section three of General Orders No. 100. "If American troops capture a train containing uniforms of the enemy," and the commander considers the garments usable, he may "distribute them for use among his men," but "some striking mark or sign must be adopted to distinguish the American soldier from the enemy."[44] Thus for the U.S. government, wearing a Confederate uniform was acceptable as long as it was modified in some way to identify the soldier as Union, or at least as not Confederate.

THE CRUMBLING CONFEDERATE SUPPLY CHAIN

Union soldiers and officials found some stability to lessen their supply struggles through the later war years, but the Confederacy did not enjoy such a reprieve. Its need for uniforms orchestrated southern commerce, politics, and international relations. The garb of warfare proved a crucial part of Confederate policy, monopolizing time, money, and effort. Men, women, European companies, and this fledgling experiment of a country risked fortunes to clothe southern troops. Confederate officials' attempts to uniform white soldiers in 1863 and 1864 took on various forms, including blockade-running to Ireland, England, and Mexico; a surge of efforts to obtain them from southern factories; and the continued theft of Union uniforms.

With the Confederacy desperate to clothe its soldiers and feeling the stress of the mounting costs and cargo losses, uniforms served as a driver of blockade-running. As the war continued and the Union blockade tightened its coils, the harder it became for steamers to make it to an operating Confederate port. In May 1863 the *Baltimore Sun* reported that since that March, twenty-six steamers had left Nassau "to run the blockade, of which ten were driven ashore and destroyed, and one supposed to have been lost." These losses "enhanced the rate of freights and wages," making firms a "little shy of the business" of slipping past Union ships.[45]

Despite the risks and considerable financial blow with each lost ship, the Confederacy still spent significant amounts of its already limited funds on contracts with European firms for uniforms. Negotiations between its purchasing agents and Peter Tait & Company, a uniform supplier from Limerick, Ireland, began in late 1863. Peter Tait & Company consisted of three different British clothing firms: Peter Tait & Company in Limerick, Ireland; Herbbert & Company from London; and Alexander Collie & Company in Manchester and London. Major James L. Tait offered to sell the Confederacy precut sets of cloth for uniforms that only required sewing. According to an order for one of the first shipments to the South, Peter Tait & Company supplied in bales the precut material for caps, great coats, uniform jackets and "trowsers," and flannel shirts. It offered this clothing for higher prices than the Confederacy normally paid.[46] In October 1864 Tait also secured contracts with Alabama quartermaster general Duff Green, stationed in Montgomery. For supplying its regiments with clothing, Alabama paid the company in cotton, which was taken back to England and sold to mills. The materials shipped to Alabama were precut and required seamstresses and tailors to assemble them. The uniform pieces were made of blue-gray broadcloth and typically had a shorter jacket that mimicked that of the British Army. Many Tait jackets had an eight-button front, with buttons that had the mark of the company on the back. Those that arrived assembled were a machine-sewn, five-piece body with an Irish linen lining. Trousers were made of matching blue-gray cloth with a twill cotton lining.[47]

This connection with Alabama prompted the Tait Company to take a risk by purchasing a share in the blockade-running steamship *Evelyn*. The particular order motivating this was shipped on the ill-fated *Condor* and the *Evelyn*. The *Richmond Dispatch* reported that the *Condor* "was deceived by the wreck of the *Night Hawk* and ran aground." The Confederate agent aboard the vessel, Rose Greenhow, an important spy for the rebels, tried "to come ashore from her [the *Condor*] in a boat" but drowned. "Under the guns of Fort Fisher," the vessel's crew cautiously unloaded the cargo while "the Yankees made an attempt to board the *Condor* to destroy her." They were repulsed by a Lieutenant Sowiee of Company A, Thirty-Sixth North Carolina and a detachment of men. The *Annie* delivered the cargo recovered from the *Condor* safely to Wilmington, North Carolina. The *Evelyn* left Limerick to arrive in Bermuda, from where it was twice unsuccessful when attempting to run the blockade. Eventually, the vessel arrived in Wilmington in December 1864 with 170 bales of uniforms, or approximately 25,500 articles of clothing.[48] Clothing companies, state governments, and blockade-runners took large risks to sneak past the Union blockade, absorbing the cost of vessels and cargo on ill-fated trips to fill Confederate soldiers' uniform needs.

Blockade-running for uniforms from S. Isaac, Campbell, & Company continued throughout 1864, even though the Confederacy already owed the clothier a large debt, for which it wanted payment in cotton. As might be expected, the continued material support by British companies inflamed the relationship between northerners and the United Kingdom. The author of one article argued that the Emancipation Proclamation "convinced England that we could be bullied and browbeaten with impunity," encouraging Englishmen to aid the rebels and even supply them with munitions of war. The Union accused Britain of building "pirate ships for the Confederacy" and fitting out "fleets of blockade runners to supply them with guns, uniforms and necessities of every kind."[49] The business relationship between the Richmond government and British firms was rocky because of an investigation by Secretary of War Seddon into the mishandling of accounts and funds by Agent Huse, who spent and promised large sums to companies but rarely received the product. Despite this, as of December 1864 Huse ordered another fourteen bales of gray wool shirts from S. Isaac, Campbell, & Company.[50] As reported in the *Houston Tri-Weekly Telegraph*, a vague source designated "An English paper" stated, "we understand that all the uniforms for the Confederate army are now being made in England—a considerable portion, indeed, in London."[51]

Running the Union blockade was only part of the battle of getting uniforms to soldiers. Once the items made it through the blockade, cargo could get stuck in a port city because Confederate leaders there claimed the garments for their own or their state's troops. If shipments made it past a port city, then it was difficult to transport large loads of heavy articles over land past Union forces or riverine blockade patrols to reach Confederate troops.

Despite these obstacles, or perhaps because of them, southerners continued to place great value on their uniforms. When any did arrive in a southern city, it sometimes led to a celebration. Nurse Kate Cumming wrote in her diary in late February 1864, "Mobile never was as gay as it is at present; not a night passes but some large ball or party is given," benefiting the soldiers, who seemed to enjoy them. She stated that the city was filled with the veterans of many battles and, while attending the parties, noted that "the gray jackets were conspicuous." A few men wore "citizen's clothes, but it was because they had lost their uniforms." Cumming observed that "the Alabama troops are dressed so fine that we scarcely recognized them." Their uniforms came from "a large steamer, laden with clothes" from the Peter Tait & Company, that "ran the blockade lately, from Limerick, Ireland."[52]

While the struggle to run the Union naval blockade concentrated in the Southeast, the Southwest—primarily the Texas border with Mexico—presented opportunities for the Confederates to export cotton and import uniforms overland. In 1863 and 1864 trade involving Mexico, either through goods that passed through from Europe or those directly from that country, proved somewhat successful for the South and profitable for Mexico. Because the Union blockade closed the Gulf of Mexico ports, trade across the Rio Grande flourished, becoming the easiest method for transporting cotton out of the Confederacy. To underscore the area's importance, the *Philadelphia Inquirer* reprinted an article from "the Camden (Ark.) *Herald*" that claimed to have "credible information that seventy tons of English goods, for soldiers' clothing, have arrived at the landing on Red River, through Mexico, for the Confederate States." This economic relationship benefited from the continued sympathy of the Mexican authorities toward the southern cause. For them, industry grew out of this relationship: the state of Nuevo Leon y Coahuila possessed eight factories that processed over 1 million pounds of cotton annually. They produced brown sheeting fabric, which was sold to Texans for their enslaved persons.[53]

Union authorities made a notable change to the blockade that bene-fited southern efforts to import uniforms through Texas. In February 1864 the War Department issued General Orders No. 69, which directed that the April 1861 blockade would now be "relaxed with advantage to the interests of commerce." Because of the current state of the war, Lincoln decided to allow ships to carry goods to and from Brownsville, Texas, in order to col-lect duties on commercial goods. But proclamation did not "authorize or allow the shipment or conveyance of persons in or intending to enter the service of the insurgents, or of things or information intended for their use, or for their aid or comfort." Aid or comfort items included, but were not limited to, mortars, firearms, pistols, saddles, and "clothing adapted for uniforms."[54] While federal authorities knew that Brownsville was a major export center for cotton and that southerners continued their attempts at running the blockade for war supplies, they were willing to risk docking ships there to increase government revenues even if doing so could mini-mally benefit the Confederacy.

Despite this slight opening in the blockade, relatively few uniforms came through the port of Brownsville. This supply and those made avail-able elsewhere proved insufficient, prompting the Confederacy to adopt more desperate strategies. In January 1864 Lieutenant Colonel W. A. Broadwell issued a call for nine actions because of the "scarcity of sup-plies, the difficulty in procuring cotton, [and] the previous want of system and efficiency in the management of Government business on the Mex-ican frontier." The majority of these dealt with cotton transactions, con-tracts, and dealings with Mexico, but the last item on the list discussed the requirement of "quartermasters to collect a tithe of the cotton and wool and turn it over to the Cotton Bureau." This appeared to be a fairly nor-mal request until Broadwell instructed the bureau to purchase three or four cotton and woolen factories from Mexico, relocating them to "eligible points" in Texas, to manufacture this "tithe into army cloth." Late in 1864 the French invaded Mexico, but the trade relationship continued with the Confederacy because the French determined that they benefited econom-ically from it. Eventually, this relationship failed along with the southern war effort. According to historian Ronnie Tyler, sample cargoes that the Union army confiscated during the latter part of the war included arms, ammunition, powder, cloth, and readymade uniforms, which were "among the most important items that the South received" during the conflict.[55]

During the winter of 1863–64, the Confederate government looked inward to assist with the process of manufacturing uniforms for their troops. Officials procured up to 43 percent of the cotton goods and up to 69 percent of the woolen materials manufactured in the South. The Commissary Bureau gained control of local looms to turn tax-in-kind cotton into cloth for clothing and uniforms. The number of garments or amount of cloth that a local manufactory could produce was a topic of conversation between army officials. Commanders worried about the numbers produced from tax-in-kind materials and if they would meet expectations. They blamed "recent raids of the enemy, driving off or capturing many of the collectors," as a significant problem when producing items for the Confederate war machine.[56] As the process progressed, officials proudly noted that the Quartermaster's Department received ten to twelve bales of jeans and linsey per week from factories, "which are at once converted into clothing," or that the quantity of garments manufactured weekly there varied from 1,000 to 1,500 pieces. These exciting reports on new factories or how much a factory could produce were encouraging for officials during a time of immense struggle to properly clothe troops. By May 1864, many of the mills surveyed produced the equivalent of about 250,000 uniforms to date, although the Confederate government acquired fewer than two-thirds of the garments. Purchasing agents and textile-mill owners struck deals as part of their contracts to obtain enough uniforms while allowing the mill to make money on the open market. While many states were happy to supply their own troops, there were disputes throughout the South about providing uniform assistance to other states.[57]

While the textile mills helped partially fill the need for uniforms, they also deprived the Confederate military of needed soldiers. Although many southern textile workers were women, men entered that segment of the labor force in a variety of ways, specifically in higher-ranking jobs that allowed them to remain on the home front. Occasionally, soldiers deserted the battlefield and also found their way to working at a factory. While the mills deprived the Confederate military of manpower, the inverse was also true. According to historian Harold S. Wilson, military recruitment also hurt textile manufacturers' skilled labor specifically because it "drained workers from the factories."[58] This was such a concern that mill owners from South Carolina and Virginia petitioned their state governments for a certain number of men to receive service exemptions.

As the number of mill workers and uniform production increased in Confederate-held areas, the Union recognized the military value of the textile mills and targeted them. Writing to Major General William Tecumseh Sherman in September 1864, Major General Henry Halleck, the chief of staff of the U.S. Army, noted having "tried three years of conciliation and kindness [toward the rebels] without any reciprocation," so he now had no qualms concerning total war on the Confederates. "I would destroy every mill and factory within my reach which I did not want for my own use."[59] On top of the growing success of the naval blockade, Sherman's March to the Sea, which cut a swath of desolation from Atlanta to Savannah before turning north through the Carolinas, was a devastating blow to the southern uniform production. Sherman began his march in November 1864, leading approximately 100,000 Union soldiers on a mission of destruction that ranged from setting fire to cotton fields and freeing enslaved persons to burning textile factories and expelling their workers.[60] In one instance, Sherman noted the contribution of the Roswell Factory in Fulton County, Georgia, which he ordered burned because it had "been engaged almost exclusively in manufacturing cloth for the Confederate Army." He wrote that its fabric was "tainted with treason" and wrote of his intention to "send all the owners, agents, and employes up to Indiana to get rid of them here." In his next communication with Brigadier General Joseph Dana Webster, his chief of staff, Sherman explained having "ordered the arrest of the operators at the Confederate manufactories at Rosewell [sic] and Sweet Water, to be sent North"; once there, they were to be "turned loose to earn a living where they won't do us any harm." He noted that the male laborers were exempt from conscription because of their skill but that "the women were simply laborers that must be removed from this district."[61] By relocating the employees to a northern state, Sherman would take away a portion of the Confederate uniform labor force and further reduce the South's ability to clothe its men.

The Union's continued sinking of blockade-running vessels and confiscation of uniforms often forced southern soldiers and their families to find other ways to clothe themselves. In one 1863 newspaper article, a Philadelphia reporter questioned prisoners about the Confederate government, services, and supplies. The men interviewed wore "homespun, or 'Virginia stuff,' . . . which, they said, was woven at their own private houses, or at mills, in the Confederacy." The prisoners described the fabric as "rough and coarse, but excellent for wear." They told the reporter that "the Confederate Government gives employment to all the soldiers' wives who are willing to work on soldiers' uniforms." These women were involved in "spinning the wool, weaving it into cloth, or making it into garments." The men exclaimed that the "women work with an enthusiasm they have never shown before."[62] Many of these coarse, homespun garments were dyed with butternut-tree bark, which gave them a yellow-brown appearance.[63]

Because good uniforms were expensive and the blockade was effective, many Confederates used their resourcefulness to procure new uniforms, often resorting to unusual tactics and creating a piecemeal garment. In March 1863 Confederate soldier Green Berry Samuels wrote to his wife that his uniform was "pretty good yet and will answer for some months yet." He added, "uniforms are very expensive costing $200.00" because of severe inflation. Samuels stated that he would purchase a "couple of grey blankets and have them made into a uniform," which would be a "much cheaper" alternative since he was "soon to be a man of family."[64] Sir Arthur Fremantle described another example of resourcefulness that June concerning the appearance of Arkansas troops. He believed that the men were "good-sized, healthy, and well clothed, but without any attempt at uniformity in color or cut," as most were "dressed either in grey or brown coats and felt hats." The troops told Fremantle that "even if a regiment was clothed in proper uniform by the Government, it would become parti-coloured again in a week" because they "preferred wearing the coarse homespun jackets and trousers made by their mothers and sisters at home," with the "Generals very wisely allow[ing] them to please themselves in this respect."[65]

Due to the crumbling supply chain and increasing desperation, southerners found another means of obtaining the clothing they needed: stealing from the enemy. Theft of Union uniforms by Confederates occurred for two reasons. First, the soldiers needed them so they did not have to fight without proper clothing. Southerners obtained enemy items in simple ways, such as following behind a Union regiment and picking up discarded pieces of clothing. Often, because of the weight and the distance to their destination, "enough clothing was thrown away for Rebels to pick up to supply a whole brigade." Union soldier David Lane then mused in his diary, "no wonder so many Rebel regiments are dressed in our uniforms." The Michigan man did not discard any of his own items during one challenging march and was proud of carrying a "load enough that day to down a mule."[66] Lane's observation provides an example of how Confederates would obtain Union uniforms without the stigma of taking them from dead bodies or stealing them from supply trains. When they did obtain enemy clothing, soldiers bleached the fabric, attempting to change the color to blend in with their peers.

A more nefarious reason for Confederate soldiers to have Union uniform pieces was to disguise themselves. This allowed the rebels to appear to be Federal troops for sneak attacks or to traverse the countryside undetected. Union soldier Charles H. Lynch, stationed at Berryville, Virginia, under the command of Captain Martin V. B. Tiffany, recounted one day in September 1864. His regiment was "detailed to guard the wagon train," Lynch noting that he "don't like that kind of duty" but that he and his unit "must take our turn at it." Guerrillas kept them busy because "many of them dress in blue uniforms" so Union forces could not tell them from their own men. The disguised rebels were so successful that "sometimes they manage[d] to cut out of a train three or four wagons loaded with supplies."[67] On another occasion, Major General William Rosecrans detailed to the Indiana legislature the atrocities of war, specifically when rebel forces violated flags of truce and stripped the Union sick and wounded of their supplies, after which his army would be "met in battle by rebels wearing our uniforms and carrying our colors."[68] Occasionally, Confederate soldiers also donned Union uniforms and infiltrated enemy camps as spies.

But Confederates caught wearing Federal uniforms faced dire consequences: execution. A report noting a "successful expedition" of Rosecrans's army also mentioned that "several rebels [disguised] in federal uniforms were shot during the past week" around Lebanon and Carthage, Mississippi.[69] Similarly, a New York newspaper reported that two men dressed in Union garb had entered a camp claiming to be "Colonel Anton, Inspector General and Major Dunlap, Assistant." They claimed that Acting Adjunct General Edward Townsend had given them an "order to inspect outposts." But the Union soldiers found the men's conduct singularly focused, so they arrested them. The article reported that, upon discovery, the soldiers confessed that they were officers in the Confederate army, which sealed their sentence of being hanged.[70]

Stealing uniforms created another set of problems for Confederates:

disease. The fear of sickness was palpable in a circular distributed by G. M. Sorrel during the winter of 1864. He cautioned Lieutenant General James Longstreet's troops to avoid using all Federal clothing because of the "invisible danger lurking in the creases and folds of Union soldiers' uniform coats"; a reference to live smallpox pustules feared present within the garments. Whether the uniforms were taken from prisoners or from the dead, Confederate authorities discouraged the use of Union blues because their porous fibers allowed for bodily fluids to soak into the garment and transmit any diseases they might carry. This was an understandable fear and problem because men often wore their uniforms for weeks at a time without washing them. If a soldier donned infected clothing, he risked not only illness himself but also contaminating the other men of his unit.[71]

Throughout the war, the Union and the Confederacy struggled to uniform Black, Indigenous, and white troops. Even with Richmond's agents forging contracts with foreign clothing manufacturers and mills, the Union struggled less. For both sides, wearing the uniform made soldiers feel more official in their roles, even if their garments were stolen, bleached, dyed, or homespun because it united them with their peers. It set them apart from others because their patriotism and sacrifice were visible to all, even if they did not look resplendent. Soldiers and civilians alike began identifying themselves or others as "blue coats" or understanding that the gray or butternut uniforms denoted the color of the rebels. Soldiers and civilians began linking their identities to what they saw and what they wore because it evoked emotion and added to their shared experience. The struggle to uniform troops was important, especially for Black and Indigenous soldiers as well as for the Confederacy in general, because those exertions and how soldiers dressed during the war proved significant to issues men and women felt on all levels.

SENTIMENTAL STITCHES

T he ideal uniform should be of such character as to cause the officer and soldier who wears it to be proud of it for itself, aside from that which it typifies," asserted Captain Oscar Long in 1895.[1] Although uniforms are physical tools of warfare, they evoke sentimental feelings of pride as well as joy and attachment and are knitted to soldiers' and community members' identities. They can be a source of frustration or used as a reward for exemplary service. Lieutenant Colonel Wilder Dwight skillfully conveyed the electric feeling in the air when troops were under review, an occasion when a "brigade burnishes its equipments and perfects its uniform." On this occasion the soldiers donned their "gayest plumage of pride" with their "hats and feathers and epaulettes" where even the "sun vied with their splendor." They felt "ambitious, confident, [and] elate[d]" because "pride was at the helm."[2]

But in the nineteenth century, these were not the feelings shared by all in uniform, nor was it representative of white men and women's feelings about Black men wearing them. Nonetheless, uniforms elicited emotion. They stirred almost intimately those closely connected to these symbols of war. Complicated feelings of pride, joy, frustration, anger, and resentment enveloped the soldiers, crafters, and observers of uniforms. These garments provided people with connection, identity, and the symbolism of legitimate personhood otherwise denied those who did not identify as white males; there was a cultural understanding that wearing military uniforms could transform them. Many hoped that donning them would grant themselves status and respect, but these depended upon the viewpoint of those around them, as a uniform could retain multiple meanings and evoke strong and contradictory emotions. Those simple, hard-to-obtain garments crafted Black, white, and Indigenous communities during as well as after the war. Examining their symbolism and the sentiments attached to uniforms shows that they were more than just a necessity, tool, or phenomenon of war. Uniforms were also the foundation for individual and group identities and tangible building blocks for cultural and political representation.

THE SENTIMENTS OF SOLDIERS

Soldiers experienced everything from frustration and anger to joy and pride about their uniforms and in seeing the enemy, community members, or women in uniform. While some may not have expressed joy about their uniforms outright, they did enjoy the praise, acts of generosity, and attention they received by wearing them. Union soldier Josiah Favill recorded similar sentiments about "the utmost attention from everybody" who exhibited "wonderful enthusiasm and loyalty" toward himself and other men in uniform. He found it to be impossible for "a man in uniform to pay for anything he wants" because civilians filled his pockets with cigars and money, some even throwing a party in his honor before he left for war. Wearing his uniform and the attention he received because of it instilled in Favill a sense of happiness and pride.[3] Confederate soldier Howard McHenry expressed similarly deep feelings about his uniform, which was being made in "the pride of my heart." He was elated about being seen in his uniform, having his picture taken and sent home to commemorate the event.[4] Even General Robert E. Lee took joy in seeing well-dressed men in uniform. In a March 1864 letter to Miss Margaret Stuart, he commented that Major General Jubal Early had returned from home and was looking "handsomer than ever." Lee was impressed with his subordinate's appearance because he had obtained new garments that gave Early "the air of a gay Cavalier."[5] Numerous Union and Confederate soldiers dressed in their uniform had their image taken, creating thousands of ambrotypes, tintypes, and cartes de visite.[6] Dressing in his uniform and spending money to have an image taken, printed, and sent home speaks volumes about how each soldier felt wearing that garment. With their photos, these men created something that outlasted many of them and their apparel.

Yet while they took pride in what they wore, soldiers often lamented the cost and style of uniforms. These necessary tools of warfare elicited frustration from men like Union sergeant John Russell, who in a February 1862 letter provided insight into the degree to which uniform costs could undermine morale within the ranks. Russell reported "considerable trouble" within his regiment concerning "the clothing which we received from the State [of Illinois]." The men were upset because they were led to believe that their uniforms were "a gift of the State," no mention ever being made of paying for them. Nobody gave it any thought until the payroll came and the men realized they were "charged for the clothing from the pay which was due." In addition, their captains thought the soldiers had been "charged exhorbitant [sic] fees" and "called for a board of survey." Russell noted that this board eventually found "the value of our clothes as 11 dolls [dollars]."[7]

The financial burden that uniforms placed on Black soldiers was a topic of public concern in the North and exemplified how much the fight for freedom meant to them. General Orders No. 247 included, among other things, modifications to the chaplain's uniform. It now consisted of a "plain black frock coat, with standing collar, one row of nine black buttons on the breast, with 'herring bone,' with black braid, around the buttons and button holes," complete with "plain black pantaloons" and a "black felt hat, or army forage cap, with a gold unbraided wreath in front, on black velvet ground, encircling the letters U.S. in silver, old English characters." The secretary of war instructed these uniform modifications for all Union chaplains, but it was a point of concern for the chaplain of the First USCT, Reverend H. M. Turner. In a letter published in a Philadelphia newspaper, Turner narrated his response to the order, calling it "fine enough for any man; indeed, it is too fine," because "black cloth is the worst in the world for field service." He explained that rain and dusty rides would "soil it more than five times [than] the same amount of exposure [would] blue cloth." The chaplain was irritated that he could not "buy this suit [readymade] in any store, but must always have it made to order." His chief complaint was the expense, being unable to "get such a suit, with the rest of the necessary attire, for less than one hundred and twenty-five dollars." In addition, he required "four suits a year, (or be an ashy-looking chaplain)," estimating his total cost at five hundred dollars annually.[8]

Not only could the unexpected cost of uniforms upset those who wore them, but the changes in uniforms also elicited frustration from senior officers. Rear Admiral David Farragut voiced concerns and frustration to Assistant Secretary of the Navy Gustavus Fox in April 1863, praying, "do not let those officers at Washington be changing our uniform every week or two." Farragut believed that there should have been only one change, while "adding on stripes until they reach a man's elbow" was "a great error" because it blended the grades of officers. He continued his rant against the uniform, stating that if officials were going to make those changes, just have sailors wear "the simple blue coat with Navy buttons." His own "rule though life" was to vote against uniform changes unless necessary; the garment must be "easy to procure—not expensive—easily preserved—and the grades distinctly marked."[9]

The positive feelings described by those who donned Union blue or Confederate parti-colors spoke to the importance of those articles to their personal service and to the community members. In a letter to a friend in the fall of 1861, Union soldier Oliver Norton discussed the busyness of camp life and the work of "perfecting themselves in all the duties of the soldier." But he took specific pride in his regiment earning "a suit of fancy uniforms (Zouave)" because it was the "best drilled regiment in his division" (the Eighty-Third Pennsylvania) out of an estimated fifteen to twenty thousand troops. Norton was proud because they were a newer regiment and beat out thousands of men, even the "far-famed 'Ellsworth Avengers,'" earning "the post of honor and of danger that of rifle skirmishers." Four days later their uniforms arrived with a French agent, and each man was fitted, with the measurements sent to France so "exact fits" would be made. Norton proudly told his sister that they were "to have the most complete outfit ever seen in this country," adding that the "boys are overjoyed at their good fortune."[10]

The boys were not the only ones who were overjoyed to get into uniform. Women also joined the fray, donning military gear for a number of reasons, including safety, fear, love, and adventure. They took pride in their uniforms, their service, and the respect and freedoms they were afforded for putting on pants. Union and Confederate women also considered it their duty as patriots to fight for their country. These "would-be Amazons" assumed new names and got "into soldiers['] clothes." One such example, Mary Jane Prater, put on the uniform and spent seven months in the Thirty-Second Ohio, under the name John Crocket, before her capture for desertion.[11] According to historians DeAnne Blanton and Lauren M. Cook, more than 250 women donned uniforms and fought for either the Union or the Confederacy. The loose cut and fit of uniforms, combined with being in a "male space" and wearing pants, made hiding their bodies easier since it was not socially acceptable for women to wear pants.[12] One Cincinnati newspaper regaled readers with a scandalous story of a young woman with "sparkling eyes and raven hair" who followed her fiancé into camp, providing "herself with the uniform necessary to a volunteer." Those around her deemed the woman brave and virtuous for being proud to serve near her love.[13]

Community members and fellow soldiers often recorded positive feelings or thoughts about the discovery of female soldiers. In multiple cases they described them as "discovered in the disguise of regular uniform" and as "good fighters," with a man named Prentice affirming that "women who wear the breeches always were."[14] Many did find it shocking to uncover a woman in a soldier's uniform. A correspondent for a Minnesota newspaper counted more than 150 female recruits who were discovered and forced to "resume the garments of their sex." He reported that almost half of them were officers' servants and that several wore "blue blouses and pants." Many times men felt deceived by these "martial demoiselles" who willingly "substituted themselves" for war in league with men who were examined by surgeons and accepted into the service.[15]

Sarah Rosetta Wakeman enlisted in the 153rd New York Infantry in August 1862. She wrote in letters to her parents that she joined partially to provide money for them—she told her father that she would send home her wages to "pay your debts"—and because she "got tired of staying in the neighborhood."[16] Wakeman seemingly had no fear of being discovered and likely kept her gender secret for her two years of service. She purposely encountered men she knew from before the war, and none revealed her identity. In August 1863 she wrote her parents of guarding prisoners at Carroll Prison in Washington, D.C., among them three women: two who were Confederate spies, while the other, like Wakeman, served as a man—a major with the Union cavalry—until she was arrested for "not doing accordingly to the regulation of war."[17]

While her uniform allowed Wakeman to hide her gender, the clothing came at a significant expense. In November 1863 she complained to her parents that she had recently been paid, but "my clothing bill was so much that I didn't get but 12 dollars and 50 cents, and I can't let you have any of it."[18] Despite the risks of discovery—a February 1864 regimental order instructed company commanders to make all soldiers "strip and wash themselves thoroughly"[19]—and being arrested for her impersonation, like the former major she guarded at the Carroll Prison, in addition to the high cost of the uniform, Wakeman enjoyed her experience as a soldier. She wrote, "I have enjoyed myself the best I have since I have gone away from home than I ever did before in my life," and she planned to sign up for another five years.[20] Sadly, Wakeman never had the chance to reenlist. In May 1864 she contracted chronic diarrhea while participating in the Red River Campaign in Louisiana, dying the following month in New Orleans. Incredibly, even with a month-long stay in the hospital, she somehow kept her gender secret and was buried under her male alias, Lyons Wakeman, at the Chalmette battlefield outside New Orleans, presumably still dressed in the uniform that provided her with freedom and hid her identity.[21]

A contested figure, Loreta J. Velazquez donned the Confederate uniform during the war and wrote a book afterward about her experiences. Men such as General Early questioned her account after its publication, as do some historians, yet how she reflects on her service and her uniform remain beneficial. From the beginning of her book, Velazquez reassures her reader that she did nothing to disgrace her uniform, demonstrating the esteem with which she held it. She was proud because it provided her a passport to a life she never would have known otherwise. Throughout her story, Velazquez explains that "clothing, and particular cuts of clothing, have a great deal to do towards making us all, men or women, appear what we would like the world to take us for." In her case, dressed in an officer's Confederate gray, she was powerful.[22]

The number of female soldiers buried in their gray or blue uniforms will never be fully ascertained, but it is clear that hundreds served and enjoyed the opportunities that their military apparel provided. Sarah Edmonds, known as Frank Thompson, wrote from the battlefield at Fredericksburg, Virginia, that she had volunteered to be the aide-de-camp to "General H.," proudly stating, "I wish my friends could see me in my present uniform!" Later in her memoir Edmonds states that once she arrived back in Cairo, Illinois, she "procured female attire, and laid aside forever (perhaps) my military uniform; but I had become so accustomed to it that I parted with it with much reluctance."[23]

While women, African Americans, and Indigenous Peoples all served for different reasons, many sought a new level of equality or sovereignty that they could acquire by putting on uniforms and performing the same duties as white men. The uniform provided Black men with their new identity and collectively allowed them and their communities a tangible source of hope and optimism about the future. From the time that enslaved people were first imported into the British colonies and into the early years of the republic, enslavers clothed Black people in low-quality fabrics such as plain kinds of cotton or fiber mixes of cotton, wool, and flax. Enslaved males typically wore loose shirts, short jackets, and trousers that allowed movement for physical labor. Often, enslaved persons wore tattered and dirty clothing because of their work life.[24]

Union soldiers forced those who self-emancipated into their lines during the war to continue wearing these same clothes in freedom. In his report of June 1863 on the condition of African Americans in the "contraband" camps, John Eaton Jr. described many of the refugees as "having hardly enough to cover their nakedness."[25] Even those who worked for the army as laborers faced the same issues. Lieutenant Charles Stevens wrote to his commanding officer that African American men who lived at the contraband camp in Kenner, Louisiana, and repaired the levees had labored every day for the past three months with no days off, lived in "filthy conditions" in an old barn, and "were in a shocking condition in regards clothing." He described most of the men as barefoot, "others with no shirts and a majority without pants except in the most ragged state," and the women as "in even a worse condition than the men as regards clothing." Stevens noted that "hardly an article of clothing has been issued," which contributed to the high rates of illness and death at the site, a common condition at such camps during the war.[26]

For Black soldiers, many formerly enslaved, Federal uniforms were the first quality clothing of their lives, despite the "shoddy" reputation of the early iterations. Beyond their physical quality, the uniforms served as manifestations of pride and the men's claims to the privileges that accompanied their status as soldiers. The January 1863 edition of *Douglass' Monthly* described these men "mustering into the army" as the First South Carolina

Volunteer Regiment, being brought before the headquarters of Brigadier General Rufus Saxton, and "proudly shouldering their guns, as they stood in their red pants, blue coats, and caps," not the standard uniform but the spare for USCT members. Saxton joined them in full "military costume," but "grouped around [them all] were parties of scoffing soldiers—here and there an officer, whose curled lip and upturned nose told the whole story." But also observing the presentation of the new Black soldiers were "groups of negroes, of all ages and sizes," and they "filled up the circle watching with alaring [*sic?*] eyes." The general spoke to the group for a few minutes and then, turning to the crowd, "with a clear voice he pronounced them all free—they, their wives, children, fathers, brothers and sisters—'and all your relations.'" The article ended with the declaration, "they were free: [the] Government had acknowledged their manhood."[27]

Similarly, Lieutenant Colonel William Gould Raymond, one of the white officers who formed the First U.S. Colored Infantry Regiment, told a "war meeting of the colored folk" at John Wesley Church in Washington, D.C., in June 1863 that the previous day had been the "happiest day of his life." He had "witnessed what he never saw before—colored men in uniform." To the applause of the crowd, he detailed that the Black soldiers in their uniforms "seemed to have more dignity than he had ever seen in the ranks before, and appeared to realize they now were *men*."[28] The transformation of Black males into soldiers and thus, as they saw it, men could not have been performed without donning the Union uniform. Watching the swearing-in ceremony and seeing their fellow African Americans in uniform meant something important to the Black community.

Because of the clothing of their prior condition, wearing a Union uniform or seeing African American men in one contributed to a physical and mental transformation. Accounts of heroic actions permeated Black newspapers: in one account the author described how a "single black man" delivered "victory" to Union forces at Roanoke Island, North Carolina, because he could guide the commanding general, Ambrose Burnside, where his men should march, having "mapped out" the terrain better than "an engineer could . . . have done . . . in a month." Because of his bravery, that African American "stands at the right hand of Burnside, clad in uniform."[29] In a "Negro Battle Hymn," the verse "They look like men of war, All arm'd and dress'd in uniform," exemplifies the Black soldiers' newfound identity.[30]

Freeman Thomas, a private in the Twelfth U.S. Colored Infantry, demonstrated the significance of the uniform to this identity. Thomas was born enslaved in Tennessee in 1845. Late in life he told an interviewer that as an enslaved child he wore poor-quality clothing, distributed by his enslaver, that offered little protection against the cold winters: "'Long in the fall he'd give his darkies shoes, and he'd have 'em half soled once a year. We'd get a coat every other year, and he'd give you a thin suit and two pair of pants that winter. And he'd give you two course cotton shirts to carry you through the winter. Little children wore what their parents put on 'em." When the Union army captured Nashville in 1862, Thomas self-emancipated to its lines, where the military forced him to work on building fortifications. Thomas faced difficult living conditions in the refugee camp, including inadequate clothing. He soon enlisted in the USCT and received his uniform, later detailing the importance of the moment: "This was the biggest thing that ever happened in my life. I felt like a man, with a uniform on and a gun in my hand." Thomas served with the Twelfth Infantry until the unit was mustered out in January 1866. He survived the harsh conditions when his regiment built the Nashville and Northwestern Railroad, a bout of mumps, and a severe leg injury received during the Battle of Nashville. He later married, had children, built a home, and became a respected leader in his community. Yet it was that point in 1863, when at the age of seventeen he donned his uniform for the first time, that he described as "the biggest thing that ever happened in my life" and the moment when he "felt like a man."[31]

The new identity that Thomas and other African Americans experienced when they put on their soldier's uniform fostered a desire in many for equality and the rights of citizenship.[32] As stated by Frederick Douglass in his continuous push for Black soldiers and Black equality: "Let the black man get upon his person the brass letters, U.S.; let him get an eagle on his button, and a musket on his shoulder and bullets in his pocket. . . . [T]here is no power on earth which can deny that he has earned the right to citizenship in the United States."[33] Black soldiers heeded these words. Speaking to the June 1863 "war meeting of the colored folk" in Washington, USCT soldier George W. Hatton told the crowd that he was "determined to have his rights and liberty." Hatton specified several "rights" he intended to exercise and stated that "when he would get his uniform he was going down in

Maryland to see his mother, and the man who would insult him he would feel it his duty to kill."[34]

Hatton also told those assembled that he planned to refuse to ride the capital city's streetcars until they allowed African Americans to sit inside the covered part of the vehicle rather than standing on the uncovered section with the conductor.[35] For Hatton and other Black soldiers, respect was not enough—they hoped to use their status as uniformed soldiers to push for the end of discrimination. The experiences of Dr. Alexander T. Augusta exemplified these issues and the importance of the uniform to this push for equality. Born in 1825 in Virginia as a free person of color, Augusta earned his medical degree in Canada and became the first African American major in the army.[36] When Augusta attended an event in April 1863 celebrating the anniversary of capital's emancipation day, the *Washington Star* reported, "the appearance of the colored man [Augusta] in the room wearing the gold leaf epaulettes of a Major, was the occasion of much applause."[37]

While African Americans lauded Augusta as a hero, he experienced the same discrimination that Hatton hoped to end. In May 1863 Augusta boarded a train from Baltimore to Philadelphia. A group of white men assaulted him, ripping the epaulets off his uniform. Augusta exited the train, reported the incident to the provost marshal, and returned with another officer to arrest his assailants. They were able to arrest one of the men who damaged the major's uniform, but whites continued to attack the doctor as he brought the prisoner to jail. Augusta wrote to the *Christian Recorder* detailing why he was determined to ride on the train in his uniform and punish those who injured it and his body. The major acknowledged that in Baltimore, "even Union men do not wish to see colored men wearing the United States uniform." Yet he argued that he had "higher grounds" to "justify my course." He proudly stated: "For I hold that my position as an officer of the United States entitles me to wear the insignia of my office, and if I am either afraid or ashamed to wear them anywhere, I am not fit to hold my commission, and should resign it at once." Augusta believed that his action "proved that even in *rowdy Baltimore* colored men have their rights that white men are bound to respect."[38]

Augusta helped codify these rights into law in 1864. That February he attempted to enter the covered section of a Washington streetcar on a rainy day. The conductor refused to allow his admittance and removed him from the vehicle. Senator Charles Sumner read of the incident in a New York newspaper—he noted to other senators that the white Washington newspapers did not cover the episode—and introduced a resolution to end discrimination on streetcars in the capital city. Sumner argued that the conductor's treatment of Augusta, who was "wearing the national uniform," was "worse than a defeat in battle." The bill ultimately passed, and Augusta's defense of his status as a uniformed officer resulted in substantive change for all African Americans in the nation's capital.[39]

Because direct records from Native Peoples wearing uniforms are difficult to obtain, much of what is known comes from newspapers and official wartime records, which include some Native voices. Interrogating these sources is difficult, but Indigenous stories are significant and must be shared even by reading against the grain to find their sentiment or symbolism. One such example is the Confederate Congress authorizing President Davis to present Hemha Micco, also known as John Jumper, principal chief of the Seminole Nation, "a commission without creating or imposing the duties of actual service or command, or pay, as a complimentary mark of honor." This gesture was "a token of good will and confidence in his friendship, good faith and loyalty to the [Confederate government]." With this commission, congressmen presented Micco with a complete uniform of his rank and grade, which cost the Confederacy $250 (almost $7,000 in 2022 currency). Micco had served first as major of the First Battalion Seminole Mounted Rifles and then as colonel of the First Regiment Seminole Volunteers. He participated in engagements at Round Mountain, Middle Boggy, and Second Cabin Creek in Indian Territory. The new uniform provided him with the identity of a loyal, valued Confederate citizen. Giving Indigenous leaders symbols that suggested equality to a white man won their loyalty and that of their followers to the Confederacy, stitching their identities to the white government they served.[40]

In the spring of 1863, Brigadier General William Steele wrote a letter to Confederate senator (and brigadier general) Louis T. Wigfall on the importance of conciliating Native Peoples. "The Indians must be addressed through the medium of their present wants; hence the necessity of feeding and clothing them to keep them firm in their allegiance," he argued. Providing their regiments and their soldiers' families with essential goods such as food and clothing to maintain their fidelity drove the war effort in

Indian Territory. By 1863, both armies considered the region "destitute of everything essential to an army, or to the supply of its inhabitants."[41] Similar observations appear multiple times throughout the records of both the Union and the Confederacy as they sought to maintain the loyalty of their Indigenous compatriots by extending the resources of uniforms. Clothing the Native Peoples secured their support and fostered camaraderie for Indigenous units because they saw this as an extension of sovereign or at least human recognition amid a common struggle.

Indigenous men all over the United States wanted to join the war. Historian Laurence Hauptman tells the story of a Seneca man, Newt Parker, and his multiple attempts at enlistment and ongoing frustration by rejection due to government policy. Before Parker was dismissed for a second time, he "returned to his home at Tonawanda, proudly dressed in his military uniform." This story, one of only a few examples throughout the record, assists in documenting good feelings by Native People when wearing a uniform.[42] Another instance with a hint of conversation about uniforms involved Ely Parker. The Seneca captain turned down an offer to work with Brigadier General William Smith to stay on Brigadier General John E. Smith's team and for a chance at working for his friend Major General Ulysses Grant. He reflected on how others perceived him, stating that "as for the common soldier, he does his duty and pays respect to my shoulder straps," indicating that even though Parker was Indigenous, he received respect because of wearing the Union uniform.[43]

A January 1864 article announced the acceptance of Oneida and Menomonee men into the Union army. The report counted "thirty large, young and fine-looking Oneida and Menomonee Indians, who have volunteered and been accepted as substitutes." The Native Peoples were reportedly "very proud of their new and warm uniforms and pleased with the idea of being soldiers." The commanding officer "returned to procure more" Indigenous troops because, he stated, "they are among the best soldiers in the field . . . better than those, even, who are born in the South."[44]

The patriotism expressed by these Indigenous soldiers helps explain the positive feelings about their service, especially pride. In October 1864 the General Council of the Choctaw Nation wrote an expression of "sentiments and feelings" to the warriors of their nation in service to the country. They praised their "self sacrificing and patriotic efforts" and, on behalf of their fellow citizens, "cordially and gratefully tendered their thanks and appreciations," proud of the "zeal, patriotism and fidelity" of the Choctaw soldiers. This resolution was signed by the principal chief, Peter Perkins Pitchlynn, and forwarded to the commanders of every Choctaw regiment and battalion to be read publicly to the troops.[45]

PRODUCTION FEELINGS

White women of the Confederacy diligently worked, pouring their skills, time, and money into crafting a variety of garments for their soldiers. Sewing for the cause was a very personal and patriotic act that became publicly recognized. The ladies of Greenville, South Carolina, made everything from gloves and scarves to socks and uniforms to show their support. Because they "had been told of their grandmothers' loyalty and industry during the war with England," they wanted to "show the same love to their defenders."[46] Judith White Brockenbrough McGuire recorded her actions and feelings of service in her diary, explaining that "the ladies of Alexandria[, Virginia,] and all the surrounding country were busily employed sewing for our soldiers," crafting "shirts, pants, jackets, and beds, of the heaviest material." They "must all work for our country" because the "fires of our enthusiasm and patriotism were burning." The women worked and excitedly conversed without doubts or fears about the "justice of our cause and the valor of our men, and, above all, on the blessing of Heaven." They could not be outdone by the men in their devotion, for they "must sew for them, knit for them, nurse the sick, keep up the faint-hearted, [and] give them a word of encouragement in season and out of season."[47]

White Confederate women in North Carolina publicly proclaimed their patriotism in their local newspaper upon the creation of the Stonewall Knitting Society. The president of the group, Julia Saunders, called her fellow workers "true heroines" for providing socks for their troops. The group considered it their duty to render "all the aid in their power" for their soldiers fighting for independence. They took pride in their "noble work" of knitting or receiving contributions of socks, gloves, or "any other articles" that added to the "comfort of the soldier."[48]

Much like their Confederate counterparts, young white women in the North lent their resources to the preservation of the Union. Caroline

Cowles Clarke (née Richards) kept a diary detailing the "trainloads of the boys in blew [*sic*] going to the front" and describing the patriotic articles the women wore on their own bodies, such as "little flag pins for badges"; tying their "hair with red, white and blue ribbon"; and having "pins and earrings made of the buttons the soldiers gave" them from their uniform jackets. Clarke participated in sewing for the soldiers, obtaining the garment cuts from another society. The young ladies in her group wrote notes and "enclosed them in the garments to cheer up the soldier boys."[49]

Individuals across the North banded together to assist the U.S. Sanitary Commission and its "benevolent and patriotic purposes." According to the author of an article in Vermont's *Independent Standard,* the Sanitary Commission organized to ease the "severe strain" of the "gigantic operations" required for war. Those involved took pride in the relief they provided to soldiers. The report highlighted the tremendous work performed at Gettysburg, where the Sanitary Commission distributed "more than thirty thousand articles of clothing, and more than sixty tons of provisions." The writer praised the "patriotic women whose ready hearts and hands" did "so much for the comfort of the soldiers" and encouraged readers to help the cause through donations of "shirts, drawers, dressing-gowns, stockings, and bedding."[50]

The response from women to requests upon their time, labor, and supplies was not always positive. One submitted a query to the editors of the *Chicago Daily Tribune:* "can you inform the public why it is that soldiers are dependant [*sic*] on female labor for the necessaries of life?" She explained that during the first panic of war, women were "anxious" to show their support and good will as unpaid labor, but it was then December 1861 and there were still "constant appeals to women for blankets, woolen socks, mittens, woolen shirts, &c." The writer recalled the work of women during the Revolutionary War, when the country did not have manufactories and the wool was "carded and spun by women." She wryly commented on the young women of the 1860s who "do not card or spin, and many do not knit," while their mothers and grandmothers worked tirelessly through the "cares and duties of housewifery, to get the soldiers comfortable." Still, Union soldiers cry for blankets. She believed that if women had "kept back" and only assisted with home needs, the "regular supply of manufactured articles would have, by this time found a channel more satisfactory." The author was frustrated with the situation, stating that she was "pained to learn that young men" were in want of "suitable clothing," and accused some with the Sanitary Commission of pocketing the donations sent for the suffering soldiers.[51]

Joy and intrigue best describe the African American reaction to seeing Black men in uniform. This is illustrated in African American newspapers by the language they used to tell stories of Black Union soldiers and the emphasis they put on their actions and clothing. Seeing one of their own in uniform assisted in transforming Black individual and community identity because the garment spoke for them, denoted authority, and commanded respect.

In March 1863, officers who intended to form a "colored brigade" met in Philadelphia. After an enthusiastic reaction, the officers of this group decided to send a delegate to Washington "to obtain mustering orders from the War Department." Their plan was to disperse five thousand circulars to the Black population of the city "as a means of inducing them to enlist." Several wealthy people of color indicated their desire for Colonel William Frishmuth to command the brigade "and promised him, upon the completion of the organization, $60,000" to assist with expenses. At that point the officers were "not yet certain how the men will be recruited, or what uniform they will be required to don," but "the uniforms, it is rumored, are now being made in this city."[52] Philadelphia's Black community believed that citizenship would be confirmed through military service. Putting on the brass belt buckle stamped "U.S." and the eagle coat buttons became an identity marker and a source of pride for individual soldiers and for African Americans who saw them. To them, those markers combined with the Union blue garments denoted an elevation of status and their personhood.[53]

In the spring of 1863, a meeting of Black citizens at the Joy Street Church in Massachusetts sought to awaken interest in forming regiments for the commonwealth. The meeting's president, Robert Johnson Jr., opened with a call to recruit Black men for the Union forces. He declared that the "necessity of having the black man in arms" made him "proud that the time had come when he could feel that he was an American citizen." Johnson introduced the next speaker, Judge Thomas Russell, who told the crowd that "he saw no one before him at that time who was not truly an American citizen, for the necessities of the country have reversed the

Dred Scott decision."[54] Both asserted that because the country called upon Black men to don a uniform and take up arms against the South, they were now considered U.S. citizens, contrary to their previous lived experience. The *Christian Recorder* reported an incident of a Black soldier bayoneting a white soldier in July 1863 because the man refused to listen. The paper stated that "now the white soldier thinks, as this one did say, that a n— soldier, as they are sneeringly called" by the whites, "have no rights that a white soldier is bound to respect." The Philadelphia paper acknowledged that white soldiers "think they can do as they have a mind to," but the author was thankful that the "colored soldier feels his position, and its responsibilities, and its honors too much, to take any insult from such cowardly, petty larceny thieves, as too many of these white soldiers [have] prove[d] to be." The writer encouraged Black troops not to let their names be "tarnished" but to have courage, "stand firm, and likewise remember, on them depends the complete salvation or destruction" of their race.[55] African Americans believed that if they looked *and* acted the part of American citizens, their goal was achievable.

After sending the Fifty-Fourth Massachusetts off in May 1863, the members of their local community became curious as to their situation in August. As *Douglass' Monthly* noted: "No conception can be formed of their appearance, unless they, are seen. We had long been desirous to see camp-life from an inside view." The publication described the scene: "just before you see the camp, there are men with U.S. uniforms, Who, at first sight (never having seen colored troops) would be mistaken for white men." This emphasis on the uniforms confirms their significance in the act of challenging white expectations of the African American soldiers. Throughout the rest of the account, the author delineates the jobs of the uniformed soldiers guarding the road and watching the banner presentations, describing the scene as "magnificent."[56]

Even the final images of a Black soldier were meant to invoke loyalty to country and the Union cause of freedom. To encourage the people of Philadelphia to support the Third USCT, who "with the spirit of patriots did not stop to consider the hardships attending camp life, and the horrors of war," the *Christian Recorder* published a letter addressed, "Dear Friend." The writer asks for the community to spare food or little pleasures like pen and paper, books, and smoking materials. To produce an emotional response, the letter paints the picture of soldiers carrying a comrade to his last resting place: "his blue uniform is his shroud, and a rough pine coffin is the last we see of what was once our companion in arms."[57] By leaving the reader with the image of the blue uniform on a Black man in his coffin, the writer knits together the identity of the community with the garment in calling them to engage with the war effort and support the troops fighting for their country. Each of these examples provides a deeper understanding of how connected the identities of the soldiers and their networks became with the Union uniform, which provided a path to citizenship and personhood.

THOUGHTS & FEELINGS ON SEEING OTHERS IN UNIFORM

Judgment, frustration, fear, and anger are all terms that aptly describe the emotions expressed when seeing the opposing side or those deemed inferior people in uniform. The representation of uniforms, whether Union blue or one of the various Confederate colors, not only identified soldiers on the battlefield and their side but also signaled a personhood that white men did not always accept. Due to supply issues for Confederate soldiers, their homespun garments provoked judgmental comments from white northern soldiers. In a letter to a friend, Union surgeon John Gardner Perry conveyed his interest in caring for his patients who were Confederate prisoners of war. He described one man as a wounded "thoroughbred South Carolinian" Confederate surgeon "dressed entirely in Alabama homespun, which is the ugliest snuff-colored stuff imaginable." Perry observed that the physician wore a "broad-brimmed planter's hat" and was "stained with mud and blood from head to foot."[58]

Another particularly descriptive example comes from Union soldier James Kendall Hosmer as he set out on a spy mission, specifically against units from Alabama and Arkansas whose men had been shooting at him in July 1863. He recorded in his diary the covert mission to "study the live 'reb,' and determine the category in natural history under which he should come." Hosmer found what he was looking for, "the real truculent and unmitigated reb in butternut of every shade." The men he observed wore everything from "dingy green which clothes the unripe nut, to the tawny brown and faded tan." He described the various stages of other uniforms as "butternut mixed with a dull characterless gray." Hosmer judged that "there was no attempt at uniform, yet something common, in the dress of the whole company,—a faded look, as if the fabric, whatever the original hue, had felt the sun until all life and brightness had wilted in the web and been killed out of the dye." He was impressed that the clothing was "whole" and, when he looked closer, determined that the uniforms, while unattractive, were "strong and serviceable, though very course."[59]

There was a complexity to the initial reaction of white northerners to using Black troops. Some supported the recruitment of African Americans because that meant saving white bodies. Many newspapers editorialized against Black soldiers, arguing they "wouldn't, as fighters, be worth the guns in their hands and the uniforms upon their backs."[60]

The official mustering of Black soldiers did not immediately soften the feelings of many white troops in the Union military. As reported in the *Douglass' Monthly*, a letter from New Orleans to the *New York Times* contained "rumors of some trouble at New Orleans growing out of the feeling of some of the white soldiers towards the black regiments." Before the Emancipation Proclamation led to Black troops in the army, the Native Guard from occupied Louisiana went unnoticed; afterward, white Union soldiers began insulting these and beating African American soldiers and civilians. The offending white soldiers took such action, they said, because they "cannot bear to have the United States uniform so degraded as when worn by 'n——.'"[61] There were the occasional commentaries in the newspapers that noted the plume of African American soldiers. An abstract authorized by Secretary of War Stanton and published in the *New York Herald* noted that "colored troops, taking a pride in their new position, exhibit great neatness and care of their persons, uniforms, arms and equipments, and in the police of their camps."[62]

Many whites described intense reactions to seeing Black men don the Union uniform because they now were dressed equally. In March 1863 Oliver Norton wrote to his cousin describing a letter he received from another soldier the previous week. "O.M." was near a Black regiment with Black commissioned officers, but "contact with the contraband" had "modified his ideas already that he don't like to see them in the same uniform he wears." O.M. described the Black officers as "wooly headed captains." Norton was surprised by this man's negative position, asking his cousin, "ain't you glad you wasn't born in the South where such ideas originate?"[63]

Similarly, a story from Tennessee reprinted in an Ohio newspaper recounted the violence that befell Black Union troops in a theater on a Saturday night. The next morning more violence ensued when "the soldiers resumed their attack upon the negroes—this time displaying their pugnacious propensities, especially against those negroes dressed in Federal uniform." A deputy marshal suggested to a Black soldier who had been knocked to the ground several times that he should "take off his coat" to prevent such treatment because his attackers wanted him to remove his military clothes. Once the man removed his coat, fellow Federal soldiers around him "tore it to atoms," effectively shredding his symbolic citizenship and costing him money, all of which they well understood. Several other accounts of Black Union soldiers being beaten and stripped of their uniforms followed, with the offending soldiers shredding the clothing each time. The newspaper account ends by saying "but no material damage was done." African American soldiers suffered bodily harm and physical damage, as did their army uniforms, which symbolized the manhood they welcomed and that their attackers feared because it put the Black men on par with white men.[64]

Not all white Union soldiers reacted in such a manner. Others felt satisfaction or pride in the presentation of Black men in uniform. "Yesterday I saw what pleased me" was the happy phrase from Union soldier Thomas Keenan as he described the review of the predominantly Black Tenth Army Corps. He continued, his letter by stating, "I never saw a finer body of men in uniform than on that occasion" because "every thing was in the best condition" with "clean clothes" and "bright buttons." This was the appearance of "good soldiers" who exhibited a "proud and manly bearing."[65]

The reaction to seeing African Americans in uniforms epitomizes one of the key complexities of the American Civil War. As argued by historian Chandra Manning, many white soldiers from the start of the war supported emancipation. These sentiments, however, did not translate into ideas of racial equality. African Americans like Frederick Douglass and Alexander Augusta believed that wearing the uniform would help convey rights of citizenship and equal treatment. For them, the uniforms of the USCT became symbols of pride and hope. But for many northern whites, including soldiers, the uniforms of the USCT represented a challenge to a racial hierarchy they supported, so some purposely attacked African American soldiers, targeting their uniforms, to maintain white supremacy.[66]

Unsurprisingly, the reaction of white southerners was almost univer-sally negative. At the "hint" that the Union seriously considered arming and outfitting Black troops in June 1862, a North Carolina newspaper printed a special dispatch from the *New York Herald:* "it is hinted that a portion of the extra appropriation of thirty millions, which passed the Senate yester-day, is covertly designed to defray the expenses of uniforming and arming negroes to fight on the Union side."[67] African Americans in arms and Union blues alarmed white southerners because of their understanding of their perceived racial hierarchy.

As the rumor percolated, some Confederates resorted to mocking the idea of Black troops. During military maneuvers in August 1862, Confed-erate major general J. E. B. Stuart sought to distract Union major general John Pope from spotting Major General Thomas "Stonewall" Jackson's ma-neuvering troops. Stuart and Pope participated in a tiny skirmish, so the cavalry commander and his men made their way into the enemy's camp and began "fumbling in the trunks of Gen. Pope, . . . obtaining clean linen enough to last through the season." Because Jackson and his men were able to cross another river ford and escape, the South counted the maneu-ver a success. A newspaper reported that "Stuart preformed his part well, and both rebel and national army are enjoying the practical joke he played off upon Gen. Pope." The story ends with "a burly negro, dressed in Gen. Pope's best uniform, with the stars of the major general glittering upon his shoulders," sitting on Pope's best horse. This Black man dressed in a Union uniform "rode in front of Stuart, as his famous cavalry brigade marched through the streets." The African American seemed embarrassed and did not know what to make of the procession, but the multitude of white Con-federates enjoyed his confusion immensely. The writer continued, explain-ing that "some one in the throng, however, was not disposed to treat the new major general with the respect due to his rank" and threw "two or three highly perfumed eggs" onto "the fine cloth of Cuffee and soon led him to discover that, instead of being an object of respect, he was one of the grossest ridicule."[68] This incident exemplifies the thoughts of white south-erners concerning Black men in uniform. While the display was meant as somewhat of a joke, angry southerners took it to the next level and disre-spected the Black man and the Union uniform he wore.

Southern newspapers continually degraded African American soldiers fighting in the Union army even though they were in uniform—indeed, in part because they wore the uniform. Like their northern counterparts, reports and editorialists argued that African Americans would make poor soldiers. "Quite a number of negroes were in the Yankee camp in uniform, only two of whom, however, had the courage to fight," reported one North Carolina newspaper in August 1862. Seeing Black men in uniform, clothed just like white men, forced Confederate soldiers to perform a feat of mental gymnastics because a race that had served them for so long now had a form of power that allowed them to come a step closer to regaining their humanity.[69] In fact, many of the formerly enslaved composed the ranks of the USCT, which began operating in 1863 to help subdue the rebelling states and end slavery. The *Washington Telegraph*, considered the Confederate mouthpiece in Arkansas during the war, posed the question, "How shall we treat our slaves arrayed under the banners of the invader, and marching to desolate our homes and firesides?"[70]

On January 14, 1864, the *Washington Star* reprinted the report of a *New York Times* correspondent about a Union raid of North Carolina by USCT troops. The regiment killed a group of southern guerrillas and burned or captured their supplies, including corn, horses, weapons, and Confederate uniforms. In the view of the newspaper, though, the unit's most significant accomplishment was instilling fear in local whites. "In regard to its moral and political results," the reporter opined, "the importance of the raid cannot be overestimated." The regiment freed 2,000–3,000 enslaved individuals and terrified the white residents. White residents of places invaded by the USCT became panic-stricken, causing scores of families to flee into the swamps. Proud white southerners accustomed to obedience "literally fell on their knees before these armed and uniformed blacks" begging for their lives. The report concluded that "an army of 50,000 blacks could march from one end of Rebeldom to the other almost without opposition, the terror they would inspire making them invincible."[71]

Though the correspondent's assessment was clearly an exaggeration, the danger that Black soldiers posed to the white supremacist racial hierarchy provoked violent reactions, and southern soldiers often gave no quarter to African Americans in uniform. The *Western Democrat* of Charlotte, North Carolina, reported on an encounter between Confederates and Union soldiers: "After fighting for some time," the Black soldiers "offered to surrender as a prisoner of war. They were both, with the others in uniform, very properly shot down." Black men with guns in Union blues embodied everything that southerners had feared from John Brown and the threats of other insurrectionists; now the uniforms gave the African Americans authority and made the southern white fear a reality.[72]

Because of the visceral hatred of white southerners at seeing them in Union uniform, Black troops when caught faced death or being forced back into slavery. As a dispatch from Murfreesboro, Tennessee, in April 1863 noted, "Wilder's brigade returned with many forces and sixty contrabands." The report continued, "after having caught several poor negroes," the Confederates "shot and hanged them for being found in Yankee uniforms."[73] Once a Black man put on army clothing and tasted the semblance of personhood, southerners often no longer viewed him as a usable slave. This change in mindset had to do with both parties understanding the authority imbued in Union uniforms. African American soldiers claimed personhood by wearing them, and Confederates understood a shift in mindset and condition of those soldiers: their race would no longer serve the white man.

A diary entry by rebel soldier Charles Herman describes "a perfect slaughter" and a group of his fellow southern military men toting trophies from the Battle of Fort Wagner with the Fifty-Fourth Massachusetts Regiment. He explained that on "becoming aware of the state of facts, that negroe troops were fighting against them," the Confederate soldiers "knew no quarters and began slaying right and left, until every blue coat was off or killed." His association of Black soldiers as "blue coats" provides an example of white southerners fusing African American identity with Union uniforms. Later in his diary Herman again mentions "blue coated Yankees," providing another example of how what soldiers wore became synonymous with their identities.[74]

On April 12, 1864, Confederate troops under Major General Nathan Bedford Forrest massacred Black soldiers captured at Fort Pillow, Tennessee. The account of this atrocity appeared in newspapers across the country, but the reporting in the *Christian Recorder* and the reaction of this Philadelphia African American newspaper underscore this fusion of man with material. The author describes the battle and the defenders' showing truce flags twice as only giving Confederates "the advantage of gaining new positions," which compelled the Union forces to surrender. Upon capitulating, "as fiends and blood-thirsty as devils incarnate, the Confederates commenced an indiscriminate butchery of the whites and blacks." The African American soldiers who ran were "bayoneted, shot or sabered," including women and children. But the newspaper's reaction was that "should a Union general avenge this murder in kind, the North would bow its head in shame," declaring that "never have they [Black soldiers] disgraced the uniform they wear, the cause they maintain, by such an atrocity."[75] The author uses the blue uniform to represent everything for which the Union stands—placing a symbol at the center of a cause—and claims that this attack was on the nation and not just individuals. He accounts for those wearing the uniform as part of a larger body, arguing that the behavior of Forrest's men disgraced not only the Confederate uniform but also their cause in a way that African Americans never did to the Union uniform or cause. This event demonstrated that the violent and volatile reactions to seeing Black men in uniform angered Confederates on an elevated level.

Even while denouncing and massacring Black troops—the Confederates used threats of violence as a means of preventing enslaved people from self-emancipating, all to maintain their race-based system—southern leaders debated their own use of African Americans as soldiers. Conversations on enlisting enslaved persons to fight began in 1863 and became a serious consideration by late 1864. Jefferson Davis opposed emancipation in 1864 and claimed that only states could take such action. Robert E. Lee feared exhausting the white population in the efforts to achieve independence. Instead of having their enslaved property used against them, the general privately stated in a letter to Virginia senator Andrew Hunter: "My opinion is that we should employ them without delay. I believe that with proper regulations they can be made efficient soldiers . . . [because of their] long habits of obedience and subordination, coupled with the moral influence which in our country the white man possesses over the black."[76] Most southerners disagreed with Lee's sentiments, though. The *Daily Confederate* of Raleigh, North Carolina, published an article arguing that "the employment of negroes as soldiers would produce a demoralizing effect upon the white troops so as to counterbalance the additional strength thus acquired," weakening the army instead of strengthening it. One of the causes of demoralization would clearly be seeing the formerly enslaved in uniforms worn by those who once had enslaved them.[77]

Over these fears and objections, on January 13, 1865, the Confederate Congress authorized Davis, with the permission of their enslavers, to recruit enslaved men as soldiers. Section three of General Orders No. 14 states, "while employed in the service the said troops shall receive the same rations, clothing, and compensation as are allowed to other troops in the same branch of the service."[78] As this news spread throughout the South, it created shock waves. Formerly enslaved soldiers now would be wearing Confederate gray or butternut uniforms, just like their white enslavers. The *Daily Intelligencer* of Wheeling, West Virginia, published a speech against arming the enslaved by Thomas S. Gholson, who stated that the proposal "has created despondency among our people, who have concluded our condition much worse than it really is. It has frightened our negroes, and made many of them escape to the enemy."[79]

The Richmond government justified its action as reflecting "the importance of calling into active service the whole physical strength of the Confederate States in this momentous crisis" because the "armies may be greatly increased by the enlistment of negroes."[80] Because southerners fought the war on the premise of maintaining slavery, the desperation to win and prove their point was palpable. They were willing to risk providing some enslaved men their freedom for serving as uniformed soldiers in return for the reward of preserving enslavement.

The issues with the Union blockade and the announcement that Black men would be allowed to serve in the rebel army prompted a fraught question: if the Confederates were to employ their enslaved men as soldiers, where would they get the uniforms? The *New York Herald* reprinted an article from the *Richmond Examiner* that answered the question: "cast off uniforms, to the number of four or five hundred thousand suits, are lying piled up in government depots in Richmond and elsewhere." The story went on to explain that white soldiers objected to being served this clothing "no matter how neat and clean." Authorities did not know how to dispose of the extra garments, but with Congress authorizing Black men to serve as soldiers, "this accumulation of second hand clothing will equip [them] from top to toe, and save the government the expense." The piece ended by urging people to "hurry up the negro, and let him get into the old clothes as soon as possible" to continue the war effort.[81]

In opposition to the concept of abundant secondhand uniforms, another article in the *Richmond Examiner* and reprinted from the *Philadelphia Inquirer* declared that the Confederacy did "not want more men because we cannot feed and clothe them." This would make sense if the writer were unaware of the stores of used clothes white soldiers refused, but this article appeared in the same newspaper a week later, meaning that he had ignored or missed the earlier story, or perhaps the earlier story was inaccurate. The author continued: "what folly, then, to talk of adding more men to our army, and especially of introducing into it the very doubtful element of the negro soldier, when we cannot, for want of supplies," properly clothe anxious recruits.[82]

In March 1865 came an "appeal" made "to the people of Virginia" in light of the Confederacy authorizing the "organization of companies composed of persons of color, free and slave, who are willing to volunteer" at the behest of "our loved Commander-in-Chief." This request "recommended that each recruit be furnished, when practicable, with a gray jacket and pants, cap and blanket, and a good serviceable pair of shoes," but there should be no delay in enlistments for want of clothing. This plea resulted from "every consideration of patriotism" for "the independence of our country."[83] Recruiting officers were asking the southern people both to furnish the army with their enslaved property and to provide them with the uniforms in which they would fight Union forces. As with white recruits, the Confederates organized a "parade of a battalion of troops from Camps Jackson and Winder, including two companies of negroes," in Richmond. The battalion marched through the capital's streets with a band and reportedly "produced quite a sensation, chiefly among the negro population."[84]

The irony of this being an image the Confederacy feared—militarized African American men—should not be lost. Yet "the interest of the occasion was lessened by the failure of those in authority to uniform and equip the negro soldiers," although they were "armed with muskets and went through the manual as well as could be expected for the short time they were drilled."[85] Another account of Black men in Confederate uniforms also comes from Richmond, where "a company of blacks in Confederate uniforms paraded in the streets to attract additional volunteers." Among those witnessing the spectacle was John S. Wise, a Confederate officer and the son of a former governor of Virginia. "Ah!" he thought as he watched the "Confederate darkeys" drill in Capitol Square, "this is but the beginning of the end."[86]

Mustering formerly enslaved men into the military became a tactic designed to perpetuate the war and the Confederacy, but it was ultimately inconsequential. The Black soldier fighting for the South in any substantial capacity is a myth. Still, it is important to note the continuing discussion of Black Confederate soldiers and the speculation—only a few historical documents address this topic—about what they would wear, both for what it meant to southern society at the time and what was to come during the creation of the "Lost Cause" theory. Much like their feelings about properly outfitting their white soldiers, southerners voiced concerns about providing uniforms for their potential Black soldiers, even if it was just for show. While those items provided for the formerly enslaved men at the depots were not of the quality intended for the white soldiers, General Orders No. 14 stipulated that Black soldiers would wear the same clothing as their white counterparts. This could be interpreted as some southerners feeling that it was important for Black Confederates to look the part of soldiers since it played into the notion of the uniform as a central focus of Confederate identity. In turn, this assists General Lee's arguments about the value of African Americans and on a certain level begins the transformation of Black southerners into people—a transformation that the Lost Cause would seek to change, with uniforms at the heart of the discussion.[87]

I dentity and control were central to Civil War uniforms, and they in turn were central to those goals. Clothing Indigenous troops allowed both the Union and the Confederacy to exercise dominion and authority. While Indigenous soldiers saw their uniforms as a bond of unity, neither of the governments had that understanding. The Union blues became a symbol and signal of freedom and personhood for the Black community that would entrench itself into African American memories and provide something for veterans to cling to after the war, amid the thoughts and actions of their white counterparts and enemies and the unrealized promise of Reconstruction. For both Indigenous and African American troops, serving in uniforms during the Civil War became a part of their individual and community identities that lasted through Reconstruction and fueled their need for memories of the war. The fact that the governments and the civilians of both the Union and the Confederacy continued dedicating precious resources of the war effort to uniforming soldiers signifies the importance of the issue to the warring powers at large. The need for women from both sides to work in factories and mills or in sewing circles demonstrates their dedication to their cause and shows how uniforms became central to the female understanding of the war, themselves, and their participation. For many during the Civil War, uniforms and identity proved inseparable. And this formed the basis of their continued or changing relationship to the garments after the war.

4

COCKADES,
BADGES & FLAGS

A simple report in a Tennessee newspaper regarding happenings in Baltimore in April 1861 perfectly encapsulated the brewing strife, division, and "indignation" that would soon become a civil war. The Union feeling in that city was "unmistakeably displayed" because men wearing "cockades and Secession emblems" were chased by crowds and required protection by police. When a "Secession flag" flew above the *Fannie Fenshaw,* some in the crowd asked a boy working on the vessel to take it down. After the youngster did so, the captain of the *Fenshaw* "rehoisted" the flag, thereafter requiring a detail of police to protect the ship because all others in the harbor flew the U.S. flag.[1] By publicly battling with their chosen emblems, Baltimoreans not only professed their political loyalties but also demonstrated the emphasis that nineteenth-century people placed on their material identity. They understood the metaphorical weight of such items and the intensity with which many reacted at being confronted with those of the opposition. Material pieces became more strongly attached to political identity during the Civil War, with versions of wartime badges and flags becoming exceptionally prominent in postwar celebrations.

Like uniforms, badges and flags not only served a practical purpose but also promoted a personalized group identity. A psychological study published in 2016 describes why and how individuals commonly attach themselves to physical symbols in an attempt to display their personal identity to others. Group settings also strongly foster this mentality. The authors concluded that "group members strategically emphasize symbols when they are motivated to convey an impression of their groups as unified and intimidating to others." This works well with the concepts of militarism and patriotism. At the same time, flags, uniforms, and badges served (both then and now) "as reservoirs of realness." As physical touchstones, they have played an important role in shaping, managing, and displaying the social identity of those who identified with the Union and those who identified with the Confederacy.[2] When ships fly flags, they signal to others their place of berth. Whether state or national, such a banner symbolizes power and has the backing of the government it represents. To deny a ship docking rights because of its flag is to deny its legitimacy.

The historical use and positions of badges and flags in the antebellum United States were incorporated into the manufacturing, use, and sentiment of the Union and white Confederates. But their physical construction came with a cost to those who made them. These material objects spoke for their wearers, showcasing their identity, place, position, and military unit. The objects represent also the work, sacrifice, and patriotism of women during the war and how they exhibited their personal politics at a time when they were not considered overtly political.

THE HISTORY OF BADGES & FLAGS

Badges, buttons, or ribbons have been used to publicly display positions and opinions for hundreds of years. Ribbon wearing for political purposes became common in Restoration England in the late seventeenth century. These ribbons provided an "imagined consensus" for the individuals who wore them, making many political statements through graphic or print culture. They are printed pieces of politics worn on the human body for public consumption. Political badges or ribbons supporting specific candidates were popular in the United States throughout the first half of the nineteenth century. Politicians' faces were printed or painted on ribbons and distributed to supporters.[3]

Badges or cockades became popular within the military during the American Revolution. Noncommissioned officers wore badges to distinguish them from privates. Many soldiers wore cockades of red or pink on their hats, others used green, and captains specifically wore yellow or buff. The cockades were in the form of rosettes created from leather or silk.

Changes to the American uniform occurred in 1821, including the adoption of "leather caps with bell crowns, gilt scales, yellow eagle in front," and a "black leather cockade."[4]

Secession cockades were created and worn by men, women, and children to demonstrate dissent with the Union. Southerners wore them in the streets and proudly posed for pictures wearing this subversive attire. Secession cockades could be as simple as a red velvet rosette crafted from a looped bow or as elaborate as five rows of red ribbon tightly folded and stitched together with a brass military button in the center.[5] During the secession crisis, white citizens adopted their own specific versions of secession cockades. The *Weekly Mississippian* reported on the design of "Carolina" designated as a "blue rosette." The cockade was two and a half inches in diameter, with a "military button in the center," and was "to be worn upon the side of the hat."[6] Some cockades were made at home, but others were manufactured in unexpected locations. The *White Cloud Kansas Chief* ran a story that some of these cockades were of "Yankee manufacture." One cockade the journalist described had a palmetto button in the center with the secession motto. The back of it bore the imprint of the Scoville Manufacturing Company, located in Connecticut. The report concluded with the snarky comment that the "secessionists prove their dependence on the North, even when asserting independence."[7] In Baltimore the *Daily Exchange* reported on the U.S. government's plan to "put a stop to the secession cockades and other emblems" people wore or flew in the city, stating that "those found wearing them in future will be arrested as traitors against the government."[8] But the wearing of secession cockades by the wrong people could result in social unrest. An Arkansas newspaper reported an incident at Yale College, where boys "raised a Palmetto flag" atop the alumni tower. This was in retaliation for a "supposed insult" by someone who "employed negroes to wear the secession cockade" in front of white southern students, who found it unconscionable for Black bodies to wear their symbol of discontentment.[9]

In addition to secession cockades, those who wished to see the United States remain intact sported Union cockades. On New Year's Day, 1861, President James Buchanan hosted a reception at the Executive Mansion filled with government officials, military officers, and court officials. Many from the public attended, some wearing secession cockades and others with Union cockades, both men and women alike. One Washington newspaper reported that those wearing secession cockades were "endowed with more partisan bitterness than good manners," declining to shake the president's hand.[10]

Just like badges, flags are imbued with meaning as tangible representations of national or regimental patriotic sentiments, but they also represent personal attachments. As historian Michael Scot Guenter has put it, Americans imbue the U.S. flag with strong meaning, emotionally responding to it "with varying degrees of loyalty, patriotism, and nationalism."[11] The Continental Congress created the first Flag Resolution, crafting the national banner and its specifications, on June 14, 1777—thus the annual celebration of Flag Day on that date.[12] Flags serve several purposes, including designating allegiance and identification of soldiers on the battlefield. During colonization, the English government gave Native People flags at meetings to encourage their support and ensure peace, instilling such meanings into these material gifts. According to Guenter, in many Native cultures, Indigenous People believe that what a warrior carried absorbs some of his power, so he forms a personal connection with some of his items. This concept assists in illustrating how the flags that Native People carried in battle adopted a personal meaning or significance. Militiamen carried regimental colors in several shapes, sizes, and designs. According to Guenter, Revolutionary-era colonists did not have a strong sense of national identity in terms of a flag, but they would have identified to their individual regiment's standard. Several flags were popular during this period, such as the snake symbol with "Don't Tread on Me." The Continental colors of the Grand Union Flag became the first flag for general use. This banner bears thirteen alternating red and white stripes, symbolizing colonial unity with the rebellion and the crosses of Saint George and Saint Andrew. In May 1777 the Pennsylvania State Navy Board paid Elizabeth "Betsy" Ross to make flags, which feeds the myth born in the 1870s of Ross creating the first U.S. flag.[13]

Leading up to the 1860 presidential election, men such as Sherman L. Miller, a sailmaker by trade, manufactured flags with the names of presidential nominees so citizens could show their political support for their chosen candidate.[14] Smith, Ezekiel, & Bladd also advertised of being "prepared to furnish flags (with likeness of candidates, or plain)" for those interested, boasting that it could produce them in large or small quantities at low prices.[15] Once the threat of secession became a reality, women living at the Shemwell House in Fayetteville, North Carolina, crafted their own U.S. flag, which they displayed from their balcony to a large cheering crowd, with brief remarks made by a local lawyer. A reported stated that it was a "pleasure . . . gazing upon that bright and beautiful Banner of Freedom" and that sadness "moistened many an eye" at the thought of "blotting this star or that from its azure field" at the removal of a seceded state.[16]

During the secession crisis, southerners began flying numerous combinations of bunting. Often, these flags could not be made in the South, so orders were forwarded to New York, where "flag-makers were busily employed in filling them," with "over one thousand flags" dispatched in a month.[17] These banners include the palmetto tree, originating from South Carolina, and the Bonnie Blue Flag, a blue banner with one white star in the middle. According to historian John Coski, some southern states adopted the Bonnie Blue as their national standard and a few regiments as their own battle flag.[18]

THE LOGISTICS OF BADGES & FLAGS DURING THE WAR

The U.S. flag is easily recognizable, but Confederate flags have a complicated history. Not only were there several versions, each symbolic of a "new nation," but they also represented a confederation of sovereign states. Throughout the war, regiments flew state and regimental flags, many of which represented the tangible crafting of both larger and individual personal identities because they had to be handmade. During the eighteenth and nineteenth centuries, flag making was a tedious and expensive process. Many banners were made out of silk during this period because of fabric durability and weight.[19] Women typically sewed them during the Civil War for their local regiments, imbuing each flag with a sentimentality that also stamped them as physical examples of women's Civil War service.

While the U.S. flag was decided on during the Revolutionary period, the Confederacy obviously had no longstanding emblem, so questions about the design of a national flag circulated throughout the government. Southerners felt as northerners did about their fidelity to and identity with their flags. Early in 1861, the provisional government in Montgomery created a committee to "select a proper flag for the Confederate States of America." After considering many designs, members first wanted to "copy and preserve the principal features of the United States flag, with slight and unimportant modifications." Although they voluntarily seceded from the United States, they wanted to keep certain aspects of the "glories of the old flag" because they considered themselves the true inheritors of the American Revolution.[20] Retaining a portion of that identity became part of the Confederate rhetoric of sloughing off an unjust government and maintaining the tradition of their forefathers, even though they had to give up the flag and "symbolically depart" from their tradition.

Throughout the brief existence of the Confederacy, the nation operated under numerous flags—all of which were based on the colors red, white, and blue and employing the star symbol. The first flag was known as the "Stars and Bars," a "Blue union, with seven white stars; three horizontal stripes, red white red." As described by a North Carolina newspaper, "the first [stripe] red and the [next one] white extending from the union to the end of the flag, and the lower red stripe extending the whole length of the flag." This version was hoisted above the first Confederate capitol in Montgomery, Alabama, and remained in use for two years. This ensign was designed and chosen by the Confederate Flag Committee.[21]

A standard battle flag, known as the "Southern Cross," was later created to avoid confusion with Union troops in combat. It has a red field, with a blue cross, and white stars for each Confederate state. The Naval Jack is the rectangular version of this flag. While the Southern Cross acted not as the national flag, but as the banner raised during engagements, it became part of the 1863 design for a revised national flag. Achieving standardization of the battle flag proved difficult. Some flags had borders, while the stars were closer together on other flags. In 1863 the Confederate Congress again debated designs of the national flag. General P. G. T. Beauregard was an active participant supporting the battle flag as the canton of their national symbol on a field of white with a blue stripe. Newspapers reported the senators' flag discussions, describing their preferences for the flag with a different field of red or with a blue stripe. According to the journalists in Wilmington, North Carolina, this version was "better than our present flag," meaning the First National flag (Stars and Bars).[22] Others supported the change, stating that the white field signified "purity, truth and freedom."[23] On May 1, 1863, President Davis signed the bill into law, establishing the new national flag with a white field and the battle flag, because it was a widely known and respected symbol throughout the Confederacy, as the canton.[24]

One Iowa newspaper provided its readers with an appropriate take on the struggles of the Confederacy in designing and sticking with a flag. One article captured the litany of issues from the beginning, stating that "the rebels have had a painful time" creating a national flag. They began with state flags and progressed to the "Stars and Bars," but even that flag "looked too much like the 'old flag,'" which they considered an imitation of the U.S. flag. The discussion then turned to the standard battle flag and its popularity, making it a logical choice as the canton for the revised Confederate flag with a white field. But critics called for a change because "it too closely resembled a flag of truce" when it drooped on the staff. As a result, and, ironically, just weeks before its formal surrender, the Confederacy modified this "flag of truce" by adding a red bar extending the width of the banner.[25]

The national Confederate flag underwent several changes, but the constant and supported emblem was the standard battle flag, which is why it was incorporated into the national design. It had become a recognizable symbol that southern women made. And because of its association with service, Confederates instilled meaning into its folds.

MANUFACTURE & LABOR

In both the Union and the Confederacy, many of the flags flown during the war were handmade by the mothers, sisters, wives, and sweethearts of soldiers. When regiments first left for the battlefield in 1861, the homemade silk flags crafted by women in their communities flew over them in battle. Once the war got underway, much like clothier companies, northern flag makers advertised their wares in newspapers, claiming that they could supply items "at short notice" and "on the most favorable terms." They could furnish silk flags for companies "according to Army regulations, at very low rates."[26] An advertisement placed in the *Gold Hill Daily News* in Nevada alerted silk manufacturers that "1,050 hands are now employed—mostly females—whose annual payrolls amount to 150,000." The newspaper stated that the silk arrived from China and Japan.[27] Others in the East advertised for women to "sew flags" both by hand and by machine.[28]

The Union relied on flag, sail, and tent makers to create their banners, but many regiments carried and flew homemade colors. Women provided the materials and the time to craft flags for their local units as a show of patriotic support and as a token of gratitude for their departing townsfolk. Often, the type these women cut and sewed were the Stars and Stripes. To demonstrate their dedication to the cause, Caroline Clarke stated, the girls in her society were willing to make a "flag bed quilt" with each of the "girls' names on the stars" for any of them who had to send a family member to war. She also wrote of the "little flag pins" she and the others wore as badges.[29]

Newspapers took favorable notice of the efforts of women and their flag making. The *Philadelphia Inquirer* notified its readers that the "young ladies of the Girls' High and Normal Schools have prepared a neat, beautiful silk flag, to be presented to the National Guards" and to be "borne by this splendid regiment wherever the fray is hottest and the fire thickest." It was made of "the finest texture" and "the richest quality, and the colors are bright and pure."[30] A general order for the First Corps, Army of the Potomac announced, "A new banner is entrusted to-day as a battle-flag to the safe keeping of the Army of the Potomac." To stir emotion, it proclaimed: "Your mothers, your wives and your sisters have made it. Consecrated by their hands, it must lead you to substantial victory."[31] Such language assisted in fusing both male and female identity and loyalty to the flag the women had made and the men now carried.

When African American women from their state presented a flag to the First North Carolina Colored Volunteers on July 24, 1863, the material itself and how it came to be demonstrated the item's importance to the identity of Black men and women alike. "Contribution of the negroes in this place" went to purchase the flag, and a newspaper report declared that they were "entitled to great credit, for, with their limited means, they did nobly." Designed by Harriet Beecher Stowe, who was already well known for *Uncle Tom's Cabin* and her commitment to abolitionism, the Boston-made flag cost $150 and featured "the Goddess of Liberty crushing to the earth a snake of the copperhead variety" on one side and on the other "the rising sun, casting its bright rays upon the dark clouds opposite; while in the bright azure appears the word 'Liberty,'" beneath which were the words, "The Lord is our sun and shield." The president of the Colored Ladies' Aid Association of North Carolina, Mary Ann Starkie, gave a speech at the occasion, stating, "they will take it [the flag] with them as an incentive to duty," and when they come home, they will show everyone "that they have stood by it with their lives in the cause of freedom." Colonel James C. Beecher, brother of Stowe and the Reverend Henry Ward Beecher, explained the meaning of the flag to the troops, discussing the Goddess of Liberty and the iconography surrounding her. He closed his speech with, "this is the flag we fight under—fight for liberty, not for one, but for *all*, as God has made them." He called the banner the men's "rallying point." He concluded, "Let it be sacred, and its influence, will grow day by day," proclaiming that the flag and what it represented was "the most sacred trust that has ever passed through my hands since I was born."[32] Raising funds, designing, and presenting flags to regiments was another way for African American women to be involved in the symbolism of the war effort.[33]

Such is the case with a story from *Douglass' Monthly,* which reported on the commissioning of a flag for the Fifty-Fifth Massachusetts, a Black regiment. The flag was "manufactured by J. Shillito & Co., of Cincinnati" and was said "to be of heavy silk, and elegantly painted and embroidered." The phrase upon the regimental banner stated, "Liberty or Death." The story concluded with the flag being taken to Columbus, Ohio, to be exhibited to Governor David Tod and then to the camp at Readville, "where Mr. Langston will present them in the name of the colored ladies of Ohio."[34]

When the fighting was over, these same women who had cut and sewed for regiments and their communities displayed their handiwork in their own homes. Days after the war ended, Jane Woolsey wrote to Eliza Howland proudly stating that she pinned a "pretty silk flag" made by a relative named Abby in one of their windows, with another smaller one in another window nearby. The Woolseys also proudly displayed a large flag on their front door in celebration of Lee's surrender.[35]

As with their Union counterparts, women of the Confederacy were called upon to "render more service than one to their brothers in the field." While actively engaged in making uniforms, they also sewed flags for local regiments. Prior to their departure, the Louisiana Guards "were presented with a beautiful flag by Mrs. H. D. Seaman, at her residence on Magazine

Street." In her speech she stated, "we have worked with our own hands this flag, which you will accept as a token of our allegiance and devotion to the cause of southern independence," adding that the women "confide this banner to your keeping, feeling that your stout hearts will never falter while it floats over your ranks."[36] Women made "little rebel flags" as keepsakes for Confederate officers, sewing them into their caps and collars. Union officers later confiscated such flags as "trophies to be sent to their friends in the North."[37]

Female support and diligence in flag making extended into Indian Territory. In June 1863 James Penney wrote to Peter Pitchlynn of the Choctaw Nation, notifying him that the ladies of their town had made a flag for a Captain Hamilton's company. The women wanted to present the flag to the unit, so Penney attempted to arrange a meeting with the Choctaw soldiers "to receive the Ladies and Flagg."[38]

Just like northern women, white Confederate women sewed homemade battle flags, often crafting them from silk. But men and women employed in Confederate quartermaster depots throughout the South typically made battle flags out of wool bunting and issued them to regiments. Because of this and a variety of other factors, it was as difficult to achieve standardization of the battle flag as it was with uniforms.[39] The inconsistency can also be attributed to limited practical sewing skills among those creating the banners. According to Victoria Ott, young ladies possessed ornamental and needlework training, not the day-to-day skills of high-demand items such as socks, shirts, and larger textile projects needed for war.[40]

Flags and badges were an integral part of military operations for both the Union and the Confederacy. Each side used flags for multiple purposes throughout the war, from national and regimental flags to red hospital flags and white flags as signals for a temporary ceasefire. Unit and regimental flags indicated the position of troops on the battlefield, which assisted in maneuvering. The governments and armies took flags seriously, making the provision that "the use of the enemy's national standard, flag, or other emblem of nationality, for the purpose of deceiving the enemy in battle, is an act of perjury by which they [the offenders] lose all claim to protection of the laws of war."[41]

The iconography of Union flags also served as a recruiting tool for African American soldiers. On an 1863 broadside designed to encourage enlistment, a depiction of a uniformed Union soldier holding the Stars and Stripes and standing on the Confederate flag declares, "Freedom to the Slave." The intricate background is busy, with African American troops marching and holding a U.S. flag, a broken set of shackles laying in the foreground. The enslaved in front of the Union soldier are tearing the Confederate flag. The back of the advertisement states, "All SLAVES were made FREEMEN BY ABRAHAM LINCOLN, PRESIDENT OF THE UNITED STATES, JANUARY 1ST, 1863," and it urges the reader, "Come, then, able-bodied COLORED MEN, to the nearest United States Camp, and fight for the Stars and Stripes."[42] The brightly colored image and the encouragement to "fight for the Stars and Stripes" provoked a sense of opportunity and the chance to exercise manhood.

The use of flags for traditional purposes, such as ships signaling their place of berth, remained important, but what happened when Confederate flags were not recognized as symbols of a legitimate nation? According to a report from the *Christian Recorder*, the secession palmetto flag did not "find favor" in one French harbor. The newspaper told the story of the *Matilda*, from Charleston, attempting to dock in the harbor of La Havre in April 1861. The vessel was not allowed to stay "until she hauled down the rebel abortion, and hoisted in its place the 'Stars and Stripes.'"[43] This simple action demonstrates not only the significance of flags to those who flew them but also their practicality.

Much like flags, badges had a practical purpose for both the Confederate and the Union military throughout the war. According to General Orders No. 9 issued by the Confederate War Department in June 1861, enlisted men were assigned badges from the *Uniform and Dress of the Army*. As previously discussed, this manual provided detailed answers to every question about the appearance of a Confederate soldier. Confederate officials determined badges to distinguish rank positioned on the "sleeve of the tunic" by an "ornament of gold braid." Lieutenants wore one braid, captains two, field officers (majors, lieutenant colonels, colonels) three, and general officers four. Officials specified that each braid had to be one-eighth of an inch wide. General officers were distinguished by a wreath of stars embroidered in gold on their collar arranged in a specific layout. Noncommissioned officers were marked by chevrons on each uniform sleeve on their tunics and their overcoats, the number of stripes corresponding with the man's rank. These badges were made of "silk or worsted binding" approximately half an inch wide and the same color of the edging on their tunic. In January 1862 the Adjutant and Inspector General's Office issued General Orders No. 4, regulating aspects of the forage cap, specifically the "marks to distinguish rank" with colors. The number of the regiment had to be "worn in front, in yellow metal" as a badge to mark every soldier.[44]

In early 1863, in the aftermath of the notorious Mud March, Major General "Fighting" Joe Hooker, the new commander of the Army of the Potomac, gave his troops a needed morale boost by designating "insignia badges for each corps." According to historian James McPherson, this simple task instilled "unit pride" among the Union soldiers.[45] Officers and enlisted men alike wore corps badges. Hooker instructed the chief quartermaster to "furnish, without delay" the badges for the First, Second, Third, Fifth, Sixth, Eleventh, and Twelfth Corps. Within the First Corps, whose badge was a sphere, the First Division wore it in red, the Second in white, and the Third in blue; this pattern of red, white, then blue was replicated throughout the army. The other corps badges were a plain cross (Sixth), a Maltese cross (Fifth), a diamond (Third), a trefoil (Second), a crescent (Eleventh), or a star (Twelfth). With this army order, the corps were provided with paper patterns demonstrating the shape, size, and color needed. Hooker was specific about the location of the badges, which should be "securely fastened upon the centre of the top of the cap." Should a badge be "lost or torn off," it must be replaced immediately. By the end of the war, nearly every other Union corps had adopted its own badge. Some were a bit ambitious or fancy with their designs. The badge selected by Major General Ambrose Burnside for his Ninth Corps was a cannon "made of gold bullion at Tiffany's" that was "scarcely practicable for the rank and file to obtain." Some soldiers put thought into the design of their badges: tradition has it that the men of the Fourteenth Army Corps selected an acorn as their badge because of their corps nickname, *Acorn Boys,*" for when rations had been dismal and they had to gather acorns and roast them to supplement their meals.[46]

The public praised this concept because it enabled soldiers of each division to distinguish themselves with a "special badge." A newspaper article reported that each corps would have a "certain figure" and each division a specific color, thus distinguishing a "soldier who straggles, deserts, is cowardly or brave" and allowing officers to punish or reward according to his deeds. The journalist wondered "how many poltroons have escaped the brand of disgrace" and "how many heroes have been deprived of just praise" because officers did not know their names. He concluded that "if the badges could be made sufficiently diverse," then their significance to the service would be "greatly enhanced."[47]

THE MEANINGS & SENTIMENTS OF BADGES & FLAGS

After the long, hard years of war, badges and flags became deeply connected with those who used them, the communities that made them, and those who saw them. These simple items were useful in providing instruction for war. But because of their constant use, the soldiers and community members linked these physical items to their own identities, oftentimes promoting positive feelings and sentiment. Occasionally, these objects, specifically flags, also became points of frustration.

Because of their personal nature, badges often were seen as a personal point of pride. Like uniforms, they were physically attached to their wearer, identifying his regiment, which told a story of the battles in which the soldier engaged. Orders from Major General Godfrey Weitzel described the badge adopted for the Twenty-Fifth Army Corps as a square, stating that "wherever danger has been found and glory to be won, the heroes who have fought for immortality have been distinguished by some emblem to which every victory added a new lustre." He felt that those men "looked upon their badge with pride, for to it they had given its fame." Weitzel encouraged his troops: "Soldiers! To you is given a chance in this Spring Campaign of making this badge immortal." The iconography of these badges became so important that they were not only worn by the infantrymen in the corps but "also painted with stencil on the transportation of a corps, its wagons and ambulances." According to Massachusetts soldier John Billings, the men of the Army of the Potomac were "so devotedly attached to its badges," looking upon them "with pride," because they were the first to adopt them (at least a year if not more before everyone else). He believed that once the war ended, the veterans "desired" an "enduring form of these emblems, so familiar and full of meaning to them." This is why veterans later wore these badges pinned to them or "suspended from a ribbon[;] the dear old corps badge, modelled in silver or gold, perhaps bearing the division colors" in enamel or stone, inscribed with the battles in which the unit fought. Billings posited, "what is such a jewel worth to the wearer?" Because of his attachment to his own badge, he wrote, "I can safely say that, while its intrinsic value may be a mere trifle, not all the wealth of an Astor and a Vanderbilt combined could purchase the experience which it records."[48] Soldiers' service and sacrifice became linked to their badges. These simple, unassuming pieces of material told their stories and represented their experiences in a way words never could.

Just as their uniforms and badges mattered deeply to them, the battle flags of many Black regiments and units were unique and became markers and ties to their identity. Like their badges, their flags were symbols that conveyed the stories of their courage, manhood, service, and sacrifice. While white troops had a connection to their material items as well, the connection Black soldiers and community members had with their objects was a prominent focus of conversation in newspapers and correspondence. Some flags displayed a hopeful tone. The 127th USCT flag depicts an African American soldier standing next to Columbia holding a U.S. flag beneath a banner reading, "We Will Prove Ourselves as Men."[49] Taken together, a Black man in uniform—the garb of a white man—and the phrase present a central goal for African American soldiers: to be seen and taken seriously as men. On the flag of the Forty-Fifth Regiment, a Black soldier holds the U.S. flag while standing next to a bust of George Washington, the men of the unit charging into battle beneath this banner proclaiming, "One Cause, One Country," demonstrating their ties to U.S. history.[50] In the background of the Sixth USCT flag is a house and an African American woman sitting on a bale of cotton, with happy children behind her. In the foreground is a Black soldier next to Columbia holding a flag. Above this image is the phrase "Freedom for All."[51] The Twenty-Fourth USCT regimental flag bears the words "Let Soldiers in War, Be Citizens in Peace," with the image of a uniformed soldier reaching out to an item with the words "Fiat Justitia," meaning let justice be done, while other soldiers mimic the motion in the background on a broken battlefield.[52] As a final example, the Third USCT flag depicts a defiant Black soldier and Columbia holding a U.S. flag between them with a military encampment as the background. Its title, "Rather Die Freemen, Than Live to be Slaves," frames the scene.[53] Such depictions of Black uniformed soldiers on battle flags exemplifies African Americans' perceptions of manhood and citizenship through respectable dress and of their desire of becoming their own heroes through military service. Some regimental banners, however, carried a more vengeful tone. The Twenty-Second USCT flag is a prime example. "Sic Semper Tyrannis" is the headline, and the picture it carries shows a Black soldier in full Union uniform bayoneting a fallen white Confederate soldier.[54]

Other flags were less ornate, though their designs reflected no less determination. The First Kansas Colored Infantry flag includes an eagle with wings spread, a sash with the words "E Pluribus Unum" held in its beak, and the U.S. shield on its chest against a field of blue with thirty-four gold stars arching overhead. It also has emblazoned the names of the battles in which the regiment participated. The Second Kansas Colored Infantry flag is much the same, though with fewer battles listed.[55]

When a soldier is featured on a flag, he is clean and well dressed in a Union uniform, the antithesis of bondage. These banners depict the transformation from enslaved human property to valuable uniformed citizens eager for service. In contrast, the Twenty-Fifth USCT flag shows a Black man, not in uniform, but in the clothes of an enslaved man, with broken shackles directly behind his feet. Holding a parchment in one hand, Columbia hands the man a musket with fixed bayonet with her other hand, arming him in his fight for freedom. The words on this flag are no longer entirely clear, but the legible portion reads, "Strike for God and."[56]

These flags and their descriptions are central to the concept of identity because the African American soldiers on them represented well-dressed formidable opponents. In turn, these aided and assured the preservation of the memory of the Black troops' combat experience. They sent a message to the men who fought under them, to other Union soldiers, to the Confederate enemy they faced, and to the African American civilians who saw them. Even those who could not read the flag understood what their images represented, the courage and tenacity of the men in these units. The Black soldiers' goal, proudly displayed to everyone through these mottos and their missions, was to fight for the African American cause.

Confederate soldiers also viewed their own flags as emblems of their cause and ambassadors of their manhood. In his journal W. W. Heartsill documented the occasion on which his company received "a splendid FLAG" from the ladies of Marshall, Texas. He describes the First National flag crafted by these women in great detail. The eight stars were emblematic of the states that had seceded to that point. On the opposite side, the women painted the emblem of their state, the "LONE STAR"; the phrase "SEMPER PARATUS"; and the unit's name, "W. P. LANE RANGERS." The care with which Heartsill records every detail of the flag suggests his excitement at its presentation and gratitude to the women who made it. He also refers to the tone of the event and the address given by Sallie O. Smith as "beautiful, and her sentiments patriotic." In June her address appeared in a newspaper, and Heartsill procured it for his journal. Smith hailed the "chivalry of Texas" and its brave sons, whose "patriot hearts" swelled with "generous pride." She wished that she could "tender to each" of the soldiers a "talismanic Flag" for their safety. She presented the ensign "in the name of the FAIR and the BRAVE," hoping that in battle their foes would "cast his eyes upon those stars and contemplate their import." This flag was not only meaningful to those who received it but also to those who made it. Like many others, Heartsill pledged to stand by it through the duration of the war, offering his loyalty and devotion to what that flag represented. Aligning it with the South's war effort, he considered it a "FREE and independent FLAG of the SOUTHERN CONFEDERACY."[57]

The new Confederates saw the flags as consecrated pieces of their identity and could not abide them being desecrated or used for something else. In one instance Union troops adopted a trick of "raising the Confederate flag and imitating the secret signals of the Confederates," which southerners deemed "unprecedented in civilized warfare" and depraved because it was "such a cowardly and wicked trick." This behavior so angered them that they vowed that "every Yankee captured under the Confederate flag or making Confederate signals, should be hung upon the battle field forthwith, and his miserable carcass left to feed the vultures."[58]

The flags the Indigenous troops carried into battle also provided them with the identity of loyal Confederate citizens. The First Cherokee Mounted Rifles, led by Stand Watie, carried their own flag that closely resembled that of the Confederate States. In the First National pattern, the canton is blue with a circle of eleven white stars, symbolizing the Confederate states. Inside that circle, five red stars represent the Five Tribes, with the larger center one being that of the Cherokee. The center white stripe bears the moniker "CHEROKEE BRAVES."[59] The imagery of the stars representing the Five Tribes safely nestled inside of those representing the southern states paints an image of misplaced acceptance and security when thinking about their place within the Confederacy. During the summer of 1861, an Indigenous woman's husband requested that she "make a fine Confederate flag." Although finding material proved difficult, she ultimately crafted one out of "silk handkerchiefs," which "cost $5.00." The flag was a gift for the Confederate soldiers the couple camped with "who were Choctaw Indians."[60] This story illustrates that Native Peoples supporting the South understood and took seriously the symbols and symbolism of the Confederate flag.

Union sergeant Isaac Newton Parker wrote to his sister Martha in August 1863 about Camp Hoffman's new flag. He was excited when the men received the "post-colors of the first quality" and called the fifty-by-twenty-foot banner a "large splendid flag." Flags became a portion of Parker's identity during the war because of his position within the outpost. In a December 1863 letter to his wife, Parker wrote that his appointment as "Sergeant Color Bearer" meant that he carried the "United States Colors" into battle. His letter ends abruptly, and he was unable to sign his usual endearing closing or express his feelings about his new position. Parker struggled because of his Seneca heritage but eagerly joined the Union army and wrote fondly of his uniform, duty, and service. This thread connected his pride of service to his appreciation for his new position and the emblem that he guarded, his duty as a color-bearer being to protect the flag at all costs, including his own life.[61]

Soldiers like Parker took the role of color-bearer seriously; many were "shot down" with their flags "bathed in their blood."[62] As reported in one Louisiana newspaper, Confederate soldier B. W. Clark took his role as color-bearer for the Delta Rifles to heart, stating, "I receive this beautiful flag, with a due sense of the responsibilities resting on me as its custodian." Soldiers so honored readily "sacrifice[d] themselves for its [the flag's] safety." Clark continued in his public proclamation that his charge was the flag of our "glorious Southern Confederacy. Made of the finest silk," it was without exception "one of the most beautiful we have ever seen." He and others saw it as their duty to protect and if necessary bleed and die for their banner, which makes it easy to see how soldiers, flag makers, and community members could stitch these emblems to their identities.[63]

Women of the South felt the same alignment of identity with the flags they sewed. Those banners flew over their loved ones and represented their devotion to the essence of who they were and their cause and country. According to historian Victoria Ott, "a popular activity among young women was sewing a flag to present to the local company of volunteers." Doing so "filled [them] with pride," gave them a sense of community, and provided an acceptable form of "political expression for teenage girls." Ott includes examples of young women using "their clothing as political expressions" by making Confederate flags to wear as aprons "as statements of loyalty."[64] Eleanor S. Turner Ivey described in her memoir how local ladies and young girls in South Carolina were "busy as bees, making a Confederate flag." She observed: "Oh! How many hopes were stitched into the folds of those Stars and Bars!" Ivey recalled that they worked "often with bleeding fingers" and, when the flag was completed, "proudly" watched the townsmen run their banner up the pole.[65] Within their domestic realm, these women performed every patriotic task they could afford, demonstrating their support and loyalty to the soldiers and their cause. These sentiments and actions would not stop with the war's end but would continue into Reconstruction and beyond.

Flags were objects that bound not only the Confederates but also the members of African American communities fighting for their freedom from them. They promoted a common thread and identity between soldiers, makers, fundraisers, and community members. For USCT units, receiving their flag, or "colors," was an occasion for celebration that typically involved pomp and circumstance. The place of presentation or the flag itself symbolized more than convenience or a piece of silk—it was meant to make a political or identity statement. As with soldier's uniforms, African American women assisted in finding and fundraising for flags suitable for USCT regiments. Under the Miscellaneous section of *Douglass' Monthly*, news regarding the Fifty-Fourth Massachusetts stated, "a circle of young ladies are exerting themselves to procure a suitable flag for the Massachusetts 54th (colored) raiment." If someone wanted to reach the ladies, the publication provided a name and address.[66]

While women made flags, they also raised the money to purchase banners, which was an intentional sacrifice on their behalf. A moving article in *Douglass' Monthly* discussed a Mr. X who traveled to raise Black regiments in North Carolina during the fall of 1863. While there, an African American woman tried to get his attention. When she was finally permitted close to him, her minister in tow, she handed him a "brown paper parcel that jingled." She explained that this was one hundred dollars collected from the "colored Ladies of Newborn to get a standard for the 1st Regiment of North Carolina Volunteers." He attempted to argue with her, saying that the women needed the money more and that the government would provide their regimental colors. But this rebuttal of their kindness "distressed her," and with "tears in their eyes" they stated that "it was their privilege and right to get the flag." The collection was of small silver coins "from the scanty savings of the slave subscribers." The newspaper stated that this was "the first subscription made by slave women in the United States for a flag for colored soldiers." It reprinted the woman's handwritten plea for a flag, which stated that she and the others wanted to "purchase a decent flag for our Colard Solders" because their husbands and sons "fight our Battles and gain our Libatys."[67] To this woman and her community, their tiny coins saved from enslaved labor were a worthy sacrifice, and they felt that the flag for this regiment, in which their husbands and sons served, was a symbol of hope and liberty. It was their privilege and their right to contribute to the war effort, and it would be their evidence that they had done so.

Later that month a correspondent for the *Christian Recorder* wrote of the flag presentation by the "Colored Women's Union Relief Association of Newbern, N.C." for the "First Colored Regiment of North Carolina Volunteers." The writer called them "noble women" who "kindled a spark in the breast of the colored warriors that can never be quenched" because they gave their soldiers a feeling of self-dependence and pride. Their flag was a "presentation of the emblem of Liberty" and thus a gateway to their "natural rights as a symbol of heavenly virtue." The correspondent concluded by declaring the "beautiful banner" to be "worthy of the respect and confidence of the world."[68] That flag represented the respect and confidence of the men who carried it by symbolizing their sacrifice, manhood, and willingness to take a stand for their race. The importance of flags as symbols of citizenship to African American women translates to what Black men felt as they fought under these banners.

Throughout the war, these communities acknowledged badges and flags as important pieces of their identity. Their creation, presentation, and meaning resonated for many community members in both positive and negative ways. The flag presentation for the Sixth USCT at Camp William Penn, Pennsylvania, was a fiery, celebratory occasion. Friends gifted the banner to the regiment. It was, according to a news report, made of "the finest silk, with the American eagle in the front, over it the words, 'freedom for all'"; on the reverse it said, "Presented by the colored citizens of Philadelphia." Adjutant General Lorenzo Thomas, speaking at the ceremony, noted that "the negro soldiers repulsed the enemy" at Milliken's Bend, Louisiana, and lauded the sacrifice of those who fought with Colonel Robert Gould Shaw. Mr. Robert E. Purvis, aide-de-camp to a Major Stearns, handed Col. Louis Wagner the flag, saying, "Receive this standard. . . . Soldiers, under this flag let your rallying cry be for God, for freedom and our country. If for this you fall, you fall the country's patriots, heroes and martyrs."[69]

Other ceremonies evoked similar responses. The presentation of the "3d Regiment of the United States Colored Troops" took place at Sansom Street Hall in Philadelphia, with a crowd of "both colored and white people" in attendance. The *Christian Recorder* proudly stated that "the flag was painted by our excellent and gentlemanly Mr. Bowser, who is a colored man and an artist No. 1." The "patriotic colored ladies of Philadelphia" ordered the flag prepared and presented on their behalf. The closing remarks of the article stated, "this meeting was creditable to our race."[70] On March 5, 1864, the Twentieth USCT received its "colors" at the Union League Club House in Union Square, New York City. Those who bestowed the flag used the presentation as a symbolic attempt to reclaim a public space after the 1863 New York City draft riots.[71] Wrapping the African American soldiers in the U.S. flag and their regimental flags with this celebration aligned them with their country and, as understood by the freedpeople who purchased and commissioned the ensigns, promoted them to citizens.

In the face of adversity, many people proudly wore their badges or stood up for the flag that represented their allegiances. In an attempt to recruit Black soldiers, meetings were held early in 1863. As reported in the *Washington Evening Star,* the forty or fifty soldiers present in the capital city "marched along, with red, white and blue badges on their breasts" while some wore "a cockade composed of the same colors." These men met with jeering, some of which came from members of their own community. While they did not have quarters, uniforms, or arms, they bore "their honors well."[72]

The condition of battle flags after the war ended spoke volumes about the service, sacrifice, and experiences of soldiers, especially African American troops. Shortly after Appomattox, Thomas Keenan described a company review he witnessed, adding, "I must not forget to mention their flags." He marveled that the flags of this Black regiment were in "perfect shreds, torn in pieces, and one instance only the bare staff." Keenan explained that a "soldier always looks to the flag for evidence of service," and this group of "colored soldiers can bear theirs with pride." He even mentioned that "it must have been galling" to the white inhabitants of Raleigh, North Carolina, to "see their former slaves proudly marching through their streets, conscious of their new position—they the masters!"[73] In conveying the purpose and meaning of flags to those in service, this story touches on a significant theme: these flags were not only symbols to those who bore them but also to those—namely, white residents—who had to view them as a message of authority. In addition, tattered flags were a sign of hard-fought service. While many white Americans did not think that Black men would be fit for service and disliked seeing them in uniform, the condition of their flags was an undeniable mark of valor even to the staunchest objectors.

Men were not the only ones who demonstrated bravery or valor when protecting their flags. Annie Wittenmyer later told the story of a woman named Mrs. Brownlow living in eastern Tennessee who "floated a large Union flag." Most of their neighbors flew Confederate flags, but the Brownlows were loyal to the United States and proudly waived their Stars and Stripes. Wittenmyer described Mrs. Brownlow as a "quiet, lovely little woman," who demonstrated courage one day when she defended the flag. On that occasion, Mrs. Brownlow was "beautiful and stately" with a drawn pistol, challenging the men who were sent to take down her flag. Wittenmyer characterized her as the "perfect personification of the Goddess of Liberty" when her "eyes flashed fire and her words rang out clear, full, and emphatic," forcing the men to leave. Brownlow watched and defended her U.S. flag until Union forces arrived. Wittenmyer stated that seeing the single U.S. flag among the sea of Confederate flags gave the troops the "inspiration" to take the town.[74]

In a heartbreaking account written in 1861, Margaret Sumner McLean conveyed her encounter with a soldier on his death trestle. She described his "noble traits of character and his gentlemanly breeding" as he lay dying. McLean saw the young man after death, lying in his coffin, "with the Confederate flag folded over him." It was at that moment that she "felt for the first time that those colors were sanctified," then posited, "how dear must they be to those who have sacrificed their all to it?"[75] In linking that young soldier's service and sacrifice to the flag under which he served, McLean demonstrated an understanding of these emblems to those who wore them, carried them, fought under them, and were buried because of them.

Seeing a battle and instruments of war made an impression on people, even if they were children when the war raged. Lucinda Davis, a formerly enslaved woman in Indian Territory, told her story in August 1937 at the age of eighty-nine. She was purchased as a child by her former enslaver, a Creek man named Tuskaya-hiniha, to care for his new baby boy. Davis recollected her experience with the Battle of Honey Springs in July 1863, watching Native troops ride as fast as they could with a flag. She described the banner as "all red" with a "big criss-cross on it dat look lak a saw horse." Davis watched as a man carried it and "rear back on it when de wind whip it," flapping around the horse's head as the animal reared like he knew something was going to happen. She watched soldiers and heard gunfire. After the battle she returned to her enslaver's home, but the image remained in her mind years later.[76]

Reactions to flags and what they represented were not always positive. In April 1862 Captain Henry W. Morris sent a detail ashore in New Orleans to raise a U.S. flag over the mint. This venture faced a rocky start when an upset crowd gathered. Several "spirited" observers, including a Mexican-American War veteran named William Bruce Mumford, removed the flag. The *Pocahontas* fired on the men, but the group walked through town with the captured flag as members of the angry crowd tore pieces from it.[77] For this act of defiance, Mumford was arrested and placed on trial before the Military Commission. Major General Benjamin F. Butler ordered the execution of Mumford, who was "convicted of an overt act of treason, in pulling down the American flag from the Mint" after it was raised by order of Captain David Farragut.[78] A large crowd gathered to witness the execution at the mint.[79] This simple act of defiance cost Mumford his life. Citizens on both sides of the conflict paid the ultimate price in service to the emblems that reflected their political beliefs.

The history, practicality, and sentiment associated with badges and flags influenced the perceptions and identities of soldiers and community members throughout the war. Badges and flags represented their identities in a personal way that was inherent during the nineteenth century. These emblem connections continued into the postwar Reconstruction era and became a functioning and meaningful part of the memory of the war, specifically as markers of service and sacrifice with the development of memorial societies.

5

SOLDIERS &
THEIR UNIFORMS
AFTER THE WAR

O n April 9, 1865, Confederate general Robert E. Lee surrendered the
Army of Northern Virginia to Union lieutenant general Ulysses S.
Grant at Appomattox Court House, Virginia. Lee's terms of surrender and Grant's response were widely circulated in newspapers across the
country, which commented on the mood and attitude of the event. While
speculating on what was to happen to the Confederate soldiers, journalists
were especially interested in how Grant and Lee, and their attending officers, compared in their respective uniforms. The *New York Herald* reported
that General Lee, while "quite reserved and sad," was "dressed in full uniform, with an elegant sword, sash and gauntlets," while "General Grant was
in full uniform, with the exception of his sword." The commanders' hour-
long conference was "a singular spectacle," with the shaking of hands and
passing of whiskey among the group. In addition, the "rebel officers were
all elegantly dressed in full uniform," which was not something for which
Union officers were noted. Each of the different newspaper accounts mention what one called the "strange mingling of blue and gray uniforms in the
streets." Upon agreeing the terms of surrender, Lee's officers were "enabled
to obtain their blankets and the change of clothes."[1] Reports detailing what
officers wore would prove important to the memory of this occasion by providing a marker for the fusion of southern identity and honor to the Confederate uniform. These men in their uniforms at this momentous occa-

sion laid a foundation for postwar memory of southern gentlemen gallantly dressed better than their northern counterparts, even in the face of defeat.

The close of the Civil War brought a disruption but not an end to the service of the citizen-soldiers. As these men phased into becoming veterans in their civilian communities, their uniforms, flags, and other beloved material objects were remade into items of remembrance or granted another life. While the Indigenous soldiers from both the Union and the Confederacy after Appomattox sought to assimilate their wartime experiences, the Union's African American troops faced continued ramifications for donning the uniform. Specifically, the formerly enslaved who continued life as soldiers while policing and attempting to secure the defeated and war-torn South during the first years of Reconstruction endured problems and even violence as white southerners reacted to their presence. And while strawman arguments to justify anger at African American authority in the postwar years were never more than flimsy, former Confederates became members of white terrorist groups to intimidate Unionist and Black communities, donning their wartime uniforms as both a scare tactic and a source of authority to regain control of the South and subvert northern influence.

BITTERSWEET VICTORY & "SECESH IMPUDENCE"

The Union victory was bittersweet for the North because of the tragedy that soon struck the nation. On April 14, 1865, at Ford's Theatre in Washington, D.C., John Wilkes Booth shot and killed President Lincoln. As reported in one Connecticut newspaper, a story emerged of Booth on the run with accomplice David Herold. Both men sought to pass for Confederate soldiers on their way home after the war, "dressed in confederate grey new uniforms," which would allow them to move about with less suspicion.[2]

Lincoln's death and the ensuing mourning turned the country's attention away from the stories of Appomattox, but newspapers slowly drifted back to the terms of Lee's surrender. The "day Lee surrendered his army at Appomattox" was the beginning of "each officer and man" of his army being "allowed to return to their homes" with the understanding that the beaten Confederates were "not to be disturbed by United States authority so long as they observe their parole and the laws in force where they may reside."

According to scholar Carrie Janney, terms of surrender and parole were confusing and complicated afterward.[3] The sight of former Confederate uniforms, however, immediately offended northern sensibilities. Two days after Appomattox, reports of "about fifty Rebel officers and several hundred Rebel soldiers" in Richmond "prowling around" in their uniforms proved too much for loyal Americans. One newspaper published an order issued by local authorities that gave the former rebels twenty-four hours to "report to the Provost Marshal, take the oath, or go to Libby" Prison, adding, "if they take the oath the Rebel uniform must be discarded," although that specification was not in the agreed terms of surrender. To reunite the nation, northerners believed that it was time to *put an end to the parading of Confederate uniforms as a matter of 'glory and honor'*" because that was the only way to abate the bitterness of war and restore order.[4] Historian Bradley Clampitt argues that the experience of Confederates returning home in uniform assisted in establishing the "ideological underpinnings of the Lost Cause."[5] To U.S. officials, allowing the symbols of a failed rebellion, such as uniforms and badges, to remain in the public eye kept war wounds open and prevented healing. This alone demonstrates the centrality of uniforms, badges, and flags to the identities of both sides. Forcing Confederates to put away their treasonous symbols caused frustration and anger throughout the southern white population, resulting in pushback. This resentment laid the foundation for reusing uniforms, badges, and flags during the "memory machine" phase of the late nineteenth and early twentieth centuries.

On April 26, 1865, Union soldier Ebenezer Gilpin recorded in his diary that he "wrote letters to the [War] Department, transmitting flags and other captured trophies." One such battle flag, captured by Private Andrew Tibbetts of Company I at Austin's Battery in Columbus, Georgia, was inscribed with "the names of battles of Shiloh, Chickamauga and Murfreesboro. Each flag had its history." What came next in his account was reflective, Gilpin stating that he "stacked them all in the corner of the tent thinking if they could speak they would have heroic tales to tell." While some of the banners "were almost new," others "were torn and tattered, lashed by tempests of shot and shell. The fortunes of war have separated them from their brave defenders, and there is no one to even tell to whom they belonged." He stated that the flags "have fought their last fight, and made 'unconditional surrender.' Never again at the 'Reveille' to unfurl in the morning light." Gilpin closed this entry by writing that he "put them all away gently, reverently, as became a soldier," tying those Confederate flags with the identity of the men who fought under them. He believed that the flags would remain stored "unless mayhap their muffled folds should stir and thrill to the softly-blown bugles of memory." Gilpin understood what those flags meant to their previous owners, and his personal thoughts imbued them with meaning, identity, and significance.[6] Confederate chaplain Father Abram Ryan expressed similar sentiments in his June 1865 poem, "The Conquered Banner." Much like Gilpin, Ryan's phrasing merges the battle flag with those who carried and fought under it: "'twill live in song and story, . . . / Furl that Banner, softly, slowly! / Treat it gently—it is holy."[7] This imagery and feeling resonated with Confederates and foreshadowed Lost Cause sentiment.

The effort of peacefully putting away uniforms failed. The women of Richmond did not take kindly to their men being told to discard their military attire. One reporter discussed a service at the Episcopal church in Richmond where "one [woman] had two rows [of] Confederate buttons upon a black silk sack, and another wore upon her sleeves the gold braid, indicating the rank of a Colonel." At that service "about a dozen Rebel officers attended in full uniform, and two or three minus one arm or leg were wearing *Confederate grey*."[8] "Impudence," as the reporter phrased these actions, continued to be the popular term when referring to those who continued to wear their rebel gray. Edward Crapsey stated that southerners "still flaunt their grey before our eyes on the street, as if it were the badge of honorable service instead of what it is, the livery of a defeated, crushed, whipped-out Rebellion." He posited that "some of them seem to act as though they expected to wear it during their natural lives and to glory in it forever." Crapsey concluded with the recommendation that "southern chivalry may on this point be taught a lesson in good manners."[9]

Those who continued to wear their rebel uniforms throughout the rest of April and May 1865 faced staunch opposition from citizens and the federal government. Attorney General James Speed added stipulations to Lee's surrender terms that "wearing the rebel uniform by officers in the Federal lines is considered incompatible with the agreement, and will be regarded as an act of hostility," much like those who wore secession cockades in previous years.[10] Speed added that the former Confederates "have as much right to bear the traitor's flag through the streets of a loyal city as to wear the traitor's garb. The stipulation of surrender permits no such thing" because Confederate uniforms and flags both represented treason and hostility.[11] In May an article published in the *Philadelphia Inquirer* noted the restoration of commerce "without restraint" to the former secessionist states. Although the supposed "halcyon days" had finally arrived, the newspaper also reported on southern issues with "Yankee perfidy and tyranny" by the War Department because of "the paroled men of Lee's army not being allowed to settle North and flaunt their uniforms in the faces of the loyal" due to federal restrictions.[12] Generals began giving the former Confederates adequate timeframes within which to "procure other clothing" besides their military apparel. While former rebels were not allowed to wear "their uniform or any badge reminding of their treason," they were "given thirty days from the time of their coming into" a certain district to stop wearing their Confederate uniforms.[13] Those who refused to comply with the moratorium were often arrested for violating parole. In the instance of Colonel James Nelligan, who wore "a uniform badge upon his hat and wore a Confederate metal badge upon his coat," his refusal to remove the insignia left the arresting officer little choice. Nelligan became "quite belligerent and abusive during the colloquy" but was released on bail shortly after the incident. The reporting newspaper and local authorities "earnestly advised" other former rebels to comply with the rules to "save themselves much inconvenience and needless mortification."[14]

Georgian Eliza Frances Andrews recorded in her diary the scenes she witnessed of men going home in uniform. She mentioned how difficult it could be to distinguish between some ex-Confederates in "dark, bluish-gray" uniforms and occupying soldiers in federal blue, while stating that "as a general thing our privates have no uniform but rags." Andrews described the Confederate uniform as "beautiful" and proclaimed that she "shall always love the colors, gray and gold, for its sake—or rather for the sake of the men who wore it." At the rumor that paroled officers were "going to be ordered to lay aside their uniforms," she wrote, "it will be a black day when this habit that we all love so well gives place to the badge of servitude." In a later entry Andrews noted seeing a Mrs. Elzey "cutting off the buttons from the general's coat" because "the tyrants have prohibited the wearing of Confederate uniforms," but "those who have no other clothes can still

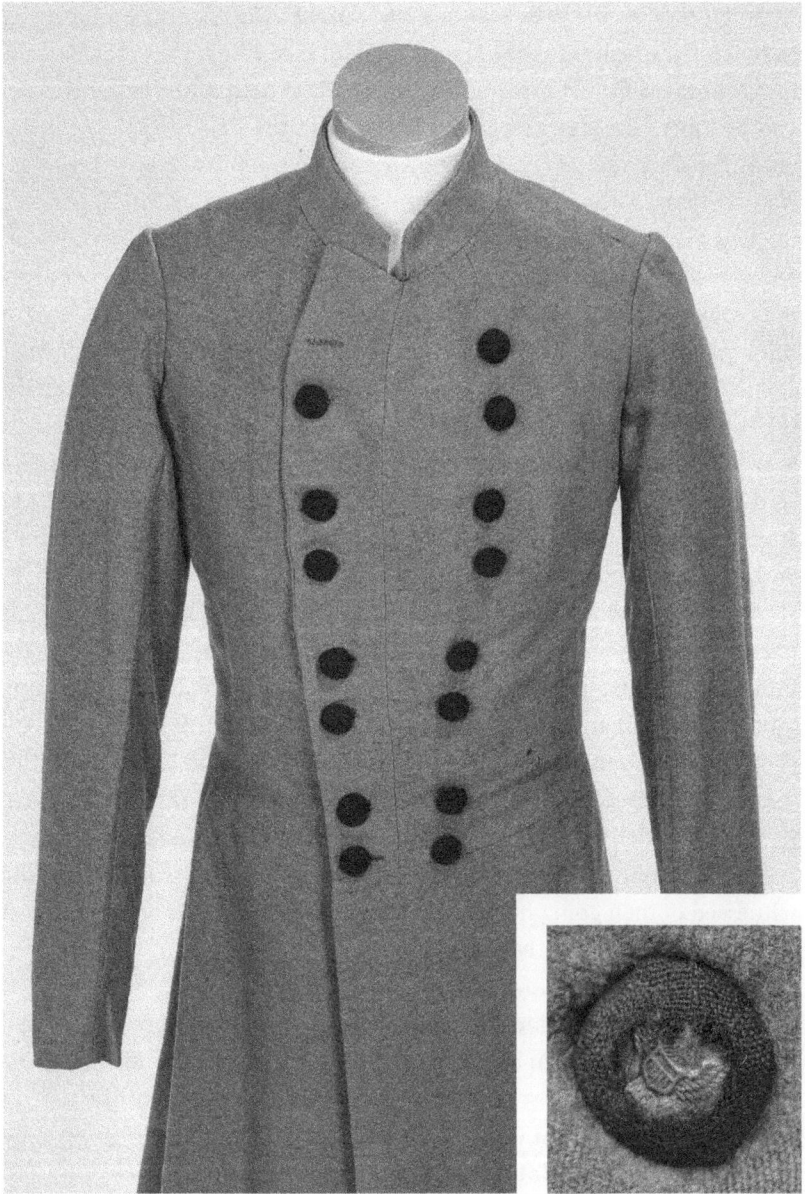

Confederate uniform with crepe-draped buttons.
Courtesy North Carolina State Museum.

wear the gray, but must rip off the buttons and decorations." She stated that people everywhere were "ransacking old chests" as the men hauled out the clothes they wore before the war. Those garments to her looked "funny and old-fashioned, after the beautiful uniforms we had all gotten used to!" Wearing their antebellum garments meant that the returning soldiers were "too poor to buy new clothes."[15]

Similar sentiments and reports are found in a June diary entry of Susan Bradford Eppes, a Tennessean, discussing her first group riding lesson for around thirty women and men, who all "came dressed in our beloved gray." She proclaimed how "proud" they were of the Confederate army and how much they "love the gray uniform." Eppes could not believe how their "heroes of the gray" were insulted when both officers and privates were told that they "must remove from their uniforms all brass buttons and every insignia of rank." She understood that it was the "intention of the military to order the gray uniform to be discarded," but "many of these men had nothing else to wear." Eppes ended with the thought that the Union soldiers "aught to be ashamed of themselves!" She also noted what a "pity" it was that her cousin Henry's new "magnificent suit of French broadcloth," which her uncle purchased through a blockade-runner while his son was in prison, must now have all insignia or rank and buttons removed or covered. Events recorded in her next entry made Eppes's "blood boil." While running her errands in town, she visited with friends and saw that every button from Church Croom's uniform "had been cut and replaced by large orange thorns." She claimed to be "perilously near tears when cousin Henry came, wearing the splendid uniform of the day before" but "over the Major's star on his collar, the thinnest of crape had been sewed; the chevrons on the sleeves were covered with the same material," and even "the buttons, too, were wearing morning [sic]." She saw a Lieutenant Eppes next, and the "gold lace had been ripped from collar and sleeves; the buttons were covered with black bombazine, but where the braid had been removed, the unfaded gray showed his rank as plainly as ever." Eppes noted that she "saw many others during the day who had obeyed this order" and modified their uniforms, which she claimed "has reflected no credit on the power that be but has only served to make them ridiculous."[16]

The examples of Andrews and Eppes as well as the women in Richmond demonstrate the attachment that southerners formed to the Confederate uniform. It became an important indicator of identity postwar and an excellent item to use as a form of resistance, which occasionally turned violent, because what they were wearing—gray, butternut, or somewhere in between—was unmistakable. This was a tangible way for defeated Confederates to maintain a "lost" identity, which became central to the success of the Lost Cause ideology. By that time, the Confederate uniform in its variety of colors and tatters became the embodiment of lost southern honor, and the forced alterations by U.S. officials created a further point of contention and resistance for the beaten rebels.

The anti-southern attitude of northern citizens was particularly apparent in their view of Confederate uniforms. While it became a common sight to see soldiers trekking home after the end of the war in their uniforms, the *Chicago Journal* published what it called a "Queer Proposition": urging that the authorities of different states immediately "declare that the Confederate uniform be henceforth the garb of all convicts sentenced to the State Penitentiaries for ordinary crimes." The article suggested that "uniforms worn by Confederate officers be that for criminals of higher grade," associating a "cut-throat or murder" with the Confederate rank of "lieutenant general" and clearly expressing an inflammatory view held by a few northerners that those still wearing the uniform "did not want a restoration of peace."[17] This commentary clearly positions former Confederates as criminals and traitors to the United States. Eliza Andrews was infuriated by this decree, by calling those who advocated it "wretches" and declaring: "As if it was in the power of man to disgrace the uniform worn by Robert E Lee and Stonewall Jackson! They couldn't disgrace it, even if they were to put their own army into it."[18]

By October, even some southerners began to express concerns. People in New Orleans began complaining to Major General Henry Davies about men wearing their service uniforms as everyday attire. In an attempt to address this matter, Davies proclaimed, "sufficient time has now elapsed for all peaceable and well-disposed citizens to dress according to their proper stations, and therefor[e] the wearing of the Confederate uniform will no longer be permitted in public." Gesturing at equality, he added, "all persons not connected with the army are forbidden to wear any portion of the United States uniform."[19] This mandate expressed respect for the government's order against wearing Confederate uniforms in public and a desire for peace among the citizens of New Orleans. It also demonstrates the difficulties in reuniting a nation after a civil war without explicitly stating that the losing side committed treason. Putting away the garb of "traitors" and those who were no longer directly involved in the military might assist in smoothing relations, but negotiating who was still allowed to wear a uniform continued as a point of contention.

The North's concerns about wearing the Confederate gray extended well beyond the average soldier. Once Robert E. Lee was indicted for treason in June 1865, comments about his clothing began circulating again.[20] One newspaper reported, "it has been ascertained that Robert E. Lee has been furnished with an entire new suit of grey Rebel uniform." This suit and "over one hundred [additional] new uniforms" for "officers and men to air themselves in and preserve the evidences of their crimes forgiven before atoned for" were made in Richmond.[21] Another paper reported that Lee "still wears the rebel uniform, without insignia of rank," even to church services.[22] A Texas newspaper claimed that Lee financially "is in the most destitute condition" and had "no change of outer clothing," which explained why he was "compelled to go to church in his old grey uniform."[23] The former general wearing his uniform without insignia or military buttons aligns him with other ex-Confederate military officers who used their uniforms after the war as daily clothing because it could have been the nicest or only pieces they possessed. Newspapers continued to comment on Lee's appearance at his last battle and the surrender ceremony into the fall of 1865. During the final battle before Appomattox Court House, reports stated that Lee "never appeared more calm." He dressed in "full uniform, with his gold-hilted sword, and [bearing a] perfectly quiet look," as if he was attending a military parade. The writer stated that the general's "'dress' costume was assumed" and that "he had dressed himself that morning" with "scrupulous care and buckled on his finest sword, declaring that if he was captured he would be taken in full war panoply."[24] Given how much care Lee put into dressing himself in his nicest uniform, it is fair to assume that he knew that coverage surrounding any surrender or capture would record his personal presentation and demeanor.

For some, separating the rebel gray uniform from its owner became the same for the man wearing it as amputating an arm. It was who they were, and they felt no need to change to appease the federal government.

While former Confederates only wore their uniform for a few years, their garments became stitched to every portion of their identity and memory of the war. This, combined with northerners' problem with seeing former rebels in their uniforms, encouraged the militarily defeated southerners to stubbornly fight for something else.

WHITE UNION SOLDIERS

The Union released white volunteer soldiers at a rapid pace from May to mid-November 1865 in varying order according to when the 801,000 officers and men were mustered in and how long they had served. The governmental ordinances releasing them specifically stipulated that "white troops in your command whose terms of service expire between this date and September 30 next, inclusive, [will] be immediately mustered out of service." These men often traveled home via railcar and experienced a variety of situations because they did not have a direct route home; many also remained in service longer than they desired. A multitude of veterans on their journey home received assistance from civilians, who gave them fruit, meat, and vegetables to tide them over until they reached their families.[25] In June the U.S. government "adopted a regulation in reference to its discharged soldiers" that "each volunteer honorably discharged" was allowed to keep his "knapsack, haversack and canteen" and was permitted "to retain his musket upon payment of a small sum," which continued the norms of northern soldiers paying for everything they needed during the war. The columnist claimed that this would be beneficial because "the soldier becomes attached to the trusty musket which he has used in battle, and when he retains his accoutrements and his uniform, they become household treasures" that one would occasionally inspect or delightedly reminisce about. These items were to be saved and brought out for future generations in order to display the soldier's "fidelity to his country."[26] Suggesting that these items would become household treasures invokes a sentimental attachment to them because of the difficult time spent at war.

Only a month after the war ended, many white Union soldiers were lauded and welcomed home from war by parades and patriotic displays. Seventy-five thousand veterans returned to a "glorious ovation" on Pennsylvania Avenue, with President Andrew Johnson reviewing the "battle-scarred warriors." The *Philadelphia Inquirer* noted the Army of the Potomac received an enthusiastic welcome from thousands of spectators, who cheered at the "splendid appearance of the men" because their "weapons were burnished, brasses were cleaned, [and] uniforms were brushed" under the "scrupulously fastidious" inspection of their sergeants. The reporter compared Major General George McClellan's occasional review of troops and banners that "then flaunted gaudily in the sunshine," after which they would "march safely back to their encampments," with the events of this day and the current flags, which now "are tattered ribbons" but "emblazoned on those silken tatters are the names of scores of victories!"[27] During the final great review, the "old Sixth Corps" marched the route from the Capitol to the White House to be "reviewed by the President, by [Maj.] Gen. [George G.] Meade, and by the thousands." They marched to the "huzzas and shouting," toting the "flags torn and shredded by bullet and shell, and by exposure to days, and weeks, and months of sun and rain." The soldiers of one brigade, who for most of the war wore "the old Zouave uniform," discarded it and were "now equipped the same as other troops of the corps."[28] People continued to identify the soldiers with their uniforms: even as the men were mustered out and transitioned back into civilian life as veterans, their identities remained knitted with their uniforms. An advertisement for the Soldiers' and Sailors' Convention in Pittsburg during September 1866 "requested that officers and men attend the Convention in uniform" and asserted "veterans, not commissioned, are entitled by act of Congress to wear the insignia of the lieutenant's rank," demonstrating honor and celebrating their service.[29]

Union veterans wore their uniforms to events and parties at the request of the host, but they did not typically wear them every day unless they were without additional clothing and in a destitute state directly after the war. A speech by Representative John Hogan of Missouri on January 30, 1866, discussed taxes and payments to the government, but he focused mainly on pensions for Union veterans and their widows because "those who were their chief support now lie 'beneath the clods of the valley.'" Without the financial support of their men, the women were dependent "upon the cold charities of the world." Hogan employed patriotic sentiment about those who "sacrificed life itself" for the "glory and flag" of the United States. He declared that he "felt humiliated when, passing through the streets of our large cities, I have been stopped by a maimed veteran wearing the uniform of my country and bearing on his breast the badge of his corps," both noble distinctions, and now reduced to "begging each passer-by for something to meet his daily demands."[30] Much like Hogan's rhetoric, other northern politicians of this era exercised the practice of "waving the bloody shirt" by physically displaying soldiers' bloodstained uniforms as a Republican Party campaign stunt. They used these bloody coats and shirts as tools to invoke emotion by demonstrating the sacrifice of Union troops who had died. According to Eric Foner, they also discussed these bloodstained garments figuratively, using the "memory of the war" to solidify Republican electoral support.[31]

Unless destitute and in need of clothing, Union veterans generally put away their uniforms and wartime items. Because the Union won the war, its veterans and the public seemed happy to bring out their uniforms for celebrations, parades, or fond reminisces, but they did not symbolically revel in wearing one daily. While they were attached to their war items, they did not have to prove that their cause was just or righteous in the same way as the former Confederates, so it was easier for these veterans to put their items away until a special occasion arose. In addition, military service was not a pleasant experience of which every soldier was proud, so some men were glad to put the war behind them by stowing away its mementos.[32]

For those still serving, all was not peaceful and harmonious in the North or the reunited South. Several newspapers reported on "riots" between white Union soldiers and members of the African American community, which did nothing to calm the tensions felt by occupied southerners. In Norfolk, Virginia, white U.S. soldiers, "men in citizens' clothing," and Black men fought in the streets. One instance reported "twenty-five white men running after one negro" with resounding "cries of 'hang him,' 'kill him,' '—— the n——.'" Some of the men in "citizens' clothing" from the Norfolk massacre turned up at the polls the next day, and "scores of men voted who wore the Rebel uniform, brass buttons and all."[33] One southern newspaper reported on a clash between white soldiers and Black citizens in Washington, D.C., which he claimed demonstrated the "unconquerable antagonism which exists between the white race and the black race, when ever an attempt is made to make them exist on terms of equality." The reporter called it a "slander on our brave troops to say that these riots were commenced by them." He went on to explain that the "irritation of the soldiers in general, at seeing the negroes in uniform, is intense, and can hardly be repressed." They "feel wronged and degraded at being compelled to regard beings of an inferior race as equals."[34] In both of these cases, uniforms denoted authority and identity. The former Confederates participating in the massacre with Union soldiers and then attending an election in full uniform with uncovered brass buttons, which was not allowed, demonstrates not only hostility to the federal government but also that they continued to be defined by their uniform as an external manifestation of identity rather than it being merely sentimental. In the massacre in Washington, D.C., both parties wore the same uniform, which should have provided them with equal authority, but the "irritation" felt by the white soldiers continually denied their Black peers manhood and citizenship.

Legally, life for African Americans changed on December 18, 1865, when Secretary of State William Seward proclaimed the ratification of the Thirteenth Amendment to the U.S. Constitution. The amendment abolished slavery throughout the United States, giving additional credence to the Union uniform that had brought increased respect for African Americans.[35] As with the uniforms, though, this proved to be just one step rather than the completion of the process of citizenship in all its meanings.

INDIGENOUS & BLACK SOLDIERS POSTWAR

The U.S. Army mustered out the First, Second, and Third Indian Home Guards in Indian Territory on May 31, 1865.[36] There was a different mustering out process for Indigenous soldiers not from Indian Territory, depending upon with whom they served. Many were members in the USCT, thus being labeled "African American, black, or Negro." Because of this, the identities of those from New England are lost in the historical record.[37] For the Native American soldiers who served in USCT regiments recruited in the North, each was discharged with his regiment from May to July 1865. The same probably happened for those who served in white or Indigenous regiments.

Brigadier General Stand Watie and other Indigenous soldiers west of the Mississippi did not accept Lee's surrender to Grant as the end of the war. They wished to be allowed to contract their own peace, separate from the white southerners in the eastern theater. Confederate Native Peoples called a meeting at Camp Napoleon, Indian Territory, to repair their ranks and decide on a course of action. Agreeing to a peace treaty among themselves, they created an alliance and vowed that "an Indian shall not spill an Indian's blood."[38] After this meeting adjourned, Union lieutenant colonel Asa Matthews began conducting peace negotiations with each tribe. On June 18 Peter Pitchlynn of the Choctaw Nation surrendered to Matthews, who allowed those troops to go home under Union protection. On June 23 Watie surrendered his Cherokee forces, and a few weeks later the Chickasaw surrendered to Matthews, who told the Native Americans of Watie's command to go home under federal protection. The white rebel troops in Indian Territory, however, were sent to federal paroling offices.[39]

Newspapers across the country reported that these official surrender agreements stated that "acts of hostility" had ceased in May. A *New York Herald* reporter noted that all the Native Peoples of the nations "represented, and who were lately allied with the Confederate States in acts of hostility against government of the United States," agree to return to their homes and "remain at peace with the United States." The Indigenous Peoples were also cautioned against committing "any acts of hostility against the whites and the Indians of the various tribes who have been friendly to or engaged in the service" of the United States during the war. The former Confederate Native American soldiers were promised protection by the federal government if they chose to abide by those stipulations. Another columnist in the same newspaper, when referencing the former Confederate Native Peoples, stated that the "bad experiences they have met with have taught them to reverence the flag of the United States" because it provides them protection.[40] Subjugating entire nations of Native Peoples, not just those who fought for the Confederacy, and then expecting them to revere the U.S. flag failed to take into consideration that their "disloyalty" was not monolithic. Many tribes split into factions that fought for the Union or the Confederacy. Their alliances were demonstrated by the tangible objects of uniforms or flags and what those entities represented to the various peoples.

At the close of the war, the U.S. government continued its policy of opening land to western settlers and displacing Indigenous nations. The Homestead Act, passed in 1862, looked a bit different for the Five Tribes because at the beginning of the Civil War, they had signed treaties with the Confederate government, thus forfeiting their relationship and former treaties with the federal government. Because new treaties needed to be established after the war, the negotiating process favored the U.S. authority.[41] The Grand Council meeting in September 1865 laid the foundation for what the Indigenous People could expect from the government. The U.S. commissioners—Major General William Harney, Major General Francis Herron, and Colonel Ely Parker, the latter a member of the Seneca—were appointed to oversee the meeting of twenty to thirty tribes. The stated "object of the council is to restore the friendly relations heretofore existing between the Indians and the United States, and to secure peace on the Plains."[42] When the meeting commenced, only a few of the Indigenous delegates were present, specifically those "representing only the loyal tribes" because the disloyal groups "were then in council at Armstrong Academy, about one hundred and fifty miles southwest." According to one newspaper correspondent, the prime goals for the disloyal faction was to "justify their course in linking their fortunes with the Confederacy, reclaim their annuities from the United States, and demand either the continuance of slavery, or remuneration for their slaves."[43]

How Indigenous Peoples dressed played a role in how the white negotiators and the white press perceived them. When the disloyal factions arrived on September 15, they were "accompanied by an escort of cavalrymen, clad in Confederate grey." The correspondent continued to note the clothing of the Native American delegates: "let no one suppose an Indian Council of 1865 the same or even like unto those of the early days" because "instead of a group of blanketed savages, gathered around an open council fire, smoking the pipe of peace, and exchanging the belt of wampum," in a group of about one hundred fifty delegates, only "twenty or twenty-five, bore every emblem of the wild Indian of the past." The journalist also pointed to the difference that, instead of an open-air conference, they were gathered within the plastered walls of a U.S. Army fort. He described in detail how the delegates wore clothing of "breech-clout and blanket, moccasins and leggings, and various ornaments of bead, reed and horn" or were dressed in in "muslin shirts and leather shoes," but he left out the description of the clothing of the white attendees.[44] Describing the Native peoples by their attire and distinguishing how different the meeting would have been one hundred years before demeaned the Indigenous delegates, using their clothing to peg them as either uncivilized or traitorous.

Newspapers across the country covered these treaty sessions because the federal government wanted to use the Five Tribes' land for other tribes and open it for white settlement. Native Peoples constructed delegations and bartered for better treaties but had very little to bargain with because loyal members were lumped in with those who had donned the Confederate gray. In the case of the Seminoles, who reconciled their strained factions after the war, the treaty negotiated with the United States extended amnesty to all of them. The federal government thus made the entirety of the Seminole Nation responsible for the actions of its pro-Confederate compatriots and demanded all of the tribe's land.[45]

Because Washington authorities had abandoned those living in Indian Territory in 1861, portions of the tribes chose to sign treaties with the Confederacy and fight on their side. This meant that when the Union won the war, all Indigenous People there lost. Looking at the Indigenous relationship with the Union and the Confederacy through uniforms adds a new perspective to the experience of those in Indian Territory during the Reconstruction period. It provides a new facet of why the Native Peoples chose the sides they did and how their perceived idea of uniforms, or clothing, as a bond of loyalty and recognition of sovereignty influenced their decision. Yet putting on those uniforms deeply affected tribal and home life for many Indigenous soldiers and their families both at the time and long after the fighting ceased.

While the men were gone during the war, uniformed Union and Confederate soldiers raided Indigenous homes across Indian Territory, resulting in varied reactions and greetings by family members when the discharged Indigenous soldiers returned home. George Walker, who went looking for his wife and five children near Fort Scott while still dressed in his Confederate uniform, received a mixed reception. His wife was happy to see him, but his children were frightened because of the turmoil between tribes and the Union and Confederate governments. "They had been taught to fear men in Confederate uniforms" due to raiding by certain groups. Walker's children, having been very young the last time they saw him, did not remember him.[46] This story is one example of the multifaceted symbolism uniforms made on Indigenous communities on a wide scale.

Because some chose the losing side, the Five Nations experienced an arduous reunification process that left many of them landless, economically devastated, and with broken tribal nations. Federal authorities did not discriminate when punishing whole tribes for the actions of the factions that chose the South. The uniforms and flags worn by the Union and Confederate troops alike were not gifts of fidelity or loyalty but tokens of bribery; still, the Indigenous communities paid a terrible price for participating in the war. As historian Christopher Bean has stated, "a hard end date does not exist for Reconstruction in Indian Territory" or for its inhabitants; their payments for meddling in a white man's war did not end until the early twentieth century.[47] The U.S. government used the misplaced judgment of a few to reconstruct what tribal sovereignty meant for the Native Peoples in Indian Territory. What it did to "reconstruct" these tribes permanently altered the way the Indigenous communities remembered the Civil War and commemorated their sacrifice and service to both the Union and the Confederacy.

After the war, the need to decide what to do with the African American and Native American troops manifested. The fate of both groups rested in Washington, however, the outcomes would differ significantly. As the war neared its end, USCT regiments entered southern cities and, under the command of their white officers, began cleaning up debris and restoring a semblance of order. While they occupied the population centers, white Union soldiers were sent to the fight. Seeing uniformed and armed Black men disturbed white southerners, even though the Confederacy approved the use of African American troops, as it comforted newly freed formerly enslaved persons. By July 1865, white Union soldiers were being discharged from the army at a faster rate than Black soldiers because, according to General Grant, many of the former enlisted prior to the time when the latter were allowed to join the army. While this was true, it is important to understand that the formerly enslaved composed a significant portion of Black regiments. Now that those men were free, some may not have had a home to return to, so keeping them in service made sense and allowed them to be in a paid working environment. In the specific case of Charleston, South Carolina, white commanders there did not want to release African American soldiers believing that they would incite trouble from the local Black community, which viewed a Black man in uniform as a point of pride and encouragement of citizenship. No white community, North or South, really wanted the formerly enslaved in their area, so releasing southern Black soldiers into a significant free Black population had the potential to incite "riots" and openly anger the local white community. By retaining USCT regiments mustered in the South, the army was able to send white soldiers home and prevent discharged Black soldiers from freely entering southern white societies.[48] This continuing active duty, historian Andrew Lang writes, was embraced by African Americans because the "opportunities of occupation" allowed them to enforce "their conception of liberty . . . [and] challenging planter legitimacy." It provided African American soldiers the "opportunity to cleanse the South of its slaveholding character, to eliminate the symbols of white supremacy, and to erase the artifacts of plantation life."[49] The majority of northern Black regiments were mustered out during 1865, but those comprising formerly enslaved men raised in the South remained in service until 1867.[50]

Those northern African American soldiers mustered out in 1865 were welcomed home by their communities with celebrations and excitement. As announced in April 1865 by the *Christian Recorder*, "a regimental flag would be presented to the 24th United States Colored Troops" in front of Independence Hall. The president of an unnamed civic organization introduced a Mr. Catto, who stated, "we have gathered to give a God-speed to the noble men of this regiment, who are going forth to assist in establishing the law and maintaining the integrity of this Government." He noted that "a regimental flag, gotten up under the auspices of the Banneker Institute, by contributions from the public," would be presented. The speaker "paid tribute to the two hundred thousand blacks, who, in spite of obloquy and the old bane of prejudice, have been nobly fighting our battles, trusting to a redeemed country for the full recognition of their manhood in the future." The presented flag bore the words, "Let Soldiers in War Be Citizens in Peace." Catto pleaded: "Soldiers! accept this flag on behalf of the citizens of Philadelphia. I know too well the mettle of your pasture, that you will not dishonor it." The ceremony ended with the regiment's colonel expressing thanks for the flag and to the crowd for cheering Abraham Lincoln and other leaders.[51] At an event in Philadelphia, community members gathered to "express some recognition of the services of our brave colored soldiers." The festivities included a religious ceremony, reception, and dinner for the troops, with the request that they arrive "in uniform, with their muskets and accoutrements."[52] An assembly of around five thousand African Americans from West Chester and neighboring counties celebrated the Emancipation Proclamation and mourned the loss of Lincoln in September 1866 with speeches, music, and a parade, with "the colored 'Boys in Blue,' with regimental officers, and full uniform" leading the procession.[53]

For those who remained in service, the story was different. Neither President Johnson nor the white Union generals in the South supported their African American soldiers when white Union troops attacked them, which left the door open for white southerners to do the same to occupying Black troops. It also demonstrated the tepid commitment of these top officials and officers to Reconstruction. Keeping uniformed Black soldiers in the army to police white communities increased the friction between themselves and white southerners because they were no longer enslaved but rather figures of authority in Union blue.

After the war, racial tensions increased between white and Black Union soldiers. Along with this, tensions between white southerners and African American soldiers led to incidents that ranged from simple disturbances to violence. In a letter from the Third Division, USCT to the *Christian Recorder,* W. M. B. Johnson described the harsh treatment of the Black community and Black Union soldiers by men from Kentucky who "wear the uniform of *Uncle Sam*" but are "base traitors," their behavior doing nothing to discourage the southerners from committing the same "shameful" actions and who "scorned to look upon the n— soldiers." Yet their commanding general, Robert McCook, upon witnessing the Black troops' dress parade remarked on how "well drilled" they were and how they "looked as well as any soldiers he ever saw."[54] Actions such as those of the Kentucky soldiers revealed some of the remaining fractures in the Union. Personal feelings about African American soldiers now manifested in public ways, which contradicted the official stance of federal officials, and the fact that those freedmen remained in uniform played a role.

One citizen linked the treatment of Black troops to the bravery they and their colleagues had displayed in wartime. James M. Sanders, a resident of Charleston, commented on the African Americans "wearing the uniform of the United States, and drawing pay from the same source as the brave men that came to us from old Massachusetts, the 54th and 55th regiments," who continued to give their "lives for the honor and glory of our common country." Yet those loyal men often were treated "as though he alone [the African American soldier] was the traitor, while his white-faced master, just returned from the field of conflict, and wearing the gray coat of the rebellion, walks the streets, and is alike honored by the government officials and their kindred rebels." Sanders was astonished that the sacrifices and service of Black men in Union blue were trivialized, while former Confederate soldiers, still in their uniforms, were welcomed home and thanked for their service.[55] This lack of support from the U.S. government for its Black troops in the militarized South only encouraged white southerners to return to old habits and wreak havoc on local African American communities.

Southerners found it difficult, if not impossible, to respect the uniform when an African American wore it. A Georgia newspaper ran a story concerning an altercation in Tennessee in which two African American soldiers "in full uniform" on "a narrow sidewalk in this city, knocked the writer of this article into the gutter, throwing him upon his hands and knees." He claimed that he was just "trying to get out of the way" but was feeble and "moved too slowly for their ideas of progress." The writer believed "one-half of all the colored soldiers in uniforms in East Tennessee have no respect for that uniform, and do not appreciate its dignity and importance," that they "had not 'learned to respect the uniform of the army,'" and that "soldiers and officers wearing the Federal uniform ought all to be gentlemen, no matter what their color."[56] This exaggerated retelling of the writer's concerns about the conduct of the Black soldiers shows that he understood that their uniforms gave them authority but failed to think of them as men of authority. It also demonstrates the strawman constructed around the uniform and provides insight into how southerners shaped their portion of the debate regarding who belonged in positions of authority and in uniform.

Countering the southern position, some northerners fell more in line with the ideas expressed by the author of a *Chicago Tribune* article. He wrote of learning "from reliable sources that it is the policy of the Government to muster out the colored troops in nearly or quite all the Southern States because they are 'distasteful' to the whites there." The author believed that southern whites viewed African American troops in that way because they were "walking certificates that the rebellion was a gigantic blunder." He continued sarcastically, "if they are to be removed on this account, let us remove at the same stroke everything that is distasteful to the same class," such as "our white troops now pining to return to their homes, remove our officers of every kind, remove our laws and proclamations abolishing slavery, and finally remove our flag and 'let the South alone' to be ruled by Jeff Davis and his minions." The writer declared that if the "tastes" of the rebels did not control the federal government, then the government should "hold every man who was willing to fight for it in its hour of peril, as worthy to tread the soil of his native State in uniform, as any man who fought us to the last is to breath the air and enjoy the liberties of our country with impunity." Defending the rights of Black soldiers to wear the uniform and serve the United States, he asked the government not to "grow ashamed of its defenders, in order to cringe servilely to its enemies" because "it is impossible to tell how soon they may again need the former to help whip the latter."[57]

In December 1865 the *Christian Recorder* wrote of a suspected freedmen's insurrection in Ripley, Mississippi. There, freedmen "disguised themselves in Federal uniforms, and thus attained the confidence of the negroes" who were actual U.S. soldiers. White townspeople discovered what had happened and dealt with the "offenders" harshly.[58] These freedmen understood the power the uniform exuded, seeking to use it as a disguise that would have helped them gain a form of authority. In the postwar period other accounts of people using uniforms as symbols of authority and forms of intimidation arose, allowing an updated view of the stories of unrest throughout Reconstruction.

Southern newspapers accused remaining white federal soldiers in the South of unfair treatment of southern whites when assaulted by a "negro soldier." A story from Mississippi stated, "we have some of the meanest officers in our midst that ever disgraced the United States uniform" because they "encourage the negro to acts of violence, and if arrested, they rescue him from the civil authorities." The correspondent claimed that "a white man can be shot down in our streets and no steps taken in the matter, no more than if his murder[er] had shot a dog."[59] This serves as an example of southerners using the Union uniform to exploit the divisions between white and Black U.S. soldiers, picking at the racial alliances bound by a uniform.

In a newspaper report on the "population of Wilmington," the "colored soldiers on the sidewalks" were viewed with favor by the "colored damsels, in whose eyes the belt and uniform transfigure the dusky wearer into a superior being" when compared to other African American men. It continued with a discussion of the "antipathy to colored soldiers" among white southerners. While the author considered them better behaved than the white soldiers who preceded them, southerners detested the humiliation "of being placed under the control of what has theretofore been the subject race." The columnist discouraged Black troops from taking "insolent satisfaction in displaying their authority" because the "southerners are naturally sensitive" and "perceive insolence in a tone, a glance, a gesture, or a failure to yield enough by two or three inches in meeting on the sidewalk." He also claimed that "it is certain that nothing was further from the intention of the Government than to place these troops in Southern cities as a taunt or a humiliation to the inhabitants." Furthermore, he argued that it would be "far better if good, well disciplined white troops were substituted" for the Black soldiers "at as early a day as it is practicable for the Government to do so" in order to "restore harmony of feeling." The writer felt that if his warnings went unheeded, "the worst practical result" of white exasperation would befall those African Americans in the country: if a planter on business entered a city garrisoned with Black soldiers "and feels his pride galled and humiliated by the deference he must pay to the Union bayonets in dusky hands," he would be "tempted to indemnify himself, on returning to his remote plantation, by making his authority felt" by the "poor unprotected creatures left there" at his mercy.[60] The lie that peace would have been possible and immediate after the war if the North had not antagonized and humiliated white southerners was built on the foundation of Black men in Union uniforms and carrying guns, items placing them in positions of authority. Thus, tangible material objects played a role in the construction of this lie, a large piece of the southern foundation of the Lost Cause, which would have been impossible without the uniforms worn by Black Union soldiers as markers of identity and authority.

This is all in stark contrast to what the southern Ladies' Memorial Associations (LMA) were working on at the same time. Organized in 1867 to honor, bury, and eulogize fallen soldiers, the LMA worked tirelessly for the dead and the living. Memorial Days provided an opportunity for former

Confederates to honor their wartime dead and created opportunities to begin the alteration of the southern narrative of why the war was fought. Under the guise of memorial celebrations, local LMA chapters invited the African American population to attend events honoring the southern dead. Former Confederates pushed a narrative of unity with the formerly enslaved through tangible items that denoted identity.[61] These civil actions by women of incorporating local African Americans into memorialization opportunities starkly contrasted with the actions of white men, who chose to regain control with violent means.

A SLEEPING DEVIL

The anger of seeing African Americans in Union uniforms continued for southerners at the end of the war, because many of the USCT regiments comprising formerly enslaved men were used to police the southern militarized districts. On Christmas Day, 1865, a "serious" riot in Alexandria, Virginia, shook the city. A large group of men, "chiefly ex-Confederate soldiers, took it into their heads to celebrate Christmas by a general onslaught on the negroes." They imbibed freely "and having attained a very high pitch of 'Dutch courage,' resolved themselves into a sort of volunteer patrol organization." These men were armed with handguns, and "whenever they met a man with a darker skin than their own, instantly declared war against him." They took particular pleasure in badly beating "three colored soldiers belonging to Battery Rogers." A newspaper report noted that the men also burst into parties, assaulting and shooting Black people without discrimination. The author concluded that "the affair seems to have been arranged beforehand" because "the men appear to have come out in the morning fully prepared for it, many of them wearing gray uniforms and carrying pistols."[62] If the reporter was correct and those men coordinated their efforts to include wearing their wartime Confederate uniforms, they may have used them along with the alcohol to boost their courage and to intimidate their victims with those items that had once denoted authority.

For the defeated Confederates, one reporter explained, "the presence of negro soldiers in towns is looked upon as an intolerable insult offered to the Southern people." He cited such examples as "showing a pass to a negro sergeant who had been a slave in the same town," which was upsetting because they felt that "the negroes all looked upon this as a degradation of their former masters." The editorial continued, "there is a profound belief in the South that the North intends to humiliate the people to the lowest point."[63] Because of this, southern ire began shifting toward retaliation. In May 1866 the *Memphis Daily Avalanche* reported the arrest of "two negroes, supposed to be discharged soldiers," for being drunken and disorderly. This caused quite a stir: Black soldiers and civilians came to the men's aid, hurling "the most abusive and indecent language" at policeman Albert Davis, who was quickly reinforced by white citizens displaying the "gleaming barrels of several Colts." The author cautioned African Americans against coming to the defense of others again "or a sleeping devil will be aroused, against which they will find it difficult to contend." He claimed that white residents were happy to treat freedpeople "kindly, but they cannot and will not countenance such outrages" because "the uniform of the United States does not protect the disturber of the public peace, or justify a man in violating the law."[64] Southerners understood the authority woven into the identity of those wearing the army uniform but chose to respect it only when it suited their purpose.

Physical threats and unrest worsened throughout 1866 and 1867, with massacres in Norfolk, Virginia; Memphis; and New Orleans.[65] Black U.S. soldiers and local southern police officers often clashed during fights between whites and the arrests of freedmen. The Fortress Monroe correspondent to the *New York Herald* told the tale of the "First Fruits of the Civil Rights Bill" in Norfolk, Virginia, when a group of African Americans assembled for a parade celebrating the bill's passage. A subtitle to the article, "White Men Shot Down by Negroes in a Procession Celebrating the Passage of the Civil Rights Bill," summarized the feelings of the white community about African American freedom. The report ended with a brief note that "order was restored by the troops of the Twelfth United States infantry" stationed in the city.[66] According to the testimony of Brevet Major F. W. Stanhope of the Twelfth U.S. Infantry, the procession marched "in a perfectly orderly manner" to a speaker's stand. Among the group were "about eighteen (18) negroes, discharged soldiers" with "arms in his [their] possession" and about twenty-two or twenty-three "discharged cavalry men." Although it is not clear from the records, these discharged USCT soldiers were probably still wearing their uniforms because it is unlikely they would have owned a change of clothes if they were enslaved when the war began. Later that night Stanhope returned to his lodging and "saw a crowd of white men dressed in gray coming from the engine-house" and marching like an organized body down the street. The major stated about the resulting massacre that it was "almost impossible to get any definite testimony of the exact number of the negroes wounded and killed." He believed that if he had not been so well provisioned with men, the outcome would have been worse because "there were about seven hundred returned negro soldiers in the city"; he was certain that "they would have ultimately turned upon the whites and there would have been a tremendous riot." Stanhope included in his testimony that "the dress worn by some of the citizens, their manner of receiving and noticing a federal officer," brought him to the conclusion that the "spirit of that class of people is quite as hostile to the government as it ever was or ever will be," noting that "rebel uniforms are seen upon the streets at all hours of the day, and are worn by everybody." Brevet Brigadier General Henry Burton provided similar testimony, stating that "the town is full of rebel soldiers, who wear the rebel uniform and buttons, and all except the badge on the collar."[67] This was a blatant use of Confederate uniforms as pieces of authority and intimidation toward opposing groups. For white ex-Confederates to put on their wartime uniforms at the sight of former USCT soldiers was a deliberate and physical method of opposition.

The *Weekly Patriot and Union* from Pennsylvania claimed that the "the Disunion Negro press, of this State," or African American newspapers, ignored the "fact that the late Memphis riot was started by about one hundred and fifty negroes, *in the United States uniform.*"[68] The *Shreveport Southwestern* chronicled "horrible outrages committed upon our peaceable citizens by negroes wearing the United States uniform." A Major Elstner and a Mr. Ivy "were stopped by some eight or ten negroes dressed in the uniform of the United States colored troops" and ordered to "descend from the buggy" as Mr. Ivy's "person [was] searched for money." Reportedly, when the Black soldiers found nothing, Ivy "received a bayonet wound in the head about six inches long" and was robbed of "$85 in greenbacks and his memorandum book."[69] The *San Antonio Express* reported on the hopes of "bringing to trial *convicting* and *hanging* murdering thieves, who shot down negro soldiers because they wear the uniform of the United States." It admonished "the treason-monger *Herald*," and asserted that "the ghost of murdered Union men whose bones bleach in the sun between Fort Clarke and the Rio Grande, and whose bodies are 'suspended by scores from black jacks,' come up before the guilty vision of the tender toed traitors of the *Herald*."[70] The escalation of violence, specifically relating to Black men in Union uniform and those occasions attended by former USCT members, confirms the link between the animosity white southerners felt to the North's authority and to the authority federal uniforms. Southerners used Black men in uniform as a metaphor for a larger social problem. The psychological linking of these concepts of African American identity with their uniforms exacerbated the fraught relationships between southern white and Black communities to the point of killing and served as a foundation for white southerners in their quest to regain authority. If they could prove that the problem was unfit Black men in army uniforms, then white southerners could create a false foundation on which to justify their actions and change the political conversation in their states.

Events like those mentioned inspired violent retaliation by white terrorist groups and former Confederates who donned their old uniforms in pursuit of intimidation and regaining authority. The formation of the Ku Klux Klan (KKK) in Pulaski, Tennessee, during May 1866 by Confederate veterans hardened by the war years and searching for a way to restore a balance of power in Tennessee embodies the white wrath of the South's postwar experience. This group claimed innocent origins rooted in a desire for personal amusement, but the evidence suggests the contrary. The original Pulaski Klansmen devoted much time and energy into crafting their look and getting the attention of their fellow townspeople. At a picnic in the spring of 1867, members wore tall hats adorned with stars, cloaks, and tunics that reached their feet.[71] During the same period, the Klan began a more public phase, with its leader, the "Grand Cyclops," ordering through an announcement in the local newspaper an assembly of the officers and members to discuss "business of more than usual interest."[72] Its members then were involved in racial violence during the latter part of 1867, including inciting the murder of an African American schoolteacher for whipping a white male student.[73]

In the winter of 1867, other nearby newspapers began covering the group and speculating about members and origins. The *Nashville Union and Dispatch* noted "general and undefined dread among the negroes of a secret order" that had recently appeared. While nobody knew who they were—the Klansmen were silent on parade—people suspected they were "Rebel bush-wackers."[74] The *Union Flag* in Jonesboro described the KKK as a "conclave of rebel assassins, plunderers and cut throats." The editor claimed that a delegate from the Klan attended the Radical County Convention and announced that "'n—— voting and attending Conventions had played out and the white man's party intended to take the management of affairs into their own hands.'"[75]

According to white southerners, the national emergence of the KKK throughout 1868 was a direct reaction to the U.S. government policing the war-torn South with formerly enslaved men in army uniforms. By this time, the majority of African American soldiers were mustered out of service, which opened the door for the Klan to appeal to the public without fear of retaliation. One article explained that the "ignoble and mischievous work of organizing, arming and drilling the negroes of the South in military bodies, by which the white people of that section have been intimidated," exacerbated the "natural arrogance of the negro character" that had been "fostered by those leagues." The writer defended the Klan as a "secret society of white men . . . whose objects are not known to be political or hostile." He affirmed that the "'Klan' should not be held responsible for its unconscious influence upon ignorance, superstition and guilt."[76]

The appearance of the KKK gave rise to ghost stories throughout the South, specifically within African American communities. As reported in the *Nashville Union and Dispatch*, "the mysterious Ku-Klux Klan is spreading terror among the negroes everywhere, and though none of these strangely dressed prowlers have ever been seen in this city, there is no less dread of them here," specifically regarding the Black population that "exists in localities where they have really appeared." The article stated, "the general belief of the negroes is that they are the wandering ghosts of the Confederate dead, who refuse to be laid [to rest], and are particularly bent on the destruction of the voting classes." Although the freedmen seemed to identify the "ghosts" as dead rebel soldiers because the "strangely dressed prowlers" were in their "grave clothes," they were actually former Confederate soldiers wearing their old uniforms as a costume of intimidation. The article continued with an account of "an old black servant" returning from Nashville to Edgefield, screaming to her white employers that she had "seed dem tings!" When the mistress of the home asked what she saw, the old woman said "Wy, dem ghosts—de Kuck-Lux, de Kuck-Lux, to be shoo—I seed 'em prumenadin' in der grave clothes, right on de street!" This tale ends with the servant again describing what frightened her, and either the writer or the servant's employer determining that it was "the sight of four Sisters of Mercy with their snow-white coifs and somber black robes, which she had mistaken for the genuine Ku-Klux regalia and insignia of death."[77] Another newspaper told of an African American man at a politico-prayer meeting in Tennessee who surprised his friends when he told them "that the Ku Klux Klan were spirits of the Confederate soldiers killed in the late war" and claimed to have "seen one of these Ku Klux rise out of the grave of a murdered Confederate soldier, who was buried near where he lived."[78] According to historian Elaine Frantz Parsons, "many though not all, Ku-Klux wore costumes," and many of those who did "used their costumes or behavior to mark themselves as bizarre" so as to frighten their victims. The costumes of the KKK evoked rebellion and a specific response from those they encountered. And as Parsons argues, the Klan used those "costumes and performances for reasons far beyond their hopes to obscure their identities or cow their victims." The outfits did not fool freedmen or others, but they did craft a conversation around the organization, which created a new space for southern white authority.[79]

The KKK published orders to its members in local newspapers. Addressed to the "Shrouded Brothers of Memphis Division No. 60," the first general order stated: "The Great Past Grand Giant commands you. The dark and dismal hour draws nigh. Some live today—to-morrow die. The bullet red and the right are ours. To-day, the 11th of the mortal's month of March, you will begin to scatter the clouds of the grave."[80] As reported in the *Daily Memphis Avalanche*, "the good people of Knoxville were horrified last Sunday" by a notice posted in various portions of the city: "Brethren: The house of revenge has arrived! Our beloved companions of the tomb of the West have long since arisen, organized, and prepared themselves for the scared duty. . . . Another passage of the sun will seal the fate of all our enemies. Revenge! Revenge!! Revenge!!!"[81] These groups often referred to themselves as soldiers in the KKK army or troops in service to the Klan leaders.

It was difficult for the townspeople or local government to stand up to the Klan. The editor of a Tennessee newspaper called on the citizens to "beware of them" because "those fiends in human form" break peace and "terrify honest, innocent citizens." But for those in East Tennessee, "let the white and colored Radials meet them promptly and in the spirit of their own lawless mission, and disperse them"; if need be, "exterminate them." The piece concluded that the KKK should not be allowed to "run riot over our law, order, and the public safety, by these midnight raids, in disguise and darkness," but brave citizens should "pull off their viziers and expose their faces and their foul crimes at once to the light of the sun."[82]

Many southerners still loyal to the former Confederacy considered the Klan the only avenue to "remedy" the ills of the time "and save the country from [the] disaster and woe" that could be caused by African Americans who could "swear false against white citizens and try to defame their characters by promulgating infamous lies."[83] The Klan obviously targeted African Americans but also went after whites supportive of the Union or those who defended freedmen. Klansmen as well as their stories fed off the fear of their victims. Tales of the Klan were intended not only for their victims but also for a northern audience: Parsons argues they were a means to "reimpose white, male Democratic dominance" and assert their identity as Confederates and southerners.[84]

On October 12, 1870, Robert E. Lee died in Lexington, Virginia. His obituary took almost the entire front page of the *Philadelphia Evening Telegraph*, which reported that the general's "death will be a serious loss to the cause of the peaceful pursuit to which he had devoted the remainder of his lite and his unquestionable abilities." The report ended with the proclamation that Lee was "the greatest of the Confederate chieftains, in truth, one of the greatest generals of the age." His "death has thrown the whole Southern section of the country into profound and unaffected grief."[85] Lee's funeral procession drew thousands. He was escorted by "officers and soldiers of the Confederate army," a "chaplain and other clergy," his horse Traveler, pallbearers, physicians, "trustees and faculty of Washington College," "dignitaries of the state of Virginia," and people from many other representative bodies. The article reporting the event in the *Charleston Daily News* stated that "the old soldiers wore their ordinary citizen's dress, with a simple black ribbon in the lapel of their coats," but the Virginia Military Institute was "beautifully draped, and from its turrets hung at half-mast, and draped in mourning, the flags of all the States of the late Southern Confederacy."[86] According to historian Caroline E. Janney, the death of General Lee was "the first real opportunity" for southern men "to glorify their war effort and honor their own martial spirit."[87]

The postwar moratorium on wearing Confederate uniforms fostered the Klansmen's Confederate ghost costume, which became a favorite for many and a useful means of scaring their victims. Members of the KKK and other white terrorist groups dressed in old Confederate uniforms to wreak havoc on Black communities and wartime Unionists throughout the country. When the authorities apprehended them, the men claimed to "know nothing of that terrible bug bear the Ku-Klux, and that they did not know why they were thrown into prison unless to gratify the malice of some Radical or negro whom they had offended."[88] Near the end of Reconstruction, leaders of the New Orleans band of "White Leaguers," dressed "in full Confederate uniform," began policing city streets and checking with local law enforcement in case there was "trouble back of the city caused by the negroes."[89] Wearing the Confederate uniform again, especially after Lee's death in 1870, was not only an outright sign of defiance toward the federally imposed order on the South but also a defiance of Lee's example of reunion and reconciliation. For Confederate veterans, their uniforms symbolized a difficult but formative time during their lives, which they stitched to their overall identity. By wearing these uniforms to terrorize northern authority, they used clothing to reclaim authority for themselves and embody the Lost Cause concept, which developed soon after Lee's death.

6

THE MATERIAL
CULTURE OF
VETERANS'
ASSOCIATIONS &
COMMEMORATION

W hen the Woman's Relief Corps (WRC) held its annual national headquarters meeting in 1888, the *National Tribune*, the official newspaper of the Grand Army of the Republic veterans' organization (GAR), waxed sentimentally about the importance of the event. In a "tender retrospection" to stimulate the WRC to greater efforts in the future, Judge Handy stated: "This scene, these old soldiers, these ladies, and this splendid flag carry me back to the days that developed all the true manhood in men and all the pure, true womanhood in women" and praised its members for being "alive with the fires of patriotism and the love of home and country." His nostalgia for the "smoke-begrimed, bloodstained, battle-broken and blackened old flags" from the war was exceeded only by his pride in the gift of a new "beautiful flag, with its crimson stripes and heaven-fixed stars, presented by loving hands and faithful hearts" of the WRC to his GAR Post.[1] A similar point of view was echoed in the 1897 National United Daughters of the Confederacy (UDC) meeting minutes. "We call our dear cause the 'Lost Cause,' and, as such, we love it, as only women love, in sorrow and defeat," adding, "every monument reared" is to "perpetuate their glory" because "we live to honor the memory of our heroes."[2]

Both Union and Confederate veterans' groups employed the same rhetoric to memorialize the war and mobilize their following. Each mentioned physical and sentimental representations of lasting forms of memory from the war. After the war, as people tried to make sense of what they had experienced, they did so in part by remembering and commemorating the sacrifices they made. Thus, from 1866 to 1910, veterans' organizations became memory machines, deliberately crafting a new understanding of the war by shaping the ways it was commemorated and remembered, which persist even today. This formulation of the conflict's narrative looked as much to the future as it did to the past. Women played pivotal roles in these organizations, determining how veterans displayed their patriotism and represented their service in public. This included designing new uniforms, the creation of badges for veterans and women to represent their service, and other visual tokens of memory. The commemorative veterans' uniforms, badges, and flags provide a cleaner visual narrative of the Civil War by invoking sentimentality to service and memory.[3] These cleaned-up images and memories made both sides look respectable, which refocused the war as an intellectual and systematic battle between northern and southern memory machines, enabling the movement away from slavery as the central cause of the war.

While the field of Civil War memory is vast and encompasses a variety of angles, the overall memory of the war, the North's contribution to reconciliation, and the Lost Cause are most important for their ties to material remembrances.[4] Creating and supporting the ruse of reconciliation on the personal level of the organizations was accomplished through uniforms, flags, and badges, the tools used to pull off one of the greatest American lies—the Lost Cause. Regarding this, historian Adam Domby states, "a less provocative term than *lie* might obscure the purposeful creation and use of these constructions, and thereby render them innocuous." Indeed, the UDC's use of material items to perpetuate their Lost Cause narrative was deliberate.[5] Uniforms were a direct reminder of the Confederacy that purposefully evoked nostalgia while obfuscating the causes of the war. The UDC intentionally created a cleaner, noble narrative using uniforms, badges, and flags, piecing together a story palatable to the rest of the nation.

The theory of the Lost Cause, which describes the Confederate quest as a heroic one struggling against insurmountable odds, has significantly influenced the memory of the Civil War. While the federal government sought to reunify the country, cultural concepts of the Lost Cause ideology invaded the North and found a form of acceptance.[6] While there was an attempt at reunion during the late nineteenth century, naked hostility from the war persisted between these men uniformed in blue and gray, but any open conflict remained disguised as aging veterans depicted in perfect images. With the veterans' and commemorative organizations came the beginning of the transformative process from Union victory and Confederate loss to the carefully crafted narrative invention of the Civil War.

BIRTH OF THE GAR ORGANIZATIONS, 1866–1880s

After the American Civil War, the development of the GAR veterans' organization began, and women's aid societies shifted their focus from the perils of war to the care of veterans and their families. These groups acknowledged the continued importance of the Union uniforms and battle flags as powerful emotional touchstones to represent war memories and postwar identity. Despite the Union victory, northerners struggled to understand what the Civil War meant in the context of the nation's next steps. But they certainly wanted to remember and commemorate their service and sacrifice over those four years. They thus used commemorative uniforms, badges, and flags to create a living memory of the Civil War that perpetuated their patriotic identity through the celebration of their wartime service.

Instead of war-torn items, new veteran uniforms, flags, and badges were instrumental in reshaping the memory of the conflict. While the bloodstained uniforms worn in combat and the tattered battle flags held a place of pride as personal artifacts, the new uniforms helped create a contemporary identity for veterans that kept the significance of their victory alive for the United States, even as the details of the campaigns and struggles began to fade from memory. But the misconception remains that northerners did not commemorate the Civil War with the same fervor displayed by southerners, who soon subscribed to the Lost Cause ideology.[7] Yet their cultural artifacts provided a powerful avenue for men and women, North and South, to create a public representation of their private memories.

Benjamin Franklin Stephenson, a Union veteran from Springfield, Illinois, founded the first GAR veterans' post, or group, in nearby Decatur in April 1866. By July of that year, thirty-nine posts were chartered throughout Illinois, with membership quickly spreading to adjacent states. Veterans from ten states and the District of Columbia attended the first national encampment in November 1866.[8] Because of the "sacred bond of comradeship welded in the fire of battle," the creation of the GAR was a natural next step for veterans and resonated with former Union soldiers. Stephenson dreamed of "a grand organization of veterans" that continued "preserving and strengthening the bonds of comradeship," which "should be a help to all who had followed the flag." He and his comrades set up the organization much like the military, creating separate branches of command such as adjutant general, aide-de-camp, and quartermaster general. They mustered veterans in and out based on conduct and created ranks to distinguish members in the name of "embracing principles of fraternity, charity, and loyalty to our flag and country." Veterans in command had the ability to rise within the ranks of the GAR and garner higher status for their postwar service.[9]

Like an official militarized body, the GAR designed uniforms to distinguish their members' identity. The GAR National Council of Administration met in New York City on October 1, 1868, "to revise the Ritual and the Rules and Regulations" of the organization, "to consider the subject of Degrees, [and] to recommend a Uniform for the Grand Army of the Republic," with the intention of reporting these decisions at the next national encampment.[10] Among the adopted revised rules and regulations, Article IX addresses uniform and badge regulations for the organization. Section one states, "On occasions of ceremony, comrades of the Grand Army of the Republic shall wear the forage cap worn in the service, bearing on the front the letters G.A.R., enclosed in a wreath, and on the top the Corps badge." When posts or departments were appearing in public parades, comrades would have options as what they should wear: "1st, in dark citizen's clothes; or, 2d, in the United States Regulation blouse and belt; or, 3d, in the uniform worn in the service, at the discretion of the command paraded."[11] Directly after the war, wearing the service uniform made sense for

GAR meetings and celebrations because this was not prohibited, as it was among the former Confederates. Their Union uniform was a usable piece of clothing that would otherwise sit in a trunk, which also made wearing it financially responsible. But in the revised rules, wearing a service uniform became the last option and was permissible only at the discretion of the post commander. This was not the only time uniforms were the topic of discussion. The official dress worn by the GAR continued to evolve and be hotly debated throughout the life of the organization due to its growth and changing circumstances.

Adding to their official status, also under Article IX among the rules and regulations printed in the handbook, GAR veterans wore a specific membership badge, harkening back to the badges implemented by General Hooker in 1863. Adopted at a special meeting in New York in October 1869, the original badge was "cast from bronze composed of cannon captured during the late rebellion" and consisted "of a miniature strap and ribbon, to which shall be pendent the bronze star of the membership badge." The strap was "one and one-half inches in length, one-half inch in width, enameled, with a border one-eighth of an inch in width, of gold or gilt, and on it be the insignia of official position in the" GAR.[12] For the organization to create membership badges from melted-down captured Confederate cannons suggests a form of psychological warfare: it empowered the wearer with a tangible public form of victory that could be flaunted in front of the losers at a time when they could not commemorate and had no comparable spoils of war.

While the discussion of badges, their design, and how to properly wear them continued throughout the 1870s, the contentious conversation around uniforms appeared frequently in GAR reports and minutes. Opinion XVI from the November 26, 1871, meeting under the rituals section, discussed the issue of veterans' heads remaining covered during ceremonies. The recorder reminded the organization that "allowing the use of the uniform worn in the service was not stricken out, but that such uniform is still one of the optional uniforms of the Grand Army." If the service uniform "is worn, the accustomed insignia of rank will be retained," but "if civilians [*sic*] clothes or the blouse are chosen, no insignia of rank having yet been adopted by the Nation Encampment, there is no badge of Grand Army rank suitable to be worn with them."[13] Determining the correct and proper

Official GAR membership badge (*front and back*).
Author's personal collection.

clothing for participating veterans, the largest piece of their identity on display, was a difficult decision and required much debate.

To leave this decision to individual posts and provide no national regulation was hard for many to accept because the topic was repeatedly raised. Throughout the May 1871 encampment, delegates suggested a uniform for the organization, once by a "comrade Eldredge" from California but most officially by the adjutant general, William T. Collins, who addressed concerns about official GAR uniforms in his report. Collins expressed his support on "the subject of uniform for the members of the Grand Army of the Republic," which he felt was of "worthy consideration." He promised "samples of swords, belts, caps, and blouses" for submission to the delegates for inspection to urge them along.[14] During the second day of these proceedings, the uniform concept changed again: "amend Paragraph 2, by inserting 'with side arms or muskets,' so that it shall read—'in the United States Regulation blouse and belt, with side arms or muskets.'" The group also amended the third paragraph to stipulate, "'No uniform or regalia, except as above prescribed, shall be worn.'"[15] While the delegates were specific about nothing being added to what was allowed, they declined to heed the request for an official uniform.

During the proceedings of the Sixth Annual GAR National Encampment during May 1872, members of the committee proposed amending Chapter V, Article IX, Section 1, Paragraph 2d "to allow each Department to adopt its own uniform." They deliberated this point thoroughly, and by the motion of a comrade named Reynolds, "an amendment was adopted allowing Posts to select their own uniform." Yet the committee reported against the proposition to make "delegates to the National Encampment wear the prescribed uniform during the sitting of the Encampment."[16] Once posts were allowed to create their own uniform, one in California began charging a "$20.00 muster-in fee" because it was "giving to each recruit a uniform costing the Post $15.00," which allowed its members to look the same at events.[17]

The post-by-post report of the inspector general during the May 1875 encampment revealed more concerns about GAR comrades wearing uniforms. From the Bosworth Post No. 2 in Portland, Maine, reportedly "the largest Post in the Department," came accusations that their officers "neglected to uniform themselves when on duty" or at events. They attributed this "laxity of discipline and dignity" as the culprit for "a loss of interest in the meetings by some of the comrades." But since then "the matter has been corrected by the new officers" who were happy to report that "there are two hundred and one members in good standing, nearly all uniformed."[18] Reporting that veterans were uniformed was a point of pride for a post by demonstrating a commitment to their cause.

Finally, a decade after the war ended, the GAR resolved the clothing issue to the satisfaction of its members. Offered by the GAR Department of Wisconsin on behalf of the Committee of Rules and Regulations at the May 1875 national encampment, it resolved provision two, which stated "that the National Encampment prescribe by regulation a uniform to be used and worn by Posts of the Grand Army of the Republic."[19] The official GAR uniform consisted of "a double-breasted dark blue coat with bronze buttons and a wide-brimmed black slouch felt hat complete with golden wreath insignia and crowned with a cord."[20] Creating a new uniform for GAR veterans set a precedent not only for regular comrades but also for those in charge. Post commanders were to "be neat in person" and "dress in the proper uniform at Post and Department meetings."[21] Dressing in a new uniform, instead of a tattered service uniform, instilled pride, assisted GAR members in perpetuating their loyalty to their country and flag, and closely knitted the identity of veterans to what they wore and how they presented themselves. It also allowed them to establish distinctively who was and who could not be part of their organization.

BEGINNINGS OF COLLABORATION, 1870s–1880s

Throughout the 1870s and 1880s, the GAR began collaborating with new organizations such as the Woman's Relief Corps, the Sons of Union Veterans, the Daughters of Union Veterans, as well as Confederate veterans. For each of these organizations, badges became an important way to define their identities, celebrate their service, and commemorate their sacrifice. In 1884 alone the GAR issued 90,500 membership badges.[22] The Union organizations touted the U.S. flag as a symbol of their devotion to cause and country. These organizations also provided opportunities for veterans to wear their uniforms publicly at memorials, reunions, parades, and social events. The concept of a shared tragedy, because of the new acceptance that the war was fought for intellectual reasons as opposed to slavery, slowly took hold on the relationship between the North and the South. This cultivated shared commemorative events between northern and southern veterans that began reuniting the country without reconciling the differences between the two regions.[23]

When the GAR united with other groups, it fostered organizational growth. Council members of the 1881 GAR national encampment believed it to be "our honorable privilege to recognize the magnificent loyalty displayed by the patriotic women of the North during the war of the rebellion" because it was only by "their loving prayers . . . , contributions to the Christian and Sanitary Commissions, and by their womanly fidelity and devotion on the battle-field and in the hospital" that Union victory was possible. The GAR partnered with the Woman's Relief Corps (WRC), which it recognized as an auxiliary in 1883, to "perpetuate the memory of the Grand Army of the Republic" even though the women's organization had started in 1879. The WRC assisted in the "furtherance of charitable and other work" for the

GAR and petitioned the group to authorize the formation of the WRC at a national encampment. Recognition of the WRC signified "their valuable and self-imposed service."[24] At the 1884 GAR national encampment, the commander in chief noted the progress of the WRC when stating that after only a year, that group was "now much further advanced in organization" than the GAR at the same time. Some members "doubted the wisdom" of recognizing the WRC, but the women were to be the men's "Grand Army Reserve, ready to respond for efficient help in all our social and charitable work." Those "loyal women" were to be their "efficient helpers" and to enjoy the events that meant something to them, including "these meetings and re-unions of men who fought under the old flag nearly a quarter of a century ago."[25] While some grumbled, other members of the GAR recognized that they needed the assistance of the WRC to spread their mission. Women eligible to join the WRC must possess "good moral character and correct deportment, who have not given aid and comfort to the enemies of the Union," meaning that they could not be former Confederates.[26] Members considered it their duty and privilege to assist the GAR and northerners affected by the war. In a "touching and beautiful address" printed in the *National Tribune,* a WRC representative was quoted as saying, "we are proud that we have lived in a heroic age: we delight to honor the heroes of this century." She continued, "we pledge you that as long as there is a member of the W.R.C. we shall have within our hearts" charity, which "shall always prompt us to the noblest sacrifices for the soldiers, their widows and orphans."[27]

The women's active involvement in memorializing themselves, their sacrifice, and the members of the GAR through uniforms, flags, and badges was their way of stretching their limited political reach in a patriarchal society. By doing so, the WRC made itself indispensable to the veterans and the cultivation of their Civil War memory machine and identity, a relationship that gave them the network to cultivate their wartime narrative. In the minutes for the 1883 national encampment, the GAR's inspector general asked post commanders, "Have you a Ladies' Aid or Auxiliary Society working in the interest of your Post?" That simple question suggests how vital women's organizations were to the functioning of the GAR at the local level, with each post encouraged to have a WRC partner. Other important questions directed at post commanders included, "How many G.A.R. uniforms have you in your Post?" and "Do you require the officers and members of your Post to wear the G.A.R. badge at all meetings and parades?"[28] The stitching of GAR identity to uniforms and badges is evident in these questions because they were addressed to every post. This was a way for the national encampment to keep tabs on veterans and to ensure that they were properly marked as representatives of the organization and its legacy.

During the mid-1880s, the national encampment and council meetings revisited the concepts and regulations for uniforms and badges. Partially because of the expense, not all GAR members agreed on a single uniform or that one was necessary for encampments and parades. Chapter V, Article IX, Section I of the bylaws state: "Sec. I. Only the uniform prescribed by the National Encampment, shall be hereafter worn by the members of the Grand Army of the Republic." Others, however, argued that just wearing "the Grand Army button" as a uniform would be enough.[29] So, why did many not feel the need to wear a uniform in an organization celebrating their military service? One reason is that the Union won the war. Its uniforms were part of the men's identities, though only as private heirlooms or as just one symbol of their part in the victory. GAR veterans had military success on their side, meaning they had nothing to prove to anyone and making the organization and its activities purely a celebration of their service and sacrifice.

But there was another reason, as it turned out: the veteran uniform was expensive. For those who wanted to participate and wear it, numerous questions arose as to where they could purchase one. M. C. Lilley & Company of Columbus, Ohio, provided the answer. The company published a GAR uniform catalog in 1887, complete with illustrations, that was available and distributed to GAR members. The uniforms, consisting of a coat, vest, blouse, pants, and hat, were made to each man's measurements. The double-breasted coat signified for the official uniform started at $9.25 and could increase in price based on the quality of cloth. The single-breasted option ranged from $7.00 to $14.50 and pants from $4.25 to $10.20 per pair. The coats and vests were equipped with GAR regulation buttons. If a member purchased a basic complete outfit, it would cost him about $25.00 (the equivalent of $733.69 in 2022), which did not include sashes, swords, guns, pins, or extra buttons.[30]

Other clothiers advertised to GAR members. In 1887 the Cloudman

M. C. Lilley & Co. single-breasted GAR coat.
Author's personal collection.

Relief Corps No. 18 from Saccarappa, Maine, advertised a May festival. Their program boasted of "music," "merry company," "ice cream," and "braiding the May Pole." In wispy cursive the advertisement at the bottom of the beige-tinged flyer stated, "Buy Your G.A.R. Indigo Blue Suits and Regulation Hats, of Clements & Co," a "clothiers and gents' furnishers."[31] Clothiers clearly understood that they could increase profits by advertising their ability to make regulation GAR uniforms.

The $25.00 suit affected the participation of veterans. The average cost of clothing for a man between the 1870s and the 1880s must be considered. A study of comparative wages, prices, and cost of living for average families in Massachusetts and Great Britain in the late 1880s provides an example of how much the surveyed men earned annually and how much of that they spent on clothing. The study secured nineteen family budgets, or "annual accounts of expenditures," from Massachusetts. The size of a family obviously varied, but on average the household numbered between three to six people, with incomes ranging from $611 to $1,300 for an average income of $803.47 and an average clothing allowance of $77.89 for a family. If the average family in Massachusetts in 1883 spent $754.42 on necessities and luxuries, and 16 percent of that went to clothing ($120.70), with the amount equally divided among six family members, that would allow each person $20.11 for clothes for the year. Prices of clothing, family incomes, and total expenditures varied greatly because of occupation, location, and cost of living, but the Massachusetts figures serve as a means of demonstrating that the average cost of a regulation GAR uniform ($25.00) priced out men from lower-income families. This also means that it was harder for African American veterans to participate in regulation GAR events because their average income was typically lower than that of their white comrades.[32]

Uniforms were important for many post activities. The General Lyon Post No. 9 in Chicago sent postcards to members requesting them "to report, in full G.A.R. uniform, at Grand Army Hall, corner Dearborn and Adams Streets, on Wednesday Evening, October 23rd, 1889." They were to "escort COMMANDER-IN-CHIEF, R. A. ALGER and Staff to the First Regiment Armory" for a reception by the posts of Cook County. Their families were requested to attend and assist with the reception; for this event, "no tickets of admission" were required.[33]

In 1885, during the national encampment in Portland, Maine, a change was made to the reverse side of the badge "by adding on the star corps marks for Sheridan's Cavalry, Wilson's Cavalry, and Hancock's Veteran Corps." The rules explicitly state that "no other [badge] shall be worn as the badge of the Grand Army, except that prescribed for officers in Section 3, and for past officers in Section 4, and hereafter no membership badge shall be manufactured or issued, except in conformity with the above" rules because a patent protected both the badge and the button. Yet there was an exception: members could wear other badges if they were "issued under the authority of the National Encampment," which applied to navy veterans, who were permitted to wear an anchor on their badge, if desired. No member of the GAR could manufacture or sell "official or membership badges without the consent of the National Council of Administration." And it was intended for use only by a member veteran: "giving of the regulation badge to persons unauthorized to wear it is impolitic, productive of evil to the Order, and is emphatically condemned."[34] Such a strong admonition illustrates the importance of these items to the GAR's identity and public image. In the general provisions section of Article IX, point seven states that "posts are required to present each recruit with a badge," with "the cost thereof being added to the muster-in fee," meaning that veterans were paying for their own items in the GAR, just as they did as soldiers in the Union army.[35]

While they were created to assist veterans, the WRC designated its own official badge and rules for its members as a material recognition of their identity, status, and service. The manual containing the WRC's rules and regulations required from its members a specific number of supplies for each local corps upon organization. Rule fifteen states that each corps would receive "10 officers' and 5 membership" badges in the post-starter kit. Much like the GAR, admitting members to the organization required an admission fee, with the "price of badge added thereto," but the WRC also took into account that members came and went: those "leaving the Order must return their badges, for which the regular price will be paid." As for its appearance, the WRC badge, according to a resolution adopted at the July 1884 national convention, was "a Maltese cross of copper bronze, with the Grand Army medallion suspended from a bar pin, bearing the initials, 'F.C.L.' (Fraternity, Charity, Loyalty), by a red, white and blue ribbon, one and one-half inches long in the clear, and one and one-fourth inches in width."[36]

The WRC took wearing their badges seriously and used them as forms of identity and authority. Rules surrounding their use and display were intricate, strict, and explicitly stated in the WRC manual. To distinguish them from regular members, the badge of an officer included a "bar pin [that] designates the office, and the ribbon is of solid color." Only women actively serving could wear one. Once a woman no longer belonged to the order, "she certainly has no *moral* right to wear the badge." Mourning attire was added if a member died: "the badge of the Order [is] draped with a bow of black grosgrain ribbon" positioned "just above the badge so as to partly conceal it" and allow for this symbol of reverence. When attending any WRC activity, "no member shall be allowed to sit in Corps meeting or Convention without wearing the badge, unless excused by vote, in special cases." Anyone without a badge would not be allowed to cast a ballot. While there would be no penalty for this breach, unless the special exception was made, she could not retain her privileges without wearing her badge.[37]

These women entered the public sphere of memory and narrative control in a private way, emphasizing the virtue of duty. Through memorialization, WRC members were able to construct their own definition of their public and private memories and assist in telling the story to future generations.[38] In this and other organizations, they exercised their ability to control the members and their activities, which is why the first paragraph in the WRC's handbook emphasizes "good moral character and correct deportment" as well as not having helped or sympathized with "the enemies of the Union."[39] They were happy to partner with the GAR and support its veterans and their families out of loyalty to their country. The GAR's standing, prominence, and perpetuation of its own narrative relied heavily on these women and the tangible pieces of memory provided by their veteran uniforms and badges, in which the WRC played a vital role.

The GAR promoted opportunities not only for women but also for African American veterans. Because they and Native Peoples participated in the Union's victory, the GAR engaged in collaboration with these groups. It was created as a politically active interracial fraternal society that accepted Black veterans as equals at a time when other organizations shut their doors to African Americans. Thus it boasted having all–African American and integrated posts as well as all-white or predominantly Indigenous posts throughout the country, including the South.[40]

African American veterans took pride in their service and in the materials that marked them as faithful GAR members. The reports of the GAR inspector general from each region included comments on the victories and hardships experienced by the posts. While it is difficult to identify which ones predominantly comprised African American veterans, some inspectors did emphasize the achievements of their "colored" posts. From Denver, Colorado, "Post 4 (colored)" possessed one hundred comrades, which was distinguished because of race and performance in the report from the all-white posts of the same region. A post in Providence, Rhode Island, was highly praised: "Ives Post is composed entirely of colored men, who are individually poor, and they have a limited field from which to recruit," but "they deserve credit for their successful struggle for existence during a period of years."[41] Historian Barbara A. Gannon states, "African Americans appear to have been as dedicated as their white counterparts, if not more so, to following GAR guidelines."[42]

Uniforms and participation apparently were connected. Inspector General J. R. Carnahan's committee reported, in respect to uniforms, "Departments which have adopted a uniform are not only the largest in numerical strength, but [also] take a deeper interest in the Order." Its members concluded, "we believe its adoption by others will prove its incalculable worth."[43] The *Christian Recorder* reported that African American veterans "fasten their silk and gilt badges on their lapels and appear at the hotels and on the streets" for commemorative events and encampments. The author added, regarding the GAR's 1884 national gathering, "as a consequence the National Capital has had what seemed to be an army of gaudy and glittering soldiers encamped here."[44] Black veterans participated in post meetings and spent money to own proper veteran uniforms and badges because of what their wartime uniforms symbolized to them personally. This was a way for them to continue to publicly display their claim to equal status in the republic.

That being said, things often were difficult for Black GAR members, especially for those who belonged to posts in southern states. Prejudice against African American members crept into southern GAR posts and caused them problems. At one national encampment, discrimination against African American veterans was noted as "a serious problem in Southern Departments" and duly rejected: "no honorably discharged veteran should be discriminated against on account of the color of his skin," that "there must be other and valid reasons for his rejection."[45] It did not matter to some that these men had fought under Old Glory and worn the Union blue: racial prejudice took precedence for them and created a hostile environment for African American veterans.

There were two confirmed GAR posts in Indian Territory that Indigenous veterans established and ran. Cabin Creek Post No. 1, in present day Vinita, Oklahoma, was organized in the Department of Kansas. It was predominantly Cherokee and mustered on April 28, 1883, under the command of C. E. Johnson, with nineteen charter members. Despite their treatment by U.S. authorities and other GAR members, "they are none the less intelligent, and anxious to be enrolled in the Grand Army."[46]

African American GAR veteran in uniform with badges.
Author's personal collection.

The CPT White Catcher Post was established in Tahlequah, Indian Territory, in 1889. Also predominantly Cherokee, it was redesignated CPT White Catcher Post 23 on June 1, 1890.[47] The Indian Territory posts were nationally recognized and discussed in the GAR's newspaper in Washington, D.C., the *National Tribune*. Departmental encampments began happening throughout the region, and Indigenous posts such as these participated. They even voted on removal of members from national office, which demonstrates commitment to their involvement by the GAR.[48]

Creating posts this long after the war means the creators were between forty and sixty years old. Reconstruction and the blanket federal punishment of all Indigenous Peoples of the territory could have delayed efforts to commemorate their Civil War service. The 1880s–1890s were also the time of allotment and land runs in the region, involving the reallocating of Indigenous lands to private ownerships mostly acquired by white settlers. Losing their treaty lands (having replaced their ancestral lands earlier in the century) could have prompted the creation of the posts because of the need to hold on to their social heritage when what had anchored them to the place was no longer theirs.[49]

While it is difficult to track Indigenous Union veterans in northern states, these examples from Indian Territory provide insight into how seriously Indigenous veterans in those states took the materials they used to understand their service and sacrifice and to construct their identity. Thomas Kechittigo, a member of Company K, Michigan Sharpshooters, after his discharge from service went home to Omer, Michigan. He became an active member of the GAR and attended the Sculley Post No. 265 in the city. Kechittigo served as the color-bearer and presented the flag for the post in ceremonies for fifteen years. When he moved in the mid-1890s to Grayling, Michigan, he actively participated in the Marvin Post No. 240. Kechittigo was an active marshal at camp meetings and received a badge of honor for extraordinary effort in his duties. In addition to his extensive involvement, the photograph in his pension file shows him wearing a dark suit and his official GAR badges, so Kechittigo must have taken the material aspect of his duties seriously. Both of the posts he attended predominately comprised white veterans. His wife, an avid WRC member, also wore her organization badge in the pension-file photo. Many other members of Company K, Michigan Sharpshooters were involved in the GAR. Leon

Otashquabono was photographed with his official GAR membership badge and hat, as was Henry Wassagezhic in 1907, who looks to be wearing a GAR uniform jacket with badges.[50]

For women, African Americans, and Indigenous Peoples, the visual representation of their Civil War service was extremely important to documenting their participation and conveying their narrative. Tangible postwar objects allowed them continual claim on their status of service as memories began to fade. This also gave them the opportunity to assert their importance to the Union victory, which white veterans could more easily and tangibly commemorate.

TURNING THE TIDE & TENDER MEMORIES

The commemoration and celebration of service among the white, African American, and Indigenous veterans of the GAR in cooperation with the WRC fostered memory within these groups and as a whole. With the passage of time and the spread of those organizations, Union veterans grew more open to the idea of sharing commemorations with former Confederates, especially when tangible pieces of identity were involved and evoked.

The U.S. flag continued to hold special meaning in the identity of GAR veterans. A description of a veterans' parade in Maine, taken from the *Portland Daily Press,* was read at the 1885 GAR national encampment. The description of "wooden platforms," "waving banners," and "patriotic songs" painted a lovely picture. "The men marched at a quick step," and the reporter estimated "23,000 men were in line." They marched with "the torn battle flags—for several were carried in the ranks." The writer commented on how "these old veterans" had "saved the nation's life, as they proudly marched along beneath the starry folds of the old flag for which they endured so many hardships," and how many of them were "marching together for the last time until they join the Grand Army above."[51] This story, like so many others, illustrates how the sacrifice and service of these veterans was continually intertwined with the flag.

The Stars and Stripes was even used as a prop to coerce the GAR to visit the "New South." A comrade named Lawrence begged the 1885 assembly "to hear a word from Tennessee" before taking a vote on the site of a future national encampment. He offered "an invitation from the city of Nashville, and from the State of Tennessee." His masterful oration included reminding the committee that he himself came from that southern state, "which gave the country Andrew Jackson," and a state that "sent into the Union armies under great difficulties and sufferings, thirty-two white regiments and thirty colored regiments." Once the idea was posited, Lawrence attempted to make the assembly feel guilty by saying: "I come to you, comrades, from the New South. Are you not glad that your bravery, that your patriotism, gave to us a New South? Are you not glad to know that the South is now being ruled with the same patriotic sentiments that moved you to fight under the old flag?" He sealed these questions with the statement that his invitation was not only from "the numerous soldiers of the Union army, but [also] . . . from our Confederate brethren." Those men "who fought against you, and who were conquered by you, and who are now citizens of this Republic," he told them, "are filled with patriotism."[52] While Lawrence's speech met with "great applause," it was no coincidence that this southerner invoked the Stars and Stripes to encourage northern cooperation to visit the "New South," or the "reformed South." He said the former Confederates were patriotic but left dangling the cause for which they were patriotic. Tensions between the GAR and the former Confederates might have lessened, but the ex-rebels had not put their loyalty to their wartime cause behind them.

Although the effort to hold a national encampment in Tennessee failed, the GAR and local Confederate memorial groups engaged in joint forms of commemoration. On Decoration Day, April 10, 1881, "a committee of the Grand Army of the Republic" presented "a magnificent floral tribute" to "the Ladies' Confederate Monumental Association on the occasion of the decoration of the Confederate monument" to the South's "heroic dead." The flowers were an "offering of peace and good-will—the offerings of the heart." In their thank-you speech, the women responded by conjuring memories of the flags and visions of their men in gray. "And, you, whose souls swell with the proud joy of success, you whose battle-flag is still flung to the breeze, obeying the traditions of your race . . . , have come today to pay tribute to the men who marched and fought beneath the banner that was furled at Appomattox." Interestingly, the speaker highlighted the "traditions of *your* race," which she wanted to make clear was different than hers. The speech ended with a poem: "'For the blue and the gray are the colors of God, / And they meet in the sky at even'. / And many a noble and gallant soul / That wore them has passed into Heaven.'"[53] While her speech clearly reflected the battle between North and South, it ended with the happy thought that those who wore the blue and the gray will commingle in the afterlife.

Because of the moratorium on wearing Confederate uniforms after the war, meetings, monument commemorations, and reunions became safe places for Confederate veterans to gather with comrades throughout the 1880s to commiserate or reminisce about their losses, whether of battles or of friends, and their time in the service. It also allowed them to be seen in their uniforms, even if in the beginning that caused a stir. Meetings became special occasions with some pageantry, especially in the South, that allowed veterans to gather dressed in their uniforms. Doing so in these situations was more acceptable: a "meeting" was not a reunion but a private and formal gathering. Former Confederate president Jefferson Davis made a last tour in 1886, and this informal but pageant-laden event provided an opportunity for former general James Longstreet, who had angered ex-rebels by becoming what they called a "scalawag" during Reconstruction for adhering to Union rules, to appear in his Confederate uniform and sit at Davis's side. A veteran offered an explanation for the meeting, which he said "means no disrespect to any other section of the country, nor is there evidence of disloyalty in the display," adding that their only wishes were to reunite with "old comrades and the revival of never-fading memories."[54] The concepts of the Lost Cause are perpetuated easiest through culture, which makes uniforms a key tangible element in such gatherings because of their visual ability to stimulate thoughts of nostalgia and sentiment for the past. While claiming that their gathering was not treasonous, it became so, because their assembling perpetuated a subversive concept: it placed the mindset of veterans in the glorified past, fostering the desire for an unrealistic South to memorialize its cause.

Even in the South, the sight of Confederate uniforms at a time when nobody was supposed to be wearing them caused excitement. One such example involving Dr. Arch Sulled startled crowds and caused "quite a fiffle of excitement" at the stage during a reunion in Cowetta, Georgia, organized by the local veterans' association. "Looking more like Rip Van Winkle than anything else," Sulled "pushed himself through the vast throng to the speakers' stand, wearing an old confederate uniform, canteen and cartridge box, in which he surrendered in 1865."[55] By appearing in his uniform at the soldiers' reunion again connects Sulled's identity and the memory of his service because the war was an important and trying time in his life.

BIRTH OF CONFEDERATE ORGANIZATIONS, 1890S–1900S

"Close upon the heels of the war came the local organizations for giving aid to the poor and former Confederate soldiers" by the "noble ladies of the South," stated a newspaper article long after Appomattox. "Then came the organization of local bodies of former soldiers and the neighborhood reunions," along with "an occasional brigade reunion."[56] To unify those efforts, the United Confederate Veterans Association (UCV) formed in New Orleans in 1889.[57] According to their constitution and bylaws, the purpose of the organization was to "unite in one general Federation all associations of Confederate Veterans, soldiers and sailors, now in existence, or hereafter to be formed." The purpose of the UCV was to "cultivate the ties of friendship that should exist among those who have shared common dangers, sufferings and privations." Organizers claimed to hope to create "an impartial history of the Confederate side" and to "collect and preserve relics and mementoes of the war." These veterans also wanted to assist the disabled and needy; erect monuments to their "great leaders and heroic soldiers, sailors and people"; and "to instill into our descendants a proper veneration for the spirit and glory of their fathers."[58] Part of the way they sought to accomplish these goals, just like the GAR, was through material objects—uniforms, badges, and flags.

Under Article VII of the UCV's constitution and bylaws is the description of its official badge. It "is the representation in enamel of the Confederate battle-flag, on a plain metal surface . . . of an inch square," which can be mounted as a pin or button, to be worn on the left lapel of the coat."[59] In contrast to the GAR, whose members debated the precise measurements of their official badge and its regulations, the UCV badge had few regulations or formalities surrounding its use. Its purpose was clear: when worn, it made the wearer immediately identifiable as a Confederate veteran.

To make that identification and to associate with "Confederate heritage" grew in importance as the South lost more of its wartime leaders. In a column entitled "THE REBEL CHIEF" on December 6, 1889, the *Rock Island Daily Argus* printed the obituary and a small illustration of former Confederate president Jefferson Davis, touting that "Death Claims the Leader of the 'Lost Cause.'"[60] With the passing of Davis, the last of the Confederate trinity of Davis, Lee, and Jackson was gone, which meant their memory could be altered and exalted in the name of the Lost Cause. Their images could be used on badges and flags, while the iconic image of Robert E. Lee in his uniform could be a blueprint for monuments and Confederate memory throughout the country.

With Reconstruction considered over and the harsh memories of war lessening throughout the 1880s and 1890s, it began to become socially acceptable for ex-Confederates to appear in public in their wartime uniforms. The opportunity to wear these old garments, and the reduction in the opprobrium associated with doing so, involved two distinct approaches. Veterans wore original and replica uniforms to memorials, meetings, and mock skirmishes after the Civil War, and those prominent among them began requesting to be buried in their battle-worn uniforms, a politically charged decision. A frequent occurrence in the former Confederacy soon after the war, memorials and reunions presented a place for veterans to gather with comrades and reflect on their wartime experiences.

By the middle of the 1870s, veterans could often be seen in uniform at "mock skirmishes" or "sham battles." Occasionally, they wowed the crowds and participated, but often they sported their regalia on the sidelines, garnering attention from those gathered as well as newspaper writers. Sham battles, generally held in tandem with Decoration Day services or reunions, were part of the entertainment for the celebration. One such sham battle caught an artist off guard when fake troops stormed the fort he was sketching, seized him, and took him inside, accusing him of being a spy. The artist "begged to be shot, but was refused the satisfaction of a soldier's death, not being in uniform." The "mimic war correspondent" received a sentence of hanging, but it was commuted by an old veteran. The ex-rebel then agreed to participate in the "battle" and later told a story of hanging a spy in Murfreesboro, Tennessee, during the war. Once released, the reporter "interviewed" his "reb" captors: "Mosby's men . . . Mosby, J. L. Richardson, General Forrest, and—Yockey the Lieutenant." The men "were all attired in butternut blouses, high boots, and immense straw hats," mimicking wartime Confederate garb.[61]

The "Mimic War" described in an October 1890 issue of one Georgia newspaper rewrote history to the satisfaction of those in attendance, who went "wild [with applause] over Dixie and the cadets" when the University of the South team appeared in gray uniforms. Confederate veterans participated in this match by "attacking the Northern battery" and capturing it, causing the northern line, composed of another school's cadets, to flee in confusion. The reserve veterans then "charged with the old rebel yell which ten thousand throats echoed from the grand stand, and were on the point of wiping out the army of the North when a silly flag of truce appeared," which ended the "slaughter and fun" and allowed the "Gallant South" to "retake" Atlanta.[62]

In 1892 a group of southern veterans who encountered their northern counterparts, members of a GAR post, demonstrated the raw feeling that the uniforms engendered. At the unveiling of the memorial to "New South" advocate Henry W. Grady in Atlanta, Confederate veterans marched in their wartime uniforms and with their old flag beside Union veterans and, in doing so, "gave such offence" to GAR commander John Palmer. The ruffled feathers of Commander Palmer seemed to surprise the southerners and led the Alabama veterans to discard their wartime uniforms for a short while.[63] As a result, UCV commanders put strict guidelines in place concerning attire for important joint events. For the Ninth Annual Reunion of the UCV, to "keep pace with the growing sentiment," organizers asked veterans to wear "a simple and inexpensive suit, or sack only, of Confederate gray, with a dark hat."[64]

Newspapers reported that numerous former Confederates wanted to be buried in their wartime uniforms. Among them was onetime Confederate general and Louisiana governor Henry Watkins Allen, whose request prompted one northern newspaper to suggest that "probably he thought Satan would otherwise fail to recognize him" without it. Other former rebel soldiers included, to name a few, Major Willis H. Claiborne; Colonel Joseph B. Bibb, who wished to be buried in the uniform "which he wore and honored"; famed Lieutenant General Nathan Bedford Forrest, the credited founder of the Ku Klux Klan; the Reverend Charles Edward Chichester; and Smith Redford of the Virginia Light Artillery.[65]

Continuing links to the Confederate cause even at funerals was only one way in which southerners increasingly reshaped public perceptions of their actions. In 1892, according to one article, the women heading the

Memorial Association of Orangeburg, South Carolina, held a parade and invited veterans, some of whom arrived in full uniform, to speak at the Corner-Stone Monument. At this meeting former general M. C. Butler stated that the purpose of the monument was to "preserve the recollections of our civil war, but they [the monuments] preserve the best side of it." He went on to say, "we revere our dead because they are worthy of it. . . . [T]hey are patriotic, gallant soldiers" and "conducted war on a high plane of enlightened principle and died for their honest convictions."[66] This rhetoric is another example of the intellectual movement that made the Civil War about ideas and convictions instead of slavery. Through memorials, monuments, and reverence of the dead, they began erasing the political and societal reasons, ranging from slavery to government and sovereignty, for which the South fought the Civil War.

The creation of southern memorial and benevolent societies and organizations provided opportunities and a sense of authority for Confederate veterans to wear their uniforms publicly. The mission of the United Daughters of the Confederacy (UDC), founded in 1894, was to "honor the memory of those who served and those who fell in the service of the Confederate States, and to record the part taken by Southern women." Its members prioritized education, memory, and social and benevolent actions to "preserve the material for a truthful history of the war between the Confederate States and the United States of America."[67] The UDC provided opportunities for veterans to wear their uniforms and badges publicly for numerous occasions without the amount of scrutiny the men faced by themselves. Veterans creating Confederate memory could be seen as treasonous or threatening, but women gave a softer face to the movement, so their participation was rarely questioned.

The organization's constitution described "the badge to be worn by the Daughters of the Confederacy." It "shall consist of a representation of the Confederate flag (stars and bars) in white, blue and scarlet enamel, surrounded by a laurel wreath with the monogram, D.C. under the flag, and dates '61–'65 on loops of bow tieing [*sic*] wreath."[68] Like the other memorial groups, the UDC designed a badge to set itself apart from the rest of society and to demonstrate its political identity and allegiance.

In April 1898, as the United States prepared for war with Spain over Cuba, Civil War veterans and their sons lined up to participate. Their actions should have demonstrated the unity of the United States a third of a century after Appomattox, but that was not always the case. While these soldiers were all Americans, what they wore again became a contentious issue. By April 30, Colonel R. C. Marshal, of Portsmouth, Virginia, began "working up a movement to raise a brigade of negro soldiers to go to Cuba and fight Spain." Calling on Major General Fitzhugh Lee, Robert E. Lee's son, he wanted to "take eight negro companies now in Virginia, organize a few more and form the First regiment of Virginia." The brigade would be "commanded by Colonel Marshall and to be in General Lee's division." Such preparations were normal in a time of war, but according to reports, "Colonel Marshall wants the brigade uniformed in confederate gray, so they can be distinguished from other soldiers."[69] Placing African American soldiers in Confederate gray nearly thirty years after the Civil War was a bold statement that fed into the desire to keep the Confederacy alive and resubjugate Black citizens. The *New York Sun* casually reported that volunteers in Camp De Soto, Florida, were "organized thoroughly and the men have begun camp duty. Some of the companies from Georgia are uniformed in Confederate gray and are encamped close to the Ohio and Michigan regiments."[70] Some former Confederate generals such as Joseph Wheeler and Fitzhugh Lee "donned Uncle Sam's uniforms and are serving as major generals in the army of our common country."[71]

During the spring of 1898, there was a push to return captured Confederate battle flags to their respective state of origin. Joseph Benson Foraker, a Republican senator from Ohio, first raised the suggestion. He stated that "the Stars and Stripes now float over a United and patriotic Nation," and now that "we have peace," Americans needed to "wipe out the marks of war." This subject sparked extensive debate and fiery feelings throughout the country. The proposition was moderately appealing because of the change in circumstances: the United States was now "at war with a foreign nation, and no section of the country is more patriotic and zealous in the support of our cause than the South." Foraker further pointed out that "some of the most distinguished officers of the Confederate army are marching as generals at the head of our columns." He believed that because those from the North and those from the South had joined together "to win the day for their common country and to add glory and renown to the flag," it was time to blot "out the bitter memories of estrangement and strife, [and to] press forward to the future with common confidence and pride."[72] Foraker's proposition received support from Union veterans in Kansas City, who believed "the fact that old Union soldiers and former Confederates now wear one uniform, in heart as well as on the body, and fight for the same flag," warranted returning the old rebel battle flags. They apparently were unaware of the regiments wearing the Confederate gray.[73]

Capturing flags is a part of war and is important to the psychology of victory. By keeping and preserving Confederate flags taken during the Civil War, the United States signified their importance, which calls for a close look at their return. While all flags have meaning, a key element that fed the southern memory machine was the U.S. government's decision to return Confederate flags at this time. This was meant to be a gesture of goodwill and unity, but it spurred the Lost Cause narrative and provided validation of ex-rebels' feelings that they had a right to celebrate their service. This action, coupled with the actual return of the physical flags, galvanized their movement and did more work in this regard than the uniforms and badges could have accomplished alone.

Stories relating various poignant scenes involving aging Civil War soldiers were pervasive throughout newspapers during this period. Headlines such as "Old Confederate Veterans Shed Tears while They Salute Old Glory" conjured sentimental feelings and presented the vision of reunion throughout the country. While current U.S. troops were encamped in New Orleans for service in the Spanish-American War, "400 old Confederate veterans, some in their old uniforms, marched into the fair ground headed by a band and wheeled on to the track and marched past the grand stand." Pandemonium broke loose; the U.S. regulars "cheered to the echo" while the U.S. band played the "Star-Spangled Banner." The veterans' band then took up the "Star-Spangled Banner," while the army band played "Dixie" as "the old Confederate veterans saluted the flag with tears streaming down their cheeks."[74] Because of the Spanish-American War, people desperately clung to the illusion that the country was united, but Confederate veterans appearing in their old uniforms and waiving their old flags conveyed a different visual of their allegiance. While these men were happy to be part of the United States and participate with U.S. symbols, by choosing to wear Confederate garb, they clung to the concept of retaining that part of their identity, making it impossible to separate them from Confederate war goals.

Many Americans claimed that "the last gap in the chasm between the North and the South was formally and officially closed when President [William] McKinley signed the political disability bill." Combined with "Confederate flags returned, Southern soldiers marching in blue beside their comrades of the North, and all with faces set toward the future rather than to the past, a new and grander destiny awaits the American people."[75] Those who thought that "the lines of sectionalism" were again "washed out" and that the United States had returned to the time "when Washington blessed it—with no North or South, no East or West, with the Confederate gray and the Union blue blended into one color and fighting for one destiny," possessed a false sense of hope and security.[76] A snippet of an article from a Fort Wayne newspaper refuted the presumed harmony represented by returning the flags: "Who wants the confederate flags returned? And for what purpose are they wanted?" The untitled paragraph's writer goes on to state that "no one has ever yet satisfactorily answered these questions," then asserts that the "flags ought to be destroyed at once, and the memories of treason that they represent be blotted out forever."[77] Former Confederates participating in combat and celebrations of U.S. victory in this new war were patriotic, but as they showed by wearing gray uniforms next to their brothers in blue (or canvas) and with the returned battle flags, this did not trump their identity as southerners and Confederates.

These hopeful feelings, combined with "the natural outgrowth of the war with Spain," led to the concept of the first "Blue and Gray Reunion." As leaders from the memorial organizations batted the idea around, veterans began weighing in on the suggestion. Some, such as ex-Union soldier Dr. E. G. Granville, stated, "I am in favor of anything that will still more strongly unite the men who took part in the great struggle between the states." He believed that the "last vestige of sectionalism will have disappeared when such a jubilee has been held." Union veteran Frank Braynard said, "some of the best friends I have are old 'Jonnies,' and I am sure it would be a most pleasant occasion." Former Confederate captain S. C. Ragan believed: "It is a very good idea and will be favored everywhere. It will be a love feast of the blue and the gray right in the midst of where the most bloody battles of the war were fought." Superintendent J. M. Greenwood, another Union veteran, thought that the reunion would bring the country closer together. He stated, "the matter we contended for in the past is settled now and I for one do not believe in digging up old bones of contention."[78]

While the notion received ample support, some suggested that the country should put the concepts of "blue" and "gray" behind them. Union veteran D. W. C. House was not in favor of a reunion, declaring: "Charles Sumner was right when he said all possible evidences of the civil war should be wiped out. I do not believe in veteran organizations or sons of veterans. They keep up the memory of the civil war." He continued, "We do not need to do that to teach patriotism." It was fine to "keep alive the memories of our wars with other countries, but not of that war between two parts of this country." Confederate veteran colonel J. W. Moore echoed House's sentiments: "Better quit all this 'blue' and 'gray' talk and all be American citizens. We ought to drop all that G.A.R. business and all the 'gray' organizations with no standard but American citizenship." Moore concluded, "it is time to drop all animosity and have no 'blue' and no 'gray.'" Resident J. F. Liddle of Warrensburg, Missouri, was a Union veteran and agreed with House and Moore: "the sooner we quit all talk about 'the blue and the gray' and just become American citizens, the better off we will be." He thought the whole topic was not a factor in daily life and did "not believe in any reunions which keep alive this remembrance of the dissensions between the two sections."[79] The fact that the responses to the reunions focused so much on the color of the clothing denotes how much the veterans' identities were still tied to the symbols their wartime uniforms represented. Wearing either the old outfits or new veteran uniforms fostered the continuation of that concept and allowed for the country to remain divided while seemingly united.

A NEW IMAGE & UNIFORMS

At the turn of the century, there was a drive to create a cohesive narrative of southern involvement during the Civil War using materials as symbols. Since uniforms were central to the memory and concept of envisioning the Confederacy, the path the UCV and the UDC chose was to begin the conversation and then the process of manufacturing new uniforms for veterans to wear to meetings, social events, and reunions, thus creating a uniform (in both senses of the word) identity for southern pride. The conversation concerned the acceptability of having new uniforms made for veterans to wear to reunions or to wear battle-worn uniforms played out in newspapers as well as in organizational meetings during the mid-1890s. The functional notion of manufacturing new clothing concerned the quality and fit of the old uniforms due to the passage of time—by then over thirty years. The Confederacy had a variety of uniforms throughout the war, and some of those that survived had holes from wear and tear, bullets, or moths. The practical alternative was to suggest the preservation of the old uniforms as a personal keepsake and the creation of new veteran uniforms. Instead of wearing various lengths of shell jackets or great coats, officials created a cohesive vision according to rank.

As announced in the April 1901 issue of the *Confederate Veteran*, J. F. Shipp, quartermaster general of the UCV, designed the veteran uniform down to its buttons. In his report to the organization's adjutant general and chief of staff, George Moorman, Shipp reported that he believed "the most important matter for the consideration and execution by this department" to be to "formulate and promulgate a regulation uniform in compliance with the resolution adopted at the annual meeting." He insisted that "formulating an appropriate uniform for an association such as ours required much reflection and investigation." The uniform was meant to represent the varying arms of service and rank in the southern army "to perpetuate a true type of our uniform as a part of the history of the Confederate States of America." The uniform of 1861 "was the pride and glory of the young Confederacy," he declared, "now revered by all survivors, and . . . respected by the American people." For uniformity, Shipp "selected the same shade, weight, and grade of goods for all uniforms—namely, No. 1238, Charlottesville Woolen Mills," because its "regulation shade, can be worn at receptions, funerals, and other occasions, as well as reunions"; all orders "outside of the cloth" should be referred to him. Shipp mentioned that the quality of goods was "first-class, and free from shoddy materials," which was a northern supply problem during the war. He suggested that it would even "serve as a proper uniform at death."[80] Shipp's report demonstrates the significance the southern people attached to the Confederate uniform, discussing the importance of securing "the regulation uniform" for regional reunions as if these men still belonged to the army.[81] The ability to craft all-new uniforms in one shade of gray for veterans to wear at reunions, instead of varying colors of gray and butternut, became an opportunity for the UCV and the UDC to recreate their vision of the struggle, consequently feeding the southern memory machine and its control over narrative and memory of the Civil War.

The UCV had the numbers to enable it to exert that control. One of its main functions was to organize reunions and fraternal gatherings. While many local newspapers and women's organizations assisted with this mission, the UCV's major organ was the *Confederate Veteran*. This magazine, first published in 1893, continued to appear once a month until 1932.[82] In its inaugural issue, the editor wrote, "the *Confederate Veteran* is intended as an organ of communication between Confederate soldiers and those who are interested in them and their affairs," the public, and even "those who fought on the other side." The periodical published reminisces of the war, news about new monuments, and reports on where reunions would occur and what the veterans needed to wear when in attendance. But General Editor Sumner A. Cunningham specifically mentioned that the magazine was "designed to publish advertisements."[83]

By publishing stories glorifying the service of the ex-rebel soldiers in their splendid or tattered gray, the *Confederate Veteran* kept alive a vision of Confederate glory and sold altered memories that fit the South's new narrative. Another way it accomplished this was through advertisements, specifically those for uniforms and their buttons. Those for the patented UCV buttons and ladies' hatpins, uniforms, and material insignia were available in 1901 from the UCV *Quartermaster*, while outside advertisements for uniforms did not appear until 1907.

The major reason the UDC supported obtaining new uniforms was concern for the presentation of the veterans. In his 1903 welcoming speech for the annual UDC convention, Governor D. Clinch Heyward of South Carolina praised the sacrifices of women during the war, noting that when the factories were "inadequate to the emergency, the handloom was made to supply the deficiency" and how women's "fairy fingers . . . boldly seized and made the coarse garments of the soldier." He continued, "through you and through your works the suffering, the courage, the patriotism and the glory of the Confederate soldiers shall endure forevermore" because "southern women . . . refused to let time teach forgetfulness." Heyward declared that there were "no truer historians than the women of the Confederacy" and that the "old, faded uniforms, precious heirlooms now in every Southern home, can find no more loving custodians than the daughters of the men who wore the gray."[84] This language solidified the wartime uniform's transition to prized heirloom and the need for new veteran uniforms to celebrate Confederate memory.

The UDC thrived on this kind of memorialistic rhetoric in speeches and its meeting minutes, believing it "a pretty idea and if practical a worthy thing" to provide veterans with new gray uniforms. The women considered it their duty to care for these men because they were the "last living links binding us to the old South, the land of chivalry, poetry and romance, and to those old times, of which it may truly be said, that 'Knighthood was in flower.'" To them, chivalry transcended history, and they believed that the era of the Civil War had produced "men and women who iived [*sic*] up to their creed of truth, justice, honor, valor and love of country."[85] The opportunity to provide veterans with uniforms allowed these women to replace tattered garments and recollections with the glorified image of the Confederacy, thus permitting them to recast their memories and adopt a heritage prettier than the reality. Veteran uniforms fostered the notion central to the Lost Cause narrative that the Confederacy had been full of pure and noble intentions. These clothes propelled the southern memory machine and helped these women reshape the image of the Civil War.

Confederate memorialization societies put considerable thought and effort into figuring out how to get new uniforms, how much they cost, and who would pay for them. The UDC increased its fundraising and contributions because members saw it as their duty to provide for their veterans. As early as the 1890s, individual chapters began purchasing new uniforms for the men they served. The Martha Reid Chapter of Jacksonville, Florida, gave its veterans "handsome new uniforms of the dear old Confederate gray, and they [both the uniforms and the veterans] were greeted with enthusiasm" when the men appeared at a Confederate Monument unveiling.[86]

Both Confederate and Union veterans fervently commemorated the war and their service. The creation and then continuation of veterans' associations gave life to their respective memory machines, and each side fostered a strong narrative of the Civil War both for those who lived through it and for future generations. The identity these organizations embedded in tangible pieces of themselves, such as uniforms, badges, and flags, were representations to the entirety of the United States. What the members wore or waved was representative of their past and their current political identity. These items provided a foundation for women's political involvement because they were able to represent themselves and continue a narrative of their perspective of the war and its causes for future generations. This amounted to an indoctrination of the next generation, from both sides, by passing on an almost elitist heritage of their service. This acted as a class barrier to public memorialization, demonstrated through a person's ability to purchase veteran uniforms and badges, and filters which veterans could actually participate in events.

7

WOMEN'S ORGANIZATIONS & THE MANUFACTURING OF MEMORIES

At the Twelfth Annual Convention of the United Daughters of the Confederacy in 1905, Sarah Gabbett from Atlanta, custodian of the Cross of Honor, presented her report. Mentioning some highly troubling incidents involving the sacred Southern Cross of Honor and other UDC badges, she said: "The Daughters of the Confederacy do not permit our badges to be bought or sold. They represent too much. They represent the blood, the life sacrifice of the Confederate soldier. Even so our Confederate cross bears on its face one assertion, that our cause is right, and will be so proved. *Deo vendice*. God our vindicator. God will prove us to be in the right."[1]

Gabbett's statement is a strong example of a political and cultural heritage claim that was prevalent throughout the early 1900s. Because they wore and bestowed their badges as physical representations of their Civil War service and sacrifice, veterans and their supporters invested these items with sentiment and sought to remove them from commoditization.[2] Both the Woman's Relief Corps and the UDC firmly believed in their historical truth and in the justice of their cause, using tangible items to represent their politics and identity to confirm their narratives.

Women became vital to popularizing the "Lost Cause" narrative and perpetuating stereotypes about why the South fought the war.[3] After 1900, their organizations grew rapidly and gained considerable political influence. In 1913 both the WRC and the UDC played key roles in the inauguration of Woodrow Wilson, the first southerner elected president since 1850. They used material items such as badges, flags, and uniforms to establish a tangible legitimacy to their causes and to provide women with a wearable form of political heritage. While the members of these organizations focused on assistance to their veterans, as the number of living veterans declined, the WRC and the UDC crafted new narratives for their Civil War memory machines, positioning women firmly at the center of their missions to perpetuate the true history of the war and to legitimize the Lost Cause.

Through the rise of memorial organizations such as the WRC and the UDC, women's groups funded, refashioned, and perpetuated their preferred memories through material goods. Wartime flags became relics or heritage pieces, while postwar production of flags and badges for celebration helped invoke sentiment and status. During this era, these groups expanded the manufacturing of veteran uniforms for both the Grand Army of the Republic and the United Confederate Veterans. Women's organizations played a substantial role in obtaining the garments and providing opportunities for veterans to be seen in public wearing them. During these years, Confederate organizations to some degree used African American and Native American veterans as "antiracist" props, who with the flags, badges, and uniforms they continued to emphasize, served as heritage tokens to perpetuate the South's narrative—specifically, the idea of Black Confederates and the loyal enslaved. The GAR, WRC, UCV, and UDC incorporated these groups into their organizations and "taught" their members how to commemorate "properly" by inviting these minorities to reunions, emphasizing their presence, and touting their value to the Union or Confederate cause.

THE GROWTH OF THE WRC & UDC

From the 1890s through 1912, the momentum gained by both the WRC and the UDC was profound. During this period, these groups developed their organizational goals, crafted their respective narratives of preserving the Union and the Lost Cause, and labeled themselves and their veterans through material means. Occasionally, they worked together or attended the same events, but these women often found it difficult to hide their distaste for one another because of what each group represented. Throughout the country, the WRC and the UDC promoted their aging and ever-diminishing ranks of veterans, which in turn allowed them to perpetuate their agenda and enhance their organization's influence. By incorporating badges, flags, and uniforms into everyday life, the UDC created a tangible and completely alternative narrative to the agony of defeat because these objects symbolized pride and were viewed as honorable. The WRC used the same elements to perpetuate a simpler task, but its narrative had to withstand the onslaughts of apathy in the North and of recast memory from the South to keep alive the importance of the Union's wartime victory.

Both the northern and the southern groups participated in creating badges and using wartime flags as tangible pieces representative of their culture and narrative. Such items played a critical role in shaping identity and memories of the Civil War and served "as reservoirs of realness" in the social identity of the women's societies.[4] For the WRC and the UDC, badges became a normal or acceptable physical way of expressing personal politics in a public manner. These items were tangible markers of service and sacrifice worn for all to see. Like other fraternal organizations of the period, the WRC and the UDC became avid badge makers and sellers for special events. Each of these societies expressed specific qualities through the images on their official and event items.[5] All of the organizations created badge committees and showed concern about obtaining supplies for making them or having them made as well as deciding on who was to pay for them and where to find the funds.

While the GAR prohibited its members from manufacturing or selling official membership badges without the council's consent, it permitted the WRC to make or commission its badges for specific events.[6] The WRC made commemorative event badges for monument unveilings; national, regional, or state encampments; and general celebratory events. They sold these badges to raise funds for their organization and for veterans. Much like crafting and repairing material items for the war, selling badges and raising money was a point of pride for these women, who put great effort into their creations. The badges were ornate emblems often consisting of multiple pieces and materials, including painted and printed silk ribbons, heavy metal pieces, and celluloid.[7] They could be complex, with multiple pieces linked together to identify any combination of one's state, commander, status as a delegate or representative, post, or the occasion (such as a meeting, convention, or reunion).

An Iowa newspaper article provided "items of information about the order of veterans," demonstrating how much ceremony and material culture mattered. The author not only discussed the typical GAR uniform and how it can vary but also devoted space to outline the badges worn by the members. The article stated that "on parade the veterans wear the badges of the army corps in which they served during the war, army society badges, regimental badges and the G.A.R. membership badge." It described the badge as "an honorary decoration bestowed upon each comrade at the time of his muster into the order." The article also covered the significance of the GAR button: "the bronze button worn by veterans in the coat lapel is a badge of recognition, being a conspicuous evidence that the wearer is a member of the GAR." The column noted, "it is unlawful for any person not a member of the order to wear either the G.A.R. button or official badge."[8]

Women also created special badges for themselves to wear to GAR events or for their own national conventions. Like the men, they were required to wear their official badge to events, but they crafted creative and beautiful devices for special occasions. The WRC Michigan delegate badge for the Fourteenth National Convention, held September 1–4, 1896, in Saint Paul, Minnesota, was adorned with a painting of a dusty pink Michigan rose cutting. Its silk ribbon has a poem at the bottom about the virtue of a Michigan rose.[9]

Badges symbolized sentimental pieces of identity for the men of the GAR and the women of the WRC. In 1895 GAR commander in chief Harvey M. Trimble accepted an invitation to attend the Thirteenth National Convention of the WRC. He thanked the women for the "great services" rendered by their departments and national staff. After his speech the national president of the WRC, Belle C. Harris, thanked "comrade" Trimble, stating that his attendance "will long be treasured by every member present" and that he had bound himself "inseparably to the memory and affections of the Woman's Relief Corps." To demonstrate her appreciation, Harris announced, "I present you with my own badge," and she "took off her badge and pinned it on the Commander-in-Chief's coat." Trimble replied,

Women's Relief Corps badge. Author's personal collection.

"I have enough badges to make a crazy quilt, and when that quilt is pieced, if it ever shall be, I shall look with many pleasant recollections at the block in which this badge is placed" because it "will bring to me the memories of [the] highly appreciate[d] loyal support" from the WRC.[10]

The Whitehead & Hoag Company, prominent "makers of badges, buttons, signs and advertising novelties" from Newark, New Jersey, made many of the GAR and WRC badges. These were typically constructed of grosgrain ribbon or celluloid.[11] A popular supplier, Torsch & Minks Badge Company from Baltimore, incorporated in May 1899 and, by that October, created the commemorative badge for the Reunion of the Blue and the Gray at Evansville, Indiana. The small, round celluloid pin is a little larger than a poker chip, with a printing of a Confederate soldier in gray uniform shaking hands with a Union soldier in blue uniform on a cream background.[12] Pins like this one demonstrate the change in understanding the reconciliation process. Opening the door to joint Union and Confederate veteran imagery visually rejoined the two white groups but silenced the effect and participation of African Americans.

Commemorative badge for the Reunion of the Blue and the Gray, 1899.
Author's personal collection.

The WRC and the UDC spent a significant amount of money and time crafting badges. References to badges in national convention journals convey their sentimental meaning to the women and their veterans. The quantity of badges possessed by one individual and the occasions for which they were created give insight into their owner's status within the organization. An abundant collection denotes active participation for the cause, and possessing such badges as the presidential or vice presidential badge suggests a deeper commitment and greater wealth than an average member. Because of how records were kept, state conventions better describe the financial benefits and costs of badges for these organizations on a smaller scale, but they are still difficult to distinguish. While they kept meticulous records of what materials each department received, quantities of items produced, and where the money went, the WRC frequently lumped in badges with other materials. This makes it difficult to calculate exactly how much money was spent and made on badges, preventing a financial statistical analysis.[13] The WRC and UDC sold badges to fellow members, to veterans, and to the public on specific celebratory occasions. Both organizations had rules prohibiting the sale of membership badges to outsiders, but the UDC experienced trouble with their manufacture when it came to their badge patent.

According to the UDC's annual meeting minutes, Mr. S. E. Theus of Savannah, Georgia, created the design of the group's badge, which was accepted during their first general convention. The UDC made a contract with the Theus Brothers for the "manufacture and sale of these badges at a cost of $2.75 each. Later Theus Bros. agreed to furnish these badges at $2 each when ordered in lots of fifteen." While no order was that large, by 1901, the enterprise filled all orders at the $2 price because both brothers were "Confederate Veterans, who love the Stars and Bars, and the matter is one of patriotism with them." But the UDC ran into a problem with a New York firm counterfeiting their official badges. This firm "manufactured and placed on the general market" their badge, but, according to the UDC, "the workmanship and material are not equal to those of the official badge," so they were instead selling "inexact imitations." While the committee was angry that a northern firm was selling knockoffs, they were kindly disposed toward those who bought them because they were either "a lover of the Confederacy or eligible to membership in one of the Confederate organizations." Unfortunately, "many true members of our order have purchased these counterfeits in good faith." Even these ersatz badges were significant because they identified the wearer as a Confederate daughter, "a member of a united body of women" who understood their "sense of the high purpose for which they were organized." While these items were used to hold other ribbons for specific events, they were also the physical manifestation of their wearers' ideological underpinnings for a world built on strict class structures. To be an active member of the UDC, its requirements suggest that a woman had to have a certain amount of money. These badges insulated their wearers' social standing and identity.[14]

UDC members acknowledged that their badges and what they represented were not always favored. As recorded in meeting minutes, one delegate from Missouri mentioned, "in St. Louis your badges may not always provoke the pleasant smile that greeted us on every hand in Charleston— they may even subject you to unfriendly glances." But she begged her fellow ladies to remember that "the hearts of your sisters here are as responsive as they are in the South."[15]

To obtain a badge, members of the UDC could submit orders, but they "must be accompanied by a permit, signed by the President and Secretary of the Chapter in which the purchaser holds membership."[16] To these

United Daughters of the Confederacy badge.
Author's personal collection.

women, the badges and medals with which they adorned themselves and their veterans were the "most precious possessions—'badges of honor.'" In a speech to the assembly, Sarah Gabbett of Georgia compared them to what the Danes wore when they had invaded England hundreds of years before. Their badges and medals "were intended to preserve the memory of great deeds, grand achievements, or faithful performance of duty. They are, in reality, memorial coins."[17]

During July 1898, Mrs. Alexander S. Erwin designed what became known as the "Southern Cross of Honor." The UDC chose the cross because it "is the universal symbol of the highest dignity, honor, and self-sacrifice." The front of the medal features a cross with the Confederate battle flag encircled by a laurel wreath and the inscription "The Southern Cross of Honor." On the back, the motto "Deo Vindice," which means "God our Vindicator," and "1861–1865" are next to the inscription "From the U.D.C. to the U.C.V."[18] It was one of the most prestigious awards given by the UDC. Veterans who received this award wore it with their other badges as a mark of honor "to stand as a record for all time of the memory of those men who represented all that was lofty in principle, pure in patriotism, and dauntless in courage" for the Confederate cause.[19]

Because the Southern Cross of Honor was so coveted, people occasionally created fakes. Spotting a fake badge is easy for those who have seen and held an authentic example. Often, the creator of a counterfeit did not use the same metal as an original, so the weight and the color would be off, or the forger did not accurately print the wording.[20] Schwab & Company, "who furnishes the U.D.C. with crosses," intentionally "manufactured bogus crosses by the thousands." This was discovered because the president of the Florence, Alabama, UDC chapter took a "bogus cross . . . from the coat of a negro." Schwab reproduced the crosses and "so carefully avoided a perfect imitation that the patent law was avoided." Thus, the UDC could not take legal action against the company or stop the production of more fakes but could only "challenge any one wearing a bogus cross" and "insist on its destruction."[21] The sentiment and value imbedded in the Southern Cross of Honor meant that allowing fakes to exist diminished its value and harmed the organization's narrative.

Because there were no Confederate government awards, southern veterans clearly coveted the real crosses. In an instance recounted by a UDC delegate at the Twelfth Annual Meeting, "a veteran called at my house to ask directions as to the way he could obtain the cross." She referred him to the president of the Atlanta chapter, "explaining the necessity of a certificate of service, with proper endorsement." This man wanted to obtain the cross the honorable way instead of obtaining a fake, unlike "two men who wore the cross [who] had said to him: 'Why take the trouble, you can buy them? We bought ours for 40 cents each at the reunion at Louisville.'" He proudly stated, "a cross I could buy with money would be worth nothing to me."[22] This story oozes with the concept of southern honor these women perpetuated: the veteran pursued the more difficult path to obtaining the Southern Cross through legitimate channels instead of paying forty cents to a vender. The memory machine was working.

Unpacking the idea that someone would replicate the Southern Cross of Honor illustrates not only the significance of these medals and badges to veterans' identities, memories of their service, and concepts of heritage but also the power the Civil War memory machines held over the nation. It specifically speaks to how important loyalty to the Confederacy remained more than thirty years after the war. The fact that a "bogus cross" was taken from an African American man's coat is another matter entirely. It was during the counterfeit troubles with Schwab & Company that Gabbett "received an envelope containing a clipping from a newspaper, the photo of a negro in [Confederate] uniform, and an article stating that the negro would be given a Cross of Honor." She also received "in a batch of certificates an application from a camp for a Cross of Honor for a negro" and reassured her fellow members that she "of course . . . refused the application."[23] This quick refusal to acknowledge African American participation, however, would not always be the case for UDC chapters. Because there were no Black Confederate soldiers, the idea of an African American man wearing a Confederate veterans' uniform and receiving the highest badge of honor in the early 1900s seems absurd, but this example highlights the importance of material representations of identity. Those objects help illuminate the exclusivity of Confederate organizations through the eyes of UDC members and how that shifts as time progresses and agendas change. These women were in it to win the nation when it came to the memory war. With exclusive access to badges and uniforms, they attempted to preserve the southern fairytale, and the only way that could succeed was to find room for African Americans in their narrative whether Black people wanted to be there or not.

When the UDC held its Eleventh Annual National Meeting in Saint Louis, Missouri, in October 1904 during the World's Fair, which lasted until December, they created a special ribbon to commemorate the event. On a white ribbon the gold lettering denoting the event, organization, place, and year slants in the center. The ribbon has two red stamps in opposing corners. The top contains bears and the slogan "United We Stand Divided We Fall," with Roman numbers underneath. The bottom stamp is larger, denoting "Universal Exposition" at the top and "Commemorating the Louisiana Purchase 1903" underneath it. A figure holding a sign, reading "PAX," completes the lower stamp.[24]

Many times throughout the meeting, when discussing the World's Fair, delegates referred to Saint Louis as "the greatest city of the Louisiana Purchase." Those from Missouri were proud to host both the UDC and the World's Fair at the same time. The president of the Missouri Division, Mrs. A. W. Rapley, remarked, "each delegation will find on the World's Fair

grounds a rallying place representative of their State." As she listed the
highlights of Tennessee, Georgia, and New York, she listed several states
in rapid succession and noted that "every one of these States has United
Daughters chapters, and a cordial welcome will be extended to you all" as
an encouragement for them to visit the properties. Lastly, Rapley recognized Mississippi, which created "a replica of Jefferson Davis' last home,
Beauvoir," as part of its exhibition. She declared, "there is none of Southern blood who see it that their hearts do not swell with pride when memory recalls our dead chieftain," assured that this structure "would be more
pleasing to him than the loftiest monument in marble or bronze." Rapley
ended with a poem: "When bronze and granite shaft shall crumbling line
/ In ages hence, in Southern women's hearts will be / A folded flag, a bril-
liant page unrolled, / A deathless song of Southern chivalry."[25] Having a
strong presence at the 1904 World's Fair allowed former Confederates to
celebrate their Lost Cause in physical architecture. People from all over the
world were able to see the structures that mattered to former Confederates
and to see members of the UDC proudly wearing their badges and waving
their rebel flags, which elevated their profile and gained them international
attention.

UDC members proved adept at raising money for their veterans and
their cause. They often did this through the sale of badges. This was successful because of the variety of souvenir badges they could sell not only to
themselves and their veterans but also to the public for commemorative
events such as monument unveilings. The organization understood the
importance of these items for fundraising, so they allotted specific lines
in their budget for them and lauded selling achievements. Buttons alone
raised $25.54 at the UDC's Tenth Annual National Meeting.[26] At the Four-
teenth Annual Convention, after contributions from twenty-six people, often just $13.00 per person, the "Badge Fund" totaled $426.50. Proceeds
from these items went toward funding monument and caring for veterans.
From November 1907 to November 1908, the Jefferson Davis Monument
Association earned $26.00 from badge sales.[27] While these numbers seem
small—the WRC had similar sales—badges were one of the cheapest and
most readily available items that could generate revenue.

The same northern companies—Whitehead & Hoag, Meyer's Military
Shop, Torsch & Minks, and others—that manufactured badges and rib-

bons for the WRC and the GAR also manufactured items for the UDC, the United Confederate Veterans, and their Confederate memorials and commemorative celebrations. A letter written by the manager of Whitehead & Hoag requested "a picture of the home of Jefferson Davis" for reproduction on "a handsome badge, suitable for distribution among the ladies attending [the] next Reunion in June 1905." While its main office and factory were based in New Jersey, the company had offices throughout the country, including in southern cities. These badges were often ordered in large quantities; for the 1905 Louisville reunion, one camp ordered "13—State Vice Presidents [badges,] 6—National Officers [badges, and] 200—Delegates [badges]" on gray ribbon printed in black.[28] For a profit, these companies assisted in selling Confederate memory and heritage not only to the UDC and UCV but also by proxy to anyone who saw former Confederates proudly wearing their badges celebrating their version of sacrifice and heritage. Making those items publicly raised awareness for the southern cause and gave tangible validity to the Confederate identity.

In addition to the importance of the badges as a method of fundraising for veterans' organizations, they became an important signifier of those who had endured the struggles of the Civil War.[29] While men wore badges made by women's organizations, women wore them as a way to display their heritage and the exclusive nature of the group to which they belonged. Such women viewed themselves as part of a special group, and only those who had lived through the war and followed their organization's rules could wear their badge or be in their club. These badges physically allowed them a way to delineate class apart from financial means.

FUN WITH FLAGS

On February 23, 1905, the Senate Committee on Military Affairs agreed with a House resolution "to return to the proper authorities certain Union and Confederate battle flags." The War Department at the time stored 544 flags of different states, with approximately 100 belonging to the Union "and about 440 Confederate flags recovered at the fall of the Confederacy." Prior to this resolution, various secretaries of war had returned 22 Union flags to states, while "22 Confederate flags had been delivered, mostly to the organizations in the Northern States who had captured them during the war." In anticipation of future requests, Congress ventured to return "all flags (Union and Confederate) to the authorities of the respective States in which the regiments which bore these colors were organized, for such final disposition as they may determine." Lawmakers acknowledged that "all civilized nations of the world" took trophies in "war against foreign enemies" to be "carefully preserved and exhibited as proud mementoes of the nation's military glories." By this time, however, "over twenty years have elapsed since the termination of the late civil war," and "many of the prominent leaders, civil and military, of the late Confederate States are now honored representatives of the people in the national councils or in other eminent positions" whose "talents" administer "affairs of the whole country." In hopes of "treading the broader road to a glorious future," the government gave back the flags.[30]

Releasing these flags was a symbol of unity and hope for the future, but it gave back to former Confederates a tangible representation of memory from their service. In 1887 President Grover Cleveland was against this idea, citing the "war of the rebellion by the Confederate forces"; when asked his preference, he had requested that "no further steps be taken in the matter, except to examine and inventory these flags and adopt proper measures for their preservation." Because the president left the decision to Congress, restoration to the states passed, although almost twenty years later. Interestingly, the congressional measure concludes that "the loyalty of the Southern States is nowhere questioned" because the "sons of the men who carried many of these flags have entered the Army of the United States." It cites the "organizations of men who wore the blue, as well as men who wore the gray," and how happy they would be "to have again in their keeping the ensigns under which they marched to victory or defeat."[31] Multiple petitions to return the flags had failed previously, but Congress now deemed it best to release the trophies of war during a time of reconciliation in the early twentieth century. Returning these material tokens of Confederate identity demonstrated the importance of tangible representations of self and shows the successful development of northern sympathy for the southern cause. This action provided fodder for the main argument of the pro-Confederate narrative and validation of the feelings that southerners had a right to celebrate their service, that it was "national history."

The preservation of flags after the war and the making of new ones for memorialization meetings became a strong tie to how women and veterans viewed their place in society. At Florida's capitol, a "strange and beautiful ceremony of the Restoration of the Battle Flags" took place. Confederate veterans "stood, in two lines, about the speaker's desk to receive the eight men, old and gray, clad in the faded uniform of the Confederacy, and bearing in their hands, sturdy and resolute, all that remained of Florida's captured flags." The banners were "tattered, hanging in shreds, some with a broken staff, all smoke-begrimed, riddled with bullet-holes, blood-stained." The room was silent, which "made audible [the] stifled sobs and sighs," then came a "voice of prayer, asking the God of Battles to bless a reunited country."[32] This event perfectly illustrated Confederate feelings: southerners felt vindicated in their actions and used these material objects vested with sentiment in justifying their position.

Another example of displaying returned flags was during the 1905 UCV reunion in Louisville, Kentucky. UCV secretary of the Finance Committee, R. E. Hughes, wrote to Major John H. Leathers, expressing the desire to create "a very attractive feature" for the reunion by "securing, through the Veterans' organization or otherwise, these war-torn silken banners of the stars and bars, for display under glass in some Louisville hall during reunion week." He was "convinced this feature alone would add several thousand visitors to the attendance."[33] Welcoming their reacquired tattered emblems while wearing their old gray Confederate uniforms or displaying the "war-torn" flags at a reunion would speak volumes. Those tangible pieces of material, what they had carried and what they had worn in battle, were not just items of memory but physical representations of their current identity.

At the Thirty-First National Convention of the WRC, one member recounted an encounter with the UDC. She recalled that this woman "leveled her lorgnette on the flag I was wearing, and with a sneering laugh said, 'We do not recognize that in the South. I am from Jawja.'" The WRC member admitted that her retort was just as impolite as the southern lady's: "Oh, I do not have to be told that. . . . [Y]our dialect is exactly like that of your negro field hands." The northerner defended her response to her audience, saying, "I think it fairly matched [given] the gratuitous insult to the flag," then furthered her defense with the statement, "men have been hung in time of stress for less treasonable utterances than those of this woman."[34]

This story illustrates the ties created between a region's wartime flag and its identity. The northern woman felt personally insulted because the physical representation of her identity was disparaged. Members of the UDC felt with a similar intensity: the North Carolina branch deemed the "Southern Cross" the "most sacred of all flags," stating that "no other flag can ever take its place in our hearts."[35] Not only did they promote their version of history and their cause but also in this case could blatantly and publicly state their opinions without facing the typical consequences that men who exhibited the same sentiments and actions would have faced.

The flags were important to these organizations because they assisted in furthering the "true history" they wanted to preserve. WRC members loved the U.S. flag, which they viewed not only as a patriotic symbol but also as a tangible object to preserve their memory of the Civil War. They held it as a sacred symbol to "remind us of our obligation to its defense," and their "love and veneration for it . . . [grew] stronger" because it helped them realize "what it has cost" and what "that glorious emblem stands for."[36] These women believed that it was the states' duty to honor, love, and teach the story of the U.S. flag because they needed to impress "upon the minds of the boys and girls their duty to 'Old Glory'" in order to remember the sacrifices and perpetuate their patriotic agenda.[37] According to a speech given during the WRC national convention in 1913, a member found herself at a "patriotic" event that winter in Washington, D.C., at which she viewed a deliberate insult to the U.S. flag. The Daughters of the American Revolution had loaned the UDC their hall one evening for their event, which President Wilson attended. The flagrant foul of the evening was the presentation of the "rebel flag" to the UDC from the man who supposedly created the design. She stated that the woman who presented the flag used "absolutely treasonable language" and "deliberately waved the flag over and around the head of the President of the United States," whose first memories as a child included Sherman's March to the Sea and whose later historical writings helped inspire the prosouthern film *The Birth of a Nation*.[38]

In one edition of the North Carolina UDC meeting minutes, a member pays special tribute to the woman who sewed the first Confederate flag. The caring way the author describes the stitched "stars and bars on a field of blue" that "wrought the emblem that our fathers fought under" conveys a connection to identity. It illustrates the love and memory of that flag and the desire for their children to "love [the flag] until the South forgets, which the South never does."[39] At one national meeting of the UDC, the opening speaker described the mission of their organization: "under the flag of the victor," they now assembled "to commemorate the heroic deeds of our dead and hand down true history to our children."[40]

UNIFORMS

During the first decade of the twentieth century, the need for veteran uniforms expanded in both the GAR and the UCV. While both organizations strongly suggested or even required their members to have one set, the discussion about men attending public events in uniform grew. While many factors explain this surge, the public nature of the events they attended and the ability of their uniforms to distinguish identity and loyalty to their wartime side was crucial. These groups appeared happily "united" once more, but they were united separately by the color of their material culture.

For GAR members, parades were the most common type of public event arranged to display their uniforms, specifically those for Memorial Day. The *Omaha Daily Bee* described the scene of "aging veterans of the civil war" lined up and marching in the Chicago Memorial Day parade in 1900. They gathered in front of the Chicago Art Institute "in their faded blue uniforms," marching toward burial plots in cemeteries, where they "decorated the graves of their comrades." At the same time "Confederate veterans held a service at their monument in the confederate plot." Marching through "the Grand Army of the Republic plot," the old rebels "passed through the lines of federal veterans" and "laid their tributes of peace on the graves of their former enemies."[41] While they had not been comrades in arms, the respect demonstrated in this story highlights the difference between the generation who fought and the generation who observed.

After the death of President McKinley, a Civil War veteran, the GAR announced a special event and issued orders to "the veterans of the Department of the Potomac." The comrades of the organization were to escort the president's "remains from the Executive Mansion to the Capitol," with "post colors properly draped" and wearing "the usual badge of mourning." All "comrades must appear in uniform, if possible, or dark coat and hat, and under no circumstances will those wearing straw or light colored hats be permitted to participate."[42] Confederate veterans also participated in escorting McKinley's body. They were "attired in civilian dress, but marching with a soldierly bearing and alacrity that gave indisputable evidence that the men who were marching there had seen military service and plenty of it." These men were last in line and concluded the military portion of the parade.[43]

Not every southerner supported the ex-Confederates wearing "a uniform of gray." As Leon Jastremski noted in his response in the *Opelousas Courier,* the editor of the *Shreveport Caucasian* had voiced his frustrations with the management of Confederate reunions. That newspaperman had argued for "solemn assemblages" instead of "pleasurable and noteworthy Confederate reunions." Instead of wearing a uniform for reunions, he had suggested a preference to "substitute for the uniform of gray 'the button' on the lapel of the coat." This inspired mocking from the editor's critics—Jastremski was one—who asked on "what kind of coat" would he suggest a button be worn. Jastremski acknowledged the *Caucasian*'s editor "to have been a good soldier and a good citizen," but "he was never considered an authority on dress and the fashions," so his "opposition to the uniform of gray should be considered from the standpoint of good taste as a strong argument in its favor." He continued, explaining that "the rules of the United Confederate Veterans merely prescribe uniforms which they may wear, if they choose to get them, at their own expense," but "veterans who prefer other clothes are welcomed at the reunions as heartily as if they had uniforms." Jastremski reported that "the cost of a uniform ranges from $6 to $25, and as as [*sic*] uniform will answer for every purpose, for traveling or to attend functions and parades, the veteran with one is fitted out for years." That being said, there were numerous reports of UDC chapters raising funds and paying for Confederate veteran uniforms as a service to their cause.[44]

Jastremski continued his argument in favor of gray uniforms by reminding his readers that "the old antagonists of the U.C.V.'s, the Grand Army of the Republic, are a uniformed body," like many other fraternal orders and organizations. He added, "last, though not least, our brave old comrades at the Soldiers' Home" also wore "the same 'uniform of gray' that the chronic objector has so roundly denounced." Jastremski argued that "a mass of valuable records, trophies and mementoes" stored at Memorial

Hall in New Orleans expose "the falsehoods which had received widespread circulation throughout the country, by which the youth of the South were being taught to regard their fathers as traitors and bushwhackers." Thus, material things, such as uniforms, badges, flags, and war objects, assisted in cultivating the knowledge of the Confederacy's "true history" and providing a counternarrative for their children and their former enemies. He concluded that the "records, the monuments, and the history of the Southern cause,"—again, all tangible objects—"will be preserved by faithful and loving guardians, and that the heirlooms that they will soon leave behind them, shall not pass away, 'unwept, unhonored, and unsung.'"[45]

The *Yorkville Enquirer* of South Carolina reported a story about former general Joseph Wheeler being "snubbed" at a Confederate reunion. His fellow ex-Confederates were unpleasant to "'Fighting Joe' Wheeler, the dashing cavalry leader of the South in the Civil War," at a recent reunion in New Orleans because he "appeared in the uniform of a brigadier-general of the United States army," which he wore during the Spanish-American War. Wheeler was questioned about his choice in clothing, with one man asking what he thought "Lee and Jackson would say to your appearance at a Confederate reunion in that uniform?" The general was "deeply hurt by the attitude of his old comrades" and stated that he wore it "to show the veterans that sectionalism was indeed over, when a general officer of the Confederacy had the right to wear the uniform of a general of the United States army." But the veterans believed that "the uniform was out of place at their reunion" because "all the veterans wear Confederate gray on these occasions," and many times the officers appeared "in the uniforms they wore in the sixties" as they "marched beneath Confederate battle flags." Clearly, Wheeler misjudged his fellow "ex-Confederates" and how their identity was more entangled with their uniforms than he realized. An editorial comment below the story sarcastically noted, "Oh, yes, they have buried the hatchet and shaken hands across the bloody chasm!" Then it concluded with the statement, "they are rebels now, as they have always been."[46] The rejection of Wheeler in his U.S. uniform at the Confederate reunion betrays the reconciliatory notion of the time and further illustrates the importance of worn physical representations of identity to Confederates.

Because of this importance, some local UDC groups convinced their state to pay for new veteran uniforms. The General George Burgwyn Anderson Chapter in North Carolina declared that since "these men gave four years of splendid service and self-sacrifice to the Commonwealth," North Carolinians owed it "to their [veterans'] dignity and self-respect to clothe them in new and suitable garments."[47] It became a point of pride at both regional and national meetings of the UDC for chapters to proclaim how they supported veterans in purchasing new uniforms. In 1903 the Robert E. Lee Chapter in Louisiana "undertook a sunshine work in defraying the expense of three veterans to the reunion, giving each a new suit of gray." Shortly before the reunion, one of the three men "was called to the great reunion beyond the skies," so the women "saw to it that he started on the long journey dressed in his suit of gray."[48] When recounting the yearly financial report for the fourteenth annual convention of the North Carolina Division, each chapter was asked, "What have you done to aid and support Veterans?"[49] Several representatives confidently replied that they had furnished uniforms to a number of veterans for the upcoming reunions, thereby fulfilling their duty and furthering the "true" memory of the Civil War.[50]

These organizations, both Union and Confederate, obtained their veteran uniforms from a number of different companies. Established in 1885, Burton-Pierce placed multiple advertisements in the retailers' newspaper *Men's Wear.* In them they showcased a number of styles, including those worn by the Confederate veterans, and boasted, "we guarantee every suit to be all wool, indigo dyed in the wool high tensile strength, [and] identical in shade with every other suit."[51] This was exactly what the UCV and UDC wanted—even if it came from a northern manufacturer. Another supplier, M. C. Lilley, established in 1865, devoted itself to the exclusive manufacturing of military uniforms and equipment for the active-duty military, fraternal organizations, and eventually veterans.

Levy Bros. was a clothing company located in Kentucky, a Union border state during the Civil War that also provided troops to the South. When a UCV reunion and parade were scheduled for the summer of 1905, the company provided "goods sold to the Reunion Committee," requesting payment of "$5.00 for the suit and $.90 for the hat." A June letter to William Haldeman from the company requested that he petition the UCV Executive Committee to reconsider the parade route because "about fifty retail merchants doing business on Market Street" asked the committee's chairman "to have the parade pass their doors," not out of any selfish motive, but "merely to see the parade." But the company added, "you no doubt are aware that the main reason this body is brought to Louisville is to benefit our retail as well as our wholesale trade," and the merchants "have given liberally to your cause and will decorate appropriately in order to make our houses attractive."[52] The Retail Merchants' Association in Louisville purchased a subscription from the UCV for $2,000. This transaction benefited the merchants and their bottom line, helped underwrite the UCV's costs for the reunion, and promoted the efforts of the Lost Cause by providing a place for Confederate veterans—in veteran uniforms—to publicly present themselves.[53]

Levy Bros. created their own pamphlet, *U.C.V. Regulation Uniforms*, also highlighting their location in Louisville. The detailed instructions describe the "time necessary to complete Uniforms" as "ten days or two weeks," provide diagrams on how to self-measure and where to record measurements for fit, and explain that the regulation uniform "consists of Coat and Trousers only" and vests are an additional cost. It also includes descriptive diagrams for insignia of rank, just like the 1861 Confederate uniform manual. The pamphlet even provides fabric samples and pricing together so veterans could feel the quality of the material they would wear. Every suit included UCV buttons as "adopted by the U.C.V. Association," meaning every veteran was guaranteed basic buttons but could purchase extra. They could select their style of coat, ranging from a regulation blouse to a double-breasted military cut. The basic coat and pants were as little as $5 for the lowest quality cloth and up to $16.50 for the best quality and most ornate veteran's uniform, not including the vest or an extra pair of trousers. The pamphlet even lists the various sundries veterans could order, including hats, caps, hat cords, leggings, flannel shirts, UCV buttons, stars, bars for their pants, and UCV wreaths.[54] Adding "sundries" such as stars, bars, or trouser stripes assisted in distinguishing veterans by class: The more ornate the uniform, the more money that veteran had to assist in crafting the Lost Cause narrative perpetuated by southern memorial organizations. The finer the uniform, the cleaner the image of noble Confederate service.

The physical process of obtaining these new uniforms embodies an even deeper contradiction because northern clothiers manufactured many of them. For a profit, as with the badges, northerners fed the southern memory machine, assisting Confederate veterans by remaking white, rebel, martial manhood and peddling their interpretation of the war as represented by pristine new veteran uniforms to the rest of the country. The narrative that "former" Confederates simply wanted to remember their sacrifice during the time of joint struggle and forget that they fought for slavery was wrapped in a blue-gray uniform coat and sold for eight dollars. Cheaper uniforms meant that more people could and would purchase their way into this exclusive club. While veterans and memorial societies bought the new outfits and promoted uniformity, the rest of the country consumed this narrative that a staged "heritage" was more important than the truth. For the companies that manufactured veteran uniforms, their overall goal was not to perpetuate the memory of one organization or the other but to make a profit off of both the GAR's and UCV's sympathetic leanings toward their respective causes. Through monetary transactions, manufacturers simply provided the tools necessary for each group to create a cohesive sectional memory, one blue or gray uniform at a time.[55]

The references to "new suits of gray" and placing its veterans in new veteran uniforms helped the UDC in its effort to perpetuate their "true" history of the war because it streamlined the vision of the Confederate in gray. This reality was harder to achieve than expected because the new uniforms physically demonstrated the financial and class differences of Confederate veterans. Listed above are the ideal versions of their veteran uniforms, but they do not accurately represent all of them. At the turn of the century, according to the M. C. Lilley catalog, purchasing an entire uniform cost approximately $25 (over $700 in 2022).[56] Understanding that those who could afford that were the exception instead of the average leaves a slightly different image. If a veteran was working within the confines of a budget, he made choices in the quality of cloth, type of buttons, and cut of the clothes. Even poor veterans were willing to sacrifice to visually participate in the organization, but concessions such as forgoing more-expensive UCV buttons resulted in them using replica general-issue CSA or new state buttons. Some opted not to line their coat because they lacked the fabric or the funds to pay for it. Those who prospered after the war and participated in veterans' events were distinguishable, which meant their class was showing. Even within the confines of the UCV uniform, there were more exceptions to the rule and less uniformity than was reported or desired.

The *Confederate Veteran*'s news sections and advertisements for reunions stated that "efforts are being made to induce all who attend to secure uniforms," but they did not tell the men how to obtain them.[57] In February 1907 the first uniform advertisement, "Pettibone Uniforms," from the Pettibone Brothers Manufacturing Company of Cincinnati, Ohio, appeared in the magazine. The graphic was a veteran in full garb resting his arm on a cannon wearing a pin with the U.S. and Confederate flags crossed. Those who ordered from this company were specifically told to mention seeing the ad in the *Confederate Veteran*. Pettibone Brothers also manufactured items for the GAR.[58] The spring 1907 UCV reunion in Richmond, Virginia, the former Confederate capital, was set for that May 30–June 3, and the organization wanted it to be a spectacle. M. C. Lilley & Company purchased its first advertisement in the magazine in March, offering catalogs and proclaiming, "we are official manufacturers of uniforms and goods you need."[59] With every subsequent edition, uniform advertisements became more and more frequent. In 1910 Levy Bros. began advertising uniforms in the magazine. The "Levy's Special" included a regulation UCV coat, trousers, and buttons for $8.00 and even offered "special terms for outfitting whole camps." Once Levy Bros. began advertising with pricing, Pettibone began doing the same, with "prices from $7.50 Up."[60]

Some women also donned uniforms to demonstrate that they were a "True Daughter of the Confederacy." One example, Mrs. Anna M. Knighton, was a nurse, a scout for Brigadier General John Morgan, and a mother whose son had served in the war; she appeared prominently in a scrapbook from the 1905 UCV reunion in Louisville. Priding herself on being a "rebel," at age eighty-two Knighton "ordered a suit of Confederate gray," which she wore during the reunion. She had it created to "conform as nearly as possible to the gray uniforms worn by Confederate veterans, even to the trimmings and the buttons," completing the outfit with a "scarf or tie of red and white."[61]

Much like during the war, the idea of women in this garb was not well received. As reported in the minutes of the Fifteenth Annual Convention in the report of the president general, "information has come to me that one of the most influential Camps, U.C.V., has adopted resolutions strongly disapproving of the wearing of Confederate uniforms, and the assumption of military titles by individual or bodies of Southern women." She stated, "no loyal woman of the South desires to usurp the prerogatives of our dear old Veterans or to incur their displeasure." She then presented the solu-

United Confederate Veterans' coat.
Author's personal collection.

tion: "let the [women's] uniforms be white—emblematic of the purity and truth of Southern womanhood."[62] Men wearing their old uniforms or newly manufactured veteran uniforms were an acceptable aspect of society, but women attempting to wear gray Confederate-like outfits were not—to do so encroached on male identity and blurred the lines between their service and sacrifice from the war. These women "needed" to embody the ideal of southern womanhood. By climbing down from their pedestal, women made the claim of men fighting for their honor a shaky pillar of the southern argument.

AFRICAN AMERICAN & INDIGENOUS VETERANS

African American and Indigenous veterans and their families continued to commemorate their Civil War service throughout the early twentieth century. White members of the GAR, WRC, UCV, and UDC publicly recognized their efforts to celebrate their sacrifice. In some cases both sides praised their efforts and their involvement in the organizations with the tone that parents tend to use to praise children. These groups took the memories and actions of people of color and added them to their own list of successes in an attempt to demonstrate white superiority and that the "others," who had to be taught how to commemorate properly, emulated them.

Much like the GAR, the WRC had African American–run departments in charge of local GAR assistance and memory preservation. During the Twenty-Ninth National Convention of the WRC, Assistant National Inspector Julia Mason, from Layton, Virginia, presented her findings after her travels through "Virginia, North Carolina, South Carolina, Florida, Georgia, and Tennessee hunting up the colored Corps." She explained to the convention, "there is a difference between being dumb and being ignorant," adding, "the colored people are not dumb, they are just ignorant— many of them." Being of mixed heritage herself, Mason believed that it was "going to take a good deal of teaching before some of the colored Corps walk just like our Rules and Regulations tell us." She believed, however, that "the strongest characteristic of the Negro race [was] loyalty." Many of the African American divisions she visited had not been inspected in years, and some charters still had their original supplies. She spent "two and three days drilling" the presidents and their officers "in the manner in which the ritualistic work" was to be administered.[63]

Mason believed that she could teach the African American WRC members "better than a white inspector" because her mother was half "Indian" and Mason herself was born into slavery; to free her, Mason's father had to pay $250. She believed that it was easier for freed Black members to ask her questions because they were not afraid of her. Mason claimed that "the colored are money-makers, too. The women just love to work to raise money for a good cause." She gave the example of corps who "buy the flowers and the flags to decorate the graves of the Union soldiers on Memorial Day." At one division in Florida, she found "twenty-two earnest loyal black women; although only two of them could read and write." Mason "had them memorize the ritual, and instructed them in the flag work." Because of her ethnicity, she also faced hardships while searching for Black divisions of the WRC. She had to sit in the Jim Crow–segregated railcars and was not allowed to wait in the ladies' waiting room at depots.[64]

African American veterans continued to participate in veterans' events and wear their identities on their bodies and on their lapels into the twentieth century. Historian Barbara Gannon has compiled an extensive list of African American and integrated GAR posts, one of which was the integrated W. W. Perkins Post No. 47, Department of Connecticut.[65] Whitehead & Hoag made a badge for the comrades of this post. About five inches long and two inches wide, it is made of red silk, with silver lettering and a blue strip centered diagonally and bearing "G.A.R." in bold silver letters. Both African American and white comrades of the post would have worn this badge on their coats.[66]

Black veterans took the material culture of their identity as GAR veterans seriously and endeavored to display their service and sacrifice like their

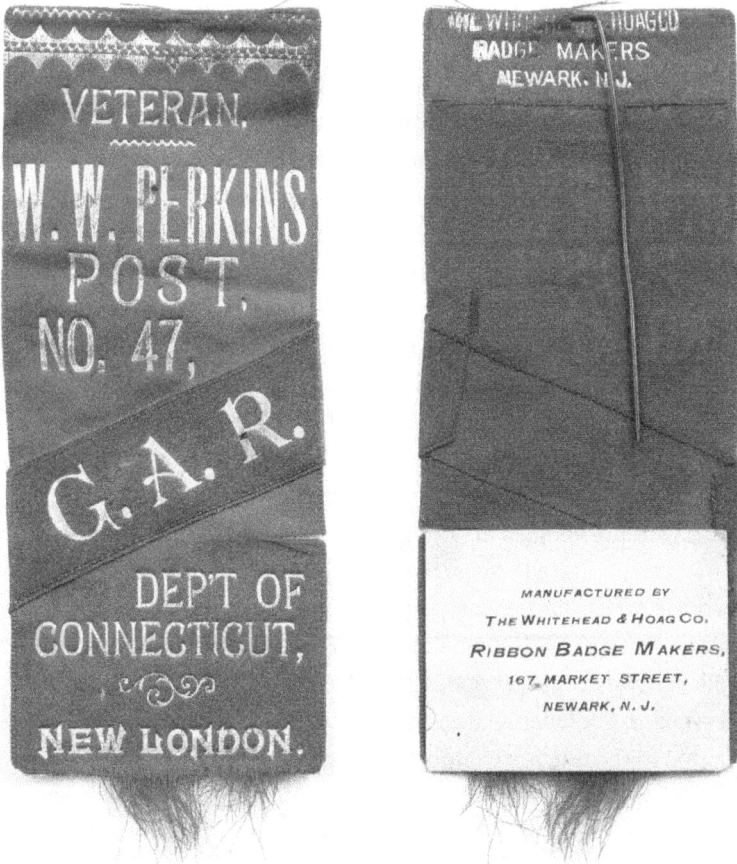

GAR badge created for the W. W. Perkins Post No. 47 (*front and back*).
Author's personal collection.

white comrades. In a photograph taken at a 1909 encampment, an African American GAR post in Lawrence, Kansas, demonstrates perfect compliance with the organization's uniform and badge regulations. The reunion picture was originally black and white and was later hand-colored to bring out the detail of the official dark blue suits, the striking red and blue on the U.S. flag, and the gold, red, and blue of the badges worn by some of the veterans.[67]

Gradually, the UDC began accepting African Americans claiming Confederate military service and lauding their sacrifice and service. The Fourteenth Annual UDC Convention heard tales from the New Orleans Chapter No. 72, which maintained "a small benevolent fund, used for emergency cases for needy Confederate soldiers and their families." Many calls were made upon the fund "for old negros, whose friends claim for them service in the Confederate army." The delegate from Louisiana concluded that those men were "probably body servants, having served their masters faithfully." Therefore, the ladies contrived "outside aid" because they did not "feel justified in using chapter funds" to assist them.[68] This story illustrates the evolution in how the UDC viewed African Americans claiming Confederate service and also set a precedent for how their perceptions and actions toward creating Black Confederate "veterans" changed after 1912. By assisting these African Americans with outside funds, the UDC was beginning its effort to wrap people of color into their Lost Cause narrative. Following their reasoning, if African Americans fought for the South, then it detracts from the Confederacy's war goal of protecting slavery and feeds into the narrative of the happy loyal slave and the principled enslavers fighting simply for their own rights and those of their states.

Indigenous Peoples also participated in Civil War commemoration throughout the United States. Some men joined the UCV while the women joined the UDC. This was especially popular in Indian Territory, which became the state of Oklahoma in 1907. They often participated with white people in these groups, attending meetings, celebration days, and reunions while waving Confederate flags. Yet their participation here, like their participation in the war, is a complicated narrative because it is very difficult to tell why they took part. Some wanted to commemorate their own service or the service of their family members, but others may have joined in Confederate events out of coercion by white people in the community.[69]

One newspaper article detailed the preparations for the reunion held in Louisville that year, noting that Indigenous veterans would attend. The journalist mentions that Brigadier General J. M. Ray from North Carolina arranged to bring a "big delegation" to the event, "accompanied by a squad of Cherokee Indians, members of the Soo-no-knee Camp of the United Confederate Veterans." They "expected to bring along two or three . . . old flags," specifically "one borne by the Rough and Ready Guards, the company enumerated by Senator Zeb Vance," and another "under which the Indians marched," purposefully paraded around by Indigenous veterans for everyone to see.[70] A report directly before the event again emphasized that Native American Confederate veterans were coming from North Carolina and were bringing their flags. The article touts that the veterans were "full-blooded Cherokee Indians" and that the "inspector General [Colonel W. W. Springfield] of [Brigadier General J. M. Ray's] staff, are going out to the Indian reservation to arrange for the attendance of the braves who fought for the Stars and Bars."[71] This story also plays into the idea that the races were congenial and, by linking the Indigenous veterans with the sentimental wartime battle flags, were attempting to add justice and validity to their narrative.

In 1910 the *Indian School Journal* highlighted tales of a Memorial Day celebration in Chilocco, Oklahoma. An article notes that "the Indian was no exception to the rule" in this event because "they took sides as well as the whites. But at this late day, when the passions of men have become cooled and reason has again been enthroned, all classes and all races can sit down together and discuss the dark period of our history without hatred and without rancor." The school gave an entire day to "patriotic devotion." People in uniform "all participated in the beautiful and impressive ceremony of 'the flag salute,'" and "the band opened with the 'Star Spangled Banner.'" Superintendent John R. Wise gave a speech about the origins of Memorial Day and explained that it was "set apart to honor the dead of those who died defending the Union, and latterly extended so as to inculcate patriotism and love of country among all our people," both "Union as well as Confederate."[72] This is an example that makes understanding the actions of Indigenous People's Civil War commemorations difficult: these are Native American students forced to participate in Memorial Day observations at an "Indian School" established and operated by white people.[73]

The UDC especially highlighted the role of Native People. At the Ninth Annual Meeting, the recording secretary of the Julia Jackson Chapter in Durant, Indian Territory, Maggie Darwin, said, "I feel proud to represent the grand country of the Choctaw Nation" because "in the war of '65 the Choctaw and the Chickasaw Nation furnished the Confederate Army seven brigades and seven full companies." She stated that "the Choctaws still hold their battle-worn flag," which "was presented and adopted June, 1863, by the Confederate Congress."[74] At the next annual meeting, another member of the Indian Territory UDC proudly reported at the Tenth Annual Meeting that they had a "baby division" that possessed "a fine record of work." The UDC considered this division "remarkable" because it included "wives and daughters of the original Americans, the noble red men themselves, the Choctaws and Cherokees, who fought in the Confederate Army."[75] Along that line of thought, at the Eleventh Annual Meeting, Mrs. W. T. Culbertson, president of the Indian Territory Division of the UDC, was introduced as "granddaughter of a half-breed Cherokee Indian," and the delegates "greeted her with applause." Culbertson described the UDC activity in Indian Territory as a "little star" that "has grown brighter and brighter." The first annual meeting of the Indian Territory UDC "was held August 23–25, at Checotah, Creek Nation, and was an harmonious and enthusiastic meeting." At that time the Stonewall Jackson and Jeff Lee Camp Chapters "presented 21 Crosses of Honor" at their memorial service for General John B. Gordon.[76]

Southern heritage groups in Oklahoma latched on to Native Peoples' representation, specifically Brigadier General Stand Watie, "our only Indian general," as the main symbol of Confederate identity in Indian Territory and Oklahoma. At the Twentieth Annual Convention, members from the Oklahoma Division described their endeavor to "locate and move the body of General Stand Watie" from "its burial place near the Kansas line to Tahlequah, his old home." They wanted to "erect a monument to the memory of this noble Indian soldier." They explained that their "committee is composed of three Cherokee Indian women, Mrs. Anderson, Mrs. Culbertson and Mrs. Pendleton, General Stand Watie himself having been a Cherokee."[77] At this same meeting, the historian for the Oklahoma chapter, Mrs. G. A. Brown, stated having found "valuable information regarding Indian tribes who served in the War Between the States on the Confederate side" and created "sketches of men and women who made Oklahoma great."[78] The next year the report by the same group stated that this committee was now "headed by a niece of this brave man [Watie]." She "compiled a history of his life," which was to be published as a pamphlet and sold for twenty-five cents each to raise funds for the monument. This section of the division's report finished with praise for "Oklahoma Daughters in honoring the memory of Gen. Stand Waitie, [who] honor not only a native Oklahoman and a great Confederate soldier, but [also] a man who stood for all that was noble and honorable." They claimed, "we show to the world that Oklahoma Daughters do not forget."[79] These statements ignore the fact that Watie came from Georgia and relocated to Indian Territory because of Indian Removal Acts of the 1830s and 1840s. Native soldiers were courted but not well provisioned by the Confederacy, so they were not a central component to the southern cause and not highly valued during the war. But because Watie was Cherokee and fought for the Confederacy, those who moved to Indian Territory, or Oklahoma, after the war and still loyal to the Confederacy, such as members of the UDC and the UCV, propped him up as their symbol and used his "Indian-ness" as authority in their identity and heritage claims.[80] Such actions complicate the commemorative narrative of the Civil War because people claiming Indigenous heritage were active in these organizations, which begs the question, how beneficial was this relationship for them?

MOVING FORWARD

After the election of Woodrow Wilson in 1912, the matter of inaugural festivities took an unexpected turn. Pro-Confederate organizations wondered whether it would be "permissible that the men who wore the gray in the conflict of half a century ago should find a place in the inaugural parade." The GAR declared it would "contribute its share in the parade by mustering as many as it may of the men who fought fifty years ago and who are still able to wear the old uniform and march this distance," that is, from where the president was sworn in at the Capitol to where he reviewed the parade at the White House. The "authorities in charge of that parade have come to the decision that there is no reason why the veterans should not march in uniform," so "Confederate veterans have been extended an invitation to participate in the ceremony."[81] Allowing both GAR and UCV members to march in the inaugural parade presented a façade of unity, but the event elevated the visibility of both organizations and memorial groups by making it nationally acceptable to view all Civil War veterans in their wartime uniforms.

While preparations were made for camps of Confederate veterans to attend the inaugural parade, members of the WRC became infuriated because those men wanted to carry their Confederate flags, soon making sure "that there would be no rebel flags in line" during the parade. The UDC also made plans to "sell silk Confederate flags during the parade" on Pennsylvania Avenue, but with the aid of the War Department and the chief of police, "not a rebel flag was sold."[82] These opposing situations for the same event provides examples of how each of these groups understood the wearing or waving of their identities through material objects. The men wore their veteran uniforms and came together to celebrate an important national event, while the women's organizations butted heads over which flag was acceptable to wave during the festivities. These illustrate the different feelings between those who fought and those who served in another capacity and their struggle for recognition of their service during the Civil War. If a uniform was just an article of clothing and a flag was just a piece of fabric, then there would have been no argument about which styles were permissible at a presidential inauguration. What each of those items meant ideologically and socially was clear and well known within their groups and across the nation. Confederate veteran uniforms and flags at the inauguration of the president of the United States were suspicious because they were the symbolic representations of a traitorous identity.

Many scholars have noted that Wilson's presidency led to the segregation of federal offices and promoted a chivalric narrative of the South during the Civil War and Reconstruction. But Wilson, or at least his inauguration, also appears to have affected how the public remembered those who were part of that narrative. These groups only continued to grow in numbers, prominence, and tension after the 1913 inaugural parade. The next large event of that year with both GAR and UCV veterans—the fiftieth anniversary of the Battle of Gettysburg—sparked a much larger debate about the suitability of wearing uniforms and waving flags and the symbolism behind those actions as well as who was welcomed to participate in such events.

8

THE BLUE &
THE GRAY

eadlines splashed across the *Evening Star* of Washington, D.C., told of "Thousands in Blue and Gray" erasing the "Mason-Dixon Line" at they gathered at Gettysburg, Pennsylvania, for a "Gay Reunion." As the nation prepared for the seventy-fifth reunion of the Battle of Gettysburg in 1938, newspapers across the United States touted the "joyous cavalcade" of veterans and spectators who flocked into the welcoming village. While the veterans from the North and South encamped separately, "no longer was there thought of a Mason-Dixon line." Grand Army of the Republic veteran John Sumer declared, "I love the old Confederates," as he headed across the street to their camp for a visit; "we're here not so much for a jolly time as to demonstrate our nation is one united." A reporter stated that Sumer's views were typical of both the Union and the Confederate veterans attending what everyone thought to be the final grand reunion.[1]

As lovely as those sentiments may be, the Woman's Relief Corps, the United Daughters of the Confederacy, and the Sons of Union and Sons of Confederate Veterans organizations harbored none of those thoughts and feelings. Instead, through the ever-present material culture of uniforms, badges, and flags, the GAR and UCV veterans taught future generations a different lesson than what they verbally espoused. Through uniforms and arguments over when it was appropriate to fly Confederate flags, veterans provided a continual example of separation between Union and Confederate descendants that still divides the United States in the twenty-first century. Because the memory machines of the North and the South provided symbols now encrusted with ideals, the wound of divisiveness remain open and festering.

The period from 1913 to 1938 witnessed the deep involvement of symbolic material objects in relation to the fiftieth and seventy-fifth anniversary commemorations of the Battle of Gettysburg.[2] What was worn then established a wider consumption of the reconciled-but-still-separate narrative, documenting the growth and decline of northern and southern memorial organizations. The contemporary conversation over the highly publicized film *The Birth of a Nation* also influenced reunions and the narrative of the organizations. The stories told in conjunction with the new technology of film established an even greater reach for the Lost Cause narrative, giving the story a veneer of legitimacy. Due to dwindling veteran numbers, the torch-carrying control authority over memory, identity, and narrative passed to the Sons and Daughters organizations toward the end of the 1930s. The culmination of the memory machine was the seventy-fifth anniversary of Gettysburg in 1938, when the display of the last few elderly veterans solidified the acceptance of wearing what was traditionally wartime garb during a time of peace.

THE 1913 GETTYSBURG REUNION

Preparations for the fiftieth anniversary of the Battle of Gettysburg began with an act of Congress on May 13, 1909. As 1913 began, the reunion became a daily topic of conversation in newspapers across the country. The *Chickasha Daily Express* in Oklahoma stated that "local veterans of the Civil War are taking great interest in the coming reunion of the Blue and Gray on the battlefield of Gettysburg next summer." Expectations were that the state legislature would offer financial assistance to "the old soldiers who are not able to pay their own expenses." The *Confederate Veteran* announced that "all surviving soldiers of the war of the state, north and south, shall be requested to take part as invited guests, under the direction of the commander in chief of the Grand Army of the Republic, that of the United Confederate Veterans, and under such order as these officers in connection with the commission may direct the United States flag only to appear."[3]

Unpacking these statements reveals a variety of meanings. Legislatures stepping in to assist veterans unable to pay for their travel to and stay in Gettysburg suggests that they were financially supporting the men from both sides residing in their state, while the appearance of this call in the *Confederate Veteran* may be a reminder that southerners continued to feel the economic effects of the war fifty years later. Funding provided by the states was in addition to the $100,000 that Congress appropriated for the celebration and the $250,000 the state of Pennsylvania allotted for the festivities. Most of this money went for tents, food, and camping accommodations, with several veterans sharing a tent. The nation was allotting thousands and thousands of dollars under the pretensions of reunification when that was not the reality of the situation.[4] A truly harmonious reunion would mean that white, Black, and Indigenous veterans from both sides were welcome, which was neither what happened nor the story that newspapers conveyed to the public. Last but not least, only the U.S. flag was to fly at the reunion. That statement sparked controversy and incited debates throughout the country, implying that Confederates would accept the United States and its flag as their sole symbol of identity instead of having a dual loyalty as U.S. citizens who continued to harbor the idea of southern Confederate nationalism.[5]

It did not take long after the announcement of the U.S. flag as the symbol of the event for Confederates and others to begin questioning the decision and voicing concerns about the restrictions. The *New York World* posited, "who are these Grand Army veterans that object to the presence of the Confederate uniform at the Gettysburg celebration in July?" After listing several battlefield positions there where these critics could not have participated, the writer states, "perhaps these objectors to the Confederate uniform were not at Gettysburg at all; but in any event they have missed the meaning of the semicentennial celebration," which was not a "gathering of Northerners or of Southerners, but of American citizens, with one flag, one nation and one history, and common memories of the most momentous struggle in the annals of human liberty."[6] That being said, the journalist then argued that to show they were American citizens from one nation, the rebel veterans needed to wear their Confederate uniforms and wave their Stars and Bars, both of which were material constructs resulting from and representing treason. The *New York World* was affiliated with the Democratic Party, as was President Wilson, which was strongly supported in the South. This could have been a reason for the newspaper to make these contradictory arguments: supporting the southern heritage of the president when he would be speaking at the event could have contributed to the push for allowing Confederate veterans to wear their uniforms.

Other advocates of allowing Confederate uniforms used various methods to make their point. Referencing the *New York World* article, the *Hattiesburg News* in Mississippi eagerly stated that the "evidences of the increasing solidarity of the country, in spirit as well as in law, and of the growing esteem of the Confederate soldier in all sections of the country" had rapidly multiplied. Union army veteran Henry C. Freeman from the Sixty-Fifth New York Volunteer Infantry weighed in on why GAR comrades would find "the wearing of the Confederate uniform" objectionable. He claimed that "the sight of the old gray uniform and the memories of the 'Rebel yell,' which latter no doubt still lie smouldering [*sic*] in their brain, [would] give rise to the fear of a resurrection of the civil war," and the old veterans would have to fight without the "chance of getting to the rear before being killed." In short, he verbally threatened the southerners' manhood by calling them chicken. Freeman even invoked the iconic image of Abraham Lincoln by contending, "were he alive today to attend the celebration it is plain that he would be the first to give a welcome to his old antagonists in gray."[7] In life, Lincoln believed that the United States comprised a single body politic, which allowed him in life to promote liberty as the lifeblood of the republic. Since Lincoln's death, however, his memory was used to invoke support or molded to fit into whatever image was needed to prove a point or champion a cause, such as what Freeman here argued.[8]

In February 1913 "a group of Confederate veterans, their tanned and wrinkled faces sometimes quivering with emotion," petitioned the commissioners organizing the fiftieth anniversary of Gettysburg "for the privilege of wearing their old gray uniforms at the reunion in July." A Union veteran on the Gettysburg reunion commission, Colonel Charles Burrows, had introduced a resolution "that no military uniforms be worn at the celebration by survivors of either army" in order to prevent fractures at the event. At the same meeting, a Texas veteran, Major General Felix H. Robertson, "begged for the privilege of carrying the old Texas battleflags in the celebration," to which "Union hands applauded." Robertson claimed no ill intentions, stating simply that the "reunion is not to celebrate a victory" but to "celebrate peace." He continued, explaining that southerners "quit fighting because we thought it was a hopeless job," but as for himself: "I love the Confederate gray. If I get the nerve to wear it on July 4 I want to wear it." Robertson concluded, "if you're going to celebrate a victory, all right, keep away the gray coats, but if you're going to celebrate peace, why, we helped to make it." After hearing such pleas, Burrows withdrew his resolution prohibiting uniforms and flags at the reunion. While excluding such items was no longer the popular sentiment for the majority of Union veterans, the attitude that Burrows expressed about uniforms and flags evoked emotional responses from veterans, committee members, and the general public.[9]

While the prospect of Confederate soldiers wearing their uniforms to national reunions caused a stir with a few northern representatives on the Gettysburg committee, it was quickly settled. When addressing the committee delegates, Governor John Tener of Pennsylvania "assured them that all veterans will be welcome and nobody will look at their clothes—they could wear garments in which they felt comfortable."[10] He stated, "we shall go there as survivors of a war which no human power had been able to avert," and the "victors in blue will greet with open arms the vanquished in gray, who fought there for a cause they believed was right, and they fought well." Confederate C. Irvine Walker concurred. "We shall go to Gettysburg, not to battle but to seal a lasting peace, wearing our gray and bearing the banners which we so gallantly followed on that gory field," he declared, adding that former Confederates were "willing to bury forever the bitterness of the past."[11]

In March 1913, Confederate veterans from the Lee Camp in Virginia were concerned about their ability to carry their "battle flags to the Gettysburg reunion." While there was "no prohibition of the use of such banners," the topic was "sidestepped in a way that led some of the veterans to think the flags" would not be permitted, which was "resented in no small degree." Virginia attorney general Samuel W. Williams expressed dissatisfaction with the concept of allowing only the U.S. flag, stating that "if the spirit of harmony of the occasion were marred . . . it would be because of opposition in the North." He declared that "he distrusted the good will of any man who preached good fellowship and then objected to the flag."[12]

Most Union veterans did not share New Yorker Burrows's distaste at seeing Confederate gray commingled with Union blue. In a letter to Dr.

Samuel Eastman, Colonel J. A. Watrous, a retired Union veteran, noted, "speaking for myself, I would vote to have them coming [with] their old uniforms or new uniforms in gray and bring along their voices" to indulge in a rebel yell. He wanted to "see the uniform and hear the yell when it will not scare the life out of me as they used to do [during the war]."[13] Still other newspapers, many southern, published articles admonishing the GAR veterans on the committee who fostered the "surviving hatred and rancor" toward those who fought on the other side fifty years later.[14] Many critics equated denying these men the right to wear their veteran uniforms with denying them their rights to nostalgia and sentimentality. Union veterans argued that seeing Confederate veterans in these new uniforms would be nostalgic, albeit a little twisted, for them, providing a chance to view them without the fear of death. Interacting with fully uniformed fellow veterans provided an opportunity to remember their own struggles and time served in the war, which fostered camaraderie because of shared experiences. Symbolically reliving combat experiences with former foes fed their egos, solidifying the justice for which they fought and the harmony they now experienced. Without the uniforms, the Gettysburg reunion would not have had the same atmosphere, while the photos from the event would not have produced the same effect or memory function. Survivors appearing in their veteran uniforms created the possibility of representing reunification. Yet those tangible pieces of identity underlined the continued reality of separation and conflicting ideals.

Local veterans leaving for the Gettysburg reunion were a point of excitement that appeared in newspapers across the country. Columns proudly proclaimed "Delegation Fully Uniformed" as they described the excited, cheer-filled farewells for the old-timers. The heads of the organizations requested "as many wear uniforms as possible, [and] nearly all the old soldiers wore replicas of the uniforms they had fought in during the war." The *Salt Lake Tribune* stated that "most of the Confederate veterans wore the gray uniform and broad-brimmed light hat of the south, and those who did not have uniforms wore suits of gray material." Nearly every Union man "dressed in their bright blue uniforms, with brass buttons and the wreath of the G.A.R. on their blue hats."[15] The *Evening Journal* of Wilmington, Delaware, described the conditions and numbers of veterans the state sent by allotting nearly $2,000 for travel. Out of the nearly three hundred veterans, "twelve men who fought for the Confederate side, and eighteen colored veterans of Union" participated; all were expected to be in their respective uniforms.[16] The *Philadelphia Tribune* also reported on the "reunion and annual meeting of the Department of Pennsylvania," with the "old soldiers dressed in the honored blue uniforms" for their train ride to the national encampment.[17]

Continuing the conversation on what to wear, the *National Tribune,* according to one New England newspaper, advised "all veterans who attend the reunion at Gettysburg . . . to wear some kind of a badge indicating their company and regiment."[18] As advertised in the *Evening Journal,* Colonel Lewis E. Beitler, secretary of the Delaware State Commission, urged "all veterans [to] wear badges of their army corps, division, brigade and society."[19] Vermont comrades were to report "immediately on arrival at Gettysburg" to "register and procure badges furnished expressly for this celebration."[20] The official souvenir badge for the fiftieth anniversary was a small button pin about the size of a poker chip and carried the dates "June 29th to July 6th 1913." It included a soldier in gray and a soldier in blue shaking hands underneath a banner of two American flags, with the face of Robert E. Lee beside the man in gray and the face of Abraham Lincoln beside the man in blue.[21]

Flags received ample attention throughout the fiftieth-anniversary reunion. An announcement in one South Dakota newspaper confirmed that

Souvenir badge for the fiftieth-anniversary reunion, Battle of Gettysburg.
Author's personal collection.

the presence of both Union and Confederate battle flags. The entire town of Gettysburg was decorated with the Stars and Stripes and the Stars and Bars, but no official event sponsored by the reunion commission decorated with the Confederate flag.[22] On July 2 South Carolina's *Edgefield Advertiser* printed a piece, written by J. Russell Wright, in the Editor Advertiser column that began: "We leave today for the Reunion of the Gray and the Blue at Gettysburg, and I will carry with me the Battle-Flag of the 7th S.C. Regt. And let it float once more over the same ground that it did so proudly, just 50 years ago." He noted that the banner had received its "baptism of fire and blood" at the Battle of Fredericksburg in 1862 and its color-bearer was wounded at Gettysburg. Wright stated, "I love this flag, as a mother loves her first born." And although declaring "I stand ready to strike down to the death any foe, who upholds insult in any way to the United States flag," he admitted, there "never will be a flag, that floats on land or sea that I can love as I do this [battle flag]."[23] The extended discussion and pleading before the reunion about uniforms, flags, and badges grounds the importance of these material constructs to the tangible memory, identity, and narrative control of northern and southern memory machines. While these veterans were celebrating peace, they remained physically divided by the same material items they carried or wore during the war.

REUNION & REACTION

Beginning on June 29, the town surrounding the historic Gettysburg battlefield "stepped 50 years backward" as again "an army of Blue and an army of Gray" met on its doorstep to celebrate "the greatest battle of the War Between the States and to show the world that scars are not so deep as the feeling of American brotherhood." Veterans "in Blue and Gray trooped into the little town" on more than thirty special trains and then dispersed to the 5,000 tents in which they would stay during the reunion.[24] Some veterans marched in "with great military stride," while boy scouts assisted "others hobbling along with [the] aid of cane or crutch," with many of the veterans in attendance now seventy years and older.[25] The first three days of the reunion were to be "given over to the reminiscences" of the battle, while the fourth was set to "formally seal that forgiveness which long ago was granted."[26]

On July 1 Governor Tener welcomed the "Blue and Gray" to Gettysburg, proclaiming, "we are to-day on the greatest battlefield of the civil war of the world, not to commemorate a victory, but to rather emphasize the spirit of national brotherhood and national unity." This statement was verbal confirmation of the more than "5,000 veterans, for whom provision had not been made" by those organizing the reunion, who had arrived in the hot, humid Pennsylvania summer to commemorate the battle and celebrate the peace. Some of those unplanned arrivals were former Confederates who came to "silence the croakers" who believed that they "would stay away from the anniversary of the battle" because of its outcome. This contrasted the precedent set by the authority of the U.S. Army, the state of Pennsylvania, and "the enemy, in blue" because the rebels were "treated with a distinguished attention," not as traitors.[27]

The speeches by Commander in Chief Alfred Beers of the GAR and General Bennett H. Young, commander in chief of the UCV, were well received on the first day. Young addressed the crowd: "If any southern man who comes here clad in the gray uniform so dear to him and those of his blood, believed he would be expected even in thought to question the memories connected with the heroic past he would go out from these tents and quickly march away." The UCV leader made it clear that "when the confederate comes here he comes with his heart still loyal to the south and those who made the four years of the confederate nation's life resplendent with heroism and glory and noble sacrifice."[28] He also stated in the *Confederate Veteran*, "if any Confederate soldier came here with even the thought in his mind that in that great struggle he was wrong, his uniform should be torn from him and he should hang his head in shame" for disgracing it. According to the magazine, a staff correspondent for the *Philadelphia Ledger* said of Young: "There is a new hero of Gettysburg. He wears the gray" and has "poured an oratorical cement into the wounds of a half century's duration and has made a nation whole."[29] But that "oratorical cement" actually held open the country's wounds, while the comment from the Philadelphia correspondent assists in confirming the overall triumph of reunion sentiment and the acceptance of tangible Confederate identity symbolism into U.S. culture as American heritage.

By day two, "the armies of the blue and the gray began to melt away under the compelling influences of a torrid sun and the discomforts of camp life." The goal of this day was to revisit the maneuvers of the battle that took place on July 2, 1863, but the heat began driving some of the old veterans home. A significant oratorical event occurred in the "big tent," where Barry Bulkley from Washington, D.C., read Lincoln's Gettysburg Address for the crowd.[30] Yet while it was hot, the added layers of three-piece veteran uniforms only added to the discomfort the aging men felt amid the rising temperature and humidity.

On July 3 "Pickett's survivors and the remnants of the Philadelphia brigade" enacted "the bloody charge up to Stone Wall in the Emmittsburg road as part of the Governors' Day celebration." But "instead of the clash of bayonets, the shriek of shells, and the hand-to-hand battles at the peak," the old veterans "clasped hands in the bond of friendship." The survivors of Pickett's Division carried "old flags" and marched as quickly as their "aged limbs would allow, up to the stone wall, behind which were the survivors of the valiant Philadelphia brigade." The reporter then described the "old flag" as "a faded Confederate flag, its red field pierced with many holes, its crossbars dim and its shaft colored with the sweat of many a man who had died that it might fly high in that last desperate effort to pierce the Union lines." When the southerners reached the top of the ridge at the Angle, the northerners from the Philadelphia brigade "arose with outstretched hands and each Union man pinned a memorial badge upon a gray coat." Each of the veterans from the event received a silk U.S. flag. As the crowd watched, the "Stars and Stripes was unfurled," and the lines of those in blue and those in gray stood across from each other, shaking hands over the wall.[31]

The following day, July 4, President Wilson spoke "to a crowd estimated at 10,000 veterans in uniforms of gray or blue" at the Gettysburg battlefield.[32] Newspapers printed photos of Wilson being "Escorted by the Blue and the Gray," with both the U.S. flag and a national Confederate Flag pictured. Wilson's speech focused not on the Civil War, but on the efforts of togetherness and peace throughout the country, claiming that the "quarrel forgotten—except that we shall not forget the splendid valor, the manly devotion of the men then arrayed against one another, now grasping hands and smiling into each other's eyes."[33] Approximately fifty-three thousand Union and Confederate veterans attended the fiftieth anniversary of Gettysburg, which is close to the same number of men who were wounded, declared missing, or died during the three-day battle.

Union and Confederate veterans shaking hands at the fiftieth-anniversary
Gettysburg reunion. Library of Congress.

Historian Barbara Gannon has explained why this battlefield reunion
illustrates how Civil War memory had morphed in the years since Appomattox. She argues that northern veterans attending the gathering approved of the transformation to accept the Confederate narrative, which
allowed them to assume amnesia about slavery and emancipation as the
central cause of the Civil War.[34]

Veteran's uniforms, badges, and flags assisted in contributing to this
narrative. At the Gettysburg commemoration, aged men in regulation
GAR and UCV uniforms with badges pinned to their coats and fluttering
in the breeze, stepping off trains, talking together, walking to their tents,
or shaking hands across a hedge—each of these images gave the public a
glimpse of "true peace." Reading descriptions in local newspapers of "veterans in Blue and Gray, arm in arm," hobbling over the Gettysburg battlefield
fostered the illusion that the country had healed. Specifically in northern
newspapers, photos and descriptions of regiments resuming "old positions"
as "the thin gray line advanced and as the Union veterans awaited them

at the 'High Water Mark' and other points" played out in people's imaginations while reading that the groups, "emotion stirring in the breast of each veteran," shared "tears, hand-clasps, and embraces."[35] Such stories and photos of Confederate veterans in gray entered homes across the country through newspapers, validating the notion that these veterans in uniform were harmless because they just wanted to remember their struggle and their heritage of noble fighting, overlooking the fact that they fought in war to protect slavery.

Newspapers were inundated with touching stories of veterans finding friends or meeting those from the other side who had saved their lives. What is most noteworthy in the majority of these accounts is how the men were described, specifically by what they were wearing. Throughout the event, coverage referred to the veterans as being either blue or gray, rendering their identities inseparable from the colors or garments they wore. When men such as I. E. Tibben from Pennsylvania and William H. Turpin from Virginia embraced, the "whole crowd looked on and applauded" because "these two old chaps were dressed in the uniforms they wore on the day of the fight." Tibben "had on his old blue coat and trousers, his blue forage cap with its white clover leaf above the visor," while "Turpin wore the oldest, most faded gray coat in the world, tied together with soiled cotton strips in lieu of buttons. A tattered campaign hat crowned his gray-brown head, and his feet were bandaged in old burlap, in strips of cotton and in parts of old socks." His outfit served as a reminder of the "destitution as well as the desperation attending Confederate campaigns."[36] Printed in the *Fort Mill Times,* one story told by A. T. Dice, vice president of the Reading Railroad, described "a veteran in gray and a veteran in blue" who arrived at Gettysburg. After the reunion, weeping, they departed together for the train station. Dice said he was unsure of how they reached this decision, but as they stood waiting on the platform, "they slowly stripped off their uniforms and exchanged them there while the curious flocked to see them." The story ends with the "Oregonian who came proudly to town with a coat of blue" leaving "with one of gray," and the Louisiana veteran "who boasted the gray of the south" swelling with pride "in his new uniform of blue."[37] This account illustrates the harmonious feelings intended to come from this reunion and exemplifies the distinction between the feelings of those who fought and those who observed. The actions of the veterans at the train station were a departure from the narratives and agendas of the women's organizations on either side. These men were able to exchange their uniforms and form a bond, while later generations and organizations used those blue and gray veterans' coats as a way to take firmer control of the Civil War memory.

Reports of and reactions to the Gettysburg reunion echoed in various media sources throughout the country. Governor W. H. Mann of Virginia was pleased with the "friendship" displayed at the commemoration. He supported the gathering and "participated with pleasure and pride" because of its efforts to "cement kindly relations and to further the idea that all are American citizens."[38] A writer for the *Bristol Press* in Connecticut proclaimed that the Gettysburg reunion was "a heavy tax on the strength and health of many of the veterans who attended, but it has been worth the cost" because of the "complete reconciliation of sections." He added, "nothing could be more cordial or genuine than the greetings of 'Johnny' and 'Yank'"[39] The members of the Virginia UCV A. P. Hill Camp returned home from Gettysburg "highly pleased with their trip." They reported that the "Confederate flag carried by the camp to Gettysburg was greatly admired by GAR men," who "begged the camp to lend it to them for special ceremonies," which pleased the southern veterans, the flag being one of their "most highly treasured possessions."[40]

Immediately after the reunion ended, speculation about a seventy-fifth anniversary reunion began. A column in one Kansas City paper planted the seed of hope for another epic celebration. The author wrote, "the veterans at Gettysburg seem old but it is certain that some of them will be there twenty-five years hence to celebrate the seventy-fifth anniversary of the battle," adding that the "pension bureau estimates name 1955 as the year in which the last soldier of the Civil War will die." Given that the "seventy-fifth anniversary of Gettysburg will be in 1938, there ought to be a fairly good rally of timeworn veterans on that memorable field."[41] While the article was hopeful that there would be an official gathering for the seventy-fifth anniversary of the Battle of Gettysburg, it brought up a solid point: the veterans and their memorial associations were aging. With the death of more veterans and their supporting female auxiliary who had lived through the war, it would be up to the Sons and Daughters organizations to take control of the memory machines.

CONTINUED COMMEMORATION, 1913–1920s

After the 1913 Gettysburg reunion, the memorial organizations returned their memory machines to business as usual, raising funds, holding commemorative events, and spreading their narratives. But the veterans and their organizations were now in a state of decline. With this, Black and Indigenous veterans had to carve their own space of recognition while still used as props by Confederate organizations. But this ended with the rise of the Sons and Daughters organizations.

Scholars often overlook the participation of African American GAR veterans at the fiftieth anniversary of Gettysburg because they rarely appear in photographs of the event. That is true in connection with white-owned newspapers. But contrary evidence appears in African American newspapers and in an archived photograph of the Gettysburg reunion that features two Black GAR veterans in their blue uniforms and GAR logo hats, with the official GAR badge and post badges pinned to their coats. Only African American newspapers covered the participation of their veterans at the Gettysburg fiftieth anniversary. According to one Philadelphia newspaper, more than three hundred Black veterans attended the reunion. Besides a couple of newspapers mentioning that these men were on a train to the reunion, African American participation in the event was purposefully overlooked because their presence did not jive with the narrative the GAR and UCV groups needed to tell.[42]

For fear of their role being forgotten, African American veterans began advertising a fiftieth anniversary reunion at Fort Wagner, South Carolina. This specific battle was important to many, according to one journalist, because of "the valorous deeds of the colored soldiers and the white soldiers of the brave 54th Massachusetts Volunteer Regiment." The writer declared the "spirit of the celebration was that of freedom and equality in all things," which is contrary to the "raising of the stars and bars under which soldiers went out to war to destroy the United States and perpetuate slavery."[43] In hopes of drawing a crowd, organizers announced that "all Colored veterans of the Civil War are wanted, all are invited." They specifically wanted "survivors of the 54th and other Massachusetts Colored Regiments" to attend and asked for the addresses and information of those interested in doing so.[44] The same call appeared in other African American newspapers, both announcing the event and giving instructions as to what veterans should wear. The Fort Wagner reunion was to take place July 18, 1913, and all commissioned officers were "expected to appear in uniform (coat and heat [*sic*] or cap); non-commissioned officers' (coat or blouse, hat or cap); privates (blouse and cap or hat, G.A.R. uniform)."[45] Even fifty years after the war, the call for African American GAR comrades to wear uniforms to an event demonstrates their commitment to their cause and highlights how closely their identities were tied to their uniforms.

One Salt Lake City newspaper reported in August 1913 that Levi Miller of Relief, Winchester County, Virginia, "bears the distinction of being the only colored Confederate veteran of the civil war in attendance at the anniversary celebration of the great battle of Gettysburg." The Confederate camp—which one exactly is unknown—"sent Comrade Miller to the celebration at its expense," and "he wore his gray uniform and received marked attention." In 1921 Miller was mentioned in the *Confederate Veteran*. The article told his story of being born into slavery as a "mulatto" and "faithfully" following his young enslaver throughout the Civil War, "nursing him with devotion when wounded" during the Wilderness Campaign in 1864. The story claims that his enslaver's comrades in arms were so impressed by his devotion that they "had his name added to the pension roll of that State," meaning that Miller "was honored and cared for by the old commonwealth to his death." It reports that his "casket was draped with the Confederate flag, which was later raised over his grave." The piece ends with the question, "could an institution under which such affection was created be other than beneficent in greatest part?"[46] Miller was placed in a Confederate veterans' uniform and claimed by former Confederates after the war, during a time of racial tension, so he could be re-enslaved for another cause. He has been used frequently since 1910 as proof and propaganda for the UCV and the Sons of Confederate Veterans that Black Confederate soldiers existed. Draping his casket in a rebel flag claimed Miller even in death as a symbol that the white southerners he represented were proud to display, proving that they accepted southern Blacks, who in turn accepted their status—that a beautiful relationship of love and devotion underpinned the institution of slavery.

The mental gymnastics in which southerners engaged to use formerly enslaved people as props for their narrative is illuminating. The use of Levi Miller demonstrates their evolution from not acknowledging African American support during the war, to honoring body servants and giving them funds outside of those meant for veterans from the UDC and UCV, to dressing a Confederate "colored veteran" up in a gray uniform and sending him to the fiftieth anniversary Gettysburg reunion is astounding; it demonstrates the Confederate willingness to adapt their principles to ensure their narrative.

Jefferson Shields, in uniform with medals and top hat.
Liljenquist Family Collection, Library of Congress.

Sometime between 1900 and 1918, Jefferson Shields, an African American, sat for a formal portrait in a full Confederate veterans' uniform, with numerous badges and a top hat in his hand. During the Civil War, Shields was a personal servant to Colonel James Kerr Edmonson from the Twenty-Seventh Virginia Infantry Regiment. Voted in as a member of the UCV Stonewall Brigade in Staunton, Virginia, he attended several reunions. When he died, Shields was buried at Evergreen Cemetery in Lexington, Virginia, with a military grave marker designating him a private in Company H, Twenty-Seventh Virginia Infantry, Stonewall Brigade, part of the Confederate Army of Northern Virginia. But he was no private. This man was used as propaganda to perpetuate the loyal-enslaved narrative. The photograph and the fact that Shields was voted as a member of a UCV camp demonstrates how much the positions of the UDC and the UCV had changed, from strictly prohibiting Black members to using material objects to name and claim them as their own. Dressing Black men like Shields and Miller in Confederate veteran uniforms and adorning them with badges incorporated them into the southern memory-machine narrative and presented the story the South wanted to tell of the Civil War, venerating the Lost Cause while minimizing the importance of slavery. It was not that southerners were trying to subjugate an entire race; they believed or wanted to believe that they fought for states' rights and that loyal Black men fought side by side with their white masters, proudly wearing the Confederate gray.[47]

BUSINESS AS USUAL

After the Gettysburg reunion, organizations returned to their regular duties and interests of furthering the mission of their memory machines. At the 1914 national UDC meeting, the Florida Division reported an "extreme financial depression of the past several months," which made it difficult to contribute to the monument funds. Its members instead focused their finances on their "benevolent work of love and duty" to the veterans, boasting of "supplying the men with uniforms and many little amenities of life not otherwise possible for them," totaling the "contributions for Confederate work of all kinds" to nearly seven thousand dollars.[48]

For a few years prior to 1920, the WRC became focused on ensuring protection of their sacred emblems. The Thirty-Fifth National Convention of the WRC inaugurated a "campaign for singling out the United States Flag from all other[s] by capitalizing it when we write." This also provided WRC members with the authority to "intercede with writers and newspapers everywhere to capitalize the word 'Flag' or 'United States Flag' in print." They began petitioning Congress to create a national law "to protect our Flag from desecration." These women also resolved that the WRC must "correct this title whenever and wherever possible by referring to the War of 1861–1865 by its true name, 'The War of the Rebellion,' or 'the Civil War,'" but they must "never permit this libel 'War between the States' to be uttered" in their "presence without protest."[49] Their efforts were in response to an education initiative by the UDC (discussed below).

After the camaraderie during Gettysburg's fiftieth anniversary, the September 1913 GAR parade in Chattanooga, Tennessee, hurt those peaceable feelings. Members from the Nathan Bedford Forrest Camp of the UCV "accepted disappointment in good grace" because the GAR rules barred all persons except Union soldiers from participating in the parade, even though "an invitation to join in the parade had been tendered to Col. L. T. Dickenson," commander of the Forrest Camp. The UCV members appeared at the parade "clad in their gray uniforms" and "preparing to form in the line of march with Forsythe Post No. 15 of Toledo, Ohio," when they were stopped. The commanding officer stated that "the Confederate camp was not excluded because its members were former Confederate soldiers, but because it is the policy of the Grand Army of the Republic to have only its members in the parade." The Forrest Camp extended an invitation to the "rank and file of the boys in blue" to visit their headquarters to show "that there is no ill feeling toward any of them," but the invitation was only to the rank and file, not to the leaders who kept the Confederate veterans from participating.[50]

There would be additional hurt feelings, and rewriting of the historical narrative, through another development that shaped the Lost Cause argument and the use of material culture to remember the Civil War. Thomas Dixon, author of *The Clansman,* saw his novel brought to life by filmmaker D. W. Griffith as *The Birth of a Nation* in 1915. This story is based on the premise that abolitionists started the Civil War and that only the Ku Klux Klan could save young white women from the evils of the African race. The film glorifies the Confederacy and its soldiers in uniform. According to historian Caroline E. Janney, many GAR posts denounced the movie, although some Union veterans received complimentary tickets to the film from at least one local newspaper.[51] The WRC called the movie a "lying representation of a critical period in the Nation's history." It charged *The Birth of a Nation* with "corrupting the minds of the youth of the Nation; grossly attacking the memory of our comrades who gave their lives for the maintenance of this Nation."[52]

The GAR and its auxiliary organizations had a vastly different reaction than many members of the UCV, UDC, and Sons of Confederate Veterans (SCV). The SCV asked for an "exhibition of motion reel" in Washington "because of its educational value in connection with an historical revival undertaken by the Sons of Confederate Veterans."[53] Newspapers throughout the South praised the movie, and many UCV members attended showings in groups. An advertisement for the movie in the *El Paso Herald* reported "the old 'rebel yell'" emanating from the "throats of over sixty veterans from Lee Camp, Soldiers' Home, who had gathered" to view it.[54] According to the *Hattiesburg News,* "a private subscription" paid for twenty Confederate veterans of Forrest County, Mississippi, to view the film.[55] Sidney Levy, the manager of the Opera House in Pensacola, Florida, "offered free admission to all Confederate Veterans" who wished to see "the grand spectacular play, 'The Birth of a Nation.'" All the men needed to do was to notify the adjunct of Camp Ward. The "veterans will wear badges and uniforms if possible," the local newspaper reported, and would assemble at a nearby monument on the night of the viewing.[56]

The Birth of a Nation may seem of questionable relation to uniforms, flags, and badges of the Civil War and subsequent years. But putting on screen the concept of the Lost Cause and the Ku Klux Klan as the salvation of southern white society was crucial to the process of desensitizing future generations to the images so dear to the Confederacy and its aftermath by promoting the acceptability of these items. *The Birth of a Nation* showed rebels in their gray uniforms and beneath their flags taking a seemingly righteous stand. Further, the film cited the work of a scholar who had defended the South and criticized Radical Reconstruction and those who supported it. That historian, President Wilson, had only recently celebrated the peace at Gettysburg in 1913.

In 1916 the GAR celebrated its own fiftieth anniversary. During that year and the few short years after, the organization began making comments about its own mortality and of its numbers "fast fading." General Orders No. 4 in April 1917 had many instructions for Memorial Day and Flag Day, one of which was a call upon all GAR members to "visit public and private schools in their vicinity on one or more days" preceding Memorial Day "to instruct the boys and girls in the lessons of the great Civil War." The general order prompted comrades to remember that "they are living apostles of patriotism, and that they are teaching the youth of the land by example as well as by precept" because "children are keen critics and scan actions more than words." Those who visited the children were ordered to "wear the uniform of the order whenever possible."[57] For northerners and southerners alike, exposing young people to the important symbols of their cause that the uniform exemplified mattered immensely.

In preparation for the last GAR parade in Boston, as the fifty-first annual encampment of the GAR was held there, General Orders No. 6 went out to the organization. Item XII states: "It is desired that every member of the Grand Army of the Republic present in Boston will make an effort to participate in the parade, whether he has a uniform or not, but it is hoped that all will make an effort to appear in the regulation uniform of the order." The next item instructs that "no flags or standards except the national and State flags" or "department and post flags and standards" were allowed in the parade. The men could not divide by regiment, only by state or post, but they all had to be under the U.S. flag. On the day of the parade, the group met with "so much enthusiasm." Newspaper articles included in the record reported that "Boston saw a mirage to-day—a ghost picture of ghost armies of '61 sweeping triumphantly to victory," but "now and then in the thin lines of Blue," a "gray uniform" could be seen. The reporters believed the comingling of the two was an "ultimate sign of a final peace to come" because "the North and South of our own fair land are welded together now in lasting union."[58]

The importance of the GAR's attachment to continuing to appear in uniform is striking. More than fifty years past the end of the Civil War, these men continued to knit their identities to their uniforms in public, especially and purposefully in front of children. The question is, what example did continually wearing a uniform provide for future generations?

Claiming unity but using tangible markers of identity separation only encouraged divisiveness. While the GAR had a right to be proud of fighting for the maintenance of the Union, its continual wearing of uniforms, despite their words of unity, encouraged the same behavior and friction from the southern groups, which was problematic for societal progression.

THE SONS & DAUGHTERS, 1917–1930s

The transition of authority to the younger auxiliary gave memory, narrative control, and identity authority to the Sons and Daughters organizations. According to historian Karen L. Cox, American entry into World War I benefited the UDC because it "offered the Daughters a unique opportunity to bring attention to the South's particular brand of patriotism." Its members classified their patriotism and role in the war-relief effort as comparable to that of their parents. Participating in relief work also meant that the focus of the organization shifted to a current issue instead of fundraising for monuments and the Confederate cause. An extremely important concept that Cox highlights is that the relief work "gave publicity to the UDC in Europe," which allowed them to spread the "gospel of the Confederacy" to others in the form of brass plates on hospital beds in the name of Confederate veterans.[59] They also developed a Southern Cross of Honor for World War I veterans who were "lineal descendants of Confederate Veterans." The state and chapter historians of the UDC were in charge of collecting the doughboys' histories and ensuring legitimate lineage.[60]

This award provided another example of a material connection to the Confederate past and contributed to forming the identities of the rebels' descendants as part of their ancestors' cause. The cross given to World War I veterans is about the same size as those given to Confederate veterans but with a different phrase, a raised center, and the Stars and Bars between "1917–1918." During this initiative, the UDC rallied around five concepts. Among them was caring for their veterans, "as this glorious opportunity for service to our heroes is fast slipping away" and their "deathless, unquestioned courage was a priceless heritage to their sons in the World War." They also dedicated themselves to the "children of the Confederacy, as our future as a great patriotic society rests with them," to the "Marianna Monument," and to "education, as the living monuments in the minds of Southern boys and girls should claim our attention."[61] Because of the decline in needy Confederate men and women by the 1920s, the UDC was able to turn its attention to the upcoming generation of southerners by incorporating flags, photos, and new uniforms for the children of the Confederacy into southern education, further perpetuating their illusion. While the UDC had long indoctrinated children in the Lost Cause, this new project of working in southern classrooms and using material culture as tangible anchors to textbook renovations was a new step in spreading "true" history.[62] The UDC tried to push a bill through Congress asking for the Civil War to be known as the "War Between the States,'" an effort that did not end in their favor.[63]

In August 1929 E. H. Pitcher from the Sons of Union Veterans of the Civil War reached out to General Richard A. Sneed, the commander in chief of the UCV in Oklahoma City, to "promote a Grand Reunion between the Blue and the Gray" in 1930. Pitcher stated that the purpose of this reunion and movement was "to create a better understanding between these two bodies of brave men, their auxiliaries and friends, also to set an example for the younger generations that will tend to further the common weal of the Republic." To convince Sneed to participate, he included several statements from a general survey throughout the country supporting this venture, stating that "the curse of sectionalism, caused by the Civil War and its aftermath, shall be forever crushed beneath the divine potency of Charity and Brotherly-love."[64] Sneed accepted the invitation to join in a national reunion of GAR and UCV members, which greatly pleased the Sons of Union Veterans. When the conditions were explained in a following letter, however, problems arose. Edwin Foster, commander in chief of the GAR, declared that "the Boys in Blue have always been ready to extend the hand of fellowship to our southern friends, and never more than now." He stated that there was "one condition which will stand in the way of our coming together," but as the head of his organization, Foster asked Sneed to "pledge to us that the Stars and Bars, or your Confederate Flag, shall have no place in the parade, either by organizations, or individuals, but that you will march under the Stars and Stripes, 'Your Flag and My Flag,' today as true American citizens."[65]

Acknowledging the letter Sneed sent Foster in November, Foster's reply in December was not hopeful. He agreed that "a gathering together of the boys in Gray and the boys in Blue would be a beautiful testimonial to the perfect reconciliation," which was "in the hearts of all." Unfortunately, the complete "disagreement as to the flags to be displayed is apparently too wide spread to be compassed by you and I." Foster did not "presume to criticize the sentiment" that Sneed and his "comrades cherish for the colors, in behalf of which" they "strove so valiantly." Nonetheless, he declared himself "sure it is a fixed conviction among the vast majority of the Boys in Blue, that only the ensign of the United States of America must float in any of their encampments or processions as Organizations." Foster warned that "any joint reunion based upon compromise of the flag dispute, or upon the abandonment of ground by either North or South," might arouse "a revival of bitterness and an unhappy denunciation of the genuine friendliness which now obtains." So, he regretfully came to the conclusion that "further attempt at the joint reunion project would be unwise and that we should abandon any effort to bring about a gathering which was undoubtedly suggested in a spirit of wholesomeness and tenderness, but which would be dependent for its felicity upon unanimity of idea."[66] While Foster wished the UCV well, he could not compromise on flying the flag of traitors at a reunion involving the GAR.

Throughout the decades after the war, the UCV was clearly willing to love and accept the U.S. flag as its American identity symbol, though not at the exclusion of their Confederate banners. To do so, UCV members believed, would be to deny the other half of their joint identity and concede a portion of the control of the narrative to those who won the war. The proposed reunion was supposed to be an example of unity for auxiliary organizations and the youth, but the commanders of the GAR and UCV could not agree on displaying material representations of identity. That being said, how could these groups expect to set a good example for future generations?

SEVENTY-FIFTH ANNIVERSARY
OF THE BATTLE OF GETTYSBURG, 1938

On June 10, 1937, the forty-seventh reunion of the Confederate army took place in Mississippi. Although fewer in number, the veterans were "still fired with memories of the war" as they marched to Winters Woods to dedicate a park. One of the main topics of the reunion was to decide on the offer from the remaining Union veterans to the remaining Confederates "for a joint reunion next year at Gettysburg." Brigadier General W. M. Buck from Muskogee, Oklahoma, emphatically replied "no," but other commanders in the "dwindling army voiced approval.[67]

To "commemorate the seventy-fifth anniversary of the Battle of Gettysburg and the final reunion of the surviving veterans of the war between the states," the U.S. government minted a half-dollar featuring the "Stars and Bars of the Confederacy" next to the Stars and Stripes, separated only by a battle-ax.[68] The significance of the coin is that both identities, Confederate and Union, are represented through flags and the different uniforms of the veterans depicted.

Numerous chapters of the WRC began planning their trips to see and assist at what would undoubtedly be the final reunion of the blue and gray.[69] Just like the fiftieth anniversary, the seventy-fifth created considerable excitement concerning who was going and what was expected. Three aged veterans attending from Henderson County, North Carolina, made headlines. A newspaper estimated that "400 of the aged soldiers from the south will meet together with the Grand Army of the Republic." The official festivities were to begin on a Friday and conclude on "July 4, but [their] departure date has been set for July 6, again allowing time for rest before the home journey." This time veterans and their attendants were given individual tents with board floors and electric lights.[70]

From June 29 to July 6, the final reunion of Civil War veterans took place in Gettysburg. While there were only a few thousand left compared to the 55,000 in attendance twenty-five years before, the event promised to be a momentous occasion. Officials from Pennsylvania and the federal commissions spent $1 million on the commemorative program. Dr. Overton H. Mennett, the 89-year-old commander in chief of the GAR, excitedly "clasped the hand of the first Confederate veteran to arrive," 105-year-old James Robert Paul from Charlotte, North Carolina. Mennett observed: "Veterans of that war are just as friendly as other people. We are all Americans." Paul commented, "I hunted all over three Southern cities to find a gray suit" because "my uniform went to pieces long ago, while we were chasing Grant around Washington, but I wanted to come to this reunion in gray."[71]

Two thousand "gallant survivors—Union and Confederate—marked the second day of their final reunion on the battleground where 75 years ago their comrades struggled through the scarlet hell." Drums, bugles corps, and uniformed veterans of more recent wars "crowded Gettysburg's diamond and the narrow streets" of the town to "parade in honor of the surviving veterans." As representatives from Pennsylvania spoke from the platform, rain began to fall. Dr. Mennett proclaimed: "Three quarters of a century has passed and those of us who remember this place so well are old. The wounds are healed. Let us who suffered here plead for mutual peace and tolerance." He continued: "The Blue and Grey are assembled to-day under one flag, the Stars and Stripes. Under this one banner we march together into the sunset of our lives."[72]

On July 4, President Franklin Delano Roosevelt spoke at Gettysburg "to 1,800 Blue and Gray clad veterans of the War Between the States." As he finished speaking, "two aged men—one in blue and one in gray—trudged to the hill top and grasped the edges of a 50-foot flag suspended there." As they tugged the flag free, they revealed "a towering memorial dedicated to 'peace eternal in a nation united.'" The fifty-one-foot Gettysburg peace monument is topped by an eternal flame.[73]

Reported in the African American publication *New York Amsterdam News,* the seventy-fifth "reunion at Gettysburg between the men in blue and gray" was "a most significant event in our history." The writer noted, "a few Negro soldiers who fought for the preservation of the union as well as the freedom of the race were present." He stated, "if the Confederates had done the right thing they would have brought along with them some Negro veterans of the defeated Confederate States of America, for many Negroes were forced to fight by the rebels during the war." The writer concluded this thought with the tale of meeting "one old Negro veteran of the Confederate Army" in Richmond a few years prior "and another one" in Louisville. He claimed that "both were hale and hearty, but neither was happy over having fought for the Confederacy."[74]

The button commemorating the seventy-fifth anniversary looks much like the one from the fiftieth. About the size of a poker chip, this pin has a blue soldier shaking hands with a gray soldier on a battlefield, the Stars and Stripes and the Stars and Bars over their heads, with the bright rays of sunshine in the background. What is notable is the Confederate flag on the commemorative pin.

Newspapers covered this last reunion at Gettysburg in depth, documenting the day not only with the written word but also through a large

Souvenir badge for the seventy-fifth-anniversary reunion, Battle of Gettysburg.
Author's personal collection.

number of photographs. Images of the reunion filled newspapers throughout the country, displaying iconic old veterans in their uniforms, wearing their badges and waving their flags. Featured on the third page of one
Washington, D.C., newspaper, Durant Hatch, a ninety-three-year-old Confederate veteran from Oklahoma, watches the parade and waves his Confederate flag.[75]

Fewer veterans attended the anniversary reunion in 1938, but those
who did still wore their veteran uniforms. Images of ninety-plus-year-old
men in Confederate gray increased the reach of the southern narrative further into society because they perpetuated the ideal heritage of the Confederacy for generations to come. The GAR and UCV veterans in uniform
proved not a relic of a divided past, but a tangible representation of a nation still at war with its past.

The seventy-fifth anniversary of the Battle of Gettysburg was a closing
moment in the chapters of Civil War memory. After this event, things
changed. While living veterans dwindled, it was one of the last big events
with men dressed in veteran uniforms as physical representatives of all
those who had worn the blue or gray, with badges pinned to their chests,
and flags floating above their heads. This memory of how those men looked

is solidified as fact in popular memory because of works such as Margaret Mitchell's *Gone with the Wind,* published in 1936 and adapted to film in 1939. The one-hundredth anniversary of the Civil War in conjunction with the civil rights movement opened another chapter, this time with memorial organizations but without living veterans. Even in the early twenty-first century it remains linked to the purpose of perpetuating the Lost Cause narrative with symbols of treason and hate. But Americans are now in another pivotal moment, when actual reconciliation of U.S. history is possible if those who hold on to these problematic symbols can let go of their material representations and bury them with the past.

CONCLUSION

B ecause of the desire to commemorate their service, the Grand Army of the Republic, the Woman's Relief Corps, the United Confederate Veterans, and the United Daughters of the Confederacy were inherently divisive. Their memory machines maintained and even expanded and encouraged the schism that personal and political views and actions kept from closing. The uniforms and badges created by these organizations were physical representations of a national wound that could not heal. By being allowed to remain open, it festered and fed the worst of humanity through racism and allowed people to alter the story of how and why the war was fought. Even the "Blue and Gray" reunions, meant to demonstrate unity, pushed the country farther apart by providing a separate visual of ex-Confederate and ex-Union instead of all Americans. Because of each side's distinctive sectional identities, the country never mended, and the wound remained. Northern and southern memory machines went to war with each other from the 1860s and remain so today, battling over narrative control of the conflict and perfecting their narratives through physical objects. Men and women of the respective organizations strategically crafted their own material items of uniforms, badges, and flags; orchestrated public events where they wore and displayed these items, keeping the United States visually separated by Union blue and Confederate gray; and systematically promoted their narratives of why the war was fought and how their sacrifices should be remembered. The GAR, the WRC, the UCV, and the UDC created specific methods to convey their personal and organizational truths to future generations throughout the United States. This spans from forms of patriotic nostalgia and forms of resistance to the opposing narrative to the business of creating a usable past. Their memory machines worked. Present-day battles over understandings of heritage and identity stem from the long life of these physical items and affect our ability to come to terms with the reasons the Civil War was fought. Even in the twenty-first century, people still actively participate in purchasing Civil War and veteran paraphernalia. The ability to purchase memorabilia or veteran uniforms, badges, or flags continues to link our memory, identities, and understanding of the era with the tangible links offered by the material culture from that period.

Veterans' badges are plentiful on sites such as eBay and Etsy and are the most common items found under the search "Civil War veteran." But it is important to try a variety of search terms, such as "badge," "medal," "pin," or "ribbon," if looking for something specific from any organization. GAR, UCV, WRC, and UDC badges range across a variety of materials, styles, and prices. GAR badges usually begin at $9, depending on the item's age, its condition, and how ornate its appearance. Most sell for between $30 and $100. While some cost more, they are typically rarer designs or from more elaborate occasions.

UCV badges are a different story. While the same search terms apply when specified to the UCV, these items typically begin at around $75 and often end in the range of $200–$700. Even UDC items outsell WRC badges and ribbons by the same ratios as UCV to GAR. WRC badges begin at $9, sometimes less, and usually end auction under $100. UDC badges, which are scarce, begin at around $50 and sell for up to $350.

Civil War veteran uniform coats and hats are also available on eBay and other private auction sites, but it is extremely rare to find a full set that includes a coat, vest, and pants. A recently purchased, longer GAR coat came with a full set of buttons, a delegate pin, and moth holes because of its age. The label in its collar is difficult to read but has a name written inside. While the list price was $642.52, it sold for $300.00 after being on the market for a month. A well-lined M. C. Lilley veterans' coat with the manufacture label, full buttons, and a GAR lapel button sold for $350.00, complete with authentication and veteran verification. Private auction sites are more likely to have UCV uniform items and will charge two to three times what a GAR coat commands.

Finding flags is rare, but they usually sell for a high price. A "very rare

Civil War Confederate Veteran U.C.V. Banner" sold on eBay for $407.02. The flag had several holes, but its connection with the UCV made it valuable to several bidders. At 9.5 by 5.75 inches, a forty-eight-star U.S. flag with "GAR 1918" printed in the center and looking as though it was previously used in a parade had a starting price of $195.00. Some flags are stamped with the organization and date, like this one, denoting a specific event or the chapter to which the object belonged.

The importance placed on an item by its previous owner or organization relates to the market for such items today. GAR badges and objects, which are more plentiful on these auction sites, sell for less, while the scarcity and the romantic notions of the Lost Cause for Confederate veterans' items often provoke a bidding war and a higher yield.

There are ethical quagmires when purchasing such items because of the issues discussed herein. The materials I have obtained personally are now part of my teaching collection, giving students an opportunity to create a museum exhibit and to handle these objects for study. This book is meant to open a conversation about the past, place, and future of these objects in American society. Once we understand why we are drawn to these items, the door opens to the conversation about their true meaning: who they have helped, who they have hurt, why they were created, and how we move forward with a new narrative about them and the war that prompted their creation.

NOTES

INTRODUCTION

1. "Grant and Lee," *Daily Ohio Statesman* (Columbus), Apr. 13, 1865.

2. "The Meeting of Grant and Lee," *Green-Mountain Freeman* (Montpelier, VT), Apr. 18, 1865.

3. Degruccio, "Letting the War Slip through Our Hands."

4. Masur, *Sum of Our Dreams*, 113–14.

5. Auslander and Zahra, *Objects of War;* Cashin, *War Matters.* Also see Gleeson, "Waving the Black-and-White Bloody Shirt"; Janney, *Ends of War;* and Taylor, "Texts and Textiles in Civil War Kentucky," 219–24. A substantial number of books consider uniforms from an antiquarian perspective, such as Adolphus, *Imported Confederate Uniforms of Peter Tait & Co.* Adolphus provides in-depth descriptions of fabric content, the cut of the uniform, and what units of the Confederate army wore products made by this specific manufacturer. Smith and Field, *Uniforms of the Civil War,* provides a brief history of the Civil War while giving a comprehensive overview of every kind of northern and southern uniform imaginable. Hadden, *Reliving the Civil War; Arms and Equipment of the Confederacy; Arms and Equipment of the Union;* and *Illustrated Atlas of the Civil War* each provides knowledge of the material but does not analyze the overall role uniforms played in the lives of those who wore them or their effect on society.

6. Wilson, *Business of Civil War,* 1–33. Wilson begins his introduction and first chapter discussing April 1861.

7. Giesberg, "Waging War Their Own Way," 16–27; Ott, *Confederate Daughters;* Attie, *Patriotic Toil;* Scott, *Southern Lady;* McCurry, *Confederate Reckoning.* McCurry argues that women and Black people tore the Confederacy apart from the inside. Because of poor wartime conditions, southern women took matters into their own hands and began raiding local stores for provisions, specifically food and materials to make clothing. Because the enslaved began abandoning their posts, white residents in the Confederacy had splintered home lives.

8. For more works on material culture, see Schlereth, *Material Culture Studies in America;* Lubar and Kingery, *History from Things;* Trentmann, *Empire of Things;* Fussell, *Uniforms;* and Cashin, "Trophies of War." Fussell's study examines not only military uniforms but

also wedding dresses and postal uniforms, among other articles of clothing, and contemplates how what people wear corresponds with their views of themselves and their value.

9. Edwards, "Textiles," 197–99; Edwards, *Only the Clothes on Her Back*, 2. To fully understand the importance of Civil War uniforms during the war and their transition to tools of identity and sectionalism, we must first create a central understanding of their value. To accomplish this, see the following foundational works on the spread of consumer-culture goods and their various political, social, and cultural meanings: Bushman, *Refinement of America*; Breen, "Empire of Goods"; Dublin, *Women at Work*; and Halttunen, *Confidence Men and Painted Women*.

10. Weicksel, "Fabric of War," xv; Weicksel, "Current Project: The Fabric of War," Research, https://sarahjonesweicksel.com/projects/.

11. Gibson, *Memory of Clothes*, xiv–xv.

12. For a comprehensive account of Reconstruction, see Foner, *Reconstruction*. Although published in the late 1980s, Foner's book remains the critical text for understanding the period. But it has been subject to some revisionism. See, for example, Richardson, *Death of Reconstruction*; Downs and Masur, *World the Civil War Made*; Downs, *After Appomattox*; Janney, *Ends of War*; and Clampitt, *Lost Causes*.

13. See Wilson, *Baptized in Blood*; and Prince, *Stories of the South*. Prince offers an explanation similar to that in Silber, *Romance of Reunion*, but he makes the case that culture mattered as much as traditional politics during the period 1865–1915, when northerners and southerners struggled to define the "Southern Question." See also Harris, *Across the Bloody Chasm*. For more on the Lost Cause, see Foster, *Ghosts of the Confederacy*; Gallagher and Nolan, *Myth of the Lost Cause and Civil War History*; Gallagher, *Jubal A. Early, the Lost Cause, and Civil War History*; Blight, *Race and Reunion*; Faust, *This Republic of Suffering*; and Loewen, *Lies across America*. For other instrumental works regarding the development of memory in the South, see Edwards, *Scarlett Doesn't Live Here Anymore*; and Domby, *False Cause*.

14. Janney, *Burying the Dead but Not the Past*; Janney, *Remembering the Civil War*; Cox, *Dixie's Daughters*; Cox, *Dreaming of Dixie*; Gannon, *Won Cause*; Kachun, *Festivals of Freedom*; Fortney, "Lest We Remember." In addition, many essays in Marten and Janney, *Buying and Selling Civil War Memory in Gilded Age America* highlight the significance of material objects to this evolving society.

15. Stewart, *On Longing*, 132–35.

1. ASSUMING THE CLOTH OF WAR

1. "The War Began," *Macon (GA) Daily Telegraph*, Jan. 12, 1861.

2. Gordon, "Novices in Warfare," 194–223 (quote, 198).

3. Gordon, "Novices in Warfare," 194.

4. Long, *Changes in the Uniform of the Army*. The prices of clothing during the Revolutionary War are not available, but Long created a comparison chart from 1816 that showed they were comparable to prices during the War of 1812. Long believed that they adopted the color blue as a nod to the Whigs, a British political party that opposed the Court.

5. Common Threads Army (online); Long, *Changes in the Uniform of the Army.*

6. Long, *Changes in the Uniform of the Army.* The clothing list includes a cap, flannel shirt, cotton shirt, shoes, stockings, blanket, and coat.

7. U.S. War Department, *General Regulations for the Army 1847,* 186–215; Franklin, "Menswear," 1840–1849, Fashion History Timeline, Mar. 26, 2020, ; Long, *Changes in the Uniform of the Army.*

8. Wilson, *Business of Civil War,* 8.

9. *Washington (DC) Constitution,* Feb. 15, 1860.

10. *Macon (GA) Daily Telegraph,* Feb. 14, 1860.

11. *Baltimore Sun,* Mar. 15, 1860.

12. *Macon (GA) Daily Telegraph,* Feb. 15, 1860.

13. Grinspan, "'Young Men for War,'" 357–78.

14. On January 9, 1861, Mississippi seceded, followed on the tenth by Florida; on the eleventh, Alabama; on the nineteenth, Georgia; on the twenty-sixth, Louisiana; and on February 1, Texas. On February 8 the Montgomery convention began.

15. "A Plea to the Public," *Anderson Intelligencer* (Anderson Court House, SC), Dec. 20, 1860.

16. *San Francisco Daily Evening Bulletin,* Feb. 18, 1861.

17. "The Fourth Ward Meeting," *National Republican* (Washington, DC), Jan. 8, 1861.

18. "The Emmet Guard," *Philadelphia Inquirer,* Jan. 10, 1861.

19. Advertisement, J. W. Aderhold, *Macon (GA) Daily Telegraph,* Mar. 23, 1861.

20. Notification, *New Orleans Daily Picayune,* Feb. 8, 1861.

21. Notification, *Baltimore Sun,* Feb. 13, 1861.

22. Matthews, *Statutes at Large of the Provisional Government of the Confederate States,* 45–47.

23. Mendelsohn, *Rag Race,* 162, 164; McPherson, *Battle Cry of Freedom,* 323.

24. McPherson, *Atlas of the Civil War,* 20–27; Wilson, *Business of Civil War,* 24. Wilson notes that at this point neither the states nor the federal government had enough uniforms on hand to clothe new regiments.

25. Matthews, *Statutes at Large of the Provisional Government of the Confederate States,* 104, 118, 119.

26. *Biographical Encyclopedia of Ohio,* 186.

27. Wilson, *Business of Civil War,* 17.

28. Mendelsohn, *Rag Race,* 175; McPherson, *Battle Cry of Freedom,* 324.

29. Wilson, *Business of Civil War,* 19–20. Many of these bids were given to larger clothiers and manufacturers that were well established and had connections with government officials.

30. Rockaway, *Jews of Detroit,* 14.

31. Wilson, *Business of Civil War,* 18.

32. Wilson, *Confederate Industry,* 160.

33. Wilson, *Business of Civil War,* 37.

34. Common Threads Army (online) .

35. T. W. Park to Hon. Erastus Fairbanks, *Saint Johnsbury (VT) Caledonian,* June 7, 1861.

36. "Off for the War," *Watertown (WI) Republican,* July 19, 1861.

37. "The Eighth Maine Regiment," *New York Herald*, Sept. 12, 1861.

38. "Indiana Troops for Virginia," *Cincinnati Daily Press*, May 31, 1861.

39. "Carl Schurz's Cavalry Regiment," *Mineral Point (WI) Weekly Tribune*, May 28, 1861.

40. *Arms and Equipment of the Union*, 88.

41. "Shameful Treatment of Ohio Volunteers," *Highland (OH) News*, June 6, 1861.

42. "Camp Scott. At York," *Philadelphia Inquirer*, May 20, 1861. For more on shoddy or unusable uniforms, see Wilson, *Business of Civil War*, 24.

43. *Burlington (VT) Free Press*, June 14, 1861.

44. "Camp Dennison Matters," *Cincinnati Daily Press*, May 31, 1861.

45. Hicks, "Organization of the Volunteer Army in 1861 with Special Reference to Minnesota," 338.

46. Dwight, *Life and Letters*, 77.

47. "Dead Fish," *Gallipolis (OH) Journal*, Sept. 12, 1861. This story was reported in newspapers throughout Wisconsin, Michigan, Iowa, and Ohio.

48. *Revised Regulations for the Army of the United States*, 169–72.

49. "The State in the Tin Cup Business," *Cadiz (OH) Democratic Sentinel*, June 19, 1861.

50. "General Order 20," *Daily Ohio Statesman* (Columbus), May 24, 1861; *Delaware (OH) Gazette*, May 24, 1861.

51. Castleman, *Army of the Potomac*, 288 (Sept. 10, 1861).

52. "Below the Grade of Lieutenant," *Indiana State Sentinel* (Indianapolis), May 1, 1861. This information was obtained by the newspaper and notes the 1860 monetary information from the army register. *Pomeroy (OH) Weekly Telegraph*, Nov. 1, 1861.

53. "Clothing of Soldiers," *Cleveland Morning Leader*, May 20, 1861.

54. Wilson, *Business of Civil War*, 18.

55. Gladys Storm, "Lowell in the Civil War," in Lowell Historical Society, *Contributions of the Lowell Historical Society*, 183.

56. Giesberg, "Waging War Their Own Way," 22–23.

57. U.S. Bureau of Labor, *Report on Condition of Woman and Child Wage-Earners*, 262.

58. Weeks, *Report on the Statistics of Wages in Manufacturing Industries*, 52–53.

59. Benjamin Franklin Butler to Winfield Scott, Aug. 13, 1861, in Butler, *Private and Official Correspondence*, 669.

60. Giesberg, "Waging War Their Own Way," 20.

61. Attie, *Patriotic Toil*, 33, 95.

62. "The Work of the Patriotic Women," *Philadelphia Inquirer*, Apr. 23, 1861.

63. "Narrative of Mr. H. C. Ferrell," *Charlotte (NC) Western Democrat*, Dec. 3, 1861.

64. "Municipal Legislation," *Nashville Daily Union*, Oct. 19, 1864.

65. Matthews, *Statutes at Large of the Provisional Government of the Confederate States*, 196.

66. The example of southern women freely sewing uniform items for the Confederacy assists in combating the narrative that they did not help with war tasks on the home front. Other works that respond to and combat the southern "damsel in distress" narrative, which began appearing in the 1970s, include but are not limited to Scott, *Southern Lady*; Clinton, *Plantation Mistress*; Fox-Genovese, *Within the Plantation Household*; Bynum, *Unruly Women*; Clinton and Silber, *Divided Houses*; McCurry, *Masters of Small Worlds*; Edwards, *Scarlett Doesn't Live*

Here Anymore; Whites, *Civil War as a Crisis in Gender;* Faust, *Mothers of Invention;* Curran, "'Making War on Women' and Women Making War"; and Glymph, *Women's Fight.*

67. "Pantaloon Makers," *Wilmington (NC) Daily Journal,* June 14, 1861.

68. Advertisement, *Richmond (VA) Daily Dispatch,* Apr. 30, 1861.

69. Advertisement, *Abbeville (SC) Press,* Aug. 8, 1861; For further examples of women's assistance, see *Richmond (VA) Daily Dispatch,* Apr. 24, 1861.

70. Johnston, *Story of a Confederate Boy,* 33.

71. Ashby, *Valley Campaign,* 28.

72. J. R. Wilson, Letter to the Editor, *Abbeville (SC) Press,* July 12, 1861.

73. "New Volunteer Company," *Richmond (VA) Daily Dispatch,* June 7, 1861.

74. Zenas T. Haines to unknown, Sept. 6, 1862, in *Letters from the Forty-Fourth Regiment M.V.M.: A Record of the Experience of a Nine Month's Regiment in the Department of North Carolina in 1862-3* (Boston: Herald Job Office, 1863), 121.

75. Confederate States of America, *Uniform and Dress of the Army of the Confederate States,* 226.

76. "The Young Guard," *Memphis Daily Appeal,* Apr. 19, 1861.

77. Thornton and Ekelund, *Tariffs, Blockades, and Inflation,* 48–57.

78. Wilson, *Confederate Industry,* 146.

79. William Gregg to Whitin and Sons, Apr. 18, 1861, Records of P. Whitin and Sons, South Caroliniana Library, University of South Carolina.

80. "Seizures in New York," *Yorkville (SC) Enquirer,* May 7, 1861.

81. S. Isaac Campbell & Co. invoices, Aug. 12, Dec. 23, 24, 1861, Colin J. McRae Collection, South Carolina Confederate Relic Room and Military Museum; Mendelsohn, *Rag Race,* 179.

82. Wilson, *Confederate Industry,* 162–63.

83. Vandiver, *Confederate Blockade Running through Bermuda,* xvi.

84. For a list of Confederate government officials and their relationships with the southern planter class, see Hubbard, *Burden of Confederate Diplomacy,* 2–12. Jefferson Davis, Alexander Stephens, Robert Toombs, Leroy P. Walker, Christopher G. Memminger, Judah P. Benjamin, Stephen R. Mallory, and John H. Reagan each had plantation connections or understood how plantation finances operated.

85. Slavery was the base of the southern plantation economy. Planter economics without the ability to sell slaves to get out of debt meant that their economic system could not work. To revisit these and other concepts of that system, see Neptune, "Throwin' Scholarly Shade." For more information on plantation economics and the early United States, see Elkins and McKitrick, *Age of Federalism.*

86. The Confederate Congress allotted $648,780 to clothe the army on March 11, 1861, and an additional $200,000 specifically for South Carolina troops and $133,860 for the navy on March 15. Matthews, *Statutes at Large of the Provisional Government of the Confederate States,* 58, 69, 72, 126, 150, 196. According to historian Mark Wilson, by 1861, several northern states had spent a total of $25 million on military goods, but it is unclear how much of that went to uniforms for soldiers. Wilson, *Business of Civil War,* 12.

87. Letters 11, 15, 16, and 18, 1862, Alfred Ward Grayson Davis Papers, South Caroliniana Library, University of South Carolina.

88. Wilson, *Confederate Industry*, 43–44.

89. Wilson, *Confederate Industry*, 215.

90. For more on the statistics of Confederate textile factories during 1862, see Wilson, *Confederate Industry*; and Duffey, "Not So Ragged Confederates."

91. Thornton and Ekelund, *Tariffs, Blockades, and Inflation*, 29. For further discussion of the economic devastation in the South due to the blockade, see the entirety of *Tariffs, Blockades, and Inflation*.

92. Barry and Burt, *Suppliers to the Confederacy II*, 50–51.

93. U.S. War Department, *War of the Rebellion*, ser. 4, 2:190–91 [hereafter cited as *OR;* all references to series 1 unless otherwise stated]. "Confederate cotton bonds were 20-year securities with a 7% coupon payable in British [pounds] sterling." Weidenmier, "Market for Confederate Cotton Bonds," 78.

94. Vandiver, *Confederate Blockade Running through Bermuda*, xx.

95. Thompson, *Confederate Purchasing Operations Abroad*, 108; Fisher, "Blockaded State," 265. Unfortunately, the records for the Trans-Mississippi War Department were not well kept in terms of supplies brought in from Mexico, so it is difficult to know the quantities of goods exchanged.

96. "An Appeal to the Women of the South," *Spirit of the Age* (Raleigh, NC), Apr. 14, 1862.

97. Avary, *Virginia Girl in the Civil War*, 164, 167–71.

98. "Military Laws," in Confederate States, *Digest of the Military and Naval Laws, 93.*

99. "Rebel Atrocities," *Cleveland Morning Leader*, Jan. 16, 1862.

100. "The Situation," *New York Herald*, Oct. 13, 1862.

101. Steiner, *Report*, 20, 43 (Sept. 10, 1862).

102. Diamond, "Imports of the Confederate Government."

103. Gibson, "Americans and the Civil War."

104. Matthews, *Statutes at Large of the Provisional Government of the Confederate States*, xiv.

105. Albert Pike to Congress, Dec. 12, 1861, Confederate Documents Collection, Research Division, Oklahoma Historical Society.

106. Matthews, *Statutes at Large of the Provisional Government of the Confederate States*, 238.

107. Ostler, *Surviving Genocide, pt. 1.* Ostler provides a thorough account of interaction between Native Peoples and settler colonialists. While he mentions providing food or clothing to Native communities during times of war, they were never given uniforms for service.

108. Warde, *When the Wolf Came*, 117.

109. Yarbrough, *Choctaw Confederates*, 117, 137.

110. Hauptman, *Between Two Fires*, 109–10; Crow, *Storm in the Mountains.*

111. Shier, *Warriors in Mr. Lincoln's Army*, 1–10. Shier provides detailed wartime and pension records for the men in Company K, First Michigan Sharpshooters.

112. Warde, *When the Wolf Came*, 117–18.

113. Conneole, "Why They Fought"; Warde, *When the Wolf Came*, 97–98.

114. Confer, "Hardship at Home."

115. Lincoln, *Collected Works*, 296–97.

116. "Chronology of Emancipation during the Civil War," Freedmen and Southern Society Project, last revised Apr. 21, 2023, http://www.freedmen.umd.edu/chronol.htm; Lincoln, *Collected Works*, 357; Weicksel, "To Look like Men of War," 126, 137. Weicksel discusses the role clothing played in the transformation process for African American soldiers during the Civil War.

2. THE COST OF WAR

1. "The Cost of Uniforms for the Rebel Army," *Philadelphia Inquirer*, Feb. 13, 1863.

2. Emancipation Proclamation, Jan. 1, 1863, Online Exhibits, National Archives, https://www.archives.gov/exhibits/featured-documents/emancipation-proclamation.

3. Dyer, *Regimental Histories*, 997–1720.

4. "War Department General Order 143: Creation of the U.S. Colored Troops (1863)," Milestone Documents, National Archives, May 22, 1863, https://www.archives.gov/milestone -documents/war-department-general-order-143.

5. "The Colored Soldiers in Kansas," *Douglass' Monthly* (Rochester, NY), Jan. 1863.

6. *Christian Recorder* (Philadelphia), May 30, 1863.

7. "War Department General Order 143," https://www.archives.gov/milestone-documents /war-department-general-order-143.

8. For more on camp and equipment conditions, see Grant, "Fighting for Freedom"; Washington, *Eagles on Their Buttons;* and Berlin, Reidy, and Rowland, *Freedom's Soldiers.*

9. Taylor, *Black Woman's Civil War Memoirs*, 41–42.

10. Luke and Smith, *Soldiering for Freedom*, 67.

11. *San Francisco Evening Bulletin*, Apr. 7, 1863.

12. "Help to Raise Colored Soldiers," *Douglass' Monthly* (Rochester, NY), Mar. 1863, 804.

13. *Christian Recorder* (Philadelphia), Dec. 17, 1864.

14. For more on Black troops and their struggles with payment and camp life, see Luke and Smith, *Soldiering for Freedom.*

15. Higginson, *Army Life in a Black Regiment*, 288. Thomas Higginson was an officer with the Thirty-Third USCT. The Militia Act of July 1862 "enabled the President to pay black soldiers the full $10, [but] most did not receive this pay adjustment for up to eighteen months after it was approved." Whitehead, *Notes from a Colored Girl*, 73.

16. Lorenzo Thomas, *Official Price List of Clothing, Jan. 1, 1863*, Gilder Lehrman Collection, *Gilder Lehrman Institute of American History*, online at American History, 1493–1945, Adam Matthew Digital, http://www.americanhistory.amdigital.co.uk (subscription required). The list of clothing accounted for is as follows: uniform hat, feather, cord and tassel, forage cap, and cap cover; uniform coat, great coat, trousers, one flannel shirt, one knit shirt, flannel drawers, knit drawers, and stockings; and bootees, bootees pegged, and leather stocks. Each man could have two pairs of trousers and up to three each of flannel shirts, knit shirts, flannel drawers, and knit drawers. This does not include blankets, which counted toward the clothing allowance and were $3.60 each. In 2023 the same uniform expenses would be $1,388.49 annually, leaving a yearly take-home pay of $2,022.42.

17. "Injustice to Colored Troops," *Hartford (CT) Daily Courant,* Jan. 25, 1864.

18. Abel, *American Indian in the Civil War,* 250–51.

19. *OR,* 22(2):140.

20. *OR,* 22(2):166.

21. *OR,* 22(2):1078.

22. *OR,* 22(2):1104.

23. *OR,* 22(2):1095–96. Scott attempted to assuage the frustrations of Creek leaders for their soldiers by asking for more guns instead of the better clothing they requested.

24. Indian Home Brigade, Company Orders Book, 1863–65, Research Center, Oklahoma Historical Society, 12–17. In April 1865 dollar amounts appear underneath each article of clothing issued. Captain Downing and his company served as the personal bodyguard for the John Ross family. Minges, *Slavery in the Cherokee Nation,* 145.

25. *Baltimore Sun,* Mar. 17, 1863.

26. Advertisement, *New York Herald,* June 5, 1863.

27. Advertisement, *Middletown (CT) Constitution,* Mar. 3, 1863.

28. Advertisement, *Hartford (CT) Daily Courant,* Mar. 4, 1863.

29. "Military Matters in New York," *Hartford (CT) Daily Courant,* June 18, 1863.

30. Advertisement, *Philadelphia Inquirer,* June 18, 1863.

31. "The Zouaves of the 165th Regiment of New York State Volunteers," *New York Herald,* Feb. 3, 1864.

32. U.S. War Department, *Revised United States Army Regulations of 1861,* 134, 170–72.

33. Quarter Master Stores Papers, 1861–Oct. 1863, Clapp Civil War Papers, Massachusetts Historical Society.

34. Wilson, *Business of Civil War,* 91.

35. Robert Walker to Patience Walker, Nov. 14, 1863, in Walker, *Letters,* 19, available at https://babel.hathitrust.org/cgi/pt?id=loc.ark:/13960/t1jh40124&view=1up&seq=23. Walker was a white soldier from Ohio. He died at the age of twenty-three from wounds sustained on December 15, 1864, during the Battle of Nashville.

36. Lane, *Soldier's Diary, 42 (Apr. 13, 30, 1863).* Lane was a white soldier from Michigan.

37. Thomas, *Official Price List of Clothing, Jan. 1, 1863, Gilder Lehrman Collection.*

38. U.S. War Department, *Revised United States Army Regulations of 1861,* 23–24.

39. "A Martyr Fallen," *Marshall County Republican* (Plymouth, IN), Mar. 26, 1863.

40. "Our Sick and Wounded Soldiers," *Bradford Reporter* (Towanda, PA), Apr. 30, 1863.

41. *Ottawa (IL) Free Trader,* Jan. 31, 1863.

42. J. Wilcox, "Resolutions Adopted by the 7th Iowa Cavalry, March 7, 1863," *Weekly Ottumwa (IA) Courier,* Mar. 26, 1863.

43. Edward East to Charles B. Colton, Sept. 21, 1862, Henry A. Huntington Papers, Southern Historical Collection, Louis Round Wilson Special Collections Library, University of North Carolina; A. L. Stamps to Colonel Ashburn, Apr. 7, 1863, ibid.; Henry Huntington to Maj. William Wiles, July 22, 23, 1863, ibid.; Capt. L. H. Drury to "My Dear Heaney," Oct. 15, 1863, ibid.; George H. Storie to Brig. Gen. G. M. Dodge, Jan. 4, 1864, ibid.; Capt. G. D. McKinney to "Friend Harry," Jan. 28, 1864, ibid. Copies of these letters were filed in the Office of the Provost Marshal General, Department of the Cumberland as well as sent to the respective parties.

44. "General Orders No. 100: The Lieber Code," Avalon Project, Lillian Goldman Law Library, Yale Law School, https://avalon.law.yale.edu/19th_century/lieber.asp.

45. *Baltimore Sun,* May 21, 1863.

46. Adolphus, *Imported Confederate Uniforms of Peter Tait & Co.,* 9–11. The typical bale of clothing comprised about 150 garments.

47. Barry and Burt, *Suppliers to the Confederacy II,* 186, 199.

48. Barry and Burt, *Suppliers to the Confederacy II,* 218–19, "The Navy: The Wilmington Blockade," *New York Herald,* Oct. 22, 1864. Tait obtained the woolen portions of the material used in Confederate uniforms from Alexander Collie & Company.

49. *New York Herald,* Dec. 20, 1863.

50. *OR,* ser. 4, 2:647; Barry and Burt, *Suppliers to the Confederacy II,* 84–94. When the Confederacy collapsed in May 1865, the S.I.C.C. still held approximately $1,500,000 in now-worthless bonds and cotton warrants.

51. *Houston Tri-Weekly Telegraph,* Feb. 6, 1865.

52. Cumming, *Kate,* 171, (Feb. 26, 1864). Cumming lived in Alabama throughout the war.

53. Tyler, *Santiago Vidaurri and the Southern Confederacy,* 98–128, 149–51; *Philadelphia Inquirer,* Feb. 17, 1863; *OR,* 53:913, 958–59. For more on the economic advantages gained by Mexico and the Confederate cotton trade, see Tyler, *Santiago Vidaurri and the Southern Confederacy.*

54. General Orders No. 69, Feb. 22, 1864, Main Street Fine Books & Manuscripts, https://www.mainstreetfinebooks.com/pages/books/25459/general-orders-civil-war-abraham-lincoln/general-orders-no-69.

55. General Orders No. 69, Feb. 22, 1864; Tyler, *Santiago Vidaurri and the Southern Confederacy,* 150.

56. *OR,* 39(2):565–66.

57. Wilson, *Confederate Industry,* 102–3, 109, 115.

58. *OR,* 39(2):503. Wilson, *Confederate Industry,* 200, app. C, 295.

59. *OR,* 39(2):503.

60. Carr, "General Sherman's March to the Sea." For the classic account, see Glatthaar, *March to the Sea and Beyond.*

61. *OR,* 38(5):91, 92–93.

62. "Costume of the First Families," *Philadelphia Inquirer,* Apr. 25, 1863.

63. Jones, *Rebel War Clerk's Diary,* 318.

64. Green Berry Samuels to Kathleen Boone Samuels, Mar. 7, 1863, in *Civil War Marriage in Virginia.*

65. Fremantle, *Three Months in the Southern States,* 156. Fremantle, a neutral British government official, made many entries in his diary regarding soldiers from both sides. How these men were dressed was an important part of his descriptions and his understanding of the situation.

66. Lane, *Soldier's Diary,* 42 (Apr. 30, 1863).

67. Lynch, *Civil War Diary,* 121 (Sept. 4, 1864). Lynch, who was born in New York, lived in Connecticut.

68. Maj. Gen. W. S. Rosecrans, "Letter from Gen. Rosecrans to the Indiana Legislature," *Richmond (VA) Examiner,* Mar. 16, 1863.

69. "Yesterday's Dispatches," *Hartford (CT) Daily Courant*, Apr. 10, 1863. Other reports of the same incident also contend that the rebel troops were disguised in Union uniforms.

70. Col. J. P. Baird, "Colonel Baird Explains the Cause of His Suspicions," *New York Herald*, June 10, 1863.

71. Weicksel, "Dress of the Enemy," 138. For more on disease and the yellow-fever plot, see the entirety of Weicksel's article.

3. SENTIMENTAL STITCHES

1. Long, *Changes in the Uniform of the Army*.

2. Dwight, *Life and Letters*, 200–205.

3. Favill, *Diary of a Young Officer*, 4–8.

4. McHenry, *Recollections of a Maryland Confederate*, 165–70.

5. Robert E. Lee to Margaret Stuart, Mar. 20, 1864, Papers of Robert E. Lee, Acc. 1085, Special Collections, University of Virginia Library.

6. Over 5,000 such images are in the Liljenquist Family Collection of Civil War Photographs, Library of Congress, available online at https://www.loc.gov/collections/liljenquist-civil-war-photographs/about-this-collection/.

7. John J. Russell to Charles, Rolla, MO, Feb. 12, 1862, Box 1, Folder 5, Case MS 10020, John J. Russell Letters, Newberry Library.

8. "General Order Number 247," *Christian Recorder* (Philadelphia), Oct. 8, 1864. Chaplain Turner's letter was sent on August 25, 1864.

9. David Glasgow Farragut to Gustavus Vasa Fox, Apr. 22, 1863, in Fox, *Confidential Correspondence*, 453–55.

10. By 1862, the Eighty-Third had switched from the Zouave-style to "government" uniforms. Norton, *Army Letters*, 38, 42.

11. "Female Soldiers," *Daily Evansville (IN) Journal*, Jan. 30, 1863.

12. Blanton and Cook, *They Fought like Demons*, 7, 47–52.

13. "A Woman in Soldier Clothes," *Cincinnati Daily Press*, May 14, 1861.

14. "Micellaneous [*sic*] and News Items," *Soldiers' Journal (Alexandria, VA)*, Feb. 17, 1864.

15. "War Incidents," *Saint Paul (MN) Weekly Pioneer and Democrat*, June 10, 1864.

16. Wakeman, *Uncommon Soldier*, 25, 31.

17. Sarah Wakeman to parents, Aug. 19, 1863, in Wakeman, *Uncommon Soldier*, 44.

18. Sarah Wakeman to parents, Nov. 22, 1863, in Wakeman, *Uncommon Soldier*, 54.

19. General Order No. 15, Feb. 25, 1864, in Wakeman, *Uncommon Soldier*, 64.

20. Sarah Wakeman to parents, Dec. 28, 1863, in Wakeman, *Uncommon Soldier*, 58.

21. Wakeman, *Uncommon Soldier*, 82.

22. Velazquez, *Woman in Battle*, 185. DeAnne Blanton and Lauren Cook explain the caution around using Velazquez's account. See *They Fought like Demons*.

23. Edmonds, *Nurse and Spy in the Union Army*, 293, 353.

24. White and White, "Slave Clothing and African-American Culture," 153–86; "Material Culture: Subsistence & Foodways" (online). The Negro Act of 1735 suggested cheap materials as "suitable" for slave clothing. O'Neall, *Negro Law of South Carolina*.

25. Chaplain John Eaton Jr. to Lt. Col. Jno. A. Rawlins, Apr. 29, 1863, O-328 1863, Letters Received, ser. 12, Adjutant General's Office, Record Group 94, National Archives.

26. Lt. Charles L. Stevens to Lt. J. H. Metcalf, Jan. 27, 1863, enclosed in Col. F. S. Nickerson to Capt. A. Badeau, Jan. 28, 1863, Miscellaneous Records, ser. 1796, Department of the Gulf, U.S. Army Continental Commands, Record Group 393, pt. 1, National Archives. For more on the conditions at the "contraband" camps, see Downs, *Sick from Freedom;* and Manning, *Troubled Refuge.*

27. "The Black Soldiers of South Carolina," *Douglass' Monthly* (Rochester, NY), Jan. 1863, 783.

28. "War Meeting of the Colored People," *Washington (DC) Star,* June 10, 1863.

29. "What One Negro Did for Gen. Burnside," *Douglass' Monthly* (Rochester, NY), Aug. 1862.

30. Wilson, *Campfires of Freedom,* 158.

31. Jones, "Freeman Thomas 1845–1936, 12th US Colored Infantry" (accessed July 3, 2022).

32. For further discussion of the role clothing played in the transformation process for African American soldiers during the Civil War, see Weicksel, "To Look like Men of War."

33. McPherson, *Struggle for Equality,* 192.

34. "War Meeting of the Colored People," *Washington (DC) Star,* June 10, 1863.

35. "War Meeting of the Colored People."

36. Newmark, "Civil War Surgeon's Books Rediscovered" (online).

37. "The Emancipation Jubilee Last Night," *Washington (DC) Star,* Apr. 17, 1863. Dr. David Jones Peck was the first African American to earn a medical degree inside the United States, in 1847 when few medical schools admitted Black students. Theodore Corbin, "Celebrating Black History Month: Reflections on the Legacy of David Jones Peck, MD," Rush University Medical Center, Feb. 22, 2022, https://www.rush.edu/news/celebrating-black-history -month-reflections-legacy-david-jones-peck-md.

38. Alexander T. Augusta, "Letter to Editor," *Christian Recorder* (Philadelphia), May 30, 1863.

39. "Congressional," *Washington (DC) Star,* Feb. 10, 1864.

40. Matthews, *Statutes at Large of the Provisional Government of the Confederate States,* 284.

41. *OR,* 22(2):819–21 (Apr. 15, 1863).

42. Hauptman, *Between Two Fires,* 166.

43. Hauptman, *Between Two Fires,* 178.

44. "Oneida and Menomonee Indians as Soldiers," *Wisconsin Daily Patriot* (Madison), Jan. 18, 1864.

45. Resolution of the General Council of the Choctaw Nation, Oct. 10, 1864, Native American Manuscripts, Indian Pioneer Papers, University of Oklahoma.

46. Jane Carson Brunson, "A Sketch of the Work at Greenville," in Taylor et al., *South Carolina Women in the Confederacy,* 26.

47. "Excerpts from the Diary of Judith Brockenbrough McGuire 1861–1865," in *Women of the South in War Times,* comp. Matthew Page Andrews (Baltimore, MD: Norman, Remington, 1920), 75–77 (May 10, 1861), available at https://babel.hathitrust.org/cgi/pt?id=loc.ark :/13960/t0ht3dz2b&view=1up&seq=101&q1=the%20ladies%20of%20alexandria.

48. "For the Confederate," *Raleigh (NC) Daily Confederate,* Apr. 23, 1864.

49. Richards, *Village Life in America*, 131.

50. "The Sanitary Commission," *Orleans Independent Standard* Blanton, VT), Apr. 22, 1864.

51. "A Woman's Inquiry," *Chicago Daily Tribune*, Dec. 27, 1861.

52. "Colored Regiments from Philadelphia," *Philadelphia Inquirer*, Mar. 24, 1863.

53. For further discussion of the role clothing played in the transformation process for African American soldiers during the Civil War, see Weicksel, "To Look like Men of War."

54. "Meeting of the Colored Citizens," *Douglass' Monthly* (Rochester, NY), Mar. 1863, 809.

55. *Christian Recorder* (Philadelphia), Aug. 8, 1863.

56. *Douglass' Monthly* (Rochester, NY), Aug. 1863.

57. "Dear Friend," *Christian Recorder* (Philadelphia), Nov. 7, 1863.

58. Perry, *Letters from a Surgeon of the Civil War*, 4–7.

59. Hosmer, *Color-Guard*, 218. Hosmer was from Massachusetts, and many of his diary entries contain comments on uniforms and clothing.

60. *Pittsfield (MA) Sun*, Feb. 5, 1863.

61. *Douglass' Monthly* (Rochester, NY), Mar. 1863, 814.

62. *New York Herald*, Aug. 15, 1863.

63. Norton, *Army Letters*, 202–3.

64. *Cleveland Morning Leader*, Sept. 30, 1862.

65. Thomas Keenan to unknown, Apr. 20, 1865, in Post, *Soldiers' Letters, from Camp, Battle-field, and Prison*, 475–81.

66. Manning, *What This Cruel War Was Over*.

67. *Winston-Salem (NC) Western Sentinel*, June 6, 1862.

68. *Chicago Daily Tribune*, Aug. 30, 1862.

69. *Charlotte (NC) Western Democrat*, Aug. 5, 1862.

70. *OR*, 22(2):543; *Washington (AR) Telegraph*, June 8, 1864.

71. "Recent Expedition into North Carolina," *Washington (DC) Star*, Jan. 13, 1864.

72. *Charlotte (NC) Western Democrat*, Aug. 5, 1862.

73. *Macon (GA) Daily Telegraph*, Apr. 16, 1863.

74. Charles Herman Journals, July 26, 27, Aug. 27, 1863, Georgia Historical Society.

75. *Christian Recorder* (Philadelphia), Apr. 23, 1864.

76. Vorenberg, *Emancipation Proclamation*, 99–100; Robert E. Lee to Andrew Hunter, Jan. 11, 1865, Papers of Robert E. Lee, Albert and Shirley Small Special Collections Library, University of Virginia. One northern paper even discussed Lee's position on enlisting slaves as soldiers and questioned if he was a good southerner. See *New York Herald*, Feb. 28, 1865.

77. "Arming Slave," *Raleigh (NC) Daily Confederate*, Jan. 12, 1865.

78. *OR*, ser. 4, 3:1161–62.

79. *Wheeling (WV) Daily Intelligencer*, Feb. 17, 1865 (speech printed from a Richmond source).

80. *New York Herald*, Feb. 20, 1865.

81. "How the Negro Soldiers are to be Uniformed," *New York Herald*, Feb. 20, 1865. This story also appeared in the *Eaton (OH) Democratic Press* (Mar. 2, 1865) and the *New Orleans Daily Picayune* (Mar. 5, 1865).

82. *Philadelphia Inquirer,* Feb. 27, 1865.

83. "COLORED TROOPS. An Appeal to the People of Virginia," *Richmond Dispatch,* Mar. 20, 1865.

84. "From the North," *Macon (GA) Daily Telegraph and Confederate,* Mar. 29, 1865.

85. "From the North," *Macon (GA) Daily Telegraph and Confederate,* Mar. 29, 1865.

86. Litwack, *Been in the Storm So Long,* 97.

87. For information debating the validity of evidence regarding Black soldiers, see Musick, "Is There Archival Proof of Black Confederates?," 35. For more on the historical understanding of Black Confederates and how the misconceptions of this short-lived phenomenon exploded in popular memory, see Levin, "Black Confederates out of the Attic and into the Mainstream"; Levin, *Searching for Black Confederates;* and Domby, *False Cause.*

4. COCKADES, BADGES & FLAGS

1. "Union Feeling at Baltimore," *Clarksville (TN) Chronicle,* Apr. 19, 1861.

2. Callahan and Ledgerwood, "On the Psychological Function of Flags and Logos," 528, 545). The article reports on the psychological effect that "material trappings of group identity" have on people. It looks at how emblems and flags affect the attitudes of inferences of the people who adopt them. The theory of self-completion suggests that "individuals use symbols and other socially recognized indicators to communicate aspects of their desired personal identity or self-image to others." Ibid., 528.

3. Legon, "Bound up with Meaning." A growing scholarship on material culture as political signifiers is common in English and French histories. See, for example, Navickas, "'That Sash Will Hang You.'" For more on political print culture, see Knights, "Possessing the Visual"; and Haynes, *Pictures and Popery.*

4. Long, *Changes in the Uniform of the Army.*

5. Secession Cockade, 1862, "Images from the Matthew L. Oswalt M.D. Collection"; "Secession Cockade" (accessed July 4, 2022).

6. "The Minute Men," *Weekly Mississippian* (Jackson), Nov. 7, 1860.

7. *White Cloud Kansas Chief,* Feb. 6, 1862 (article reprinted from *Boston Journal*).

8. "War Items," *Baltimore Daily Exchange,* Sept. 9, 1861.

9. "Secession at Yale," *Des Arc (AR) Constitutional Union,* Feb. 8, 1861.

10. "The President's Levee," *Washington (DC) Evening Star,* Jan. 1, 1861.

11. For information on the history of the U.S. flag, see Guenter, *American Flag,* 17. Guenter compiles a historical overview of "cultural shifts in the presentation, reproduction, and use of the flag of the United States in art, music, legend, custom, and ritual" from its creation to the "codification of a code of flag etiquette." Ibid., 21.

12. Marling, *Old Glory,* 3–9. For more on the origins of the U.S. flag, see Miller, *Betsy Ross and the Making of America.*

13. Guenter, *American Flag,* 25–30.

14. Advertisement, *Cleveland Morning Leader,* Sept. 17, 1860.

15. Advertisement, *Cleveland Morning Leader,* Aug. 13, 1860.

16. "The Stars and Stripes," *Newbern (NC) Weekly Progress*, Feb. 5, 1861.

17. "The Stars and Stripes at a Discount," *Rutland (VT) Weekly Herald*, Mar. 28, 1861.

18. Coski, *Confederate Battle Flag*, 2–17.

19. Hammerstrom, "How to Make a Flag or Standard" (online).

20. "Affairs at the South—Proceedings of the Southern Congress—The National Flag of the Confederate States," *Memphis Daily Appeal*, Mar. 13, 1861.

21. *Wilmington (NC) Journal*, Apr. 30, 1863.

22. *Wilmington (NC) Journal*, Apr. 30, 1863.

23. "Confederate Congress—The Flag," *Richmond (VA) Whig*, May 2, 1863.

24. Smith, *Flags*, 6; *Baton Rouge (LA) Sugar Planter*, Mar. 9, 1863.

25. "Rebel Flags," *Tipton (IA) Advertiser*, Mar. 2, 1865.

26. Advertisement, *Cleveland Morning Leader*, Aug. 1, 1861.

27. Advertisement, *Gold Hill (NV) Daily News*, Feb. 24, 1864.

28. See, for example, advertisement, *New York Herald*, Apr. 11, 1865.

29. Richards, *Village Life in America*, 132.

30. "Flag for the National Guards," *Philadelphia Inquirer*, Apr. 23, 1861. The presentation of this flag did not take place on time because the Guards had yet to receive their uniforms.

31. Headquarters, First Corps, Army of the Potomac, General Orders No. 75, Centreville, VA, Nov. 29, 1861, *Charleston (SC) Daily Courier*, Dec. 3, 1861.

32. "The First Regiment North Carolina Volunteers," *New York Times*, Aug. 5, 1863.

33. For more examples of African American women assisting in the flag effort, see Forbes, *African American Women during the Civil War*, 77, 103; and *Christian Recorder* (Philadelphia), Nov. 5, 1864.

34. *Douglass' Monthly* (Rochester, NY), Aug. 1863, 861.

35. Bacon and Howland, *Letters of a Family during the War for the Union*, 334–36.

36. "Gentlemen of the Louisiana . . . ," *New Orleans Daily Picayune*, Apr. 26, 30, 1861.

37. "Letter and Flags Sewed in Collars and Caps," *Memphis Daily Appeal*, Mar. 2, 1863.

38. James Penney to Peter P. Pitchlynn, June 6, 1863, Native American Manuscripts, Western History Collections, University of Oklahoma.

39. Smith, *Flags*, 196; Coski, *Confederate Battle Flag*, 6.

40. Ott, *Confederate Daughters*, 35–72.

41. "Exchange of Prisoners," *Philadelphia Inquirer*, May 16, 1863.

42. Untitled broadside recruiting African Americans for military service, 1863, Item GLC04198, Gilder Lehrman Collection, Gilder Lehrman Institute of American History, online at American History, 1493–1945, Adam Matthew Digital, http://www.americanhistory.am digital.co.uk (accessed June 17, 2019; subscription required).

43. *Christian Recorder* (Philadelphia), June 8, 1861.

44. Cooper, *Uniform and Dress of the Army of the Confederate States*, 1–5.

45. McPherson, *Illustrated Battle Cry of Freedom*, 507. Long, *Changes in the Uniform of the Army*. Instead of metal, which could be lost or broken, these badges were made of cloth and also denoted the division to which the soldier belonged.

46. Headquarters, Army of the Potomac, Circular, Mar. 21, 1863, in Billings, *Hardtack and Coffee*, 258; ibid., 261, 262.

47. "Hooker's Corps of Division Badges," *Chicago Daily Tribune*, Apr. 1, 1863.

48. Billings, *Hardtack and Coffee*, 266, 268.

49. *We Will Prove Ourselves as Men—127th Regt. U.S. Colored Troops*, U.S. Army Officers and Other Persons of the Civil War Period, cph 3a24165, http://loc.gov/pictures/resource /cph.3a24165/. The flags in this discussion were painted by an African American man, David Bustill Bowser, who was an artist in Philadelphia. His paintings typically depicted landscapes, portraits, and emblems and banners for local organizations. *Philadelphia Tribune*, Apr. 13, 2006.

50. *One Cause, One Country—45th Regt. U.S. Colored Troops*, U.S. Army Officers and Other Persons of the Civil War Period, cph 3b47501, http://hdl.loc.gov/loc.pnp/cph.3b47501.

51. *Freedom for All—6th United States Colored Troops*, U.S. Army Officers and Other Persons of the Civil War Period, cph 3g06156, http://hdl.loc.gov/loc.pnp/cph.3g06156.

52. *Let Soldiers in War, Be Citizens in Peace—24th Regt. U.S. Colored Troops*, U.S. Army Officers and Other Persons of the Civil War Period, ppmsca 11274, http://hdl.loc.gov/loc.pnp /ppmsca.11274; reverse of ibid., ppmsca 11275, http://hdl.loc.gov/loc.pnp/ppmsca.11275.

53. *Rather Die Freemen Than Live to Be Slaves—3rd United States Colored Troops*, U.S. Army Officers and Other Persons of the Civil War Period, cph 3a24166, http://hdl.loc.gov /loc.pnp/cph.3a24166. For more on the concepts of manhood, see Bederman, *Manliness and Civilization*.

54. *Sic Semper Tyrannis—22nd Regt. U.S. Colored Troops*, U.S. Army Officers and Other Persons of the Civil War Period, cph 3a24164, https://hdl.loc.gov/loc.pnp/cph.3a24164.

55. "First Kansas Colored Infantry Flag," Keep the Flag to the Front: Battle Flags of Kansas, last modified Oct. 2019, https://www.kshs.org/kansapedia/first-kansas-colored-infantry -flag/10125; "Second Kansas Colored Infantry Flag," ibid., last modified Feb. 2016, https://www .kshs.org/kansapedia/second-kansas-colored-infantry-flag/10312.

56. *Strike for God and [. . .]—25th United States Colored Troops*, U.S. Army Officers and Other Persons of the Civil War Period, cph 3b47500, https://hdl.loc.gov/loc.pnp/cph.3b47500.

57. Heartsill, *Fourteen Hundred and 91 Days in the Confederate Army*, 4–6, 23–26, 262.

58. "Counterfeiting the Flag," *Winston-Salem (NC) Western Sentinel*, Jan. 3, 1862.

59. "Cherokee Braves Flag," Gallery: Native Americans in the War, Civil War Virtual Museum, http://www.civilwarvirtualmuseum.org/1861-1862/native-americans-in-the-war /cherokee-braves-flag.php. This flag was captured by Lieutenant David Whittaker of Company B, 10th Regiment Kansas Volunteer Infantry at Locust Grove, Cherokee Nation, Indian Territory, on July 3, 1862.

60. Sarah Ann Harlan, interview, Aug. 24, 1937, ID 8248, Indian Pioneer Papers, Western History Collections, University of Oklahoma, 64.

61. Parker, *Seneca Indian in the Union Army*, 81–82, 88.

62. "The Battle of Buena Vista," *Charlotte (NC) Western Democrat*, May 21, 1861.

63. "The Flag Presentation to the Delta Rifles," *Baton Rouge (LA) Sugar Planter*, Apr. 27, 1861.

64. Ott, *Confederate Daughters*, 50–53.

65. Eleanor S. Turner Ivey, "Why I Am a Daughter of the Confederacy," in Taylor et al., *South Carolina Women in the Confederacy*, 225.

66. Miscellaneous, *Douglass' Monthly* (Rochester, NY), June 1863, 847.

67. "A Story of Patriotism," *Douglass' Monthly* (Rochester, NY), Aug. 1863, 856–57.

68. *Christian Recorder* (Philadelphia), Sept. 5, 1863.

69. *Christian Recorder* (Philadelphia), Sept. 5, 1863. The financial numbers for the Sixth USCT flag were published soon afterward. The report listed everyone who donated money (forty-two people), how much making the flag cost ($1.69), how much a man named D. Bowser was paid for his services painting the flag ($150), and the advertising price ($2.81). The entire endeavor cost $152.81. Ibid., Sept. 12, 1863.

70. *Christian Recorder* (Philadelphia), Nov. 21, 1863.

71. Bernstein, *New York City Draft Riots*, 138.

72. Leech, *Reveille in Washington*, 253.

73. Thomas Keenan to unknown, Apr. 20, 1865, in Post, *Soldiers' Letters, from Camp, Battle-field, and Prison*, 475–80.

74. Wittenmyer, *Under the Guns*, 66–69.

75. McLean, *Northern Woman in the Confederacy*, 12.

76. "Lucinda Davis," in *Slave Narratives*, 53–64, online at https://www.gutenberg.org/files /20785/20785-h/20785-h.htm.

77. "The Feeling in New Orleans," *Wilmington (NC) Journal*, May 8, 1862.

78. "Our New Orleans Correspondence," *New York Herald*, June 19, 1862.

79. "Hanging of WM B. Mumford," *Memphis Daily Appeal*, June 13, 1862; "In Union Occupied New Orleans, William B. Mumford Is Hanged for Treason," House Divided: The Civil War Research Engine at Dickinson College, https://hd.housedivided.dickinson.edu/node /39051.

5. SOLDIERS & THEIR UNIFORMS AFTER THE WAR

1. "The Surrender," *New York Herald*, Apr. 14, 1865. Several times throughout this issue, reporters mention how Lee was "neatly dressed in gray cloth."

2. "BOOTH—Particulars of His Escape, His Wanderings and Death," *Hartford (CT) Daily Courant*, Apr. 28, 1865.

3. U. S. Grant, "Glorious News!—Surrender of Lee and His Whole Army!," *Hartford (CT) Daily Courant*, Apr. 10, 1865. For more on the terms of surrender and parole, see Janney, *Ends of War*. For a brief discussion of uniforms, see ibid., chap. 13 and 230–31.

4. "Railroad Communications," *Philadelphia Inquirer*, Apr. 11, 1865.

5. Clampitt, *Lost Causes*, 2.

6. Gilpin, *Diary*, Apr. 26, 1865.

7. Abram J. Ryan, "The Conquered Banner," in *Poems: Patriotic, Religious, Miscellaneous* (1884; Ann Arbor: University of Michigan Humanities Text Initiative, 1997), 187, http://name .umdl.umich.edu/BAD9548.0001.001.

8. "Secesh Impudence," *Philadelphia Inquirer*, Apr. 12, 1865.

9. "Impudence," *Philadelphia Inquirer*, Apr. 15, 1865.

10. "Exclusion of Returned Rebels," *Baltimore Sun*, Apr. 26, 1865.

11. "Important Decision of the Attorney General," *Daily State Gazette and Republican* (Trenton, NJ), Apr. 26, 1865.

12. "The Opening of Trade" *Philadelphia Inquirer,* May 1, 1865.

13. "Dealing with the Traitors," *Philadelphia Inquirer,* May 17, 1865.

14. *New-Orleans Times,* May 24, 1865.

15. Andrews, *Diary,* May 8, 28, 1865. Andrews discusses her love of Confederate uniforms and southern soldiers multiple times throughout her diary.

16. Eppes, *Through Some Eventful Years,* June 17, 18, 1865.

17. "Queer Proposition," *New Orleans Daily Picayune,* May 17, 1865 (reprinted from the *Chicago Journal*). See also *New Hampshire Patriot and Gazette* (Concord), May 24, 1865.

18. Andrews, *Diary,* May 25, 1865.

19. "Letter from Montgomery," *New Orleans Daily Picayune,* Oct. 22, 1865.

20. For more on this event, see Reeves, *Lost Indictment of Robert E. Lee.*

21. "Lee in a New Suit," *Philadelphia Inquirer,* June 8, 1865.

22. Various Items, *New-Orleans Times,* June 21, 1865.

23. "General Lee in Destitute Circumstances," *Houston Tri-Weekly Telegraph,* June 9, 1865.

24. "Lee's Last Battles," *New Orleans Daily Picayune,* Aug. 27, 1865.

25. *OR,* ser. 3, 5:57; Holberton, *Homeward Bound,* 34–80. For personal accounts of the mustering-out process of both sides, see the entirety of Holberton, *Homeward Bound;* and Cimbala, *Veterans North and South.*

26. "Honorable Memorials," *Philadelphia Inquirer,* June 17, 1865.

27. "President Johnson Reviews the Battle-Scarred Warriors!," *Philadelphia Inquirer,* May 24, 1865.

28. "Last of the Grand Reviews," *Philadelphia Inquirer,* June 9, 1865.

29. Advertisement, "The Pittsburg Convention," *New York Herald,* Sept. 16, 1866.

30. *Washington (DC) Daily Constitutional Union,* Feb. 6, 1866.

31. Foner, *Reconstruction,* 487–97. Throughout his book, Foner references the use of the bloody shirt to drum up support for the Republican Party during the Reconstruction era in an attempt to keep the South in its place.

32. For more on Union men who were glad to put the war behind them, see Dean, *Shook over Hell;* and Logue and Blanck, *Heavy Laden.*

33. "Election Day," *Philadelphia Inquirer,* June 27, 1865.

34. Malcolm, *New Orleans Daily Picayune,* June 29, 1865. Malcolm was supposedly a correspondent of the *New York News,* writing from Washington.

35. Holzer, *Lincoln and Freedom,* 192.

36. Dyer, *Regimental Histories,* 1740–41.

37. Hauptman, *Between Two Fires,* 145. According to Hauptman, by 1860, there were fewer than thirty thousand Native Americans residing in the northern United States. Ibid., 125. Determining every Indigenous Person who fought for the Union in a northern regiment would require looking through every regimental description of each person and beyond the scope of this book.

38. "The Indian Tribes—Terms of Surrender of the Rebellious Indian Tribes," *New York Herald,* July 16, 1865.

39. Connole, *Civil War and the Subversion of American Indian Sovereignty*, 180; Warde, *When the Wolf Came*, 248.

40. "The Indian Tribes—Terms of Surrender of the Rebellious Indian Tribes," *New York Herald*, July 16, 1865.

41. Connole, *Civil War and the Subversion of American Indian Sovereignty*, 177–79.

42. "Notification," *Pittsfield (MA) Sun*, Aug. 24, 1865.

43. "The Indians—The Conference at Fort Smith," *Philadelphia Inquirer*, Oct. 6, 1865.

44. "The Indians—The Conference at Fort Smith," *Philadelphia Inquirer*, Oct. 6, 1865.

45. Warde, *When the Wolf Came*, 275. For more on the financial strains of the various tribes, see ibid., chap. 7.

46. Warde, *When the Wolf Came*, 266–67. For more on treatment in Indian Territory see: Cobb-Greetham, "Hearth and Home."

47. Bean, "Who Defines a Nation?," 125.

48. Zalimas, "Disturbance in the City." For more on southern community reactions to Black soldiers, see Downs, *After Appomattox*; and Behrend, *Reconstructing Democracy*.

49. Lang, *In the Wake of War*, 160–73. For more on the federal occupation of the South during Reconstruction, see Downs, *After Appomattox*; Marshall, *Creating a Confederate Kentucky*; and Egerton, *Wars of Reconstruction*.

50. Dyer, *Regimental Histories*, 3:1720–40.

51. *Christian Recorder* (Philadelphia), Apr. 22, 1865.

52. *Christian Recorder* (Philadelphia), Oct. 28, 1865.

53. *Christian Recorder* (Philadelphia), Sept. 29, 1866.

54. *Christian Recorder* (Philadelphia), Aug. 12, 1865.

55. *Christian Recorder* (Philadelphia), June 10, 1865.

56. "Revolution of Sentiment," *Macon (GA) Daily Telegraph*, Oct. 28, 1865.

57. "Disbanding Negro Troops," *Chicago Tribune*, Oct. 7, 1865.

58. *Christian Recorder* (Philadelphia), Dec. 2, 1865.

59. "From Natchez," *Georgia Weekly Telegraph* (Macon), Apr. 9, 1866.

60. "Antipathy to Negro Troops," *Philadelphia Inquirer*, Aug. 9, 1865. At this time Wilmington, North Carolina, was garrisoned by three full regiments of USCT, the Sixth, Twenty-Seventh, and Thirty-Seventh.

61. Janney, *Burying the Dead but Not the Past*, 74–76.

62. *Daily Iowa State Register* (Des Moines), Jan. 5, 1866.

63. *San Francisco Evening Bulletin*, Jan. 26, 1866.

64. *Memphis Daily Avalanche*, May 5, 1866.

65. For more details of these massacres, see Hardwick, "'Your Old Father Abe Lincoln Is Dead and Damned'"; Carden and Coyne, "Political Economy of the Reconstruction Era's Race Riots"; Vandal, *New Orleans Riot of 1866*; Hollandsworth, *An Absolute Massacre*; and Kirk, "'No Safety for Union Men.'"

66. "Civil Rights at Norfolk," *New York Herald*, Apr. 19, 1866.

67. U.S. Congress, House, *Riot at Norfolk*, 3–6, 12. The massacre at Norfolk was a multi-day event, and the House investigation into it lasted multiple days as well. But according to one report, this was not the racial clash in Norfolk but rather an "attempted mutiny among colored troops." Important Events, *Hartford (CT) Daily Courant*, Jan. 2, 1866.

68. *Harrisburg (PA) Weekly Patriot and Union,* May 17, 1866.

69. "Outrages by Negro Soldiers," *New Orleans Daily Picayune,* Feb. 6, 1867.

70. *San Antonio (TX) Express,* May 2, 1867.

71. Parsons, *Ku-Klux,* 29–44. For more information on the KKK, see Chalmers, *Hooded Americanism;* Summers, *Ordeal of the Reunion;* Proctor, "'From the Cradle to the Grave'"; Proctor, "'K. K. Alphabet'"; Martinez, *Carpetbaggers, Cavalry, and the Ku Klux Klan;* and Rable, *But There Was No Peace.*

72. "Kuklux Klan," *Pulaski (TN) Citizen,* Apr. 26, 1867.

73. Parsons, *Ku-Klux,* 58–100.

74. *Nashville Union and Dispatch,* Dec. 18, 1867.

75. "Ku Klux Klan," *Jonesboro (TN) Union Flag,* Feb. 7, 1868.

76. "The 'Loyal League' and the 'Ku Klux Klan,'" *Harrisburg (PA) Weekly Patriot and Union,* Apr. 16, 1868.

77. "The Ku-Klux in Nashville," *Nashville Union and Dispatch,* Feb. 21, 1868.

78. *Dallas Herald,* May 2, 1868. For more on supernatural tales of the Klan, see Prince, *Stories of the South.*

79. Parsons, *Ku-Klux,* 74–84. According to Parsons, "freedmen hardly required such a supplement of terror" by Klansmen wearing costumes, but the "Ku-Klux sometimes interpreted their costumes for their victims." Ibid., 81. She notes that the KKK supplementing their identity as ghosts of the Confederacy was a common performance. Klansmen had many different outfits crafted for specific purposes and audiences, including themselves.

80. Great Grand Cyclops, G.C.T., "The Ku Klux Klan," *New Orleans Daily Picayune,* Mar. 17, 1868.

81. *Daily Memphis Avalanche,* Mar. 20, 1868.

82. "Political Violence in the South," *Georgia Weekly Telegraph* (Macon), Apr. 3, 1868.

83. *Flake's Bulletin* (Galveston, TX), May 14, 1868.

84. Parsons, "Midnight Rangers," 811–36, 814.

85. "Governor Walker's Message upon the Death of General Lee," *Philadelphia Evening Telegraph,* Oct. 13, 1870.

86. "The Funeral of Gen. Lee," *Charleston (SC) Daily News,* Oct. 19, 1870.

87. Janney, *Burying the Dead but Not the Past,* 106.

88. *Pomeroy's Democrat* (New York City), Dec. 17, 1871.

89. "The South—Excitement over a White League Demonstration in New Orleans," *Chicago Daily Inter Ocean,* Oct. 11, 1874.

6. THE MATERIAL CULTURE OF VETERANS' ASSOCIATIONS & COMMEMORATION

1. "Awakening Tender Memories," *National Tribune* (Washington, DC), Aug. 30, 1888.

2. *Minutes of the Fourth Annual Meeting of the United Daughters of the Confederacy,* 4.

3. Gibson, *Memory of Clothes,* xiv–xv.

4. See Silber, *Romance of Reunion;* Blight, *Race and Reunion;* Janney, *Remembering the Civil War;* Harris, *Across the Bloody Chasm;* and Prince, *Stories of the South.* Nina Silber ex-

amines sentiment as a cultural construction in relation to the changing views of nationhood, especially as it relates to gender, immigration, and industrial capitalism. David Blight traces the interrelationships between race and reunion in an insightful and original exploration of how Americans chose to remember the Civil War, concluding that reconciliationist narratives prevailed in popular culture by the early twentieth century. Caroline Janney argues that the narrative is much more complicated than this, arguing that veterans from both sides clasped hands but did not shrink from promoting their agenda.

5. Adam Domby argues that falsehoods and fabrications are lies created to serve a contemporary purpose and "were often passed on and repeated by others who may not have realized the truth or simply did not care." Domby, *False Cause*, 8–9. Others who address this misrepresentation include Cox, *No Common Ground;* Cox, "What Trump Shares with the 'Lost Cause' of the Confederacy," *New York Times*, Jan. 8, 2021; and David Blight, "How Trumpism May Endure," ibid., Jan. 9, 2021. Blight states, "all Lost Causes find their lifeblood in lies, big and small, lies born of beliefs in search of a history that can be forged into a story and mobilize masses of people to act politically, violently, and in the name of ideology."

6. Wilson, *Baptized in Blood*. For more on the Lost Cause, see Foster, *Ghosts of the Confederacy;* Gallagher and Nolan, *Myth of the Lost Cause and Civil War History;* Gallagher, *Jubal A. Early, the Lost Cause, and Civil War History;* Faust, *This Republic of Suffering;* Loewen, *Lies across America;* and Roberts and Kytle. "Looking the Thing in the Face," 639–84. For other works instrumental to the development of memory in the South, see Edwards, *Scarlett Doesn't Live Here Anymore;* Silber, *Romance of Reunion;* Cox, *Dixie's Daughters;* and Janney, *Burying the Dead but Not the Past*. The analysis in these books of memorial celebrations and the friction that existed between northern and southern veterans made me question what part uniforms played in their reunions.

7. This misconception was created because the push for reconciliation and the rise of the Lost Cause mythology overshadowed much of the participation of Union veterans and the WRC postwar. Scholarship that attempts to catch up the northern memory machine include, but is not limited to, Dean, *Shook over Hell;* and Fahs and Waugh, *Memory of the Civil War in American Culture*.

8. "Grand Army of the Republic and Kindred Societies" (online).

9. Beath, *History of the Grand Army of the Republic*, 10–54, 100.

10. Grand Army of the Republic [hereafter GAR], *Grand Army Blue-Book*, 9.

11. GAR, *Rules and Regulations*, 28.

12. GAR, *Grand Army Blue-Book*, 96–100.

13. GAR, *Proceedings of the First to Tenth Meetings*, 13–14.

14. GAR, *Proceedings of the First to Tenth Meetings*, 116.

15. GAR, *Proceedings of the First to Tenth Meetings*, 129.

16. GAR, *Proceedings of the First to Tenth Meetings*, 189–90.

17. GAR, *Proceedings of the First to Tenth Meetings*, 164–65.

18. GAR, *Proceedings of the First to Tenth Meetings*, 338–39.

19. GAR, *Proceedings of the First to Tenth Meetings*, 361.

20. "Grand Army of the Republic and Kindred Societies" (online).

21. GAR, *Grand Army Blue-Book*, 52, 96–100.

22. GAR, *Journal of the Eighteenth Annual Session, of the National Encampment,* 24.

23. For more on the foundational concepts of reunion versus reconciliation, see Blight, *Race and Reunion.* See also Silber, *Romance of Reunion;* Harris, *Across the Bloody Chasm;* Cox, *Dixie's Daughters;* Janney, *Burying the Dead but Not the Past;* Janney, *Remembering the Civil War.* The Daughters of Union Veterans of the Civil War, incorporated in 1885, and the Sons of Union Veterans, formed in 1881, were created to "keep green the memory" of the sacrifices made during the war. While they are significant organizations in their own right, the focus here is on the relationship between the GAR and the WRC, with the WRC providing aid to the GAR in using badges and flags.

24. Beath, *History of the Grand Army of the Republic,* 227–28.

25. GAR, *Journal of the Eighteenth Annual Session, of the National Encampment,* 29.

26. Woman's Relief Corps [hereafter WRC], *Rules and Regulations,* 4.

27. "Relief Corps News," *National Tribune* (Washington, DC), Aug. 30, 1888.

28. "Minutes," in GAR, *Journal of the Seventeenth Annual Session, National Encampment,* 107.

29. GAR, *Journal of the Eighteenth Annual Session, of the National Encampment,* 225.

30. M. C. Lilley & Company, *Grand Army of the Republic Price List.* Other manufacturers— L. Gansman & Brothers from Lancaster, Pennsylvania; Augusta Thomas and Company from Philadelphia; and Gusky's from Pittsburg; and others—advertised and made GAR uniforms starting at six dollars and up, but those in the M. C. Lilley price book were complete and readily available. Advertisements in *Lancaster (PA) Daily Intelligencer,* May 30, 1889; *National Tribune* (Washington, DC), July 11, 1889; and *Pittsburg Dispatch,* May 29, 1889.

31. Cloudman Relief Corps No. 18, May Festival program, in author's personal collection. This item, purchased from a Nevada antique store, probably survived because one side is a color print of a blonde boy with brown eyes in a red, white, blue, and yellow sailor suit sitting on the mast of a ship draped in a flag, with a sailor hat tucked into the flag. This speaks to the randomness of what is saved and what is discarded when privately collecting and preserving material culture. Without the color print, this item may have been discarded long ago.

32. Massachusetts Bureau of Statistics of Labor, *Comparative Wages, Prices, and Cost of Living,* 247–55. According to the Bureau of Statistics of Labor, a workingman with an income of between $300 and $450 a year spent approximately 7 percent of it on clothing the family annually, while men of intermediate incomes of $450–$600 spent 10.5 percent on clothing; incomes of $600–$750 spent 14 percent on clothing; incomes of $750–$1,200 spent 15 percent on clothing; and incomes of $1,200 or higher spent 19 percent on clothing.

33. GAR postcard to Mr. Herman Shimpfky (276 North Avenue, Chicago), in author's personal collection. The item was a part of a large lot of card and stamp items from the nineteenth century. The eBay vendor had purchased it from a Delaware auction house in September 2010.

34. GAR, *Grand Army Blue-Book,* 96–100.

35. GAR, *Grand Army Blue-Book,* 98–102.

36. WRC, *Red Book,* 31, 34.

37. WRC, *Red Book,* 187–92.

38. Specifically in this section, I am addressing Mary P. Ryan's works and her conclusions

about women and minorities and their relationships to urban public and private spheres. See Ryan, "Gender and Public Access: Women's Politics in Nineteenth-Century America," in Calhoun, *Habermas and the Public Sphere,* 259–88; and Ryan, *Civic Wars,* chaps. 1, 2, and 4.

39. WRC, *Red Book,* 25.

40. Gannon, *Won Cause,* 15–16. Because of how ethnic status was documented on Civil War muster rolls, it is difficult to track Indigenous veterans from the loyal states, so this study specifically focuses on those who came from or remained in Indian Territory.

41. GAR, *Journal of the Seventeenth Annual Session, National Encampment,* 72.

42. Gannon, *Won Cause,* 41.

43. Beath, *History of the Grand Army of the Republic,* 227.

44. *Christian Recorder* (Philadelphia), Feb. 21, 1884.

45. "Address of the Commander-in-Chief," in GAR, *Journal of the Thirtieth National Encampment,* 64.

46. *National Tribune* (Washington, DC), May 17, 1883; Oklahoma GAR Posts & History, Grand Army of the Republic (GAR) Records Project (online). More information for the Cabin Creek Post is in the Edward Everett Dale Collection at the University of Oklahoma, Norman. Unfortunately, those files are misplaced (as of 2023) or were taken, and the university does not have the resources or manpower to locate them.

47. Oklahoma GAR Posts & History, Grand Army of the Republic (GAR) Records Project (online).

48. "Indian Territory," *National Tribune* (Washington, DC), June 29, 1893, July 5, 1900.

49. The first land run to claim "unassigned lands" in Indian Territory took place on April 22, 1889. During this period, the Five Nations had endured immense pressure to jettison their communal ownership of territory and to allot their lands as parcels for individual ownership. This became the official policy under the Curtis Act of 1898. Article 23 of the 1907 Oklahoma Constitution uses the term "white race," which applied to all people except those of African descent. Reese, *Trail Sisters,* 9, 130–31.

50. Shier, *Warriors in Mr. Lincoln's Army,* 203, 480–83. Special thanks to Michelle Cassidy for her guidance and assistance with this information.

51. GAR, *Journal of the Nineteenth Annual Session of the National Encampment,* 305–6.

52. GAR, *Journal of the Nineteenth Annual Session of the National Encampment,* 133–34.

53. Unidentified newspaper clippings, Mrs. William J. Behan Collection on Confederate Memorials, 1800s–1940s, Folder 7, Box 2, Manuscript Collection 1058, Louisiana Research Collection, Howard-Tilton Memorial Library, Tulane University.

54. "Santa Catalina," *Idaho Avalanche* (Silver City), May 22, 1886. This story appeared in newspapers throughout the country, but this paper provided the most complete, legible example.

55. "A Regular Revival," *Columbus (GA) Enquire-Sun,* July 26, 1888.

56. Unidentified newspaper clipping, n.d., Folder 7, Box 2, Mrs. William J. Behan Collection on Confederate Memorials.

57. "United Confederate Veterans," Dictionary of American History, Encyclopedia.com.

58. United Confederate Veterans [hereafter UCV], *Constitution and By-Laws,* 1.

59. UCV, *Constitution and By-Laws,* 3. This is the same badge as later adopted by both

the Sons of Confederate Veterans and the United Daughters of the Confederacy, with the exception of the organizational letters.

60. "The Rebel Chief," *Rock Island (IL) Daily Argus,* Dec. 6, 1889.

61. "The Sham Battle," *Chicago Inter Ocean,* Aug. 23, 1879.

62. "Interstate Drill Sham Battle," *Macon (GA) Telegraph,* Oct. 25, 1890.

63. *Salt Lake Weekly Tribune* (Salt Lake City), Dec. 15, 1892.

64. "Reunion Orders," *Watchman and Southron* (Sumter, SC), Mar. 22, 1899.

65. *Hartford (CT) Daily Courant,* June 4, 1866; *Pacific Commercial Advertiser* (Honolulu, HI), Sept. 22, 1866; *Galveston (TX) Tri-Weekly News,* Sept. 10, 1869; *Daily Columbus (GA) Enquirer,* Sept. 16, 1869; *Territorial Enterprise* (Virginia City, NV), Dec. 14, 1877; *Baltimore Sun,* Dec. 13, 1898, July 18, 1899.

66. "Perpetuating Their Glory," *The State* (Columbia, SC), Apr. 13, 1892.

67. United Daughters of the Confederacy [hereafter UDC], *Constitution,* 2; Janney, *Burying the Dead but Not the Past.* The Sons of Confederate Veterans was organized in 1896 for the same purpose. Because of the UDC's active membership and contribution to the UCV, the focus here is on the women's efforts in memorializing the Confederacy through material culture.

68. UDC, *Constitution,* 6.

69. "A Colored Brigade," *Topeka (KS) State Journal,* Apr. 30, 1898.

70. "Troops Find Alligators," *New York Sun,* May 24, 1898.

71. *Santa Fe New Mexican,* May 11, 1898. For this war, the U.S. military changed its uniform color to canvas, which was a "light earthy brown," because the men were posted in a tropical climate. "This color seems to merge with the shadows and to resist detection better" than the typical dark blue. *Anaconda (MT) Standard,* June 14, 1898.

72. J. B. Foraker, "Return Rebel Flags," *Kansas City (MO) Journal,* May 25, 1898.

73. Foraker, "Return Rebel Flags."

74. "A Touching Incident," *Sisterville (WV) Oil Review,* May 25, 1898.

75. *Keowee Courier* (Pickens Court House, SC), June 16, 1898. This legislation allowed those who fought for the Confederacy but were once again U.S. citizens to participate in politics.

76. "Wroth Statements, Open Apologies," *Sacramento Record-Union,* Feb. 23, 1899.

77. *Fort Wayne (IN) News,* June 7, 1898.

78. "Blue and Gray," *Kansas City (MO) Journal,* Oct. 10, 1898.

79. "Blue and Gray," *Kansas City (MO) Journal,* Oct. 10, 1898.

80. *Confederate Veteran* 9 (Apr. 1901): 133.

81. *Point Pleasant (VA) Weekly Register,* Sept. 17, 1901; *Opelousas (LA) Courier,* Feb. 15, 1902.

82. *Confederate Veteran* Archives, Online Books Page, http://onlinebooks.library.upenn.edu /webbin/serial?id=confedvet.

83. *Confederate Veteran* 1 (Jan. 1893): 1.

84. UDC, *Minutes of the Tenth Annual Meeting,* 5–7.

85. UDC, North Carolina Division, *Minutes of Organization and of 1st and 2nd Annual Conventions,* 7.

86. UDC, *Minutes of the Fifth Annual Meeting,* 27.

7. WOMEN'S ORGANIZATIONS & THE MANUFACTURING OF MEMORIES

1. UDC, *Minutes of the Twelfth Annual Meeting*, 152–53.

2. For more on sentimentality, see Nelson, *Market Sentiments;* and Appadurai, *Social Life of Things.*

3. For more on the perpetuation of Lost Cause narratives, see Prince, *Stories of the South;* Silber, *Romance of Reunion;* and Harris, *Across the Bloody Chasm.* For more on the Lost Cause itself, see Foster, *Ghosts of the Confederacy;* Gallagher and Nolan, *Myth of the Lost Cause and Civil War History;* Gallagher, *Jubal A. Early, the Lost Cause, and Civil War History;* and Blight, *Race and Reunion.*

4. Callahan and Ledgerwood, "On the Psychological Function of Flags and Logos." See also the discussion in chapter 4, note 2.

5. For the WRC badge, see "Woman's Relief Corps Badge Symbolism," WRC, https://womansreliefcorps.org/the-wrc-medal/. For the UDC badge, see UDC, *Meeting Minutes of the Twenty-First Annual Convention*, 450. See also the discussion of each in chapter 6.

6. For more on the interdependence of the GAR and WRC, see Chamberlain and Yanus, "'Our One Great Hope'"; and Silber, *Daughters of the Union.*

7. Created in the 1850s, celluloid is a chemically processed organic material—usually wood—combined with synthetic materials to create a highly durable and malleable base; in addition, it is easy to dye. It was a popular material in fashion from the late nineteenth century through the 1930s. "Celluloid," Dictionary.com, https://www.dictionary.com/browse/celluloid (accessed Sept. 30, 2016).

8. "A Grand Army Catechism," *Denison (IA) Review*, May 25, 1900.

9. WRC Michigan Delegate Badge, 1896, author's private collection. Many of these badges were crafted from silk, and several have shattered because of their age and the conditions in which they were kept.

10. WRC, *Journal of the Thirtieth National Convention*, 291–92.

11. Four miscellaneous GAR ribbons, dates unknown, Kentucky Museum, Western Kentucky University.

12. Maryland Bureau of Industrial Statistics, *Eighth Annual Report*, 50; Reunion of the Blue and Gray pin, 1899, author's private collection. Whitehead & Hoag made badges for a variety of occasions, including the 1896 presidential campaign. The company was known for being nonpartisan and accepted orders from major political parties and organizations as well as prohibitionists, communists, and socialists. "Whitehead & Hoag Company History" (online).

13. For example, the WRC took in $5.62 "from [the] sale of flags and badges at [the] Twenty-ninth National Convention." "National Treasurer's Supplemental Report," June–Aug. 1911, in WRC, *Journal of the Twenty-Ninth National Convention*, 118. Just in the supplies furnished to various WRC departments nationwide, the national treasurer reported providing 12,045 badges in fiscal year 1911. "Report of National Treasurer," July 1, 1911, ibid., 106.

14. UDC, *Minutes of the Fifth Annual Meeting*, 52–53; Janney, *Remembering the Civil War.*

15. UDC, *Minutes of the Eleventh Annual Meeting*, 6–7.

16. UDC, *Minutes of the Fifth Annual Meeting*, 78.

17. UDC, *Minutes of the Fifth Annual Meeting*, 62–63. Gabbett's sentiment is an accurate statement, judging from the number of souvenir badges in the collections of the American Civil War Museum in Richmond, Virginia. The museum possesses a large quantity of badges in all shapes and sizes and composed of a variety of materials. They come from reunions, monument unveilings, and chapters of Confederate memorial associations. Some are hand-painted silk, others are enamel, several are different types of metal and celluloid, and a few even have brass bullion fringe, yet all are unique and ornate. Each leaves no doubt as to the identity and allegiance of the person wearing it. The museum even has a box of fifteen Southern Crosses of Honor, some of which are inscribed with the name of the owner. Most of these are stored as collections 1914.022, 1914.024.00059, 1914.024.00058, 1914.024.00060, TB-MR-122.1, TBMR-122.3, TMBR-287, 0985.07.00135r, and 0985.7.135 (part of a large, framed collection). The rest of the souvenir badges are numbered separately, 0985.7.135a–0985.7.135q and 0985.7.135s–0985.7.135hh.

18. Finding Aid, United Daughters of the Confederacy, Southern Cross of Honor Documents, 1905–1941, Special Collections, Carrier Library, James Madison University, Harrisonburg.

19. UDC, *Minutes of the Fifth Annual Meeting*, 62.

20. Counterfeit Southern Cross of Honor, author's private collection.

21. UDC, *Minutes of the Eleventh Annual Meeting*, 222–23.

22. UDC, *Minutes of the Twelfth Annual Meeting*, 152.

23. UDC, *Minutes of the Eleventh Annual Meeting*, 222–23. For information about the myth of Black Confederates, see Levin, *Searching for Black Confederates;* and Domby, *False Cause*.

24. UDC Eleventh Annual National Meeting ribbon, 1904, author's private collection.

25. UDC, *Minutes of the Eleventh Annual Meeting*, 187–88.

26. UDC, *Minutes of the Tenth Annual Meeting*, 79.

27. UDC, *Minutes of the Fourteenth Annual Convention*, 218. Because of the recordkeeping system used by each organization during their first several years, tracking UDC or UCV badge spending or income per camp/department or nationally is nearly impossible. But meticulous records from November 1911 to October 1912 show the UDC spent $2,583.77 on various badges. During Fiscal Year 1912, the UDC received $1,867.02 for badges and, after paying expenses, amassed a $470.00 profit upon those sales. UDC, *Minutes of the Nineteenth Annual Convention*, 23, 134–39.

28. Whitehead & Hoag to Secretary of the UCV, Spring 1905, UCV Records, 1899–1905, Mss. BC U58b, Folder 6, Filson Historical Society, 155, 226.

29. For discussions of foundational southern memorial groups, see Cox, *Dixie's Daughters;* Janney, *Burying the Dead but Not the Past;* and Janney, *Remembering the Civil War*.

30. Grover Cleveland, Executive Order, Apr. 30, 1887, online by Gerhard Peters and John T. Woolley, American Presidency Project, https://www.presidency.ucsb.edu/node/205379.

31. Grover Cleveland, Executive Order, June 17, 1887, online by Gerhard Peters and John T. Woolley, American Presidency Project, https://www.presidency.ucsb.edu/node/205402.

32. UDC, *Minutes of the Twelfth Annual Meeting*, 235.

33. R. E. Hughes to Maj. John H. Leathers, Mar. 1, 1905, UCV Records, 1899–1905, Mss. BC U58b, Folder 6, Filson Historical Society, 98.

34. WRC, *Journal of the Thirty-First National Convention*, 401.

35. UDC, North Carolina Division, *Minutes of Organization and of 1st and 2nd Annual Conventions*, 3. Throughout its brief existence, the Confederacy operated under numerous flags—all of which were based on the colors red, white, and blue and employed the symbol of one or more stars. Smith, *Flags*, 196.

36. WRC, *Journal of the Thirty-First National Convention*, 182. The WRC does not condone the desecration of the U.S. flag and urged all members of their organization to assist in enforcing strict flag laws in their respective states.

37. WRC, *Journal of the Thirty-First National Convention*, 205. For more information on the U.S. flag, see Guenter, *American Flag*.

38. WRC, *Journal of the Thirty-First National Convention*, 401.

39. UDC, North Carolina Division, *Minutes of the Twenty-Second Annual Convention*, 126. This is from a speech discussing the life of the woman who made the first flag of the Confederacy, Rebecca Winborne. While the orator provides a story of Winborne's life, she carefully conveys emotion for the flag, her description demonstrating the memory and identity wrapped up in this object.

40. UDC, *Minutes of the Seventh Annual Meeting*, 6.

41. "Favor the Aging Veterans," *Omaha (NE) Daily Bee*, May 31, 1900.

42. "Badge on Swordhilt," *Washington (DC) Evening Star*, Sept. 16, 1901.

43. "Confederate Veterans," *Washington (DC) Evening Star*, Sept. 17, 1901.

44. Leon Jastremski, "A Uniform of Gray," *Opelousas (LA) Courier*, Feb. 15, 1902.

45. Jastremski, "Uniform of Gray"; Confederate Memorial Hall (online). Memorial Hall in New Orleans has numerous battle artifacts, uniforms, flags, and personal items from the Civil War.

46. "Why Wheeler Was Snubbed," *Yorkville Enquirer (SC)*, May 30, 1903.

47. UDC, North Carolina Division, *Minutes of the Seventh Annual Convention*, 51.

48. UDC, *Minutes of the Tenth Annual Meeting*, 150–51.

49. UDC, North Carolina Division, *Minutes of the Fourteenth Annual Convention*, 132.

50. See, for example, UDC, North Carolina Division, *Minutes of the Fourteenth Annual Convention*, 87. As is the case for the majority of the annual meeting minutes, this one contains several pages of local chapter financial reports, which lists (among other expenses) uniforms and the cost for the grouping in addition to their narrative reports describing their contributions of the year.

51. *Men's Wear: The Retailers' Newspaper*, Feb. 6, 1907, 82, 120.

52. Invoice, Levy Bros. Company to Capt. John H. Leathers, May 12, 1905, UCV Records, 1899–1905, Mss. BC U58b, Folder 6, Filson Historical Society; Levy Bros. to William Haldeman, June 7, 1905, ibid.

53. R. E. Hughes, secretary of the Finance Committee, to John Leathers, UCV president, Apr. 20, 1905, UCV Records, 1899–1905, Mss. BC U58b, Folder 6, Filson Historical Society, 227.

54. Levy Bros., *U.C.V. Regulation Uniforms: Made to Measure Outfitters* (ca. 1901), 1–12, Virginia Sons of Confederate Veterans, https://www.scvvirginia.org/ucv-uscv-uniforms (site discontinued), pdf copy in author's possession. The lowest quality vest started at $1.25, while the highest quality vest was $2.25. Regulation-gray caps were $0.25, $0.50, or $0.75, depending on quality. Flannel shirts were $1.50 each.

55. Examples of these veteran uniforms are in archives and museums across the country. The American Civil War Museum houses one specifically manufactured for Virginian John W. Jewett. It is a five-button-front, cadet-gray, wool-cloth coat with a gold-embroidered general's insignia on the collar and gold-color UCV buttons. A similar piece is a veterans' coat, much like Jewett's, with the gold embroidery of a lieutenant colonel; the inside pocket contains the label, "Only Lexington Suitings bear this label / The Burton-Pierce Co. Boston–New York–Chicago." Collections 1982.010 and 1984.003, UCV coat, American Civil War Museum.

The North Carolina History Museum houses one full uniform of particular interest because of its label. The coat is blue-gray with a tan lining, gold "NC" state buttons, a cream collar with matching cuffs, and gold embroidery on the sleeves. The inside of the collar is black crushed velvet and has a black label with gold writing that reads, "The M. C. Lilley & Co. Columbus, O. / Military & Society Goods." The pants are the same blue-gray and with a higher-cut waist popular during the Civil War. Collections H.19XX.330.95 and XX330.95, Capt. W. H. S. Burgwyn, 35th NC, North Carolina History Museum. The curator called the elaborate gold embroidery "chicken guts." He believed that the coat was worn during the war and relined for postwar events, which would account for the sprucing that has occurred to the coat.

In the Bluegrass State, the Special Collections Library at Western Kentucky University has several veteran uniforms, including a set from local judge Jeptha Crawford Johnson, who served in Company B, 37th Arkansas Infantry and eventually attained the rank of lieutenant colonel. It is a simple gray coat with tan lining, a variety of UCV and eagle gold buttons, and stars on the collar to match his rank. Another item is a complete Confederate veterans' uniform set, with coat, vest, and pants of the same description. Collections 3180 and 2791, Manuscripts and Folklife Archives, Department of Library Special Collections, Western Kentucky University. The Kentucky Historical Society holds a 1910-era UCV coat bearing the label "Levy Bros. / Louisville" in the interior breast pocket. It is the same blue-gray wool as the others, with brass UCV buttons on the right cuff. Official Record: Uniform, Catalog 1972.3.13, UDC Collection, Kentucky Historical Society (online).

56. M. C. Lilley & Company, *Grand Army of the Republic Price List*.

57. Advertisement, *Confederate Veteran* 14 (Jan. 1906): 151.

58. "Pettibone Uniforms," *Confederate Veteran* 15 (Feb. 1907): 99.

59. Advertisement, *Confederate Veteran* 15 (Mar. 1907): 147.

60. Advertisement, *Confederate Veteran* 18 (Jan. 1910): 50; Advertisement, ibid. (Apr. 1910): 194.

61. Newspaper article, n.d., Scrapbook, UCV Records, 1899–1905, Mss. BC U58b, Folder 6, Filson Historical Society, 266.

62. UDC, *Minutes of the Fifteenth Annual Convention*, 99.

63. WRC, *Journal of the Twenty-Ninth National Convention*, 425–27.

64. WRC, *Journal of the Twenty-Ninth National Convention*, 425–27.

65. See Gannon, *Won Cause*, esp. app. 1 and 2.

66. W. W. Perkins Post badge, author's private collection. There is no proof that this particular badge belonged to an African American member, but it serves as an example of what such a man would have worn.

67. *Samuel Walker Post No. 365*, ca. 1890–1909, "Grand Army of the Republic, Lawrence, Kansas," Kansas Memory, https://www.kansasmemory.org/item/218628.

68. UDC, *Minutes of the Fourteenth Annual Meeting*, 263–64. Also see Domby, *False Cause*, chap. 4.

69. While there is some scholarship on Indigenous forms of commemoration after the Civil War, no comprehensive study puts uniforms or what these veterans wore at the center of the study. Secondary sources present the perspective that Native Peoples tried to forget the war and reunify their tribes. See, for example, Fortney, "Lest We Remember." Jeff Fortney writes, "Natives practiced self-silence in regard to public Civil War commemoration." He then states, "Natives who made critical sacrifices during the war sought to bury the past" in an attempt to reunify their tribe and deal with the political fallout from having to sign new treaties with the U.S. government because of siding with the Confederacy. Ibid., 526. Gregory Smithers, in discussing material culture, writes that because of the deep divisions in Indian Territory during the Civil War, Cherokee citizens jettisoned the Cherokee Brigade flag afterward in an effort to mend tribal relations. He notes that the Oklahoma Cherokee adopted another flag in its place as a sign of reunification for the entire tribe. Yet former veterans were active in veterans' organizations and attended Confederate reunions, while many women were also active in the UDC. Smithers even mentions a photograph of Thomas Legion Cherokees at the Confederate reunion in 1903 but provides no explanation of why those veterans held up the Confederate battle flag. Smithers, "Dumping the Confederate Flag." (online) At best, these authors demonstrate that Indigenous Peoples had a difficult relationship with their war memory and identity. Studying their use of uniforms, flags, and badges complicates the historiography and sheds new light on why Native Peoples on both sides would continue to commemorate their involvement in the Civil War through material culture.

70. "INDIANS WILL ATTEND REUNION," newspaper clipping, Scrapbook, Spring 1905, UCV Records, 1899–1905, Mss. BC U58b, Filson Historical Society, 137.

71. "Squad of North Carolina Braves Who Fought for Confederacy . . . to Bring Historic Flags," newspaper clipping, Scrapbook, Spring 1905, UCV Records, 1899–1905, Mss. BC U58b, Filson Historical Society, 137.

72. *Indian School Journal*, June 1910, 12, online at American Indian Newspapers, Adam Matthew Digital, http://www.americanindiannewspapers.amdigital.co.uk/ (accessed Jan. 31, 2019; subscription required).The journal was published by the Chilocco Indian Agricultural School in Chilocco, Oklahoma.

73. For more on this school, see Lomawaima, *They Called It Prairie Light*.

74. UDC, *Minutes of the Ninth Annual Meeting*, 40–41. No general report was submitted for the Indian Territory UDC this year, although the Stonewall Jackson Chapter from McAlester and the Julia Jackson Chapter from Durant, each only a few months old, submitted their own reports.

75. UDC, *Minutes of the Tenth Annual Meeting*, 110.

76. UDC, *Minutes of the Eleventh Annual Meeting*, 171–72.

77. UDC, *Minutes of the Twentieth Annual Convention*, 428–29.

78. UDC, *Minutes of the Twentieth Annual Meeting*, 190.

79. UDC, *Minutes of the Twenty-First Annual Meeting*, 388.

80. Historian Philip Deloria discusses the reconstruction of personal identity through the past. He explains the connection of American Indians and American identity, specifically

how white Americans coopting the identity of Indigenous People provide a link of heritage and authority. Deloria, *Playing Indian*. The dynamics of Civil War commemorative associations align well with the framework of this concept because the personal identities of white UDC members were shaped through their claiming of heritage and interactions with the past. Books that focus on memory and identity often discuss the relationships between place and memory that link a form of "boosterism" with race and identity. See also Kropp, *California Vieja;* and Kammen, *Mystic Chords of Memory*.

81. "The Essex Troop Which Will Be the Presidential Escort," *Washington (DC) Evening Star,* Feb. 9, 1913.

82. WRC, *Journal of the Thirty-First National Convention,* 402.

8. THE BLUE & THE GRAY

1. "VETERANS ERASE MASON-DIXON LINE," *Washington (DC) Evening Star,* June 29, 1938.

2. For a short history of the Blue and Gray Reunions held at Gettysburg and the beginnings of Civil War memory studies, see Blight, *Race and Reunion,* 188, 202–3.

3. *Wilmington (DE) Evening Journal,* Jan. 24, 1913; "Veterans Plan for Gettysburg Reunion," *Chickasha (OK) Daily Express,* Jan. 8, 1913; *Confederate Veteran* 5 (Jan. 1913): 21, 29. Delegations in many other states requested funds from their state government for assistance in getting veterans to the reunion.

4. *Macon (MS) Beacon,* Jan. 31, 1913.

5. Faust, *Creation of Confederate Nationalism*. Drew Gilpin Faust's study was the first to acknowledge Confederate nationalism without quantifying it, arguing that it must be studied as a cultural construct. While Faust's book is extremely helpful in assessing Confederate identity during the war and understanding the need to separate it from the Lost Cause ideology, I argue that this process continues throughout Reconstruction. For information on the history of the fluidity of American and Confederate nationalism, see Potter, "Historian's Use of Nationalism and Vice Versa"; and Kohn, *American Nationalism*. For a comparative perspective on the American North, see Grant, *North over South;* Grant, "'Charter of Its Birthright'"; and Potter, "Civil War." Historical pillars such as E. Merton Coulter, Avery Craven, and Emory Thomas began varying discussions of "Rebel Nationalism" or Confederate nationalism and the Confederacy; David M. Potter's "Historian's Use of Nationalism" came out in the middle of the development of their school of thought. See Coulter, *Confederate States;* Craven, *Growth of Southern Nationalism;* Thomas, *Confederate Nation;* Thomas, "Rebel Nationalism"; McCurry, "Women Numerous and Armed"; and Sinche, "Scripting a Nationalist Narrative." Paul Quigley argues that Confederate nationalism was a fluid process, not a static product, and, much as Charles Reagan Wilson affirms, a form of religion. See Quigley, *Shifting Grounds; and Wilson, Baptized in Blood*. This makes sense because of how southern sectionalism thrived during and after Reconstruction, highlighting the point that post–Civil War Confederate/southern and U.S. nationalism need to be in conversation with one another.

6. "At Gettysburg in July," *Richmond (VA) Times Dispatch,* Feb. 3, 1913.

7. "The Blue and the Gray at Gettysburg," *Hattiesburg (MS) News,* Feb. 18, 1913.

8. For more information on how Lincoln's body and memory have been used over time, see Fox, *Lincoln's Body.*

9. "Would Don Gray at Gettysburg," *Honesdale (PA) Citizen,* Feb. 7, 1913. This story was reprinted throughout the country; for an earlier example, see, *Charlotte (NC) Daily Observer,* Jan. 25, 1913.

10. "May Wear Old Uniforms," *Carroll County Democrat* (Huntingdon, TN), Jan. 31, 1913.

11. *Confederate Veteran* 21 (Mar. 1913): 107.

12. "Flags at Reunion Make Sore Point," *Richmond (VA) Times Dispatch,* Mar. 1, 1913.

13. *Confederate Veteran* 21 (Mar. 1913): 183.

14. "Bloody Shirt Called Down," *Charlotte (NC) Daily Observer,* Jan. 27, 1913.

15. "Veterans Leave for Gettysburg Reunion," *Salt Lake Tribune* (Salt Lake City), June 28, 1913.

16. "Delaware Survivors of Civil War to Move on Peaceful Errand Monday," *Wilmington (DE) Evening Journal,* June 26, 1913.

17. "Veterans Own Gettysburg," *Philadelphia Tribune,* June 28, 1913.

18. "Bristol," *Burlington (VT) Weekly Free Press,* Mar. 13, 1913.

19. "Delaware Vets to Fight over Again," *Wilmington (DE) Evening Journal,* Apr. 10, 1913.

20. "First Vermont Cavalry—Dedication of Monument at Gettysburg, July 3," *Bennington (VT) Evening Banner,* June 27, 1913.

21. Fiftieth Anniversary Badge, author's private collection.

22. "COLORS FLYING AT GETTYSBURG," *Madison (SD) Daily Leader,* June 30, 1913.

23. "The Battle-Flag of the 7th Regiment Goes Back to Gettysburg," *Edgefield (SC) Advertiser,* July 2, 1913.

24. "Scraps and Facts," *Yorkville (SC) Enquirer,* July 1, 1913.

25. "Six Train Loads of Veterans Leave City to Invade Gettysburg," *New York Evening World,* June 30, 1913.

26. "Gettysburg," *Denison (IA) Review,* July 2, 1913.

27. *New York Evening World,* July 1, 1913.

28. "Evidence of Greatness," *Marshalltown (IA) Evening Times-Republican,* July 1, 1913.

29. *Confederate Veteran* 21 (Aug. 1913): 370. This feeling was particularly prominent after the Spanish-American War. For more on reunion versus reconciliation, see Silber, *Romance of Reunion;* and Janney, *Remembering the Civil War,* chapter 6.

30. "Sweltering Veterans Evacuate Gettysburg," *Bridgeport (CT) Evening Farmer,* July 2, 1913.

31. "Veterans Will Reproduce Pickett's Famous Charge," *Washington (DC) Times,* July 3, 1913, reprinted in *Norwich (CT) Bulletin,* July 4, 1913; Union and Confederate veterans shaking hands, fiftieth anniversary of the Battle of Gettysburg, Liljenquist Family Collection of Civil War Photographs, Prints & Photographs Online Catalog, Library of Congress, http://www.loc.gov/pictures/item/2018652225/.

32. "President Wilson Miss Wilson Will at Gettysburg Wed in November," *Daily Ardmoreite* (Ardmore, OK), July 4, 1914.

33. "Escorted by the Blue and the Gray," *New York Sun,* July 5, 1913.

34. Gannon, *Won Cause,* 182–83. Also see Reardon, *Pickett's Charge in History and Memory.*

35. "70,000 Veterans Hobble over Gettysburg Field on First Reunion Day," *Seattle Star,* July 1, 1913.

36. "Blue and Gray Act Pickett's Charge," *New York Tribune,* July 4, 1913.

37. "Sidelights of Gettysburg Reunion," *Fort Mill (SC) Times,* July 10, 1913.

38. *Confederate Veteran* 21 (Aug. 1913): 386.

39. "A Defeat That Turned to Victory," *Confederate Veteran* 21 (Aug. 1913): 388. The *Confederate Veteran* item discusses the newspaper article. For more information on veterans' feelings and motivations for attending the reunion, see Flagel, *War, Memory, and the 1913 Gettysburg Reunion.*

40. "Veterans Return," *Richmond (VA) Times Dispatch,* July 5, 1913.

41. "GETTYSBURG REUNION IN 1938?," *Kansas City (MO) Star,* July 7, 1913. According to Richard A. Serrano, the last veteran from either side died in 1956. Serrano, "Last Civil War Veterans" (online).

42. Gannon, *Won Cause,* 183–85. Gannon's book includes this photograph, which is located in the Edgecombe County Memorial Library, Tarboro, North Carolina.

43. *Chicago Defender,* July 19, 1913.

44. "Battle of Fort Wagner Semicentennial and Reunion of 54th and 55th Mass. Regiments," *Salt Lake City Broad Ax,* July 12, 1913.

45. "All Colored Veterans Invited to Boston," *Norwich (CT) Bulletin,* July 17, 1913.

46. "Miller at Gettysburg Celebration," *Salt Lake City Broad Ax,* Aug. 16, 1913; *Confederate Veteran* 29 (1921): 358. A modern source on Miller does not support the point of view presented in the *Confederate Veteran* but tells his story as a slave and a personal body servant who traveled with his enslaver to war. See "Levi Miller (Virginia Soldier)," Wikipedia, last edited Mar. 24, 2023, https://en.wikipedia.org/wiki/Levi_Miller_(Virginia_soldier). For more information on the controversy of creating Black Confederates postwar, see Levin, "Nathan Bedford Forrest's Black Confederates" (online). Levin demonstrates that Forrest was careful never to call the slaves he impressed into service "soldiers" or to demonstrate any status change. Also see Martinez, *Confederate Slave Impressment in the Upper South;* and Domby, *False Cause.*

47. Jefferson Shields, Liljenquist Family Collection of Civil War Photographs, Prints & Photographs Online Catalog, Library of Congress, https://www.loc.gov/pictures/item/2017659670/.

48. UDC, *Minutes of the Twenty-First Annual Convention,* 351–52.

49. WRC, *Journal of the Thirty-Fifth National Convention,* 468–69.

50. "Confederates Do Not Take Part in Great Parade," *Columbia (TN) Herald,* Sept. 19, 1913.

51. *East Oregonian* (Pendleton, OR), May 1, 1916; Janney, *Remembering the Civil War,* 277–79. *The Clansman* was published in 1905.

52. WRC, *Journal of the Thirty-Fifth National Convention,* 370, 468–69.

53. "Wants Capital to See 'Birth of a Nation'," *Washington (DC) Herald,* Feb. 9, 1916.

54. Advertisement, "Cheered by Confederate Veterans," *El Paso (TX) Herald,* Mar. 15, 1916.

55. "Veterans Going to Birth of a Nation," *Hattiesburg (MS) News,* May 9, 1916.

56. Boykin Jones, "Attention Veterans," *Pensacola (FL) Journal,* June 7, 1916.

57. General Orders No. 4, in GAR, *Journal of the Fifty-First National Encampment,* 240.

58. GAR, *Journal of the Fifty-First National Encampment,* 200–201, 252.

59. Cox, *Dixie's Daughters,* 154–57. For more on the efforts to promote southern patriotism and the role of women's organizations, see Janney, *Remembering the Civil War,* 266–305.

60. UDC, *Minutes of the Twenty-Sixth Annual Convention . . . 1919,* 138, 217.

61. UDC, *Minutes of the Twenty-Seventh Annual Convention, . . . 1920,* 217.

62. Karen L. Cox provides a discussion of southern literature entering classrooms but does not provide a clear timeline for the process, which is what is established here. See Cox, *Dixie's Daughters,* 118–40.

63. UDC, *Minutes of the Twenty-Ninth Annual Convention, . . . 1922,* 212.

64. E. H. Pitcher to Gen. R. A. Sneed, Aug. 26, 1929, UCV Collection, Oklahoma Historical Society Research Division.

65. E. H. Pitcher to Gen. R. A. Sneed, Sept. 16, 1929; and Edwin J. Foster to Gen. R. A. Sneed, Oct. 15, 1929, UCV Collection, Oklahoma Historical Society Research Division.

66. Edwin J. Foster to Gen. R. A. Sneed, Dec. 9, 1929, UCV Collection, Oklahoma Historical Society Research Division.

67. "Confederate Army Meets in Jackson," *Washington (DC) Evening Star,* June 10, 1937.

68. "Stars and Bars on U.S. Coins," *Key West (FL) Citizen,* Apr. 7, 1938.

69. *Washington (DC) Evening Star,* June 26, 1938.

70. "Age-Weary Vets by Scores Plan to Go to Gettysburg," *Hendersonville (NC) Times-News,* June 28, 1938.

71. "Greets 105-Year-Old Vet," *Washington (DC) Evening Star,* June 28, 1938.

72. *Hendersonville (NC) Times-News,* July 2, 1938.

73. "Gettysburg Battlefield," *Hendersonville (NC) Times-News,* July 4, 6, 1938.

74. *New York Amsterdam News,* July 9, 1938.

75. "Photo," *Washington (DC) Evening Star,* July 3, 1938.

BIBLIOGRAPHY

ARCHIVES & COLLECTIONS

Abraham Lincoln Papers. Library of Congress, Washington, DC.

Alexander Family Papers. Manuscripts and Folklife Archives, Special Collections Library, Western Kentucky University, Bowling Green.

Alfred Ward Grayson Davis Papers. South Caroliniana Library, University of South Carolina, Columbia.

Avery, Agent John. "Hamilton Company—Boardinghouse Rules from the Handbook to Lowell, 1848." Lowell History: Nineteenth Century Documents, University of Massachusetts Lowell Library, https://libguides.uml.edu/primary_documents.

Channing Clapp Civil War Papers. Massachusetts Historical Society, Boston.

Charles Herman Journals. Georgia Historical Society, Savannah.

Civil War Uniforms, UCV Uniforms, and Civil War Flags. North Carolina History Museum, Raleigh.

Colin J. McRae Collection. South Carolina Confederate Relic Room and Military Museum, Columbia.

Confederate Documents Collection. Research Division, Oklahoma Historical Society, Oklahoma City.

Constitution of the Lowell Factory Girls Association, 1836. Center for Lowell History, University of Massachusetts, Lowell. Sourced from Mill Girls in Nineteenth-Century Print, American Antiquarian Society, https://americananti quarian.org/millgirls/items/show/54.

Daughters of Union Veterans of the Civil War, 1861–1865. Records, Special Collections, Chicago Public Library.

Gilder Lehrman Collection. Gilder Lehrman Institute of American History, New York.

Henry A. Huntington Papers, 1862–64. Southern Historical Collection, Louis Round Wilson Special Collections Library, University of North Carolina, Chapel Hill.

Indian Home Brigade. Company Orders Book, 1863–65. Research Center, Oklahoma Historical Society, Oklahoma City.

Indian Pioneer Papers. Western History Collections, University of Oklahoma, Norman.

John J. Russell Letters. Newberry Library, Chicago.

Lawrence, Agent Samuel. "Middlesex Mills—Company Regulations." Lowell, MA, July 1, 1846. Lowell History: Nineteenth Century Documents, University of Massachusetts Lowell Library, https://libguides.uml.edu/primary_documents.

Letters Received, Series 12, Adjutant General's Office, Record Group 94, National Archives, Washington, DC.

Liljenquist Family Collection of Civil War Photographs. Library of Congress, https://www.loc.gov/collections/liljenquist-civil-war-photographs/about-this -collection/.

Miscellaneous Records, Series 1796, Department of the Gulf, U.S. Army Continental Commands, Record Group 393, Pt. 1, National Archives, Washington, DC.

Mrs. William J. Behan Collection on Confederate Memorials, 1800s–1940s. Manuscript Collection 1058, Louisiana Research Collection, Howard-Tilton Memorial Library, Tulane University, New Orleans.

Native American Manuscripts. Western History Collections, University of Oklahoma, Norman.

Papers of Robert E. Lee. Albert and Shirley Small Special Collections Library, University of Virginia, Charlottesville.

Papers of William Daniel Cabell and the Cabell and Ellet Families, 1798–1955. Albert and Shirley Small Special Collections Library, University of Virginia, Charlottesville.

Postwar Badge Collections. Western Kentucky University, Bowling Green.

Records of P. Whitin and Sons Papers. South Caroliniana Library, University of South Carolina, Columbia.

Uniform, Badge, and Flag Collections. American Civil War Museum, Richmond, VA.

United Confederate Veterans Collection. Research Division, Oklahoma Historical Society, Oklahoma City.

United Confederate Veterans Records, 1899–1905. Filson Historical Society, Louisville, KY.

United Daughters of the Confederacy, Southern Cross of Honor Documents, 1905–1941. Special Collections, Carrier Library, James Madison University, Harrisonburg, VA.

NEWSPAPERS

Abbeville (SC) Press
Anaconda (MT) Standard
Anderson Intelligencer (Anderson Courthouse, SC)
Baltimore Daily Exchange
Baltimore Sun
Baton Rouge (LA) Sugar Planter
Bennington (VT) Evening Banner
Bossier Banner (Bellevue, LA)
Bradford Reporter (Towanda, PA)
Bridgeport (CT) Evening Farmer
Burlington (VT) Free Press
Burlington (VT) Weekly Free Press
Cadiz (OH) Democratic Sentinel
Carroll County Democrat (Huntingdon, TN)
Charleston (SC) Daily News
Charlotte (NC) Daily Observer
Charlotte (NC) Western Democrat
Chicago Daily Tribune
Chicago Defender
Chicago Inter Ocean
Chickasha (OK) Daily Express
Christian Recorder (Philadelphia)
Cincinnati Daily Press
Clarksville (TN) Chronicle
Cleveland Morning Leader
Columbia (TN) Herald
Columbus (GA) Enquirer-Sun
Daily Ardmoreite (Ardmore, OK)
Daily Evansville (IN) Journal
Daily Gate City (Keokuk, IA)
Daily Iowa State Register (Des Moines)
Daily Memphis Avalanche
Daily Ohio Statesman (Columbus)
Daily Southern Reveille (Port Gibson, MS)
Daily State Gazette and Republican (Trenton, NJ)
Dallas Herald
Dayton (OH) Daily Empire

Denison (IA) Review

Des Arc (AR) Constitutional Union

Deseret News (Salt Lake City)

Douglass' Monthly (Rochester, NY)

East Oregonian (Pendleton, OR)

Eaton (OH) Democratic Press

Edgefield (SC) Advertiser

El Paso (TX) Herald

Flake's Bulletin (Galveston, TX)

Fort Mill (SC) Times

Gallipolis (OH) Journal

Galveston (TX) Tri-Weekly News

Georgia Weekly Telegraph (Macon)

Gold Hill (NV) Daily News

Green-Mountain Freeman (Montpelier, VT)

Harrisburg (PA) Weekly Patriot and Union

Hartford (CT) Daily Courant

Hattiesburg (MS) News

Hendersonville (NC) Times-News

Highland (OH) News

Honesdale (PA) Citizen

Houston Daily Telegraph

Houston Tri-Weekly Telegraph

Idaho Avalanche (Silver City)

Indiana State Sentinel (Indianapolis)

Jonesboro (TN) Union Flag

Kansas City (MO) Journal

Kansas City (MO) Star

Keowee Courier (Pickens Court House, SC)

Key West (FL) Citizen

Lancaster (PA) Daily Intelligencer

Macon (GA) Daily Telegraph

Macon (GA) Daily Telegraph and Confederate

Macon (MS) Beacon

Madison (SD) Daily Leader

Marshall County Republican (Plymouth, IN)

Marshalltown (IA) Evening Times–Republican

Memphis Daily Appeal

Memphis Daily Avalanche

Men's Wear: The Retailers' Newspaper (New York)
Middletown (CT) Constitution
Mineral Point (WI) Weekly Tribune
Nashville Daily Union
Nashville Union and Dispatch
National Republican (Washington, DC)
National Tribune (Washington, DC)
Newbern (NC) Weekly Progress
New Hampshire Patriot and Gazette (Concord)
New Orleans Daily Picayune
New-Orleans Times
New York Amsterdam News
New York Evening World
New York Herald
New York Sun
New York Times
New York Tribune
North Branch Democrat (Tunkhannock, PA)
Norwich (CT) Bulletin
Oklahoma City Times
Omaha (NE) Daily Bee
Opelousas (LA) Courier
Orleans Independent Standard (Blanton, VT)
Ottawa (IL) Free Trader
Pacific Commercial Advertiser (Honolulu, HI)
Pensacola (FL) Journal
Philadelphia Evening Telegraph
Philadelphia Inquirer
Philadelphia Tribune
Pittsburgh Dispatch
Pittsfield (MA) Sun
Point Pleasant (VA) Weekly Register
Pomeroy (OH) Weekly Telegraph
Pomeroy's Democrat (New York City)
Portland (ME) Daily Press
Pulaski (TN) Citizen
Raleigh (NC) Daily Confederate
Richmond (VA) Daily Dispatch
Richmond (VA) Examiner

Richmond (VA) Times Dispatch

Richmond (VA) Whig

Rock Island (IL) Daily Argus

Rutland (VT) Weekly Herald

Sacramento (CA) Record-Union

Saint Johnsbury (VT) Caledonian

Saint Paul (MN) Appeal

Saint Paul (MN) Weekly Pioneer and Democrat

Salt Lake City Broad Ax

Salt Lake Weekly Tribune (Salt Lake City)

San Antonio (TX) Express

San Francisco Daily Evening Bulletin

Santa Fe New Mexican

Seattle Star

Sisterville (WV) Oil Review

Soldiers' Journal (Alexandria, VA)

Spirit of the Age (Raleigh, NC)

The State (Columbia, SC)

Territorial Enterprise (Virginia City, NV)

Tipton (IA) Advertiser

Topeka (KS) State Journal

Washington (DC) Constitution

Washington (DC) Daily Constitutional Union

Washington (DC) Evening Star

Washington (DC) Herald

Washington (DC) Star

Washington (DC) Times

Watchman and Southron (Sumter, SC)

Watertown (WI) Republican

Weekly Mississippian (Jackson)

Weekly National Intelligencer (Washington, DC)

Weekly Ottumwa (IA) Courier

Wheeling (WV) Daily Intelligencer

White Cloud Kansas Chief

Wilmington (DE) Evening Journal

Wilmington (NC) Daily Journal

Wilmington (NC) Journal

Winston-Salem (NC) Western Sentinel

Wisconsin Daily Patriot (Madison)

Yorkville (SC) Enquirer

GOVERNMENT PUBLICATIONS

Confederate States of America. *A Digest of the Military and Naval Laws of the Confederate States, from the Commencement of the Provisional Congress to the End of the First Congress under the Permanent Constitution.* Richmond, VA: J. W. Randolph, 1863. Sourced from Documenting the American South, https://docsouth.unc.edu/imls/digest/digest.html.

Confederate States War Department. *Uniform and Dress of the Army of the Confederate States.* Richmond, VA: Wynne, 1861. Sourced from Library of Congress, https://www.loc.gov/item/05025942/.

Dyer, Frederick H. *Regimental Histories.* Vol. 3 of *A Compendium of the War of the Rebellion.* New York: Thomas Yoseloff, 1959.

Long, Oscar F. *Changes in the Uniform of the Army, 1774–1895.* Washington, DC: Army and Navy Register, 1895. Sourced from Army Clothing History, U.S. Army Quartermaster Foundation, http://old.quartermasterfoundation.org /changes_in_the_army_uniform_1895.htm.

Maryland Bureau of Industrial Statistics. *Eighth Annual Report of the Bureau of Industrial Statistics of Maryland 1899.* Baltimore: William J. C. Dulany, 1900.

Massachusetts Bureau of Statistics of Labor. *Comparative Wages, Prices, and Cost of Living. Reprinted from The Sixteenth Annual Report of the Massachusetts Bureau of Statistics of Labor, for 1885.* Boston: Wright & Potter Printing, 1889.

U.S. Bureau of Labor. *Report on Condition of Woman and Child Wage-Earners in the United States. 19 vols.* Washington, DC: Government Printing Office, 1910–13.

U.S. Congress. House. *Riot at Norfolk.* 39th Cong., 2nd Sess., 1867. H. Exec. Doc. 72.

U.S. Special Commissioner of the Revenue. *Report of the Special Commissioner of the Revenue for the Year 1868.* Washington, DC: Government Printing Office, 1868.

U.S. War Department. General Regulations for the Army 1847. Washington, DC: J. & G. S. Gideon, 1847.

——. *Revised Regulations for the Army of the United States, 1861.* Philadelphia: J. B. Lippincott, 1861.

——. *Revised United States Army Regulations of 1861, with an Appendix Containing the Changed and Laws Affecting Army Regulations and Articles of War to June 25, 1863.* Washington, DC: Government Printing Office, 1863.

——. *The War of the Rebellion: A Compilation of the Official Records of the Union and Confederate Armies.* 128 vols. Washington, DC: Government Printing Office, 1880–1901.

Weeks, Joseph D. *Report on the Statistics of Wages in Manufacturing Industries; with Supplementary Reports on the Average Retail Prices of Necessaries of Life, and on Trades Societies, and Strikes and Lockouts.* Washington, DC: Government Printing Office, 1886.

BOOKS & ONLINE PUBLICATIONS

Abel, Annie Heloise. *The American Indian as Participant in the Civil War, 1862–1865.* Cleveland: Arthur H. Clark, 1919.

———. *The American Indian as Slaveholder and Secessionist.* Cleveland: Arthur H. Clark, 1915.

———. *The American Indian in the Civil War, 1862–1865.* Lincoln: University of Nebraska Press, 1992.

Abernathy, Frederick H., John T. Dunlop, and Janice H. Hammond. *A Stitch in Time: Lean Retailing and the Transformation of Manufacturing.* New York: Oxford University Press, 1999.

Adolphus, Frederick R. *Imported Confederate Uniforms of Peter Tait & Co., Limerick, Ireland.* Self-published, 2010.

Andrews, Eliza Frances. *Diary of Eliza Frances Andrews: The War-Time Journal of a Georgia Girl, 1864–1865.* New York: D. Appleton, 1908.

Appadurai, Arjun, ed. *The Social Life of Things: Commodities in Cultural Perspective.* Cambridge: Cambridge University Press, 1988.

Arenson, Adam, and Andrew R. Graybill, eds. *Civil War Wests: Testing the Limits of the United States.* Oakland: University of California Press, 2015.

Arms and Equipment of the Confederacy. Vol. 2 of *Echoes of Glory.* 1991. Reprint, Alexandria, VA: Time-Life Books, 1998.

Arms and Equipment of the Union. Vol. 1 of *Echoes of Glory.* 1991. Reprint, Alexandria, VA: Time-Life Books, 1998.

Ashby, Thomas Almond. *The Valley Campaigns: Being the Reminiscences of a Non-Combatant while between the Lines in the Shenandoah Valley during the War of the States.* New York: Neale, 1914.

Attie, Jeanie. *Patriotic Toil: Northern Women and the American Civil War.* Ithaca, NY: Cornell University Press, 1998.

Auslander, Leora, and Tara Zahra, eds. *Objects of War: The Material Culture of Conflict & Displacement.* Ithaca, NY: Cornell University Press, 2018.

Avary, Myrta Lockett, ed. *A Virginia Girl in the Civil War: Being a Record of the Actual Experiences of the Wife of a Confederate Officer.* New York: D. Appleton, 1903.

Bacon, Georgeanna Muirson Woolsey, and Eliza Newton Woolsey Howland, eds. *Letters of a Family during the War for the Union, 1861–1865.* Vol. 2. Privately published, 1899.

Barry, Craig L., and David C. Burt. *Suppliers to the Confederacy II: S. Isaac Campbell & Co., London Peter Tait & Co., Limerick.* Fairfield, OH: Stainless Banner, 2014.

Beard, Charles, and Mary Beard. *The Rise of American Civilization.* New York: Macmillan, 1927.

Beath, Robert B. *History of the Grand Army of the Republic.* New York: Bryan, Taylor, 1889.

Beckert, Sven. *Empire of Cotton: A Global History.* New York: Alfred A. Knopf, 2014.

Bederman, Gail. *Manliness and Civilization: A Cultural History of Gender and Race in the United States, 1880–1917.* Chicago: University of Chicago Press, 1996.

Behrend, Justin. *Reconstructing Democracy: Grassroots Black Politics in the Deep South after the Civil War.* Athens: University of Georgia Press, 2015.

Beringer, Richard E., Herman Hattaway, Archer Jones, and William N. Still Jr. *Why the South Lost the Civil War.* Athens: University of Georgia Press, 1986.

Berlin, Ira, Joseph Patrick Reidy, and Leslie S. Rowland. *Freedom's Soldiers: The Black Military Experience in the Civil War.* Cambridge: Cambridge University Press, 1998.

Bernstein, Iver. *The New York City Draft Riots: Their Significance for American Society and Politics in the Age of the Civil War.* New York: Oxford University Press, 1991.

Billings, John Davis. *Hardtack and Coffee: The Unwritten Story of Army Life.* Philadelphia: Thompson, 1888.

The Biographical Encyclopedia of Ohio of the Nineteenth Century. Cincinnati: Galaxy, 1876.

Bircher, William. *Diary of William Bircher.* 1865. Sourced from The American Civil War: Letters and Diaries, Alexander Street, https://alexanderstreet.com/products/american-civil-war-letters-and-diaries (subscription required).

Blanton, DeAnne, and Lauren M. Cook. *They Fought like Demons: Women Soldiers in the American Civil War.* Baton Rouge: Louisiana State University Press, 2002.

Blight, David W. *Race and Reunion: The Civil War in American Memory.* Rev. ed. Cambridge, MA: Belknap Press of the Harvard University Press, 2002.

Britton, Wiley. *The Union Indian Brigade in the Civil War.* Kansas City, MO: Franklin Hudson, 1922.

Buckingham, James Silk. *The Slave States of America.* London, 1842.

Bushman, Richard L. *The Refinement of America: Persons, Houses, Cities.* New York: Vintage Books, 1992.

Butler, Benjamin Franklin. *Private and Official Correspondence of Gen. Benjamin F. Butler, during the Period of the Civil War.* Vol. 1. Norwood, MA: Plimpton, 1917.

Bynum, Victoria. *Unruly Women: The Politics of Social and Sexual Control in the Old South.* Chapel Hill: University of North Carolina Press, 1992.

Calhoun, Craig, ed. *Habermas and the Public Sphere.* Cambridge, MA: MIT Press, 1992.

Cashin, Joan E., ed. *War Matters: Material Culture in the Civil War Era.* Chapel Hill: University of North Carolina Press, 2018.

Castel, Albert. *A Frontier State at War: Kansas, 1861–1865.* Ithaca, NY: Cornell University Press, 1958.

Castleman, Alfred Lewis. *The Army of the Potomac, behind the Scenes: A Diary of Unwritten History; from the Organization of the Army, . . . to the Close of the Campaign in Virginia, about the First Day of January, 1863.* Milwaukee: Strickland, 1863.

Chalmers, David M. *Hooded Americanism: The History of the Ku Klux Klan.* Durham, NC: Duke University Press, 1987.

Cimbala, Paul A. *Veterans North and South: The Transition from Soldier to Civilian after the American Civil War.* Santa Barbara, CA: Praeger, 2015.

Clampitt, Bradley R., ed. *The Civil War and Reconstruction in Indian Territory.* Lincoln: University of Nebraska Press, 2015.

———. *The Confederate Heartland: Military and Civilian Morale in the Western Confederacy.* Baton Rouge: Louisiana State University Press, 2011.

———. *Lost Causes: Confederate Demobilization and the Making of Veteran Identity.* Baton Rouge: Louisiana State University Press, 2022.

Clinton, Catherine. *The Plantation Mistress: Woman's World in the Old South.* New York: Pantheon Books, 1982.

———. *Stepdaughters of History: Southern Women and the American Civil War.* Baton Rouge: Louisiana State University Press, 2016.

Clinton, Catherine, and Nina Silber, eds., *Divided Houses: Gender and the Civil War.* New York: Oxford University Press, 1992.

Cole, Arthur C. *The Irrepressible Conflict.* New York: Macmillan, 1934.

Connole, Joseph. *The Civil War and the Subversion of American Indian Sovereignty, North Carolina.* Jefferson, NC: McFarland, 2017.

Coski, John M. *The Confederate Battle Flag: America's Most Embattled Emblem.* Cambridge, MA: Harvard University Press, 2005.

Coulter, E. Merton. *The Confederate States of America, 1861–1865.* Baton Rouge: Louisiana State University Press, 1950.

Cox, Karen L. *Dixie's Daughters: The United Daughters of the Confederacy and the Preservation of Confederate Culture.* Gainesville: University Press of Florida, 2003.

——. *Dreaming of Dixie: How the South Was Created in American Popular Culture.* Chapel Hill: University of North Carolina Press, 2013.

——. *No Common Ground: Confederate Monuments and the Ongoing Fight for Racial Justice.* Chapel Hill: University of North Carolina Press, 2021.

Craven, Avery. *The Growth of Southern Nationalism, 1848–1861.* Baton Rouge: Louisiana State University Press, 1953.

Crow, Vernon H. *Storm in the Mountains: Thomas' Confederate Legion of Cherokee Indians and Mountaineers.* Cherokee, NC: Press of the Museum of the Cherokee Indian, 1982.

Cudd, John Michael. *The Chicopee Manufacturing Company, 1823–1915.* Lanham, MD: Rowman & Littlefield, 1974.

Cumming, Kate. *Kate: The Journal of a Confederate Nurse.* Edited by Richard Barksdale Harwell. Baton Rouge: Louisiana State University Press, 1998.

Daybell, Mark, and Peter Hinds, eds. *Material Readings of Early Modern Culture: Texts and Social Practices, 1580–1730.* London: Basingstoke, 2010.

Dean, Eric T., Jr. *Shook over Hell: Post-Traumatic Stress, Vietnam, and the Civil War.* Cambridge, MA: Harvard University Press, 1997.

Debo, Angie. *The Rise and Fall of the Choctaw Republic.* Norman: University of Oklahoma Press, 1961.

Delfino, Susanna, and Michele Gillespie, eds. *Global Perspectives on Industrial Transformation in the American South.* Columbia: University of Missouri Press, 2005.

——, eds. *Technology, Innovation, and Southern Industrialization: From the Antebellum Era to the Computer Age.* Columbia: University of Missouri Press, 2008.

Deloria, Philip Joseph. *Playing Indian.* New Haven, CT: Yale University Press, 1998.

Derevenski, Joanna Sofaer, ed. *Children and Material Culture.* London: Routledge, 2000.

Dew, Charles B. *Apostles of Disunion: Southern Secession Commissioners and the Causes of the Civil War.* Charlottesville: University Press of Virginia, 2001.

Domby, Adam H. *The False Cause: Fraud, Fabrication, and White Supremacy in Confederate Memory.* Charlottesville: University of Virginia Press, 2020.

Downs, Gregory P. *After Appomattox: Military Occupation and the Ends of War.* Cambridge, MA: Harvard University Press, 2015.

Downs, Gregory P., and Kate Masur. *The World the Civil War Made.* Chapel Hill: University of North Carolina Press, 2015.

Downs, Jim. *Sick from Freedom: African-American Illness and Suffering during the Civil War and Reconstruction.* New York: Oxford University Press, 2012.

Dublin, Thomas. *Women at Work: The Transformation of Work and Community in Lowell, Massachusetts, 1826–1860.* New York: Columbia University Press, 1979.

Duncan, Robert L. *Reluctant General: The Life and Times of Albert Pike*. New York: E. P. Dutton, 1961.

Dwight, Wilder. *Life and Letters of Wilder Dwight, Lieut. Col. Second Mass. Inf. Vols*. Boston: Ticknor, 1891.

Edmonds, Sarah Emma. *Nurse and Spy in the Union Army*. Hartford, CT: W. S. Williams, 1865.

Edwards, Laura F. *Only the Clothes on Her Back: Clothing and the Hidden History of Power in the Nineteenth Century United States*. New York: Oxford University Press, 2022.

———. *Scarlett Doesn't Live Here Anymore: Southern Women in the Civil War Era*. Urbana: University of Illinois Press, 2000.

Eelman, Bruce W. *Entrepreneurs in the Southern Upcountry: Commercial Culture in Spartanburg, South Carolina, 1845–1880*. Athens: University of Georgia Press, 2008.

Egerton, Douglas R. *The Wars of Reconstruction: The Brief, Violent History of America's Most Progressive Era*. New York: Bloomsbury, 2014.

Egnal, Marc. *Clash of Extremes: The Economic Origins of the Civil War*. New York: Hill and Wang, 2010.

Elkins, Stanley M., and Eric L. McKitrick. *The Age of Federalism*. New York: Oxford University Press, 1993.

Eppes, Susan Bradford. *Through Some Eventful Years*. Macon, GA: J. W. Burke, 1926.

Fahs, Alice, and Joan Waugh, eds. *The Memory of the Civil War in American Culture*. Chapel Hill: University of North Carolina Press, 2004.

Faust, Drew Gilpin. *The Creation of Confederate Nationalism: Ideology and Identity in the Civil War South*. Baton Rouge: Louisiana State University Press, 1988.

———. *Mothers of Invention: Women of the Slaveholding South in the American Civil War*. Chapel Hill: University of North Carolina Press, 1996.

———. *This Republic of Suffering: Death and the American Civil War*. New York: Alfred A. Knopf, 2008.

Favill, Josiah Marshall. *The Diary of a Young Officer Serving with the Armies of the United States during the War of the Rebellion*. Chicago: R. R. Donnelley & Sons, 1909. Sourced from Hathi Trust, https://catalog.hathitrust.org/Record /008650512.

Flagel, Thomas R. *War, Memory, and the 1913 Gettysburg Reunion*. Kent, OH: Kent State University Press, 2019.

Foner, Eric. *Reconstruction: America's Unfinished Revolution, 1863–1877*. New York: Harper and Row, 1988.

Forbes, Ella. *African American Women during the Civil War*. New York: Garland, 1998.

Foster, Gaines M. *Ghosts of the Confederacy: Defeat, the Lost Cause, and the Emergence of the New South, 1865–1913*. New York: Oxford University Press, 1988.

Fox, Gustavus Vasa. *Confidential Correspondence of Gustavus Vasa Fox: Assistant Secretary of the Navy, 1861–1865*. Vol. 1. New York, 1918.

Fox, Richard Wightman. *Lincoln's Body: A Cultural History*. New York: W. W. Norton, 2015.

Fox-Genovese, Elizabeth. *Within the Plantation Household: Women in the Old South*. Chapel Hill: University of North Carolina Press, 1988.

Fox-Genovese, Elizabeth, and Eugene D. Genovese. *The Fruits of Merchant Capital: Slavery and Bourgeois Property in the Rise and Expansion of Capitalism*. New York: Oxford University Press, 1983.

Freehling, William W. *The Road to Disunion. Vol. 2, Secessionists Triumphant, 1854–1861*. New York: Oxford University Press, 2007.

Fremantle, Sir Arthur. *Three Months in the Southern States: April–June, 1863*. Edinburgh: William Blackwood & Son, 1863. Sourced from Hathi Trust, https://catalog.hathitrust.org/Record/011605915.

Fussell, Paul. *Uniforms: Why We Are What We Wear*. New York: Houghton Mifflin, 2002.

Gaines, W. Craig. *The Confederate Cherokees: John Drew's Regiment of Mounted Rifles*. Baton Rouge: Louisiana State University Press, 1989.

Gallagher, Gary W. *Jubal A. Early, the Lost Cause, and Civil War History: A Persistent Legacy*. Milwaukee: Marquette University Press, 1995.

Gallagher, Gary W., and Alan T. Nolan, eds. *The Myth of the Lost Cause and Civil War History*. Bloomington: Indiana University Press, 2000.

Gannon, Barbara A. *The Won Cause: Black and White Comradeship in the Grand Army of the Republic*. Chapel Hill: University of North Carolina Press, 2011.

Gibson, Robyn, ed. *The Memory of Clothes*. Rotterdam: Sense, 2015.

Gilpin, Ebenezer Nelson. *Diary of Ebenezer Nelson Gilpin*. Leavenworth, KS: Ketcheson, 1908. Sourced from Library of Congress, https://www.loc.gov/item/09003584/.

Glatthaar, Joseph T. *The March to the Sea and Beyond: Sherman's Troops in the Savannah and Carolinas Campaigns*. Baton Rouge: Louisiana State University Press, 1985.

Glymph, Thavolia. *The Women's Fight: The Civil War's Battles for Home, Freedom, and Nation*. Chapel Hill: University of North Carolina Press, 2019.

Goff, Richard D. *Confederate Supply*. Durham, NC: Duke University Press, 1969.

Grand Army of the Republic. *The Grand Army Blue-Book Containing the Rules and Regulations of the Grand Army of the Republic and Decisions and Opinions Thereon. . . .* Philadelphia: Grand Army of the Republic, 1884.

——. *Journal of the Seventeenth Annual Session, National Encampment, Grand Army of the Republic,* ... *1883.* Omaha, NE: Republican Book and Job Printing, 1883.

——. *Journal of the Eighteenth Annual Session, of the National Encampment, Grand Army of the Republic,* ... *1884.* Philadelphia: Town Book and Job Printing, 1884.

——. *Journal of the Nineteenth Annual Session of the National Encampment, Grand Army of the Republic,* ... *1885.* Toledo, OH: Montgomery & Vrooman, 1885.

——. *Journal of the Thirtieth National Encampment of the Grand Army of the Republic,* ... *1896.* Indianapolis: William B. Burford, 1896.

——. *Journal of the Fifty-First National Encampment, Grand Army of the Republic,* ... *1917.* Washington, DC: GPO, 1918.

——. *Proceedings of the First to Tenth Meetings, 1866–1876 (inclusive), of the National Encampment Grand Army of the Republic.* Philadelphia: Samuel P. Town, 1877.

——. *Rules and Regulations for the Government of the Grand Army of the Republic: As Revised and Adopted* ... *May 12 and 13, 1869.* Washington, DC: Gibson Brothers, 1869.

Grant, Susan-Mary. *North over South: Northern Nationalism and American Identity in the Antebellum Era.* Lawrence: University Press of Kansas, 2000.

Grant, Susan-Mary, and Brian Holden Reid, eds. *The American Civil War: Explorations and Reconsiderations.* London: Longman, 2000.

Green, Nancy L. *Ready-to-Wear and Ready-to-Work: A Century of Industry and Immigrants in Paris and New York.* Durham, NC: Duke University Press, 1997.

Guenter, Scot M. *The American Flag, 1777–1924: Cultural Shifts from Creation to Codification.* Rutherford, NJ: Fairleigh Dickinson University Press, 1990.

Gutman, Herbert G. *Work, Culture, and Society in Industrializing America: Essays in American Working-Class and Social History.* New York: Vintage Books, 1977.

Hadden, Robert Lee. *Reliving the Civil War: A Reenactor's Handbook.* Mechanicsburg, PA: Stackpole Books, 1997.

Hall, Jacquelyn Dowd, et al. *Like a Family: The Making of a Southern Cotton Mill World.* Chapel Hill: University of North Carolina Press, 1987.

Halttunen, Karen. *Confidence Men and Painted Women: A Study of Middle-Class Culture in America, 1830–1870.* New Haven: Yale University Press, 1986.

Harris, M. Keith. *Across the Bloody Chasm: The Culture of Commemoration among Civil War Veterans.* Baton Rouge: Louisiana State University Press, 2014.

Hauptman, Laurence M. *Between Two Fires: American Indians in the Civil War.* New York: Free Press, 1995.

Haynes, Clare. *Pictures and Popery: Art and Religion in England, 1660–1760.* Aldershot, Eng.: Ashgate, 2006.

Heartsill, W. W. *Fourteen Hundred and 91 Days in the Confederate Army: A Journal Kept by W. W. Heartsill.* . . . [Marshall, TX], 1876.

Higginson, Thomas Wentworth. *Army Life in a Black Regiment.* Boston: Fields, Osgood, 1870.

Holberton, William B. *Homeward Bound: The Demobilization of the Union & Confederate Armies, 1865–1866.* Mechanicsburg, PA: Stackpole Books, 2001.

Hollandsworth, James G., Jr. *An Absolute Massacre: The New Orleans Race Riot of July 30, 1866.* Baton Rouge: LA, Louisiana State University Press, 2001.

Holzer, Harold, and Sara Vaughn Gabbard, eds. *Lincoln and Freedom: Slavery, Emancipation, and the Thirteenth Amendment.* Carbondale: Southern Illinois University Press, 2007.

Hosmer, James Kendall. *The Color-Guard: Being a Corporal's Notes of Military Service in the Nineteenth Army Corps.* Boston: Walker Wise, 1864.

Hubbard, Charles M. *The Burden of Confederate Diplomacy.* Knoxville: University of Tennessee Press, 1998.

Huston, James L. *The British Gentry, the Southern Planter, and the Northern Family Farmer: Agriculture and Sectional Antagonism in North America.* Baton Rouge: Louisiana State University Press, 2015.

——. *Calculating the Value of the Union: Slavery, Property Rights, and the Economic Origins of the Civil War.* Chapel Hill: University of North Carolina Press, 2003.

Illustrated Atlas of the Civil War. Vol. 3 of *Echoes of Glory.* 1991. Reprint, Alexandria, VA: Time-Life Books, 1998.

Janney, Caroline E. *Burying the Dead but Not the Past: Ladies' Memorial Associations & the Lost Cause.* Chapel Hill: University of North Carolina Press, 2008.

——. *Ends of War: The Unfinished Fight of Lee's Army after Appomattox.* Chapel Hill: University of North Carolina Press, 2021.

——. *Remembering the Civil War: Reunion and the Limits of Reconciliation.* Chapel Hill: University of North Carolina Press, 2013.

Johnston, David E. *The Story of a Confederate Boy in the Civil War.* Portland, OR: Glass & Prudhomme, 1914.

Jones, John Beauchamp. *A Rebel War Clerk's Diary at the Confederate States Capital. Vol. 1.* Philadelphia: J. B. Lippincott, 1866. Sourced from The American Civil War: Letters and Diaries. Sourced from Hathi Trust, https://catalog.hathitrust.org/Record/008729844.

Kachun, Mitch. *Festivals of Freedom: Memory and Meaning in African American Emancipation Celebrations, 1805–1915.* Amherst: University of Massachusetts Press, 2006.

Kammen, Michael. *Mystic Chords of Memory: The Transformation of Tradition in American Culture*. New York: Vintage Books, 1993.

Kohn, Hans. *American Nationalism: An Interpretative Essay*. New York: Macmillan, 1957.

Kropp, Phoebe. *California Vieja: Culture and Memory in a Modern American Place*. Berkeley: University of California Press, 2006.

Lane, David. *A Soldier's Diary: The Story of a Volunteer, 1862–1865*. Privately published, 1905.

Lang, Andrew F. *In the Wake of War: Military Occupation, Emancipation, and Civil War America*. Baton Rouge: Louisiana State University Press, 2017.

Laqueur, Thomas. *The Work of the Dead: A Cultural History of Mortal Remains*. Princeton, NJ: Princeton University Press, 2015.

Leech, Margaret. *Reveille in Washington, 1860–1865*. Garden City, NY: Garden City, 1945 [1941?].

Levin, Kevin M. *Searching for Black Confederates: The Civil War's Most Persistent Myth*. Chapel Hill: University of North Carolina Press, 2019.

Levy Bros. *U.C.V. Regulation Uniforms: Made to Measure: Outfitters*. Louisville, KY, c. 1901. Sourced from Virginia Division, Sons of Confederate Veterans, https://www.scvvirginia.org/ucv-uscv-uniforms (site discontinued).

Lincoln, Abraham. *The Collected Works of Abraham Lincoln*. 9 vols. Edited by Roy P. Basler. New Brunswick, NJ: Rutgers University Press, 1953.

Litwack, Leon. *Been in the Storm So Long: The Aftermath of Slavery*. New York: Knopf, 1979.

Loewen, James W. *Lies across America: What Our Historic Sites Get Wrong*. New York: New Press, 1999.

Logue, Larry M., and Peter Blanck. *Heavy Laden: Union Veterans, Psychological Illness, and Suicide*. Cambridge: Cambridge University Press, 2018.

Lomawaima, K. Tsianina. *They Called It Prairie Light: The Story of Chilocco Indian School*. Lincoln: University of Nebraska Press, 1994.

Lowell Historical Society. *Contributions of the Lowell Historical Society: Organized, December 21, 1868, Incorporated, May 21, 1902*, Lowell, MA: Stone, Bacheller, & Livingstone, 1921.

Lubar, Steven, and W. David Kingery. *History from Things: Essays on Material Culture*. Washington, DC: Smithsonian Books, 1993.

Luke, Bob, and John David Smith. *Soldiering for Freedom: How the Union Army Recruited, Trained, and Deployed the U.S. Colored Troops*. Baltimore: Johns Hopkins University Press, 2014.

Lynch, Charles H. *The Civil War Diary, 1862–1865, of Charles H. Lynch, 18th Connecticut Volunteers*. [Hartford, CT]: Case Lockwood & Brainard, 1915. Sourced from Library of Congress, https://lccn.loc.gov/16002601.

M. C. Lilley & Company. *Grand Army of the Republic Price List of Uniforms, Caps, Swords, Belts, Banners, and Flags*. List 48. Columbus, OH, 1887.

Manning, Chandra. *Troubled Refuge: Struggling for Freedom in the Civil War*. New York: Knopf, 2016.

———. *What This Cruel War Was Over: Soldiers, Slavery, and the Civil War*. New York: Penguin Random House, 2007.

Marling, Karal Ann. *Old Glory: Unfurling History*. Boston: Bunker Hill, 2004.

Marshall, Anne E. *Creating a Confederate Kentucky: The Lost Cause and Civil War Memory in a Border State*. Chapel Hill: University of North Carolina Press, 2013.

Marten, James E., and Caroline E. Janney, eds. *Buying and Selling the Civil War in Gilded Age America*. Athens: University of Georgia Press, 2021.

Martinez, J. Michael. *Carpetbaggers, Cavalry, and the Ku Klux Klan: Exposing the Invisible Empire during Reconstruction*. Lanham, MD: Rowman & Littlefield, 2007.

Martinez, Jaime Amanda. *Confederate Slave Impressment in the Upper South*. Chapel Hill: University of North Carolina Press, 2013.

Masur, Louis P. *The Sum of Our Dreams: A History of America*. New York: Oxford University Press, 2020.

Matthews, James M. ed. *Statutes at Large of the Provisional Government of the Confederate States of America. . . .* Richmond, VA: R. M. Smith, 1864.

McCurry, Stephanie. *Confederate Reckoning: Power and Politics in the Civil War South*. Cambridge, MA: Harvard University Press, 2010.

———. *Masters of Small Worlds: Yeoman Households, Gender Relations, and the Political Culture of the Antebellum South Carolina Low Country*. New York: Oxford University Press, 1995.

McHenry, Howard. *Recollections of a Maryland Confederate Soldier and Staff Officer under Johnston, Jackson, and Lee*. Baltimore, MD: Williams and Wilkins, 1914.

McLean, Margaret Sumner. *A Northern Woman in the Confederacy*. New York: Harper & Brothers, 1914.

McPherson, Ernest Lander, Jr. *The Textile Industry in Antebellum South Carolina*. Baton Rouge: Louisiana State University Press, 1969.

McPherson, James M. *The Atlas of the Civil War*. Philadelphia: Running Press, 2005.

———. *Battle Cry of Freedom: The Civil War Era*. New York: Oxford University Press, 1988.

———. *The Illustrated Battle Cry of Freedom: The Civil War Era*. New York: Oxford University Press, 2003.

———. *The Struggle for Equality: Abolitionists and the Negro in the Civil War and Reconstruction*. Princeton, NJ: Princeton University Press, 1964.

——. *This Mighty Scourge: Perspectives on the Civil War.* New York: Oxford University Press, 2007.

——. *The War That Forged a Nation: Why the Civil War Still Matters.* New York: Oxford University Press, 2015.

Mendelsohn, Adam D. *The Rag Race: How Jews Sewed Their Way to Success in America and the British Empire.* New York: New York University Press, 2015.

Meyer, David R. *The Roots of American Industrialization.* Baltimore: Johns Hopkins University Press, 2003.

Minges, Patrick Neal. *Slavery in the Cherokee Nation: The Keetoowah Society and the Defining of a People, 1855-1867.* London: Routledge, 2004.

Miller, Marla R. *Betsy Ross and the Making of America.* New York: Henry Holt, 2010.

Mitchell, Broadus. *The Rise of Cotton Mills in the South.* Baltimore: Johns Hopkins University Press, 1966.

Nayak, Rajkishore, and Rajiv Padhye, eds. *Garment Manufacturing Technology.* Cambridge, UK: Woodhead, 2015.

Nelson, Elizabeth White. *Market Sentiments: Middle-Class Market Culture in Nineteenth Century America.* Washington, DC: Smithsonian Books, 2004.

Niven, John. *John C. Calhoun and the Price of Union: A Biography.* Baton Rouge: Louisiana State University Press, 1993.

Norton, Oliver Wilcox. *Army Letters, 1861-1865: Being Extracts from Private Letters to Relatives and Friends from a Soldier in the Field during the Late Civil War....* Chicago, 1903.

Oakes, James. *Freedom National: The Destruction of Slavery in the United States, 1861-1865.* New York: W. W. Norton, 2014.

O'Neall, John Belton. *The Negro Law of South Carolina....* N.p., 1848.

Ostler, Jeffery. *Surviving Genocide: Native Nations and the United States from the American Revolution to Bleeding Kansas.* New Haven, CT: Yale University Press, 2019.

Ott, Victoria E. *Confederate Daughters: Coming of Age during the Civil War.* Carbondale: Southern Illinois University Press, 2014.

Parker, Isaac N. *A Seneca Indian in the Union Army: The Civil War Letters of Sergeant Isaac Newton Parker, 1861-1865.* Edited by Laurence M. Hauptman. Shippensburg, PA: Burd Street, 1995.

Parsons, Elaine Frantz. *Ku-Klux: The Birth of the Klan during Reconstruction.* Chapel Hill: University of North Carolina Press, 2015.

Perry, John Gardner. *Letters from a Surgeon of the Civil War.* Boston: Little, Brown, 1906.

Pope, Jesse Eliphalet. *The Clothing Industry in New York.* Columbia: University of Missouri, 1905.

Post, Lydia Minturn, ed. *Soldiers' Letters, from Camp, Battle-field, and Prison.* New York: Bunce & Huntington, 1865.

Prince, K. Stephen. *Stories of the South: Race and the Reconstruction of Southern Identity, 1865-1915.* Chapel Hill: University of North Carolina Press, 2014.

Prude, Jonathan. *The Coming of Industrial Order: Town and Factory Life in Rural Massachusetts, 1810-1860.* New York: Cambridge University Press, 1983.

Quigley, Paul. *Shifting Grounds: Nationalism and the South, 1848-1865.* New York: Oxford University Press, 2012.

Rable, George C. *But There Was No Peace: The Role of Violence in the Politics of Reconstruction.* Athens: University of Georgia Press, 2007.

——. *Civil Wars: Women and the Crisis of Southern Nationalism.* Urbana: University of Illinois Press, 1991.

Reardon, Carol. *Pickett's Charge in History and Memory.* Chapel Hill: University of North Carolina Press, 1997.

Reese, Linda Williams. *Trail Sisters: Freedwomen in Indian Territory, 1850-1890.* Lubbock: Texas Tech University Press, 2013.

Reeves, John. *The Lost Indictment of Robert E. Lee: The Forgotten Case against an American Icon.* Lanham, MD: Rowman & Littlefield, 2018.

Richards, Caroline Cowles. *Village Life in America, 1852-1872, including the Period of the American Civil War as Told in the Diary of a School-Girl.* New York: Henry Holt, 1913.

Richardson, Heather Cox. *The Death of Reconstruction: Race, Labor, and Politics in the Post-Civil War North, 1865-1901.* Cambridge, MA: Harvard University Press, 2001.

Rockaway, Robert A. *The Jews of Detroit: From the Beginning, 1762-1914.* Detroit: Wayne State University Press, 1986.

Ryan, Mary P. *Civic Wars: Democracy and Public Life in the American City during the Nineteenth Century.* Berkeley: University of California Press, 1997.

Samuels, Green Berry. *A Civil War Marriage in Virginia: Reminiscences and Letters.* Collected by Carrie Esther Spencer et al. [Boyce, VA?]: Carr, 1956.

Schlereth, Thomas J. *Material Culture Studies in America.* Nashville: American Association for State and Local History, 1982.

Scott, Anne Firor. *The Southern Lady: From Pedestal to Politics, 1830-1930.* Charlottesville: University Press of Virginia, 1995.

Shier, Quita V. *Warriors in Mr. Lincoln's Army: Native American Soldiers Who Fought in the Civil War.* Bloomington, IN: iUniverse Books, 2017.

Silber, Nina. *The Romance of Reunion: Northerners and the South, 1865-1900.* Chapel Hill: University of North Carolina Press, 1993.

Slave Narratives: A Folk History of Slavery in the United States from Interviews with Former Slaves. . . . Vol. 13, *Oklahoma Narratives.* Washington, DC: Library of Congress Project, 1941.

Smith, John David, ed. *Black Soldiers in Blue: African American Troops in the Civil War Era.* Chapel Hill: University of North Carolina Press, 2002.

Smith, Robin, and Ron Field. *Uniforms of the Civil War: An Illustrated Guide for Historians, Collectors, and Reenactors.* Guilford, CT: Lyons Press, 2001.

Smith, Whitney. *Flags: Through the Ages and across the World.* New York: McGraw-Hill, 1975.

Smithers, Gregory D. *The Cherokee Diaspora: An Indigenous History of Migration, Resettlement, and Identity.* New Haven, CT: Yale University Press, 2015.

Stamper, Anita, and Jill Condra. *Clothing through American History: The Civil War through the Gilded Age, 1861–1899.* Santa Barbara, CA: Greenwood, 2011.

Stampp, Kenneth M., ed. *The Causes of the Civil War.* New York: Touchstone, 1991.

Steiner, Lewis Henry. *Report of Lewis H. Steiner: Inspector of the Sanitary Commission, Containing a Diary Kept during the Rebel Occupation of Frederick, Md., and an Account of the Operations of the U.S. Sanitary Commission during the Campaign in Maryland, September, 1862.* New York: A. D. F. Randolph, 1862.

Sternhell, Yael A. *Routes of War: The World of Movement in the Confederate South.* Cambridge, MA: Harvard University Press, 2012.

Stewart, Susan. *On Longing: Narratives of the Miniature, the Gigantic, the Souvenir, the Collection.* Baltimore: Johns Hopkins University Press, 1984.

Stout, Harry S. *Upon the Altar of the Nation: A Moral History of the American Civil War.* New York: Penguin Books, 2007.

Summers, Mark. *The Ordeal of the Reunion: A New History of Reconstruction.* Chapel Hill: University of North Carolina Press, 2014.

Taylor, Susan King. *A Black Woman's Civil War Memoirs: Reminiscences of My Life in Camp with the 33rd U.S. Colored Troops, Late 1st South Carolina Volunteers.* New York: Markus Wiener, 1988.

Taylor, Mrs. Thomas, Mrs. A. T. Smythe, Mrs. August Kohn, M. B. Poppenheim, and Martha B. Washington, eds. *South Carolina Women in the Confederacy. Vol. 1.* Columbia, SC: State Company, 1903.

Thomas, Emory. *The Confederate Nation, 1861–1865.* New York: Harper and Row, 1979.

Thompson, Samuel Bernard. *Confederate Purchasing Operations Abroad.* Chapel Hill: University of North Carolina Press, 1935.

Thornton, Mark, and Robert B. Ekelund Jr. *Tariffs, Blockades, and Inflation: The Economics of the Civil War.* Wilmington, DE: Scholarly Resources, 2004.

Trentmann, Frank. *Empire of Things: How We Became a World of Consumers, from the Fifteenth Century to the Twenty-First.* New York: HarperCollins, 2016.

Tyler, Ronnie. *Santiago Vidaurri and the Southern Confederacy*. Austin: Texas State Historical Association, 1973.

United Confederate Veterans. *Constitution and By-Laws of the United Confederate Veterans . . ., 1892*. N.p., 1909.

United Daughters of the Confederacy. *Constitution of the United Daughters of the Confederacy*. Atlanta, 1895. Sourced from *Encyclopedia Virginia*, https://www .encyclopediavirginia.org/confederacy-constitution-of-the-united-daughters -of-the-1895/.

——. *Minutes of the Fourth Annual Meeting of the United Daughters of the Confederacy, . . . 1897*. Nashville: Press of Foster & Webb, 1898.

——. *Minutes of the Fifth Annual Meeting of the United Daughters of the Confederacy, . . . 1898*. Nashville: Press of Foster & Webb, 1899.

——. *Minutes of the Seventh Annual Meeting of the United Daughters of the Confederacy, . . . 1900*. Nashville: Press of Foster & Webb, 1901.

——. *Minutes of the Ninth Annual Meeting of the United Daughters of the Confederacy, . . . 1902*. Nashville: Press of Foster & Webb, 1903.

——. *Minutes of the Tenth Annual Meeting of the Daughters of the Confederacy, . . . 1903*. Nashville: Press of Foster & Webb, 1904.

——. *Minutes of the Eleventh Annual Meeting of the Daughters of the Confederacy, . . . 1904*. Nashville: Press of Foster & Webb, 1905.

——. *Minutes of the Twelfth Annual Meeting of the Daughters of the Confederacy, . . . 1905*. Nashville: Foster, Webb, & Parker, 1906.

——. *Minutes of the Fourteenth Annual Convention of the Daughters of the Confederacy, . . . 1907*. Opelika, AL: Post, 1908.

——. *Minutes of the Fifteenth Annual Convention of the Daughters of the Confederacy, . . . 1908*. Opelika, AL: Post, 1909.

——. *Minutes of the Nineteenth Annual Convention of the Daughters of the Confederacy, . . . 1912*. Jackson, TN: McCowat Mercer, [1913?].

——. *Minutes of the Twentieth Annual Convention of the Daughters of the Confederacy, . . . 1913*. Raleigh: Edwars & Broughton, 1914.

——. *Minutes of the Twenty-First Annual Convention of the United Daughters of the Confederacy, . . . 1914*. Raleigh: Edwards & Broughton, 1915.

——. *Minutes of the Twenty-Sixth Annual Convention of the United Daughters of the Confederacy, . . . 1919*. Jackson, TN: McCowat-Mercer, n.d.

——. *Minutes of the Twenty-Seventh Annual Convention of the United Daughters of the Confederacy, . . . 1920*. Jackson, TN: McCowat-Mercer, n.d.

——. *Minutes of the Twenty-Ninth Annual Convention of the United Daughters of the Confederacy, . . . 1922*. Jackson, TN: McCowat-Mercer, n.d.

United Daughters of the Confederacy, North Carolina Division. *Minutes of Organi-*

zation and of 1st and 2nd Annual Conventions, United Daughters of the Confederacy, North Carolina Division. N.p., 1898[?].

———. *Minutes of the Seventh Annual Convention of the United Daughters of the Confederacy, North Carolina Division, . . . 1903.* Raleigh: Edwards & Broughton, 1904.

———. *Minutes of the Fourteenth Annual Convention of the United Daughters of the Confederacy, North Carolina Division, . . . 1910.* N.p., n.d.

———. *Minutes of the Twenty-Second Annual Convention of the United Daughters of the Confederacy, North Carolina Division, . . . 1918.* N.p., n.d.

Vandal, Gilles. *The New Orleans Riot of 1866: Anatomy of a Tragedy.* Lafayette: Center for Louisiana Studies, University of Southwestern Louisiana, 1983.

Vandiver, Frank E. *Confederate Blockade Running through Bermuda, 1861–1865.* Austin: University of Texas Press, 1947.

Velazquez, Loreta Janeta. *The Woman in Battle: A Narrative of the Exploits, Adventures, and Travels of Madame Loreta Janeta Velazquez, Otherwise Known as Lieutenant Harry T. Buford, Confederate States Army.* Edited by C. J. Worthington. Richmond, VA: Dustin, Gilman, 1876.

Vorenberg, Michael. *The Emancipation Proclamation: A Brief History with Documents.* Boston: Bedford/St. Martin's, 2010.

Wakeman, Sarah Rosetta. *An Uncommon Soldier: The Civil War Letters of Sarah Rosetta Wakeman, alias Pvt. Lyons Wakeman, 153rd Regiment, New York State Volunteers, 1862–1864.* Edited by Lauren Cook Burgess. Pasadena, MD: Minerva Center, 1994.

Walker, Robert. *Letters of Robert Walker: A Soldier in the Civil War of 1861–1865.* Edited by Clara A. Glenn. Viroqua, WI: Vernon County Censor, 1917.

Warde, Mary Jane. *When the Wolf Came: The Civil War and the Indian Territory.* Fayetteville: University of Arkansas Press, 2013.

Ware, Caroline Farrar. *The Early New England Cotton Manufacture: A Study in Industrial Beginnings.* Boston: Houghton Mifflin, 1931.

Washington, Versalle F. *Eagles on Their Buttons: A Black Infantry Regiment in the Civil War.* Columbia: University of Missouri Press, 1999.

Waugh, Joan, and Gary W. Gallagher, eds. *Wars within a War: Controversy and Conflict over the American Civil War.* Chapel Hill: University of North Carolina Press, 2009.

Whitehead, Karsonya Wise. *Notes from a Colored Girl: The Civil War Pocket Diaries of Emilie Frances Davis.* Columbia: University of South Carolina Press, 2014.

Whites, LeeAnn. *The Civil War as a Crisis in Gender: Augusta, Georgia, 1860–1890.* Athens: University of Georgia Press, 2000.

Wilson, Charles Reagan. *Baptized in Blood: The Religion of the Lost Cause, 1865–1920.* Athens: University of Georgia Press, 1980.

Wilson, Harold S. *Confederate Industry: Manufacturers and Quartermasters in the Civil War.* Jackson: University Press of Mississippi, 2005.

Wilson, Keith P. *Campfires of Freedom: The Camp Life of Black Soldiers during the Civil War.* Kent, OH: Kent State University Press, 2002.

Wilson, Mark. *The Business of Civil War: Military Mobilization and the State, 1861–1865.* Baltimore: Johns Hopkins University Press, 2006.

Wittenmyer, Annie. *Under the Guns: A Woman's Reminiscences of the Civil War.* Boston: E. B. Stillings, 1895.

Woman's Relief Corps. *Journal of the Twenty-Ninth National Convention of the Women's Relief Corps Auxiliary to the Grand Army of the Republic, . . . 1911.* Boston: Griffith-Stillings, 1911.

———. *Journal of the Thirtieth National Convention of the Women's Relief Corps Auxiliary to the Grand Army of the Republic, . . . 1912.* Boston: Griffith-Stillings, 1912.

———. *Journal of the Thirty-First National Convention of the Women's Relief Corps Auxiliary of the Grand Army of the Republic, . . . 1913.* Boston: Griffith-Stillings, 1913.

———. *Journal of the Thirty-Fifth National Convention of the Woman's Relief Corps Auxiliary to the Grand Army of the Republic, . . . 1917.* Washington, DC: National Tribune, 1917.

———. *Red Book: A Manual Containing the Rules and Regulations of the Woman's Relief Corps. . . .* Boston: E. B. Stillings, 1897.

———. *Rules and Regulations for the Government of the Woman's Relief Corps.* Boston: E. B. Stillings, 1894.

Woodward, C. Vann, ed. *The Comparative Approach to American History.* 1968. Reprint, New York: Oxford University Press, 1997.

Yarbrough, Fay A. *Choctaw Confederates: The American Civil War in Indian Country.* Chapel Hill: University of North Carolina Press, 2021.

Zakim, Michael. *Ready-Made Democracy: A History of Men's Dress in the American Republic, 1760–1860.* Chicago: University of Chicago Press, 2003.

Zevin, Robert Brooke. *The Growth of Manufacturing in Early Nineteenth Century New England.* New York: Arno, 1975.

ARTICLES & ESSAYS

Bean, Chris B. "Who Defines a Nation? Reconstruction in Indian Territory." In Clampitt, *Civil War and Reconstruction in Indian Territory,* 110–31.

Beatty, Bess. "Textile Labor in the North Carolina Piedmont: Mill Owner Images and Mill Worker Response, 1830–1900." *Labor History* 25, no. 4 (1984): 485–503.

Breen, Timothy H. "An Empire of Goods: The Anglicization of Colonial America, 1690–1776." *Journal of British Studies* 25, no. 4 (October 1986): 467–99.

Callahan, Shannon P., and Alison Ledgerwood. "On the Psychological Function of Flags and Logos: Group Identity Symbols Increase Perceived Entitativity." *Journal of Personality and Social Psychology* 110, no. 4 (2016): 528–50.

Carden, Art, and Christopher J. Coyne. "The Political Economy of the Reconstruction Era's Race Riots." *Public Choice* 157 (2013): 57–71.

Carr, Matt. "General Sherman's March to the Sea." *History Today* 64 (November 2014): 29–35.

Cashin, Joan E. "Trophies of War: Material Culture in the Civil War Era." *Journal of the Civil War Era* 1, no. 3 (September 2011): 339–67.

Chamberlain, Adam, and Alixandra B. Yanus. "'Our One Great Hope': The Interdependence of the Woman's Relief Corps and the Grand Army of the Republic." *Armed Forces & Society* 48, no. 3 (July 2022): 679–700.

Cobb-Greetham, Amanda. "Hearth and Home: Cherokee and Creek Women's Memories of the Civil War in Indian Territory." In Clampitt, *Civil War and Reconstruction in Indian Territory*, 153–71.

Confer, Clarissa. "Hardship at Home: The Civilian Experience." In Clampitt, *Civil War and Reconstruction in Indian Territory*, 38–63.

Conneole, Joseph. "Why They Fought: Native American Involvement in the American Civil War." *Whispering Wind* 39, no. 6 (January/February 2011): 12–16.

Curran, Thomas F. "'Making War on Women' and Women Making War: Confederate Women Imprisoned in St. Louis during the Civil War." *Confluence (2009–2020)* 2, no. 2 (Spring/Summer 2011): 4–15.

Degruccio, Michael. "Letting the War Slip through Our Hands: Material Culture and the Weakness of Words in the Civil War Era." In *Weirding the War: Stories from the Civil War's Ragged Edges*, edited by Stephen Berry, 15–35. Athens: University of Georgia Press, 2011.

Diamond, William. "Imports of the Confederate Government from Europe and Mexico." *Journal of Southern History* 6, no. 4 (November 1940): 470–503.

Edwards, Laura F. "Textiles: Popular Culture and the Law." *Buffalo Law Review* 64 (2016): 193–214.

Fortney, Jeff. "Lest We Remember: Civil War Memory and Communication among the Five Tribes." *American Indian Quarterly* 36, no. 4 (Fall 2012): 525–44.

Gibson, Arrell Morgan. "Americans and the Civil War." *American Indian Quarterly* 9, no. 4 (Autumn 1985): 385–410.

Giesberg, Judith. "Waging War Their Own Way: Women and the Civil War in Pennsylvania." *Western Pennsylvania History* 13, nos. 1–2 (Summer 2013): 16–27.

Gleeson, William. "Waving the Black-and-White Bloody Shirt: Civil War Remembrance and the Fluctuating Functions of Images in the Gilded Age." *e-Rea Revue électronique d'études sur le monde anglophone* 8, no. 3 (June 2011).

Gordon, Lesley J. "'Novices in Warfare': Elmer E. Ellsworth and Militia Reform on the Eve of Civil War." *Journal of the Civil War Era* 11, no. 2 (June 2021): 194–223.

Grant, Susan-Mary. "'The Charter of Its Birthright': The Civil War and American Nationalism." *Nations and Nationalism* 4, no. 2 (April 1998): 163–85.

———. "Fighting for Freedom: African American Soldiers in the Civil War." In Grant and Reid, *American Civil War,* 191–213.

Grinspan, Jon. "'Young Men for War': The Wide Awakes and Lincoln's 1860 Presidential Campaign." *Journal of American History* 96, no. 3 (September 2009): 357–78.

Hardwick, Kevin R. "'Your Old Father Abe Lincoln Is Dead and Damned': Black Soldiers and the Memphis Race Riot of 1866." *Journal of Social History* 27, no. 1 (1993): 109–28.

Hicks, John. "The Organization of the Volunteer Army in 1861 with Special Reference to Minnesota." *Minnesota History Bulletin* 2, no. 5 (1918): 324–68.

"Images from the Matthew L. Oswalt M.D. Collection: Miniature Flags and Secession Cockades." *Military Images* 39, no. 4 (2021): 36–47.

Knights, Mark. "Possessing the Visual: The Materiality of Visual Print Culture in Later Stuart Britain." In Daybell and Hinds, *Material Readings of Early Modern Culture,* 85–122.

Legon, Edward. "Bound up with Meaning: The Politics and Memory of Ribbon Wearing in Restoration England and Scotland." *Journal of British Studies* 56, no. 1 (January 2017): 27–50.

Levin, Kevin M. "Black Confederates out of the Attic and into the Mainstream." *Journal of the Civil War Era* 4, no. 4 (December 2014): 627–35.

McCurry, Stephanie. "Women Numerous and Armed: Gender and the Politics of Subsistence in the Civil War South." In Waugh and Gallagher, *Wars within a War,* 1–26.

McGuire, Brockenbrough Judith. "Excerpts from the Diary of Judith Brockenbrough McGuire 1861–1865." In *Women of the South in War Times,* comp. Matthew Page Andrews, 71–104, 155–95, 372–412. Baltimore, MD: Norman, Remington, 1920.Sourced from Hathi Trust, https://catalog.hathitrust.org/Record/000566659.

Musick, Mike. "Is There Archival Proof of Black Confederates?" *Civil War Times* 51, no. 1 (February 2012): 35.

Navickas, Katrina. "'That Sash Will Hang You': Political Clothing and Adornment in England, 1780–1840." *Journal of British Studies* 49, no. 3 (July 2010): 540–65.

Neptune, H. Reuben. "Throwin' Scholarly Shade: Eric Williams in the New Histories of Capitalism and Slavery." *Journal of the Early Republic* 39, no. 2 (2019): 299–326.

Parsons, Elaine Frantz. "Midnight Rangers: Costumes and Performance in the Reconstruction-Era Ku Klux Klan." *Journal of American History* 92, no. 3 (December 2005): 811–36.

Potter, David M. "The Civil War." In Woodward, *Comparative Approach to American History*, 135–45.

———. "The Historian's Use of Nationalism and Vice Versa." *American Historical Review* 67, no. 4 (July 1962): 924–50.

Proctor, Bradley D. "'From the Cradle to the Grave': Jim Williams, Black Manhood, and Militia Activism in Reconstruction South Carolina." *American Nineteenth Century History* 19, no. 1 (January 2018): 47–79.

———. "'The K. K. Alphabet': Secret Communication and Coordination of the Reconstruction-era Ku Klux Klan in the Carolinas." *Journal of the Civil War Era* 8, no. 3 (September 2018): 455–87.

Roberts, Blain, and Ethan J. Kytle. "Looking the Thing in the Face: Slavery, Race, and the Commemorative Landscape in Charleston, South Carolina, 1865–2010." *Journal of Southern History* 78, no. 3 (August 2012): 639–84.

Sinche, Bryan. "Scripting a Nationalist Narrative: Robert Bingham and the Construction of Confederate Identity." *American Nineteenth Century History* 12, no. 3 (September 2011): 327–46.

Taylor, Amy Murrell. "Texts and Textiles in Civil War Kentucky." *Register of the Kentucky Historical Society* 117, no. 2 (Spring 2019): 229–24.

Terrill, Tom E., Edmond Ewing, and Pamela White. "Eager Hands: Labor for Southern Textiles, 1850–1860." *Journal of Economic History* 36, no. 1 (1976): 84–99.

Thomas, Emory M. "Rebel Nationalism: E. H. Cushing and the Confederate Experience." *Southwestern Historical Quarterly* 73, no. 3 (January 1970): 343–55.

Tucker, Barbara M. "The Merchant, the Manufacturer, and the Factory Manager: The Case of Samuel Slater." *Business History Review* 55, no. 3 (1981): 297–313.

Urwin, Gregory J. W. "'We Cannot Treat Negroes . . . as Prisoners of War': Racial Atrocities and Reprisals in Civil War Arkansas." *Civil War History* 42 (September 1996): 193–210.

Weicksel, Sarah Jones. "The Dress of the Enemy: Clothing and Disease in the Civil War Era." *Civil War History* 63, no. 2 (June 2017): 133–50.

———. "To Look Like Men of War: Visual Transformation Narratives of African American Union Soldiers, 1861–1865." *Clio* 40, no. 2 (July 2014): 137–52.

Weidenmier, Marc D. "The Market for Confederate Cotton Bonds." *Explorations in Economic History* 37, no. 1 (January 2000): 76–97.

White, Shane, and Graham White. "Slave Clothing and African-American Culture in the Eighteenth and Nineteenth Centuries." *Past & Present* 148 (August 1995): 149–86.

Zakim, Michael. "A Ready-Made Business: The Birth of the Clothing Industry in America." *Business History Review* 73, no. 1 (April 1999): 61–90.

Zalimas, Robert J., Jr. "A Disturbance in the City." In Smith, *Black Soldiers in Blue*, 361–90.

THESES & DISSERTATIONS

Duffey, Davis. "Not So Ragged Confederates: A History of Confederate Uniforms and Uniform Production in the Civil War." MA thesis, University of West Georgia, 2017.

Fisher, John Phillip. "A Blockaded State: Texas during the Civil War, 1861–1865." PhD diss., Texas A&M University, 1995.

Guenter, Scot M. "The American Flag, 1777–1924: Cultural Shifts from Creation to Codification." PhD diss., University of Maryland, 1986.

Kirk, Brianna E. "'No Safety for Union Men': The Norfolk Race Riot of 1866 and Military Occupation." MA thesis, University of Virginia, 2019.

Weicksel, Sarah Jones. "The Fabric of War: Clothing, Culture, and Violence in the American Civil War Era." PhD diss., University of Chicago, 2017.

WEBSITES

Common Threads Army. U.S. Department of Defense. https://www.defense.gov/Multimedia/Experience/Common-Threads/Common-Threads-Army/.

Confederate Memorial Hall in New Orleans. https://confederatemuseum.com.

Daughters of Union Veterans of the Civil War. http://www.duvcw.org.

Franklin, Harper. "Menswear." 1840–1849, Fashion History Timeline, Fashion Institute of Technology, March 26, 2020. https://fashionhistory.fitnyc.edu/1840-1849.

Freedmen and Southern Society Project. http://www.freedmen.umd.edu/index.html.

"Gallery: Native Americans in the War." 1861–1862, Trans-Mississippi Theater Virtual Museum. http://www.civilwarvirtualmuseum.org/1861-1862/native-americans-in-the-war/cherokee-braves-flag.php.

"Grand Army of the Republic and Kindred Societies." Research Guides, Library of Congress. http://www.loc.gov/rr/main/gar/garintro.html.

Grand Army of the Republic (GAR) Records Project. Sons of Union Veterans of the Civil War. http://www.garrecords.org/.

Hammerstrom, Kristen. "How to Make a Flag or Standard." Museum of the American Revolution, May 2021. https://www.amrevmuseum.org/how-to-make-a-flag -or-standard.

Jones, Tina Cahalan. "Freeman Thomas 1845–1936, 12th US Colored Infantry." *From Slaves to Soldiers and Beyond—Williamson County, Tennessee's African American History* (blog), August 14, 2016. http://usctwillcotn.blogspot.com /2016/06/freeman-thomas-1845-1936-usct-veteran.html.

Kansas Memory. https://www.kansasmemory.org.

Keep the Flag to the Front: Battle Flags of Kansas (online exhibit). Kansas Histor- ical Society. https://www.kshs.org/p/keep-the-flag-to-the-front-introduction /10659.

Levin, Kevin M. "Nathan Bedford Forrest's Black Confederates." Civil War Memory, March 10, 2019. http://cwmemory.com/2019/03/10/nathan-bedford-forrests -black-confederates/.

"Material Culture: Subsistence & Foodways." Africans in the Low Country, Park Ethnographic Program, National Parks Service. https://www.nps.gov/ethnog raphy/aah/aaheritage/lowCountryC.htm.

Milestone Documents. National Archives. https://www.archives.gov/milestone-docu ments/list.

Newmark, Jill L. "A Civil War Surgeon's Books Rediscovered." *Circulating Now (blog)*, National Library of Medicine, April 4, 2014, https://circulatingnow.nlm .nih.gov/2014/04/04/a-civil-war-surgeons-books-rediscovered/.

Object Record: Uniform. Catalog 1972.3.13. United Daughters of the Confederacy Collection. Kentucky Historical Society. https://kyhistory.pastperfectonline .com/webobject/D1050FDF-A915-4BAF-9C51-710895323013.

"Secession Cockade." Item, Campaigns & Causes Collection, *UNC Libraries*. https:// exhibits.lib.unc.edu/items/show/2334.

Serrano, Richard A. "The Last Civil War Veterans Who Lived to Be over 100 . . . or Did They?" *Smithsonian Magazine*, November 6, 2013. https://www.smith sonianmag.com/history/the-last-civil-war-veterans-who-lived-to-be-over-100 -or-did-they-180947577/.

Smithers, Gregory. "Dumping the Confederate Flag: Natives Can Teach America How." *Indian Country Today*, July 5, 2015. https://ictnews.org/archive/dumping -the-confederate-flag-natives-can-teach-america-how.

Sons of Union Veterans. http://www.suvcw.org/.

"United Confederate Veterans." Dictionary of American History, Encyclopedia.com. https://www.encyclopedia.com/history/dictionaries-thesauruses-pictures-and -press-releases/united-confederate-veterans.

U.S. Army Officers and Other Persons of the Civil War Period, 1861–1865, comp. John White Geary. Prints and Photographs Division, Prints & Photographs Online Catalog, Library of Congress, Washington, DC. https://www.loc.gov /pictures/item/99402729/.

"Whitehead & Hoag Company History." Ted Hake Collections. http://www.tedhake .com/viewuserdefinedpage.aspx?pn=whco.

Woman's Relief Corps. https://womansreliefcorps.org/.

INDEX